China's Minority Nationalities

Edited by Ma Yin

FOREIGN LANGUAGES PRESS
BEIJING

First Edition 1989

Hard cover: ISBN 0-8351-1952-1 ISBN 7-119-00001-2

Copyright 1989 by Foreign Languages Press

Published by Foreign Languages Press
24 Baiwanzhuang Road, Beijing, China

Printed by Foreign Languages Printing House
19 West Chegongzhuang Road, Beijing, China

Distributed by China International Book Trading Corporation
(Guoji Shudian), P.O. Box 399, Beijing, China

Printed in the People's Republic of China

DISTRIBUTION OF CHINA'S NATIONALITIES

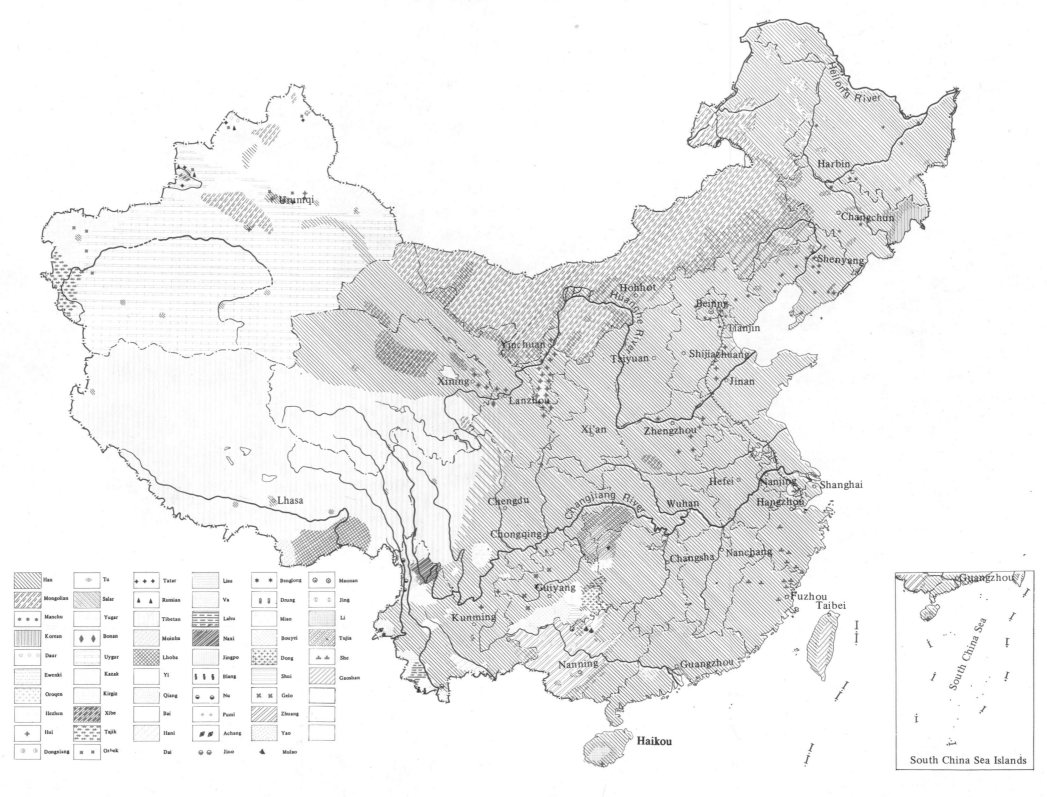

Han · Tu · Tatar · Lisu · Benglong · Maonan · Mongolian · Salar · Russian · Va · Drung · Jing · Manchu · Yugur · Tibetan · Lahu · Miao · Li · Korean · Bonan · Moinba · Naxi · Bouyei · Tujia · Daur · Uygur · Lhoba · Jingpo · Dong · She · Ewenki · Kazak · Yi · Blang · Shui · Gaoshan · Oroqen · Kirgiz · Qiang · Nu · Gelo · Zhuang · Hezhen · Xibe · Bai · Pumi · Zhuang · Hui · Tajik · Hani · Achang · Yao · Dongxiang · Ozbek · Dai · Jino · Mulao

South China Sea Islands

CONTENTS

iii

PUBLISHER'S NOTE

China's Minority Nationalities systematically surveys the 55 ethnic minorities who inhabit vast areas of the People's Republic of China. Each minority nationality is given a separate chapter describing its population, history, culture, language and customs, as well as its pre- and post-liberation forms of society. Taken together, these chapters constitute an overview of the development of China as a multi-national country, and they illustrate how the government's policies for minority nationalities have worked.

The English edition is based on the Chinese book of the same title, which was published by the People's Publishing House of Beijing in 1981. This edition, however, revises as well as translates the original text, while taking new facts and statistics into account.

The book is enlivened by close to 200 photos showing how ethnic minority groups live and the natural environment they inhabit.

The original Chinese edition was sponsored by the State Nationalities Affairs Commission. The editorial board for the book included Ma Yin as editor-in-chief, Chen Yongling as deputy editor-in-chief, and Professor Fei Xiaotong as advisor. The board has also edited four series of books on the history, languages and social development of China's ethnic minorities and the geography of the areas in which they live.

Taking part in the original book's writing and editing were teachers and researchers of the Central Institute for Nationalities, the Nationalities Research Institute of the Chinese Academy of Social Sciences and other organizations. Participants included Ma Shouqian, Wang Ersong, Wang Bin, Wang Furen, Wei Shiming, Zhu Ning, Lu Guangtian, Liu Xianzhao, Li Jinchi, Yang Xuechen, Wu Heng, Song Shuhua, Shao Xianshu, Hu Qiwang, Zhao Bingkun, Zhao Shuxun, Xiang Meizhen, Suo Wenqing, Mu Junqing, Chang Fengxuan, Huang

Youfu and Dai Qingxia. The English edition was translated and edited by Liu Qizhong, Chen Gengtao, Zhang Shuquan, Shi Songqing, Li Yao, Zhu Shida, Jin Shaoqing, Zhou Yougao, Wang Bo and Ma Jianmin.

CONTENTS

THE PEOPLE'S REPUBLIC OF CHINA, A UNIFIED MULTI-NATIONAL STATE

A BRIEF OVERVIEW OF ITS MINORITY NATIONALITIES

CHINA'S POPULATION MIX

Chinese civilization extends backwards in time some 4,000 years. Through a long period of history, China has played a major role in the development of the Orient, and made great contributions to human advancement.

China has a land mass of 9.6 million square kilometres, making it almost as large as the combined nations of Europe. China's borders reach from the confluence of the Heilongjiang (Black Dragon River) and the Wusuli River in the east to the Pamir Mountains in the west, taking in more than 60 degrees of longitude for a total of about 5,000 kilometres. From the centre of the Heilongjiang near Mohe in the north to the Zengmu Reef in the Nansha Archipelago in the south, China extends 5,500 kilometres, covering more than 50 degrees of latitude.

On this vast expanse of China's richly endowed land live 56 ethnic groups with a total population of 1,031,882,511*. In the long course of developing the land they have become an intelligent, brave and industrious people with a rich tradition. By their common work they have brought into being a collective creation, developing the Chinese economy and creating a great culture.

---

* Based on the census taken across the country July 1, 1982.

1

In China, the Han people make China's and the world's largest ethnic group, numbering some 963,000,000 and making up 93.3 per cent of the country's population.

The formation and development of the Han people was a continuous process of integration of the earliest Huaxia tribe with other related tribes and ethnic groups. It was in the Han Dynasty (206 B.C.-A.D. 220) that they adopted the name "Han"; their language belongs to the Han group of the Chinese-Tibetan language family.

A people first active along the Yellow River, the Hans later expanded and gradually moved to fill the country; the highest population concentrations are now in the Yellow River, the Yangtze and the Zhujiang River basins and on the Songhuajiang-Liaohe Plain in Northeast China. In the long course of history they have developed various political, economic and cultural contacts with other nationalities to become more advanced; Hans now play an overwhelming role in the life of the state.

The population of the other 55 ethnic minority groups adds up to 67,250,000, or 6.5 per cent of China's population. But there is a great difference in the size of these minority nationalities. The ethnic minority groups with over a million people include: Zhuang, Hui, Uygur, Yi, Miao, Manchu, Tibetan, Mongolian, Tujia, Bouyei, Korean, Dong, Yao, Bai and Hani, 15 in all. The largest of these is the Zhuang, with a total of 13,378,162 people.

Those with populations between 100,000 and one million each are the Kazak, Dai, Li, Lisu, Va, She, Gaoshan, Lahu, Shui, Dongxiang, Naxi, Tu, Kirgiz and Qiang.

Those with a population of 10,000 to 100,000 each are the Jingpo, Daur, Mulam, Xibe, Blang, Salar, Gelo, Maonan, Pumi, Tajik, Nu, Achang, Ewenki, Uzbek, De'ang, Jing, Yugur and Jino. Those whose population is below 10,000 are the Bonan, Moinba, Drung, Tatar, Oroqen, Russian, Hezhe, and Lhoba. Living in Yunnan Province and Tibet are also the Chamans and Dengs whose ethnic type remains to be ascertained.

Although small in number, the peoples of the various minority nationalities inhabit 50 to 60 per cent of the country. This area includes Inner Mongolia, Xinjiang, Tibet, Guangxi, Ningxia, Heilongjiang, Jilin, Liaoning, Gansu, Qinghai, Sichuan, Yunnan, Guizhou, Guangdong, Hunan, Hebei, Hubei, Fujian and Taiwan.

Minority nationalities live in places with the following common characteristics:

1) A wide expanse of land with a sparse distribution of population. Many minority peoples have traditionally established their villages in mountainous and pastoral areas, on high plateaus and in deep forests.

2) A wide range of products and abundant mineral resources.

3) Strategically important as border regions for the whole country.

The vicissitudes of time, war, migration and seizure of lands throughout history have produced many shifts of population in the border areas. Various nationalities live both mingled together and as separate compact communities. Some minority nationalities live widely scattered over the country, though they may also have one or two communities. A permanent presence of about 10,000,000 minority people can be found in the country's big and small cities and towns. So, with mutual influence on each other in economy, politics and culture, they have formed close ties with the Han people.

LANGUAGE

Among the 55 minority nationalities of China, only the Hui and Manchu use the Han language (Chinese). The others speak their own languages; 29 have languages in the Chinese-Tibetan language family. These groups live in central, south and southwest China. Seventeen groups have languages of the Altaic language family. These are found in northeast and northwest China. Three have languages in the language family of South Asia, and two speak Indo-European languages. In the Indonesian language family are the Gaoshan people of Taiwan, and there is one group whose language type has not yet been traced. Many times various minority groups speak each other's languages. Tajiks, Uzbeks and Tatars speak Uygur, for instance.

Before liberation in 1949 there were 21 minority peoples (including Hui, Manchu and She using the written script of the Hans) that had their own written languages. Some of these written languages are pictographic or ideographic scripts; others have alphabets or syllabic systems, such as Tibetan, Korean, Uygur, Dai and Arabic. There were also some people that used several written scripts concurrently. The Dais, for example, had four, while the Mongolians had two.

HISTORICAL ECONOMIC DEVELOPMENT

The social and economic development of the various nationalities was very uneven; this was even found among different communities within each nationality. Generally speaking, the social and economic development of the Han people in 1949 was more highly evolved than that of most of the minorities. The Hans had a well-developed feudal agricultural economy, with elements of capitalism developing within it. Wherever the minority nationalities comingled with or lived in close proximity to Han communities, their social economy had similar features, a result of the adoption of advanced Han production techniques. Nationalities that lived in isolation from external influences remained in a quite primitive economic state. Some had an economy traditionally based on primitive fishing and hunting, as the Hezhes, Oroqens, Ewenkis and Jings did; others pursued a pastoral life (Kazak, Kirgiz, Tajik, and some of the Mongolian and Tibetan peoples); still others practised slash and burn agriculture supplemented by fishing and hunting or gathering (Drungs, Lhobas, Nus, Lisus, Vas and some of the Miaos and Yaos).

For many minority nationalities iron farm implements introduced by the Han people were predominantly used instead of their own. There were also instances where some nationalities practised an economy that made no distinction between various types of life pursuits, engaging in agriculture, stock-breeding and manufacture of handicrafts simultaneously. Division of labour and economic exchanges existed among different nationalities rather than within each ethnic group.

In China before liberation the minorities presented a complex spectacle, an illustration of social development in four different socio-economic forms. A feudal landlord economy was practised, as a rule, by those groups that had social and economic structures largely identical with those of the Hans. Contrasting with these were a few others that still lived either under a feudal serf system or with slavery (Tibetans and Yis); vestiges of primitive communal society were even found among many of the small, primitive tribes.

PRE-1949 CLASS STRUCTURE

There were in 1949 more than 30 minorities that had been largely assimilated by, or had social and economic structures identical with, those of the Hans. These included the Zhuang, Hui, Uygur, Korean, Manchu, Bouyei, Bai, Tujia, Dong and Miao nationalities, as well as most of the Mongolians, Lis and a few Tibetans, altogether about 30 million people.

As with the Hans, the two main classes were landlords and peasants. The latter were subjected to exploitation by landlords, tribal chiefs, top clerical elements, secular officials and local tyrants who appropriated most of the land and livestock. Minority peasants in many places were not only subjected to exploitation by landlords of their own people but also to that by landlords of the Hans and other groups. To varying degrees elements of capitalism had developed, along with some embryonic industry among 20 of these nationalities, including the Huis, Manchus, Uygurs, Zhuangs, Bouyeis and Koreans.

Those living under a feudal serf system were the Tibetans, Dais and Hanis, altogether about four million people. Feudal lords and serfs made up the two main classes for these groups. Ruling in Tibet were the local government (Kasha), monasteries and nobles, known as "the three manorial lords." A total of 60,000 people, constituting about 5 per cent of Tibet's population, had possession of all the land and the overwhelming majority of livestock; they were served by household slaves. With their own manors set up and worked by serfs for a set part of the year, the lords let the serfs have only small patches of land divided among them as "self-managed plots," depriving them of all personal freedom and weighing them down with all manner of rents, usury and hereditary *ula* corvees.

In Yunnan's Xishuangbanna the ruling stratum was composed of chieftains and their agents at all levels. Every inch of land, mountains, forest and rivers in this homeland of the Dais belonged to the local supreme ruler, the "zhaopianling" (meaning "lord of vast tracts of land"). Manors were set up for feudal lords and land was granted as reward for services rendered by government officials, to be worked by serfs. Serfs were allowed only their tiny patches of "self-managed plots" allotted according to established communal rules. Confined to many small settlements to live a kind of communal life typical at the time, the serfs were exploited in every possible way.

In some parts of Inner Mongolia there was feudal pastoral serf-dom. The nobility and herding slaves made up the two main classes of the society. The former was composed of princes and dukes, "taiji" (lowest order of the nobility) and upper clerical elements. By using extraeconomic oppressive measures, nobles put serfs to the task of tending their herds. For those who had their own animals to manage, no exemption was made from payment of taxes and performance of corvee to their masters. From this evolved in time a different kind of exploitation: nobles rent herds to their tenders and collected animal products and newborn animals according to set ratios.

By 1949 a feudal landlord economy was well developed among most of the Yi people. But in the Greater and Lesser Liangshan Mountains of Sichuan and Yunnan provinces, slavery was practised among one million of the Yis. The slaveowners and slaves made up the two main classes; these were strictly stratified into four categories under the names of "nuohuo" (Black Yis, nobles), "qunuo", "ahjia" and "yaxi". The latter two could be prisoners-of-war or had an inherited status. Black Yis, who comprised about 7 per cent of the population, took possession of over 70 per cent of the land and most draught animals, and to various degrees, held power over the other three groups. The "qunuos," 50 per cent of the population, owned only a small amount of land and some other means of production. Tied to the land, they were forced to perform for a certain duration every year all sorts of labour for the slaveowners. The "ahjias," making up one third of the people, could be freely bought and sold or killed;

their children could be seized and taken as "yaxis."

The "yaxis" were the lowest 10 per cent, living under the domination of the slaveowners, deprived of all means of livelihood. Year in and year out, they did household chores and toiled in the fields. There were isolated cases of disgraced Black Yis becoming slaves, and the "qunuos" or "yaxis" becoming slaveowners.

As mentioned above, there were some peoples at the time of liberation who continued to live partially by primitive communalism. Among these were the Drung, Nu, Lisu, Jingpo, Va and Blang peoples living in the mountainous areas of Yunnan, the Oroqen and Ewenki nationalities in Inner Mongolia and Heilongjiang, some of the Yi people in the Wuzhi Mountains on Hainan Island, and some of the Gaoshan people in Taiwan — altogether about 600,000 people.

Although these minority groups had begun to develop individual production, giving rise to class elements and a life of private ownership, vestiges of primitive communalism remained. The means of production were publicly owned, labour was carried out collectively, and benefits were equally distributed.

Production and distribution were carried out on a clan communal basis among the Drungs living in western Yunnan and some of the Ewenkis living in Inner Mongolia. Every member and family or household in the clan could share equally with labourers in the final results. In Ximeng most of the Vas and Lisus were divided into classes with a fairly-developed household-based economy; tenant farming and exploitation through usury were practised. But vestiges of primitive communalism were still noticeable. There were economies where individual farming coexisted with collective farming.

Many and varied were the political forms found before liberation in the minority areas, suiting the different forms of social and economic structures noted above. In some parts of Inner Mongolia provinces and counties were instituted. In the meantime "leagues" and "banners" were kept as the hereditary domains of princes and dukes. In Tibet a combined autocratic rule of the nobles and monasteries was practised. In the Liangshan Mountains, a primitive patriarchal tribal system survived among Black Yis. Instead of being ruled by a unified central power, they were grouped into over 100 different lineages, each having its clearly-defined sphere of activity carved out. A barbaric slave rule persisted in this caste system. The minority nationalities in some parts of Sichuan, Yunnan, Guizhou, Guangxi and Qinghai had a tithing system ruled by clan heads and tribal chiefs.

Within some groups still practising primitive communalism, some primitive democracy was practised, with the eldest and most representative figures chosen as chiefs, and important matters being discussed and decided on by the whole membership at communal meetings.

RELIGION

Religion had and retains a wide influence throughout the minority nationality areas.

Lamaism, a Buddhist sect, has its followers mostly among the Tibetans, Mongolians, Tus and Yugurs. Hinayana, or Lesser Vehicle Buddhism, has believers mainly among such nationalities as the Bais, Dais, De'angs, Achangs, Blangs, Jingpos and some of the Vas.

Islam has a following among ten nationalities — the Hui, Uygur, Kazak, Tatar, Kirgiz, Tajik, Uzbek, Dongxiang, Salar and Bonan.

Protestantism found converts among the Miaos and Yis, and some nationalities living in western Yunnan. Believers in the Orthodox Eastern Church are found among the small groups of Russians and Ewenkis.

Primitive fetishism and polytheism, ancestor worship, totemism, witchcraft and shamanism can still find believers among such nationalities as the Drungs, Nus, Vas, Shuis, Dongs, Bouyeis, Jingpos, Gaoshans, Oroqens, Miaos, Jinos and Pumis.

Religion exerted an enormous influence among Islamic and Lamaist peoples. Before liberation in 1949, Lamaist monasteries in Tibet, Qinghai and Sichuan held large amounts of land and livestock and practised usury. Spiritual rulers not only went into political and economic collaboration with the secular feudal lords and big landlords, but worked with them as one, forming an inseparable whole in the exercise of power.

CULTURE

The minority peoples of China enjoy music and traditional dancing; many have a fine artistic tradition. They have evolved a large volume of poems, fables and legends, and a wealth of scientific writings. Many famous scientists and men of letters have come from the ethnic minorities, and many magnificent old buildings have been built in a distinct ethnic style.

But the rich store of cultural and artistic heritage was neglected in the old society; most people were denied the right to receive an education; mass illiteracy was the rule. Widespread disease and perpetual natural and man-made calamities caused the loss of countless lives, particularly in the minority nationality areas; some minority nationalities were reduced to a state of near extinction. Culture was often suppressed by exploitation.

HISTORY

The earliest histories say that the people living on the Central Plains in the Yellow River valley were called the Xia. In the area from the Huaihe River to Mount Tai in the east lived the Dongyi; in the Yangtze valley in the south, the people were called Sanmiao; in the area beyond the Yellow River to the Huangshui River in the northwest were those called the Qiang; and in the area around the northern deserts were people called the Hunzhou (including the Shanrong and Xianyun). The Xia people established links with the people of other nationalities in their vicinity.

From the Shang and Western Zhou dynasties to the Spring and Autumn and Warring States periods (16th century-221 B.C.), closer contacts developed among these nationalities. Alliances were formed between the Shang and Zhou nationalities and those of the Dongyi and Daoyi in the east, Sushen in the northeast, Nanman in the south, and the Di, Rong and Kunyi in the west and north, leading to mutual influence and eventual merging. During this period the Huaxia nation came into existence, through a merger of the Xia, Zhou and Shang with the Qiang, Rong, Kunyi, Miao and Man peoples.

The Spring and Autumn (770-476 B.C.) and Warring States (475-221 B.C.) periods saw a transition of various states on the Central Plains from slave system to feudalism. It is said that there were 1,800 "states" during the Zhou Dynasty (11th century-771 B.C.), but through war and absorption, the number dwindled to 100 by the Spring and Autumn Period. Of the hundred states, only seven remained in central China through the Warring States Period.

The First Emperor of Qin, Qin Shi Huang Di, following his unification of the country in 221 B.C., centralized the multi-national state under a feudal autocracy. The Dongyi living along the Huaihe River, the Nanman in the Yangtze valley, the Baiyue living in present-day Guangdong, Guangxi, Fujian and Zhejiang, the Zhurong in the western part of the country and such various nationalities as the Ze, Bu and Yanlang, all came under the rule of the Qin emperor. Within his domain he instituted prefectures and counties directly under central authority, establishing for the first time in China a central feudal state power. But in some places there remained rival powers, leading to lengthy, serious conflicts. Under the brief Qin rule, some small states developed among the Xiongnus (Huns) living in the north and the Wusuns in the northwest, as well as among the Qiangs living in the western part of the country and the Donghus, Xianbeis, Wuhuans and Yufus living in the northeast.

During the Han Dynasty (206 B.C.-A.D. 220), the country became further unified as the Huaxia absorbed many other tribes to become one nation known as the Han.

By the end of the second century B.C., the Han Dynasty had brought the Qiangs of the northwest under control; by the year 119 B.C., the Wusuns came into the empire, followed by the Man people on Hainan Island in the south in 110 B.C., and the southern Xiongnu in 91 B.C. The northern Xiongnu, meanwhile, began a migration into Europe that would end with numerous wars between the tribe under its leader Attila and local powers.

In 60 B.C., the Han Dynasty established a regional government in what is today Xinjiang, a step that led to the merger of more than

30 small city states. For a while, the Xianbei people, who had taken over the territory abandoned by the northern Xiongnu, posed a threat to the dynasty; after a period of internecine struggle, Chief Budugeng led most of the Xianbei into an alliance with the Eastern Han.

During the Wei, Jin and Southern and Northern dynasties (A.D. 220-581) the various major powers in China fought through 300 years of factionalism, marked by wholesale migrations and national annexation and assimilation. Toward the end of the Eastern Han Dynasty, people of many minority groups moved across the Great Wall to live comingled with the Han people on the Central Plains. The population thus formed consisted half of the Hans and half of the Rongs and Kunyis.

The years following the demise of Western Jin (A.D. 265-316) saw another period of fragmentation, with 23 local powers and seven nationalities rising in the northern part of the country and Sichuan, known in old histories as a period of "Five Tribes and Sixteen States." Living in the northeast at this time were the Fuyu and Yilou people; the Rourans, Tieles and Turkis were active in the north and northwest, and the Tuguhuns and Di people lived on the Qinghai-Tibet Plateau. Closer contacts and assimilation took place among the various tribes as a result of migration into the Central Plains. A great number of Han war refugees moved southward into the Yangtze and Pearl River valleys and northward beyond the Great Wall.

By the Sui and Tang dynasties (A.D. 581-907), China was reunited. Political, economic and cultural contacts between the nationalities were strengthened and developed as never before. Following the demise of the Sui (A.D. 581-618), the Tang Dynasty in A.D. 630 conquered the Eastern Turks living both south and north of the Gobi Desert, and in A.D. 657 the Western Turks in modern Xinjiang and Central Asia. Tang armies followed up with conquest of the Gaochang, Yanqi, Guizi, Shule and Yutian regimes formerly allied to the Western Turks. Later, after the Uygurs grew strong on the former land of the Turks, the local rulers were given the titles "Governor of Hanghai" and "Huairen Khan" by the Tang government.

In 713, the ruler of the state of Zhen, established in the northeast by the Sumo and Mohe tribes, was given the titles "Dashing Grand General of the Left Guard" and "Prince of the State of Bohai" by the Tang government.

In the Nenjiang and Heilong river valleys, the Shiwei tribe early pledged their allegiance to the Tang court. Established in present-day Yunnan Province, a strong local power called the Southern Zhao formed an alliance with the Wuman tribe, the Baiman and other related tribes, their chieftains being respectively accorded the titles "Imperial Inspector," "King of Yunnan" and "King of the Southern Zhao." Living in the southwest and in south central China, the Li, Liao, Wuximan, Siyuanman and Moyao tribes also came within the jurisdiction of prefectures, counties and *dao* (circuits) of the Tang court.

Prefectures and sub-prefectures were likewise established in most of the border areas of the minority nationalities. Tribal chiefs were set up as governors and imperial inspectors, and were granted hereditary offices and empowered to rule in the capacity of local authorities. Under the governors' offices local census lists were developed and independent taxes were collected at prefectural, sub-prefectural and county levels beyond the jurisdiction of the central treasury. There was then a system of 856 prefectures, sub-prefectures and counties established throughout China, forcing closer ties between the central Tang government and the country's multiple nationalities.

During the Five Dynasties and Ten States period (A.D. 907-979), China was again plunged into 70 years of fragmentation. These rival powers were established mainly by the Hans; the Later Tang was the only dynasty created by a minority people, the Shatuos of the Turkic people. Along with these rival powers existed the State of Qidan (Khitan, later renamed the State of Liao) established by the Qidan tribe, the State of Dali formed by the Baiman tribe and many other small states of the Uygurs, Tufans, Dis and Qiangs.

In the Song, Liao and Jin time (960-1234), an end was put to the separatist regimes. The Song (960-1279) rose in the south in direct opposition to the Qidan State of Liao (916-1125) and

Nuzhen's State of Jin (1115-1234) in the north. During the Song era the Dangxiangs of the Qing tribe established the Daxia (Western Xia) regime (1032-1227), subjecting China to another 300 years of fragmented rule.

In 1206, Genghis Khan consolidated all the Mongol tribes. A Mongolian empire was created by his conquest of the Gaochang-Uygur, Western Liao, Western Xia, Jin, Dali and Tufan states, renamed in 1271 the Yuan Dynasty (1271-1368). By 1279 the country was brought under a centralized rule of the Yuan following the final collapse of the Southern Song (1127-1279). Under Yuan rule "provincial governments" were instituted and empowered to administer areas where the minorities lived in the Northeast, Inner Mongolia, Xinjiang, Guangdong, Guangxi, Yunnan and Guizhou; special administrative departments were established to take charge of affairs in Tibet, and Penghu and Taiwan. Moreover, tribal chiefs were granted hereditary offices as local rulers and vested with administrative powers to draft soldiers, conscript labour, collect tax and exact tributes on behalf of the court. These measures brought the various localities of the minority nationalities under closer central control than they had known during the Tang and Song period of prefectures and sub-prefectures.

Provincial governments were instituted, consisting of co-administrations by local officials with hereditary titles and officials sent by the Yuan court. Above this level were posts manned by court officials, and direct control imposed by the court through officials either centrally dispatched or recruited from the ethnic chiefs.

During the rule of the Ming Dynasty (1368-1644), centralized control further eroded the powers of the individual tribal chiefs. By tightening control of the border areas and paving the way for increased commerce between various tribal groups, the Ming rulers succeeded in bringing about the collapse of the feudal economy in China as a whole. In some minority areas, however, truly feudal economic structures persisted until, and even beyond, the liberation in 1949.

In 1616, Nurhachi, a tribal chief of the Manchus, annexed the various groups of the Nuzhen tribe and established in 1635 the state of "Later Jin," which was renamed "Qing" in 1636. The years after the downfall of the Ming Dynasty saw the various nationalities further unified. In the north, the Qing unified the three Mongol groups — Southern Mongolians, Northern Mongolians (Khalthas) and Western Mongolians (Eleuts or Qirats) — living respectively south, north and west of the Gobi Desert. By putting down rebellions of the Mongolian Jungar tribe, reactionary elements among the Huis (Uygurs) and the upper classes of Tibet collaborating with the Mongolians in Xinjiang and Tibet, the Qing government consolidated its control of these areas and maintained the unity of the country.

In the process of repelling an invasion by Tsarist Russia, the Qing government strengthened its control in the northeast, especially among the minority nationalities in the Heilong River drainage. The Qing government also set up a provincial government and county administrations on the island of Taiwan, finally establishing sovereignty over the whole of China and bringing all peoples of the Chinese nation under centralized rule.

Though feudal autocratic rule bore little hope for a thorough elimination of divisions within China, the struggle for unification always stood as a central task. In the country's recorded history two thirds of the time was devoted to the establishment and preservation of unity, whereas one third was spent fragmented. With each new step toward unification, the various nationalities and their economy and culture progressed, forging a closer relationship among them.

ECONOMIC HISTORY

Many ethnic groups based their livelihood on animal husbandry and achieved great skill in raising horses, sheep and other livestock. This contributed to the development of a diversified economy in the country as the Hans were mainly farmers. Horse-raising by the Xiongnus and their ancestor tribe, the Northern Kunyis in ancient China, reached a fairly high level; they spread their knowledge of raising horses, mules and donkeys to the Central Plains peoples, exerting an enormous influence on the development of their agriculture and livestock breeding, and on the development of a system of stage coaches. Historical records show enormous numbers of livestock of the minorities being steadily drawn to the Central Plains. In one barter the Turks made with the Sui Dynasty, 10,000 horses and 20,000 sheep were involved; 140,000 bolts of silk cloth were exchanged every year for Turkish livestock by the Tang. The Wumans and Baimans were nationally known for their fine "Dali" horses — several thousand of the breed were imported every year into Yongzhou and the Central Plains during the Song. During the reign of Emperor Shen Zong (1573-1620) of the Ming Dynasty, 36,000 Mongolian horses were sold in the town of Zhangjiakou every year. In the Qing Dynasty there was a sale of 100,000 horses and as many as 500,000 sheep made by the Mongolian Khalkhas.

AGRICULTURE

A number of tribes in ancient China had a fairly well-developed agriculture. As early as the Qin Dynasty (200 B.C.) the Luoyues in south China cleared jungle land and had developed cultivation and crop irrigation. In what is now Xinjiang, grain, mulberry trees, hemp, grapes and other crops were already being grown by minority peoples 2,000 years ago. Crops such as sorghum, maize, cotton, sesame, grape, watermelon, cucumbers and carrots were introduced into the central areas from the "Western Regions." During the Tang-Song period 1,000 years ago the Wumans and Baimans in Yunnan developed water conservancy and irrigation projects on a large scale at Changshan, Dali and Dianchi. The crops of 10,000 "qing" (roughly 67,000 hectares) of land on the Dali Plain were guaranteed at the time by the "Cross Ditch" and "Jinlang River" irrigation works, part of a network with eighteen other water courses covering the whole plain. The Tufans, in what is now Tibet, had in the Tang Dynasty attained a relatively high level of development in growing wheat, highland barley, buckwheat and kidney beans and in tilling land and irrigating crops. The Fuyus and Yilous of the Han Dynasty had learned to grow cereal grains.

By enlarging their acreage from 400,000 shang (hectares) to 2,900,000 shang during the Qing Dynasty, the Manchu people inhabiting the Fengtian area of Liaoning in the Northeast became self-sufficient in food grain.

CRAFTS

There were some minority nationalities in ancient China that had reached a fairly high level in handicraft manufacture. Beautiful and elaborately-designed bronze drums were made by the Luoyues as early as the Han and Wei dynasties. Guizi, then known as an iron mining centre, supplied metal products to 36 states throughout the "Western Regions." A people expert in mining copper, iron, lead, tin, gold, silver and cinnabar, the Xinanyis particularly showed advanced workmanship in making cast gold and silver articles and jade-inlaid objects. In the north, the warlike Xiongnus were noted for their skill in making weapons, as were the Wuhuan people known for their embroideries and carpet weaving. Brocades of the Zhuangs and Dongs became known nationwide, and the cloth of the Dai, Miao and Yao nationalities was on a high artistic plane. Just as the woolen fabrics of the Tufans of Tibet found their way into Bhutan, "Dali" knives of Yunnan enjoyed a brisk market both in China and abroad.

The Li people demonstrated a high skill in cotton spinning and weaving. It was by learning from the Li people that Huang Daopo, a famous weaver of the Yuan Dynasty, improved her weaving techniques and popularized them among the people of the Han nationality.

CULTURE AND SCIENCE

Alphabetic writing systems of a fairly advanced type had already been devised and used by the minority peoples living in Yanqi, Guizi and Yutian as early as the Han Dynasty. The 11th century saw the compilation of *The Great Turkic Dictionary* by the Uygur scholar Mahmut Kashgar. Many Chinese words and expressions still in use by the Han people are assimilated from the languages of minority nationalities. The famous Dunhuang murals, the Yun-gang and Longmen caves and the Thousand-Buddha Caves of Kizir are all creations of the Xianbei, Tufan and other nationalities in the Western Regions as well as of the Han. Murals on the cliffs of the Huashan Mountain towering over the Zuojiang River in Guangxi are reportedly works of ancient artists of the Zhuang nationality, dating back to the Qin Dynasty. The thousand lively figures, ani-mals, bronze drums and gongs in the murals are of high artistic quality. In the Jianchuan Cave of Yunnan is a large collection of stone carvings done by the Baiman and Wuman peoples. The "Ten Books of Music" handed down from the Tang Dynasty can be traced to minority nationalities living in Guizi, Sule, Yutian and Gaochang of the Western Regions.

Among the folk musical instruments now in general use through-out China are flutes, *pipas*, plucked stringed *konghou*, two-stringed bowed *hu* fiddles, waist drums, copper gongs and cymbals, all of which came from minority nationalities since the Han Dynasty. There is a wealth of literary works by minority writers. Among these outstanding literary works are: *Song of the Sules* of the Xian-bei nationality, *An Anthology from Yamen* by the Hui poet Sha Duci of the Yuan Dynasty, the *Inside History of Mongolia*, the first literary work of the Mongolians in the Ming Dynasty, *A One-Story House and Weeping Scarlet Pavilion* by the Qing Dynasty Mongo-lian writer Inzanashi, *Knowledge Gives Happiness*, a long narrative poem of the Uygur people dating back to the 11th century, *Life of Gessar Khan*, an 11th-century epic of the Tibetans, *Jianggar*, a long epic of the Mongolians, *Manasi*, the epic of the Kirgiz people, and *Ashima*, a long narrative poem by the Sani people of the Yi nation-ality.

In the field of science and technology, the *Ten-Thousand-Year Almanac* published by the Yuan government was compiled by Jamal al-Din, a Hui. His contributions to astronomy included the founding of an observatory in Dadu (Beijing) and the design of seven scientific instruments, including the armillary sphere.

The design and construction of Yuan Dynasty palaces in Dadu

by the Hui architect Yehdardin had a great influence on the development of the city in Ming Dynasty and the building of the Imperial Palace now standing. A Uygur agronomist of the Yuan Dynasty, Liu Mingshan, wrote *Essentials of Agriculture, Sericulture, Clothing and Food.* And a celebrated Mongol mathematician of the Qing Dynasty, Ming Antu, wrote *A Quick Method for Determining Segment Areas.*

POLITICAL STRUGGLE

The minority nationalities have a great revolutionary tradition, having made significant contributions in the struggle against oppression under various dynasties, and in the struggle against foreign imperialism and colonialism.

In the late Qin Dynasty (A.D. 265-316) in southern China, the Man people took part in the anti-Qin struggle led by Liu Bang. The Eastern Han Dynasty saw a succession of massive uprisings among the Qiangs in a struggle to fight the feudal ruling class. The great peasant uprising of the Yellow Turban at the close of the Eastern Han Dynasty included "several thousand mounted Xiongnu soldiers."

As a protest against Western Jin rule uprisings of the Xiongnu, Jie, Di and Qiang peoples were led by Hao San, a Xiongnu, and Qi Wannian, of Di origin; the Man and Han people in Jingzhou rose under the standard of Li Chang, a member of the Man nationality.

By the time of the Northern Wei Dynasty (A.D. 386-534), Poliubaling, a Xiongnu, and Xianyuxiuli and Ge Rong led people of various nationalities in a struggle that embraced six towns in the north; people of various nationalities were fighting throughout the whole province of Hebei.

In the Tang Dynasty came uprisings of the Man living in Xiyuan, Guangdong, Guangxi and Qinzhou, and the uprising of the Shanyue. These were followed by the great peasant uprising of Huang Chao, fought by the people of various nationalities in Guangdong and Guangxi in the final years of the Tang.

In the time of the Song, Yuan, Ming and Qing dynasties and

Kuomintang rule, uprisings broke out incessantly on an ever greater scale in the fight against feudal rule. Among the best known of these were the great uprising started by the people of the Yi, Bai and Han, involving more than 100,000 people in Yunnan, the uprising by the people of the Yao in Datengxia during the Ming Dynasty, and the uprising, also during the Ming Dynasty, of the Hui and Han led by Ma Shouying of the Hui nationality.

The Taiping Rebellion[1] symbolized the awakening of the Chinese people, a movement against imperialism and feudalism started by people of the Han, Zhuang, Yao, Hui, Miao, Dong and Yi nationalities. During the Revolution of 1911[2] that overthrew the Qing Dynasty, and in the May 4th Movement of 1919[3], there were also a great number of Zhuang, Hui, Mongolian and other nationalities fighting alongside the Han people.

In 1898 in Taiwan an armed uprising put Gaoshan people alongside their Han compatriots in fighting against occupation by Japanese imperialists. Telling blows were dealt to invading British forces by Tibetans in the Battle of Lungtushan in 1884, and the Battle of Gyangze in 1904. In their invasion of Guangxi and Yunnan, the French were fought back by the Zhuang and Yi peoples.

Under the influence of the Russian October Revolution, some people of the minority nationalities became members of the first batch of Marxist-Leninist groups in China. The year 1921 saw Deng Enming, of Shui origin, hailing from Guizhou, present at the First Meeting of Communist Representatives, which proclaimed the founding of the Chinese Communist Party.

Taking part in the First Revolutionary Civil War (1925-27) were fighters of the Mongolian, Hui, Zhuang, Miao, Manchu, Korean and Li nationalities. Party organizations were developed among Mongolian, Hui and Zhuang peoples. In the years of the Second Revolutionary Civil War (1927-37), revolutionary bases were established in the area of the Zuojiang and Youjiang rivers inhabited by the Zhuang and Yao nationalities in Guangxi, in the Li area on Hainan Island, and in the Miao and Tujia areas in Hunan and Hubei. In 1934 the Red Army set out on the Long March, going through areas inhabited by the Miao, Dong, Bouyei, Yi, Tibetan, Qiang and

Hui nationalities. The revolutionary army exerted a great influence on them, helping them organize their own armed forces and establish revolutionary political power. After the outbreak of the War of Resistance Against Japan (1937-1945), many minority nationals joined the Eighth Route[4] and the New Fourth[5] armies led by the Communist Party. There were also many minority youth in Yan'an, the Communist Party headquarters. In the Northeast the United Anti-Japanese Army[6] was composed of Han, Manchu, Korean, Mongolian, Hui, Daur, Ewenki, Oroqen and Hezhe nationalities. On Hainan Island the Qiongya Column was formed of Han, Li and Miao peoples. In the Shaanxi-Gansu-Ningxia border region a cavalry regiment of Hui people was active. In Hebei, near the Bohai Sea was a detachment composed of Hui people. In the base area of Daqingshan was a guerrilla unit of Mongolians, and in Yunnan there was a border detachment formed by people of several minority nationalities.

During the War of Liberation (1946-49) led by the Chinese Communist Party, people of many nationalities joined in the decisive battle. They fought in the People's Liberation Army, an army of people of all nationalities, until the whole mainland was liberated.

But unification of the country under the leadership of the Chinese Communist Party is fundamentally different from that of old. Under the various feudal dynasties and the Kuomintang government, national oppression and inequality remained the rule, and a unified multi-national state was maintained under conditions of oppression and internecine struggle, including wars between various nationalities tormented by local separatist forces. But when the country came under the leadership of the Chinese Communist Party, the people's democratic dictatorship insured that China has achieved its true unification on the basis of equality among all nationalities across the country.

ETHNIC MINORITIES SINCE 1949

On October 1, 1949 the People's Republic of China came into being, a great family founded in principle on national equality and unity and on friendship and cooperation among all nationalities.

Before the advent of the People's Republic of China, the First Chinese People's Political Consultative Conference, which included representatives of the Mongolian, Hui, Tibetan, Uygur, Miao, Yi, Manchu, Korean, Bai, Li, Gaoshan and Uzbek nationalities, was called in Beijing. By exercising the functions and powers of the National People's Congress, the delegates developed a Common Programme which, working as a temporary constitution, systematically set forth a new policy towards the many nationalities of China.

It stipulated that "all nationalities within the boundaries of the People's Republic of China are equal. They establish unity and mutual aid among themselves, and shall oppose imperialism and public enemies in their midst so that the People's Republic of China will become a big fraternal and cooperative family comprising all its nationalities. 'Greater nationalism' and 'local nationalism' should be opposed. Acts of discrimination, oppression and dividing the various nationalities should be prohibited."

The Common Programme also stipulated that "regional autonomy should be exercised in areas where national minorities are concentrated. . . . All ethnic minorities should have the freedom to develop their spoken and written languages, and to preserve or reform their traditions, customs and religious beliefs. The People's Government shall assist the broad masses of all national minorities to develop politically, economically, culturally and educationally."

The policy towards nationalities in the Common Programme embodied the basic principles of the Chinese Communist Party for solving the ethnic minority problem and represented the common interests of all nationalities in the country. The policy was later incorporated in the Constitution of the People's Republic of China, adopted by the First Session of the First National People's Congress on September 20, 1954. As stated in the preamble and other relevant articles of the Constitution, the tasks that the country faced in its work on nationalities during the transitional period were: to consolidate the unity of the country and the cooperation of the varous nationalities in a common effort to rebuild the motherland; to safeguard the right of equality between the various nationalities and practise regional autonomy; and to help the national minorities carry out reforms in their economic, political and cultural development, so that they could all develop into socialism.

Shortly after the founding of the People's Republic, the People's Government, recognizing that there still existed misunderstandings and discrimination resulting from former policies of the reactionary government, conducted a programme of general education on national equality, unity, mutual help and friendship among the various nationalities. The government also issued a series of laws and decrees to protect the rights of national minorities and to eliminate the influence of the former system.

Between 1950 and 1952, four delegations were sent by the Central People's Government to visit the national minorities in various parts of the country. During their journeys they informed the local people about the new policy towards groups in the minority nationality areas. In the meantime, delegations were also organized by the various minorities to visit Beijing and other places.

From 1949 to 1964, the Central People's Government sent 13 delegations into the minority nationality areas to convey greetings to the people. Furthermore, during this time, 268 delegations of minority nationalities comprising approximately 10,000 people, met leading personalities of the Party and government including Chairman Mao Zedong, Chairman Liu Shaoqi, Premier Zhou Enlai and National People's Congress Standing Committee Chairman Zhu De. By demonstrating the relationship between the central authorities and people of the various minorities, these contacts helped foster understanding and strengthening of friendship between the Hans and people of various nationalities.

In May 1951, the Central People's Government issued a directive that all signs, place names, tablet inscriptions and billboards carrying derogatory terms or showing discrimination against minority nationalities should either be changed or removed.

In 1952, the Central People's Government issued the "Decision Protecting People of All National Minorities Living in Scattered Groups to Enjoy the Right of Equality." It stipulated that all minority nationality people living in scattered groups have all the rights their Han counterparts enjoy and a greater representation in state organs, with practical measures to be taken by local governments in their respective localities; and that they have the right to preserve or change their way of life, customs and religious beliefs.

In order to help the minority people take part in the management of state affairs and to ensure their participation in government administration at all levels, the National People's Congress adopted an Electoral Law stipulating that each minority nationality living in a compact community would be represented at the People's Congress of that locality. According to this law, when the total population of a minority nationality living in a compact community or in scattered groups represents less than 10 per cent of the total population in a locality, the number of inhabitants represented by each deputy from the minority nationality may be less than half that represented by other deputies to the local People's Congress. Elections could be held separately or jointly to have minority nationality deputies elected, taking account of the population composition and the relationship between various nationalities in respective localities.

Added to the Electoral Law was a new provision formulated by the 5th National People's Congress in 1979. It states that even a minority nationality with an exceptionally small population "shall have at least one deputy" to the National People's Congress.

Among the deputies to the People's Congresses at all levels and the National People's Congress, the proportion of ethnic representatives generally exceeds that of the Han population of a specific locality, so that generally every minority nationality, including those with a population of under 1,000, is represented at the national and local People's Congresses.

In some minority areas, there was considerable resistance to the national unity trend the government hoped to foster, with Hans and minorities both asserting their own cultural superiority. A specific problem was found among Han cadres, who often expressed contempt for the ethnic communities in which they worked. In 1952-53, and again in 1956, the Central People's Government conducted a nationwide educational programme on the minority equality policy, at the same time investigating the measures taken to implement it.

SELF-GOVERNMENT

Regional self-governments were established in areas where minority nationalities lived in compact communities. These governments, apart from exercising the functions and powers of normal state bureaucracies, also exercise the functions and powers of autonomous self-government within the limits prescribed by the Constitution and state laws.

Organs of self-government are formed mainly of personnel of the majority ethnic groups, with a proper representation from other nationalities in the area where they live. Self-governments in autonomous areas use one or several languages commonly used by the minority nationalities in the localities concerned.

In performing their duties, the self-governments give full consideration to the traditions, characteristics and customs of the minority nationalities, enacting specific autonomous regulations and local laws.

In managing financial matters, the self-governments in the autonomous areas enjoy greater financial power than other local governments at the same level.

In 1984, the Second Session of the Sixth National People's Congress adopted a law on regional autonomy. The law takes into account the characteristics and special needs of the country's autonomous areas and ensures the full exercise of autonomy by organs of self-government which have bigger decision-making powers than other local governments.

Clauses in the law on training minority personnel will help raise the proportion of minority cadres and workers in autonomous areas.

It is through applying Marxist-Leninist theory to the problem of multi-nationality that the Chinese Communist Party formulated its policy on national regional autonomy in light of the following actual conditions facing China:

1) China is a united, multi-national country where close political, economic and cultural ties have long existed among its various nationalities.

2) The Han nationality is the most numerous, while the minority nationalities inhabit vast regions rich in natural resources. Over the breadth of history, the people of various nationalities have come to live together with the Han people living mainly in the interior.

3) In the hundred years or so before China's liberation, people of all nationalities shared a common misfortune, being subjected to imperialist aggression and feudal oppression.

National autonomy, a policy instituted by the Chinese Communist Party, proceeds from the cooperation and mutual assistance of China's nationalities in bringing about their common prosperity.

As early as May 1, 1947, the Chinese Communist Party helped establish the Inner Mongolia Autonomous Region, the earliest and then the largest autonomous region in China. After the founding of the People's Republic of China, the policy was introduced throughout the country. In 1952 the government promulgated the "Programme of the People's Republic of China for Implementing Regional National Autonomy" and, by 1953, 47 national autonomous areas at the county level and below had been established. By the end of 1958, regional autonomy was in effect for over 90 per cent of the population in minority areas.

Tibet, the last minority area liberated, formally inaugurated the Tibet Autonomous Region in 1965. By the end of 1985, China had five autonomous regions at the provincial level, 31 autonomous prefectures, and 96 autonomous counties and autonomous "banners."

Regional national autonomy is designed to ensure the right of autonomy not only for ethnic people living in considerable numbers in dense communities, but also for those living in small communities. A minority people may have several autonomous areas in accordance with their distribution. These autonomous areas established by the various minority groups, whether large in population or small, have put an end to the centuries-long deprivation of their political rights. Living in the national autonomous areas the people of minority nationalities are now ensured an equal status in the political life of the state, and the right to manage their own affairs.

The key to exercising regional national autonomy lies in training large numbers of minority cadres (leaders and executives). Familiar with the histories, languages, customs and wishes of people of their own nationality, they provide the best link for the Party and government to maintain communications with the various minority nationalities.

Since 1951, a number of colleges for minority nationalities were inaugurated in Beijing as well as in the country's Northwest, Southwest, Central South and provinces with a big concentration of ethnic minorities.

The Chinese Communist Party and the Central People's Government not only respect the spoken and written languages of the nationalities but help them use and develop them. After the founding of the People's Republic, minority language research institutions were established at the central level and in various minority areas. Language courses were offered at institutes for nationalities and at nationality schools in the minority areas. Many people were trained for scientific research, translation and the teaching of minority languages.

In 1956 the state organized a language investigation team that included more than 700 language experts to carry out a large-scale scientific investigation into the languages of 33 minority nationalities living in 16 provinces and autonomous regions of the country. In line with the policy of "following the will and decision of the minority nationalities" and facilitating their development and prosperity, an effort was made to help the Zhuang, Yi, Bouyei, Miao, Dong, Hani, Lisu, Li, Va and Naxi peoples develop their own written scripts on the basis of the Latin alphabet. Moreover, on the basis of two different dialects in Xishuangbanna and Dehong, two schemes were designed for the Dai people to change their script. The Jingpo and Lahu peoples were also assisted in improving their written scripts. The original written languages of Uygurs, Kazaks and Yis are still in common use.

The government has specified that self-governments in autonomous regions should use the respective spoken and written languages, and that the written languages of various nationalities should be used in the election of deputies to the People's Congresses. Citizens of every nationality also have the right to use their own spoken and written languages in legal proceedings, and the commonly used languages in the minority nationality areas should be used for interrogation, announcement of court verdicts, notices, bulletins and other legal documents. Respect is given to languages being used by the minorities in daily life. These languages are also used in minority area schools and in local news releases, broadcasts and book publishing. The ethnic languages are used in books, newspapers and magazines published by central publishing departments and publishers in the autonomous areas. At the present time Mongolian, Tibetan, Uygur, Kazak and Korean are used daily by the Central People's Broadcasting Station in programmes beamed to those areas. Radio programmes are also produced with one or several minority nationality languages by regional and prefectural broadcasting stations in Inner Mongolia, Xinjiang, Jilin, Heilongjiang, Yunnan, Qinghai, Sichuan and Gansu.

CUSTOMS AND TRADITIONS

The ethnic groups of China are distinguished by their different traditions and customs in marriage, childbirth, funerals, festivals, food, housing, costume, hosting guests and recreational activities.

The people's government takes care to accord respect to the traditions and customs of the minority nationalities, and works to gain broad acceptance of these by the population as a whole, especially among Han cadres and Han people living in minority nationality areas. Serious offences against the traditions and customs of minority nationalities may be punished by a sentence of two years' imprisonment or other forms of custody as stipulated by the penal code. The government also has adopted measures to protect ethnic traditions and customs. Vacation is regularly provided for ethnic festival days; pig-raising is discouraged among Islamic groups that have traditions against eating pork; special meals are provided for Huis and Uygurs at their places of work or given subsidies allowing them to have meals at nearby Islamic restaurants; and special arrangements are made for the production and supply of specific utensils and articles needed by the various minorities.

Since liberation, many of the old customs and traditions that benefit production and prosperity have been further developed, for example, the Ongkor (Harvest) Festival of the Tibetan people, the Mongolian traditional festival, the Nadam Fair, the Corban of the Huis and Uygurs, and the Water-Sprinkling Festival of the Dais. These have become days on which people hold cultural physical activities, exchange goods and discuss farming innovations. As the political and cultural awareness of the more primitive minority nationalities rise and their economy improves, they have taken steps to voluntarily give up some ancient customs and traditions that are emotionally and physically harmful. Among these practices are such customs as the slaughter of draft animals for religious purposes, restrictions preventing men from transplanting rice seedlings and women from ploughing, prohibitions against doing field work on special days, and the practices of polygamy, polyandry, early marriage and outdoor childbirth.

RELIGION

Religious freedom is a right enjoyed by all Chinese citizens. Every citizen has the right to believe or disbelieve, the freedom to renounce or embrace this or that religious faith and sect, and the right to practise a particular religion or promote atheism. The government prohibits interference in the normal religious life of the Chinese people. The ethnic minorities are allowed to maintain their temples, mosques and churches; and famous temples, mosques and monasteries are now under state protection, with the government responsible for their renovation and repair. The government maintains that religious activities should be conducted in temples, mosques and churches, and people who disbelieve in religion may not encroach upon these religious grounds to promote atheism.

The criminal code of the state stipulates that government employees who unlawfully deprive citizens of their freedom to conduct normal religious activities shall either be taken into custody or punished with a prison sentence of less than two years in serious cases.

LAND REFORMS

As the backward social system in the minority areas hindered the development of productive forces, reform of the social system, long cherished by the minority people, was the key to achieving prosperity.

In places where minority people had the same or similar social economic structures as those in the Han areas, the people's government generally used more or less the same methods to accomplish land reform from 1950 to 1954, putting an end to land ownership by feudal landlords which had lasted for several thousand years.

In the areas of the Tibetan, Dai and Yi nationalities, still living under a slave system and feudal serfdom, positive but careful measures were taken by the state. A policy of redemption was employed towards some upper-strata elements. Reforms were carried out through consultation between the labouring people and the upper-strata elements. All forms of exploitation and privileges formerly enjoyed by the slave-owners and feudal serf-owners were abolished, with their land distributed to the land-poor and landless masses. All serfs and slaves were emancipated and given personal freedom and the right to live in political equality. Slave-owners and feudal serf-owners who accepted reforms, when their land was confiscated and their extra animals and farm implements requisitioned, were allotted a share of the land. Law-abiding and cooperative former slave-owners and serf-owners were even given certain political rights and the right to vote.

What was not to be ignored, however, was the attitude of the upper-strata elements toward the reforms. In the Dai and Hani areas peaceful reforms were carried out through consultation with the upper-strata elements who accepted the Party's policy, ending the serf system. But in Tibet, where entrenched feudalism resisted any political reform, an armed rebellion was staged in March 1959 by forces loyal to the Dalai Lama, Tibet's traditional spiritual leader. Troops of the People's Liberation Army quelled the insurrection. After Dalai Lama and his followers fled the country, land reform and the complete abolition of serfdom and exploitation were carried out.

Armed insurrection among the Yi people was also quelled.

In the pastoral areas a more relaxed attitude was adopted in carrying out social reform. A policy of rehabilitation was employed towards all herd-owners. Because pastural economy was so much at the mercy of weather and livestock breeding could easily be sabotaged, no heated struggle took place, nor was the confiscation or redistribution of their herds allowed. What was ended was the system of feudal privileges surrounding herdowners and chieftains; pasture was placed under public ownership; free grazing was extended to major herdowners and poor herdsmen alike. Government aid was given to the poor herdsmen to compensate for their former suffering.

In the course of socialist transformation, the herdsmen were relied upon to convert all who could be converted, and with a focus on the protection and development of livestock, pastoral mutual-aid teams and co-operatives were formed; herdowners were allowed to join state-private pastures and state pastoral farms.

In the areas of the Jingpo, Lisu, Drung, Nu, Blang, Va, Jino, Oroqen and Ewenki nationalities, and some Li communities retaining vestiges of primitive communalism, no democratic reforms were carried out systematically. But efforts were made by the Central Government to help in the development of production, culture, mutual-aid teams and cooperatives; changes were made in obsolete practices and backward systems that hindered economic development.

In line with China's policy on religious freedom and protecting religious relics and people's religious activities, positive but careful guidelines were worked out to distinguish religious beliefs from practices of oppression and exploitation. It was necessary to separate legitimate ecclesiastical practices from the feudal punishment system that allowed high clerical leaders to oppress the monks under their control. Active counter-revolutionaries had to be separated from those who simply clung to reactionary ideas, and it was deemed necessary to find those religious leaders who had incurred the real hatred of the guiltless masses. But it was also necessary to maintain a policy of non-interference in the normal religious activities of professional clerics.

GOVERNMENT AID

Large sums of financial aid were allotted by the People's Government to the national autonomous areas, including a wide range of relief funds, loans and subsidies to facilitate the rehabilitation and development of production. In areas where grave shortages were felt, the government provided farm implements, draught animals, seed and grain free of charge, and even exempted the people from taxes. A network of supply and marketing cooperatives and state-run trading agencies was established in minority areas to supply production needs and daily necessities and to purchase farm produce and sideline products at reasonable prices.

Increased investments were also made by the state in capital construction in minority areas. In the 33 years from 1950 to 1983 there was a total of 84 billion yuan of capital investment made by the state in state-owned enterprises in the national autonomous areas. In 1983 alone, 6.2 billion yuan were allotted by the state to the autonomous areas, in a total state budget of 130 billion yuan.

ULTRA-LEFT DISRUPTION

Things have not always gone well since liberation. The policies of the government towards national minorities were at times disrupted and retarded by "Leftist" errors.

Starting in 1957, many minority areas hurriedly adopted the "people's commune," as did most other parts of China. This phase of the Great Leap Forward impeded further progress in the development of increased production. Under the banner of intensified class struggle, and in part because of armed rebellions among the Yi and Tibetans, the policy of promoting local national identities was repudiated. Beginning in 1958, a campaign developed that called for the assimilation of the minority peoples, with a total disregard for the rights of self-government guaranteed by the Constitution.

During the Cultural Revolution (1966-1976), great calamities were suffered by people of minority nationalities along with those of the whole country. All nationalities institutes and institutions in charge of minority-related work were closed down, in a total negation and sabotage of the Party's policies towards nationalities. A great number of unjust, false and wrong cases were brought against the cadres and masses of the minority peoples, and a ban was imposed on all their normal religious life. Great havoc was wrought in the country's productive and economic work with inestimable losses to construction and development. The excesses of the Cultural Revolution not only shattered the progress of the nation as a whole, but also seriously undermined the brotherhood between the Hans and the various ethnic groups. Red Guards smashed temples and made every attempt to destroy the old and traditional aspects of life and religion that were especially important to the way of life of the ethnic minority groups. But since the downfall of the "Gang of Four" in October 1976, and particularly since the advent of new agrarian economic policies in 1979, life has been steadily improving in the minority regions as it has in the rest of China.

As part of a mass movement to recognize and rectify the incorrect policies fostered by the "Gang of Four" responsible for the ultra-Left Cultural Revolution, the original Party policy on minorities was again thoroughly publicized. After a decade of trying to force Han conformism upon the minority peoples, it was time once again to let the ethnic groups be themselves.

RECONSTRUCTION SINCE 1978

An effort was made to see that all working institutions for ethnic minorities from the central level downwards as well as nationalities institutes were reopened.

Efforts were also made to see to it that a great many minority cadres and masses who had been falsely accused during the Cultural Revolution and other disruptive periods be rehabilitated.

A readjustment was made in the administrative division of the Mongolian Autonomous Region: Three leagues and three banners which had been amalgamated into other provinces and autonomous regions during the Cultural Revolution were restored to it. The institution of the Bouyei-Miao Autonomous Prefecture in Guizhou and a number of autonomous counties in Guizhou, Sichuan, Yunnan, Hubei and Gansu provinces helped increase minority self-government.

Part of the post-Cultural Revolution rectification included the replacement of Han cadres in the minority areas with leaders of native origin. By 1978, the minority self-governments could boast of 800,000 non-Han cadres, 80 times those in 1949. By 1983, 1.3 million minority managers and executives were on the job. In the country's 5 autonomous regions, 31 autonomous prefectures and 96 autonomous counties (banners), self-governments are all headed by cadres of ethnic minority origin.

Intensified efforts were made to strengthen construction work in the border areas and assist the minority peoples in their rehabilitation and development of production.

Since 1979, restructuring of the rural economy has aided ethnic minority peoples as it has helped Han farmers in central China. By raising the state purchase price for farm produce and side-line products, encouraging individual responsibility for production and profits, and instituting private cropplots within the cooperative structure, the central government has achieved spectacular results in the rural economy. Individual family specialized enterprises and exemption from certain taxes have also helped minority peoples lead a more prosperous life.

With China's grain supply now firmly sufficient to feed its billion people, the People's Government is encouraging other lines of agriculture, livestock management and forestry, as well as taking specific measures to develop trade and specialized goods in the minority areas.

In many places monasteries and mosques have been reopened to the public, with renovations and repair work done, to reemphasize the policy on religious freedom and to give respect to the traditions and customs of the minority peoples. All traditional religious festivals and activities such as Buddhist worship, chanting scriptures, burning incense, initiating believers into monkhood or nunhood, performing services and fasting at home or in monasteries and mosques are protected by law.

With their political status restored and special allowances made in line with the Party's policy on "Forming a United Front," a large number of upper-strata people (including upper-strata religious leaders) of the minority nationalities have been rehabilitated.

In the last few years, an annually increasing output in the national autonomous areas has been achieved in industry and agriculture. In 1984 they had a gross product valued at 68.17 billion yuan (calculated according to the constant price of 1980), 13.7 times over 1949, averaging an annual increase of 7.8 per cent from 1950 to 1984. Particularly noteworthy was their development in agricultural production and livestock management. In 1984, the total output of agriculture was valued at 33.17 billion yuan, an increase of 555 per cent over 1949.

Since 1979, through a combination of sound agricultural policy and good weather conditions, very strong harvests have been reaped in the minority areas. The expansion of decision-making powers at local levels, the granting of tax exemptions and the introduction of state subsidies, and in particular the linkage of increased production with increased individual income have proven very effective.

Total agricultural product increased at an annual rate of 5 per cent (avg.) between 1949 and 1984.

At the end of 1949 farm animals in the national autonomous areas numbered 41 million head; these had increased to 182 million by 1984, averaging an annual growth rate of 4.3 per cent from 1950 to 1984.

Before liberation, modern industry was almost non-existent in the minority areas except for a little handicraft industry and some other backward industrial lines. But with the founding of the People's Republic came a speedy growth of local industry in the national autonomous areas.

In the last 35 years, there have been 37,000 small, medium-sized, and modern industrial enterprises built in the minority areas. Even some large state enterprises are in minority regions, including the Baotou Iron and Steel Company in Inner Mongolia, the Karamay Oilfield in the Xinjiang Uygur Autonomous Region, the Honghe River Water Conservancy Project in the Guangxi Zhuang Autonomous Region, and the Helanshan Coal Mine in the Ningxia Hui Autonomous Region.

In 1984, the total value of industrial output in the minority areas shot up to 35 billion yuan (calculated according to the constant price of 1980), 63 times that in 1949, averaging an annual increase of 12.6 per cent.

Because of the largely rural and agricultural background of the minority peoples, and because of an overemphasis in the past on China's heavy industrial capacity, planning for development in the autonomous ethnic areas has focused largely on light industry.

Before liberation there was no trunk railway line in southwestern China, just a narrow-gauge railway in Yunnan Province and 60 kilometres of mining rail tracks in Sichuan. In Guizhou Province there was practically no railway. But now there are a number of trunk railways, including the Chengdu-Chongqing, Sichuan-Guizhou (Chongqing-Guiyang), Baoji-Chengdu, Chengdu-Kunming, Xiangfan-Chongqing, Guizhou-Kunming, Hunan-Guizhou (Zhuzhou-Guiyang) and Guizhou-Guangxi (Guiyang-Liuzhou) railways. Altogether 5,900 kilometres long, excluding branch lines, they account for about 11.7 per cent of the country's total railway mileage to form a transportation network over the southwestern part of China.

On the vast expanse of northwest China (including Qinghai, Xinjiang and Ningxia), pre-1949 railway mileage was negligible. There was only a short railway between Shaanxi Province and Tianshui in Gansu Province, and it often collapsed owing to poor engineering. After liberation, with the completion of the Tianshui-Lanzhou Railway, the whole Longhai line, from Lianyungang on the east coast to Lanzhou, capital of Gansu, was open to traffic. Stretching across the Northwest now are a number of new trunk lines, including the Lanzhou-Xinjiang, Lanzhou-Qinghai, Baotou-Lanzhou, Southern Xinjiang and Qinghai-Tibet railways, a total of 7,000 kilometres, or

National Autonomous Regions Economic
Growth Indicators

	1949	1978	1984
Electricity		17.4 billion kilowatt hours	26.6 billion kilowatt hours
Crude oil		5.77 million tons	7 million tons
Timber		12.1 million cubic metres	16.65 million cubic metres
Cotton cloth		373 million metres	474 million metres
Cigarette		514,000 cases	1.74 million cases
Railway	3,511 km	9,018 km	12,097 km
Highway	11,400 km	208,000 km	235,400 km
Social retail sales	980 million yuan	15 billion yuan	32.6 billion yuan

14 per cent of the country's total. By linking the west with the coastal and inland provinces to make it more easily accessible to the whole of China, the new railways contribute to the exploitation of mineral and natural resources and have brought a shift in the distribution of the country's industry.

In the 35 years since the founding of the People's Republic, much has been achieved in higher education by the minority nationalities. Today 11 nationalities institutes have been established nationwide for training minority cadres. Over the years 114,300 minority cadres and specialized personnel have been trained, including many responsible leading cadres working in Party and state departments at all levels in the minority areas.

Before liberation, there was hardly any school at all in the minority areas; higher learning was virtually a blank. But with the development of the economy, great advances have been made in minority education. In June 1951, the Central Institute for Nationalities was inaugurated in Beijing. Later, nine similar institutes were set up in northwestern, southwestern and central-south China, and in Guangxi, Qinghai, Guangdong and Tibet. In 1984, the No. 2 Northwest Institute for Nationalities opened in Xinjiang.

With the improvement of conditions in teaching and scientific research in minority institutions of higher learning, many minority intellectuals now hold bachelor's and master's degrees. Minority candidates for doctorates began to be enrolled in 1984. Special training classes are open in many colleges and universities for minority nationality students. By the end of 1984, a total of 69,000 minority students were enrolled in the country's institutions of higher learning.

By 1984, total enrollment of minority students in junior and senior middle schools was 2.18 million compared to 92,000 in 1952; enrollment of ethnic primary school students grew from 1.47 million in 1952 to 9 million in 1984.

In the last 35 years the minority peoples have also made great advances in medical and health care. In 1949, only 361 medical service units were active in minority areas, but by 1984 these had increased to 29,794, a yearly increase of 13.4 per cent from 1950 to 1984; professional medical and health personnel numbered 406,880 in 1984 compared to 3,530 in 1949, an annual increase of 14.5 per cent during the period.

When all is said, work on ethnic minorities in China did not go smoothly. There were major disruptions caused by the Cultural Revolution and mistakes committed by people who showed no regard to special conditions of minority nationality areas. There have been significant economic and cultural achievements in minority nationality areas compared with their past. But in comparison with other areas in the country, ethnic minority areas are still backward. Development of China's ethnic minority areas is a long-term task.

The general task as formulated by the 12th National Congress of the Chinese Communist Party convened in September 1982: to unite the people of all nationalities in hard work and self-reliance to achieve the modernization of China's industry, agriculture, national defence and science and technology and to make China a culturally advanced and highly democratic socialist country; and in the course of the modernization drive, to take active steps to help the minoriry nationalities speed up their economic and cultural construction for a gradual elimination of the *de facto* inequality between nationalities.

NORTHEAST CHINA AND INNER MONGOLIA

The Manchus

The 4,299,200 Manchus are scattered over all of China. The largest group, about 46.2 per cent of the total, live in Liaoning Province, and the rest in Jilin, Heilongjiang, Hebei, Gansu, Shandong, Inner Mongolia, Xinjiang and Ningxia, as well as in Beijing, Chengdu, Xi'an, Guangzhou and other cities.

Like the Han nationality, the majority ethnic group in China, over 80 per cent of the Manchus are engaged in agriculture. Their main crops include soybean, sorghum, corn, millet, tobacco and apple. They also raise tussah silkworms. For Manchus living in remote mountainous areas, gathering ginseng, mushroom and edible fungus makes an important sideline. Most of the Manchus in cities, who are better educated, are engaged in industries.

Manchus have their own script and language, which belongs to the Manchu-Tungusic group of the Altaic language family. Beginning from the 1640s, large numbers of Manchus moved to south of the Shanhaiguan Pass, and gradually adopted Mandarin Chinese as their spoken language. Later, as more and more Han people moved to north of the pass, many local Manchus picked up Mandarin Chinese too.

A nationality originally living in forests and mountains in northeast China, the Manchus excelled in archery and horsemanship. Children were taught the art of swan-hunting with wooden bows and arrows at six or seven, and teenagers learned to ride on horseback in

41

full hunting gear, racing through forests and mountains. Women, as well as men, were skilled equestrians.

The traditional costumes of male Manchus are a narrowcuffed short jacket over a long gown with a belt at the waist to facilitate horse-riding and hunting. They let the back part of their hair grow long and wore it in a plait or queue. During the Qing Dynasty (1644-1911) the queue became the standard fashion throughout China, eventually becoming a political symbol of the dynasty. Women coiled their hair on top of their heads and wore earrings, long gowns and embroidered shoes. Linen was a favourite fabric for the rich; deerskin was popular with the common folk. Silks and satins for noble and the rich and cotton cloth for the ordinary people became standard for Manchurians after a period of life away from the mountains and forests. Following the Manchus' migration south of Shanhaiguan Pass, the common people came to wear the same kind of dress as their Han counterparts, while the Manchu gown was adopted by Han women generally.

In places around Aihui County, Heilongjiang Province, however, Manchu people lived by their old traditions and customs and used their own ancient language until 1949, when the People's Republic of China was founded.

Houses of the Manchus were built in three divisions, with the middle used as a kitchen and the two wings each serving as bedroom and living room. By tradition, the bedroom had three "kang" (brick beds which could be heated in winter), which were laid against the west, north and south walls. Guests and friends were habitually given the west "kang", elders the north, and the younger generation the south. With windows generally open to the south and west, the houses stayed warm in winter and cool in summer.

A favourite Manchu meal consisted of steamed millet or cakes of glutinous millet. Festivals were traditionally celebrated with dumplings, and the New Year's Eve with a treat of stewed meat. Boiled and roast pork and Manchu-style cookies were table dedicacies.

Monogamy has always been practised by the Manchus, with young people engaged at the age of 16 or 17 by parental will.

On the wedding day, the bride had to sit the whole day on the south "kang", an act inaugurating "future happiness." When night fell, a low table with two wine pots and cups would be set. The bride and bridegroom would, hand in hand, walk around the table three times and sit down to drink under the light of a candle burning through the night on the south "kang". They were congratulated amid songs by one or several guests in the outer room. Sometimes the ceremony was marked with well-wishers casting black peas into the bridal chamber before they left the new couple. On the fourth day, the newlyweds would pay a visit to the bride's home.

A variety of manners were observed by the Manchus. Children were required to pay formal respects to their elders regularly, once every three to five days. In greeting their superiors, men were required to extend their left hand to the knee and idle the right hand while scraping a bow, and women would squat with both hands on the knees. Between friends and relatives, warm embraces were the commonest form of greeting for all men and women.

The Manchus used to believe in Shamanism, which in the early days was divided into the court branch and the common folk branch. The former was generally practised by priestsorcerers in the palace. During the early Qing period, those eligible for the office of "shaman" were mostly clever and smart people with a good command of the dialect of the royal Aisin-Gioro clan. Shamans were employed to chant scriptures and perform religious dances when imperial services were held. Shamanism remained popular among the Manchus in the area of Ningguta and Aihui County in northeast China until the nation-wide liberation.

Shamans of the common Manchus generally fell into two categories: village shamans, who performed religious dances to exorcise evil spirits through the power of the gods, and clan shamans who presided only over sacrificial ceremonies. Every village had its own shaman, whose sole job was to perform the spirit dance. Only seriously ill patients saw a real doctor. Religious rite was generally performed by a shaman attired in a smock and a pointed cap festooned with long coloured paper strips half-concealing his face. Dangling a small mirror in front and bronze bells at the waist, he would intone prayers and dance at a trot to the accompaniment of drumbeats.

Military successes and triumphal marches or returns were inevitably celebrated with sacrificial ceremonies presided over by shamans. Up to the eve of the country's liberation, making animal sacrificial offerings to the gods and ancestors was still a big event among the Manchus in Aihui County.

The Manchu funeral arrangement was unique. No one was allowed to die on a west or north "kang". Believing that doors were made for living souls, the Manchus allowed dead bodies to be taken out only through windows. Ground burial was the general practice.

Jumping onto galloping horses from one side or onto camels from the rear was the most popular recreational activity among the Manchus. Another favourite sport was horse jumping in celebration of bumper harvests in the autumn and on New Year holidays at the Spring Festival.

Skating is also a long established sport enjoyed by the Manchus, as it is by the whole Chinese people. In the Qing Dynasty before the mid-19th century, skating was even undertaken by Manchu soldiers as a required course of their military training. Pole climbing, swordplay, juggling a flagpole, and archery on ice are the more interesting sports of the Manchu people.

History   The ancestry of the Manchus can be traced back more than 2,000 years to the Sushen tribe, and later to the Yilou, Huji, Mohe and Nüzhen tribes native to the Changbai Mountains and the drainage area of the Heilong River in northeast China.

As testified to by the stone arrowheads and pomegranate-wood bows they sent as tributes to rulers of the Western and Eastern Zhou period (11th century-221 B.C.), the Sushens were one of the earliest tribes living along the reaches of the Heilong and Wusuli rivers north of the Changbai Mountains.

After the Warring States period (475-221 B.C.), the Sushens changed the name of their tribe to Yilou. They ranged over an extensive area covering the present-day northern Liaoning Province, the whole of Jilin Province, the eastern half of Heilongjiang Province, east of the Wusuli River, and north of the Heilong River. Stone arrowheads and pomegranate-wood bows still distinguished the Yilous in hunting wild boar. They also mastered such skills as raising hogs, growing grain, weaving linen and making small boats. They pledged allegiance to dynastic rulers on the Central Plains after the Three Kingdoms period (220-280).

During the period between the 4th and 7th centuries, descendants of the Yilous called themselves Hujis and Mohes, consisting of several dozen tribes.

By the end of the 7th century a local power called the State of Zhen with the Mohes of the Sumo tribe as the majority was formed under the leadership of Da Zuorong on the upper reaches of the Songhua River north of the Changbai Mountains. In 713, the Tang court conferred on Da Zuorong the title of "King of Bohai Prefecture" and made him "Military Governor of Huhan Prefecture." Da's domain, known afterwards as the State of Bohai, showed marvellous skills in iron smelting and silk weaving. With its political and military institutions modelled on those of the Tang Dynasty (618-907), this society adopted the Han script. Under the influence of the political and economic systems of the central part of China and the more developed science and culture there, speedy advances were made in agriculture and handicraft industries.

Then the Liao Dynasty (916-1125) conquered the State of Bohai and moved the Bohai tribesmen southward. Along with this movement, the Mohes in the Heilong River valley made a southward expansion. Gradually a people known as Nüzhens built a powerful state in the former domain of Bohai.

The early 12th century saw a successful insurrection led by Aguoda with the Wanyan tribe of the Nüzhen people as a key force in their fight against the Liao Dynasty, founding the regime of Jin (1115-1234). After the termination of the Liao, the Jin armies destroyed the Northern Song (960-1126) and rose as a power in opposition to the rule of the Southern Song (1127-1279). Moving to live en masse on the Central Plains, the Nüzhens gradually became assimilated with the Han people.

Early in the 13th century, the Nüzhens were conquered by the Mongols and later came under the rule of the Yuan Dynasty (1271-1368). With the largest concentration in Yilan, Heilongjiang Province, they settled on the middle and lower reaches of the Heilong

River and along the Songhua and Wusuli rivers, extending to the sea in the east. The Yuan Dynasty enlisted the service of local upper-strata residents to create five administrations each governing 10,000 house-holds, known respectively as Taowen, Huligai, Woduolian, Tuowolian and Bokujiang. The Nüzhens at this time were still leading a primitive life. They developed and progressed, until Nurhachi's son proclaimed the name of Manchu towards the end of the Ming Dynasty (1368-1644).

The Ming Dynasty had 384 military forts and outposts established in the Nüzhen area, and the Nuergan Garrison Command, a local military and administrative organisation in Telin area opposite the confluence of the Heilong and Henggun rivers, was placed directly under the Ming court. While strengthening central government control over northeast China, these establishments aided the economic and cultural exchanges between the Nüzhen and Han peoples.

From the mid-16th century onwards, repeated internecine wars broke out among the Nüzhengs, but they were later reunified by Nurhachi, who was then Governor of Jianzhou Prefecture.

In 1595, the Ming court conferred on Nurhachi the title of "Dragon-Tiger General" after making him a garrison commander in 1583 and public procurator of Heilongjiang Province in 1589. Frequent trips to Beijing brought him full awareness of developments in the Han areas, which in turn exerted great influence on him. A talented political and military leader, he later proved his outstanding ability by welding together within 30 years all the Nüzhen tribes that were scattered over a vast area reaching as far as the sea in the east, Kaiyuan in the west, the Nenjiang River in the north and the Yalu River in the south.

Once the Nüzhens were united, Nurhachi initiated the "Eight banner" system, under which all people were organised along military lines. Each banner consisted of many basic units called "niulu" which functioned as the primary political, military and production organisation of the Manchu people, and each unit was formed of 300 people. Members of these units hunted or farmed together in peace time, and in time of war all would go into battle as militia.

In 1619 Nurhachi proclaimed himself "Sagacious Khan" and established a slave state known to later times as Late Jin.

Political and Cultural Development   Under the strong influence of the Han people, the Manchu slave system soon underwent a speedy development towards feudalism, accompanied by intense class struggle and social reform made from above downwards. In pursuing their goal to conquer the country, the Manchu rulers began in 1633 to institute the Eight Banner system among the Hans and Mongolians under their control.

In 1635, Huang Taiji (1592-1643, eighth son of Nurhachi and later enthroned as Emperor Tai Zong of the Qing Dynasty) chose the name of "Manchu" to replace Nüzhen for his people. In the following year, when he ascended the throne, he adopted Great Qing the name of his dynasty.

In 1644 the Qing troops marched south of Shanhaiguan Pass and unified the whole of China, initiating nearly 300 years of Manchu rule throughout the country.

The Manchus made their contributions in defending China's frontiers from foreign aggression. As early as the mid-17th century, Tsarist Russia made repeated incursions into areas along the Heilong River. In 1685, on orders of Qing Emperor Kang Xi, Manchu General Peng Chun led his "eight banner" troops and naval units in driving out the Russian invaders. The subsequent Treaty of Nerchinsk, signed on an equal footing in 1689, delineated a boundary line between China and Russia, and maintained normal relations between the two countries for more than 100 years.

Later, in the 18th and 19th centuries, troops sent by the Qing court repulsed British-backed Gurkha invasions of southern Tibet and local rebellions in Xinjiang, also incited by the British colonialists. These and other military exploits of the Manchu emperors brought into being a unified Chinese state that extended from the outer Hinggan Mountains in the north to the Xisha Islands in the south, and from the Pamirs in the west to the Kurile Islands in the east in the heyday of the Qing Dynasty.

The Manchu people have also added splendour to Chinese culture with many works of scientific significance. These include *Shu*

Li Jing Yun (Essence of Mathematics and Physics), Li Xiang Kao Cheng (A Study of Universal Phenomena) and *Huang Yu Quan Lan Tu (Complete Atlas of the Empire)* compiled during the reign of Emperor Kang Xi. *Man Wen Lao Dang (Ancient Archives in Manchu), Man Wen Tai Zu Shi Lu (A Manchu Biography of the Founding Emperor)* and *Yi Yu Lu (Stories of Exotic Lands)* by Tu Lichen are among the famous works written in the early years of the dynasty, while *Qing Wen Qi Meng (Primer of Manchurian), Chu Xue Bi Du (Essential Readings for Beginners), Xu Zi Zhi Nan (A Guide to Function Words)* and *Qing Wen Dian Yao (Fundamentals of Manchurian)* are important works in the study of the Manchu language.

While the Manchu language was enriched in vocabulary, efforts were made by the Manchus to translate important works of the Han people into their own language. Along with government documents, such great works as *Romance of the Three Kingdoms, The Western Chamber, A Dream of Red Mansions, Flowering Plum in the Vase* and *Strange Tales from a Lonely Studio* all had their Manchu versions.

Notable achievements were made by the Manchu people in writing books in the Han language. Typical of these were the poems of classical styles written in the seventeenth century by the Manchu poet Nalanxingde who became known for his vivid description of the landscapes of Inner Mongolia and northeast China.

A Dream of Red Mansions written in the 18th century by the Manchu writer Cao Xueqin is a classic that occupies a prominent place in the history of world literature. With its story drawn from the life of a Manchu noble family, the novel gives incisive analysis and exposure of all the decadence of the Manchu ruling class. By dissecting China's feudal society, the author brought the country's literary expression to an unprecedented height.

Zhao Lian's *Xiao Ting Za Lu (Random Notes at Xiaoting)*, a true account of the events, rites, personalities and institutions of the early Qing Dynasty, was a work of academic value for the study of the history of the Manchus and Mongols.

Also outstanding among the Manchus were many works by women writers. These include *Qin Pu (Music Score)* by Ke De, *Hua*

Ke Xian Yin (*Leisurely Recitation of Poems by the Flower Beds*)
by Wanyan Yuegu, *Xiang Yin Guan Xiao Cao* (*Poems from Xiang-yin Pavilion*) by Kuliya Lingwen, and *Tian You Ge Ji* (*Poems Written in Tianyou Pavilion*) by Xilin Taiqing (Gu Taiqing). Her *Dong Hai Yu Ge* (*Song of East Sea Fishermen*) won her reputation as the greatest poetess of the Qing Dynasty.

Contemporary History China was reduced to the status of a semi-colonial and semi-feudal country after the Opium War of 1840.[7] During the war, many Manchus, as well as Hans, lost their lives in fighting for China's independence and the dignity of the Chinese nation. A 276-man Eight Banner unit under Major Fu Long, fighting to the last man at Tianzunmiao in Zhejiang Province, beat back the onslaught of British invaders five times in succession. In another battle fought in Zhenjiang City, Jiangsu Province, 1,500 Eight Bannermen yielded no ground in defiance of an enemy force ten times their strength.

The Second Opium War of 1856-60[8] ended with Tsarist Russia annexing more than a million square kilometres of northeast China. Local Manchus and people of other nationalities in this area waged tenacious resistance against the aggression and colonialist rule of Tsarist Russia.

In 1894, the Japanese launched a war against China and Korea, occupying large tracts of Chinese territory in eastern Liaoning Province. This aroused nationwide protest and gave rise to strong resistance by the Han, Manchu and Korean peoples, who sprang surprise attacks on the enemy day and night. Chinese troops and civilians defending Liaoyang, Liaoning Province, inflicted heavy casualties on the invading Japanese troops.

The year 1900 marked the outbreak of the *Yi He Tuan* movement or Boxer Rebellion[9], which was composed mainly of peasants of Han and Manchu nationalities.

The Revolution of 1911 led by Dr. Sun Yat-sen won wide acclaim and support among the broad masses of the Manchu people. Manchus staged a series of armed uprisings including those of Fengcheng and other places led by the Manchu progressives, Bao Huanan and He Xiuzhai, who cooperated with the Han revolutionary Ning

Wu. Manchu and Han intellectuals in Shenyang (Mukden) formed a "Progressives' Radical Alliance." Leaders of the alliance, Manchu intellectuals Bao Kun and Tian Yabin and Han progressive Zhang Rong, a member of the Tong Meng Hui (Chinese Revolutionary League), proposed the establishment of a "coalition republican government composed of Manchu and Han people." Though executed by the Qing government, the two Manchus represented the correct position many Manchu people took in the Revolution of 1911.

On September 18, 1931, Japanese forces launched a surprise attack on Shenyang and installed the puppet "Manchukuo" government to control the area.

The rigging up of the puppet "Manchukuo" soon gave rise to strong national protest throughout China. Under the leadership of the Chinese Communist Party, anti-Japanese volunteers, anti-Japanese organisations and guerrilla units were formed with massive participation by Manchu people.

On September 9, 1935, a patriotic demonstration was held with a large number of Manchu students in Beijing participating. Many of them later joined the Chinese National Liberation Vanguard Corps, the Chinese Communist Youth League or the Chinese Communist Party, carrying out revolutionary activities on their campuses and outside.

After the nation-wide War of Resistance Against Japan broke out in 1937, guerrilla warfare was waged by the Communist led Eighth Route Army with many anti-Japanese bases opened far behind enemy lines. Guan Xiangying, a Manchu general, who was also Political Commissar of the 120th Division of the Eighth Route Army, played a vital role in setting up the Shanxi-Suiyuan Anti-Japanese Base.

With the Japanese surrender in 1945, the Chinese Communist Party led the people in the Liberated Areas in fighting against attacks launched by Kuomintang troops. The Manchu people in northeast China and Manchu soldiers marching southward with the People's Liberation Army gave active support to the liberation war and made great contributions to the nationwide victory in 1949.

Before liberation, the social and economic conditions of the

Manchu people in northeast China was quite different from those of the people in the central part of the country. In the days of Japanese occupation, most land in the northeast was in the hands of landlords and rich peasants, with large tracts of farmland under direct control of the Japanese "Land Reclamation Corps." The Manchu people were subjected to plunder and enslavement. A compulsory "grain purchasing system" was enforced. All soybean, maize, corn and millet harvested by the peasants were taken by the Japanese and Chinese puppet officials, policemen and village heads. Food grain was strictly rationed after all the layers of corruption, leaving only swill for the average Manchus. Along with this were all sorts of military services and forced labour. A physical examination was required of all young Manchu peasants at the age of 19. With the strong ones conscripted into the Japanese military or the puppet army, the weaker ones were made coolies building highways, fortifications and factories or working in the mines. Life for them was extremely miserable. Treated like beasts of burden and tortured by cold and hunger they were forced to work 15 to 16 hours a day. Many perished under the lashes of the Japanese. Massacres of press-ganged Manchu workers by the Japanese were the rule upon completion of strategic military projects.

In Shenyang, Dalian, Anshan, Fushun, Changchun and Harbin, the Japanese and their Chinese helpers opened many big mines and factories. The capitalists ruthlessly exploited the workers, Manchus and Hans alike, and deprived them of their political right and personal safety.

Before liberation, about 500,000 Manchus lived under Kuomintang rule south of Shanhaiguan Pass, most of them being workers, rickshaw men, small handicraftsmen, shop keepers, retailers and teachers, all living in poverty.

Life was no better for many Manchu intellectuals, including scientific and artistic workers, teachers and government employees, since inflation and currency devaluation made things all the worse for those with meagre pay. This circumstance left no exception for the Manchu peasants living in the countryside south of the Great Wall. A few privileged old-timers and offspring of big families under the Qing Dynasty were the only ones better off than the general run.

These were rent collectors or dealers in jewellery, calligraphy and Chinese painting.

Under the Kuomintang policy of national discrimination, many Manchus, like people of other minority nationalities, lived in dread of being identified by their real names and nationality. This situation underwent a drastic change after liberation.

In 1952, the Central People's Government issued a decision protecting the right of people of all national minorities living in scattered groups to enjoy political equality. The decision stipulates that all minority people be duly represented in governments at all levels. Under this policy the Manchu people have their own deputies to the national and local People's Congresses and enjoy equal right with other nationalities running state affairs.

Manchu Artists Since 1949 Many Manchu writers and artists have gained fame throughout China since liberation. Cheng Yanqiu was a distinguished Manchu Beijing Opera singer as well as a patriot. During the War of Resistance Against Japan, he quit the stage to show his hatred and contempt for the Japanese aggressors and returned to a quiet life on the western outskirts of Beijing. But soon after the liberation of the country, he plunged himself into the work of training young opera singers.

Lao She, widely known as a patriotic writer and people's artist, was born into a poor Manchu family and had tasted all the bitterness of life in his childhood. Before liberation he wrote *Camel Xiang Zi* (or *Rickshaw Boy*) to make a thorough critique of the old society. During the War of Resistance Against Japan, with the concern and support of Comrade Zhou Enlai, he founded the National Writers' and Artists' Resistance Association, uniting and organising Chinese writers and artists for the war against Japan. He continued to write novels after liberation. From 1950 to 1966, he wrote more than a score of plays including *Dragon-Beard Ditch, A Woman Shop Assistant* and *Teahouse*, winning wide acclaim among the people.

Luo Changpei, a famous Manchu linguist, was distinguished for his expert knowledge of the dialects and phonology of the Han language and for his studies in phonetic classification of classical Chinese, its pronunciation and its history. He also studied Chinese grammar, compiled dictionaries and promoted researches into the languages of minority nationalities. He helped create the language science of New China.

The Koreans

The Korean nationality has a total population of 1,763,900. Most of them, about one million, live in Jilin Province, 430,000 in Heilongjiang and 190,000 in Liaoning. Others are found among major Chinese cities.

The largest concentration of Koreans is in the Yanbian Korean Autonomous Prefecture in eastern Jilin Province. Under its jurisdiction are the cities of Yanji and Tumen, and the counties of Yanji, Helong, Antu, Huichun, Wangqing and Dunhua, covering a total area of 41,500 sq. km.

The Yanbian Korean Autonomous Prefecture is a beautiful, majestic land of high mountains and deep valleys. The land rises to 2,744 metres above sea level to the highest peak of the Changbai Mountains — White Head Summit. This is an extinct volcano, from the crater lake of which spring the Yalu and Tumen rivers, flowing south and north respectively, and forming the boundary with the Democratic People's Republic of Korea to the east.

The area is accessible nowadays by both road and rail, except for the mountain-locked Hunchun District. The prefecture has 1,600 km of railways and 3,700 km of highways and branch roads.

Another community of Koreans lives in the Changbai Korean Autonomous County in southeastern Jilin.

The area is one of China's major sources of timber and forest products, including ginseng, marten pelts and deer antlers. It is also a habitat for many wild animals, including tigers.

Copper, lead, zinc and gold have been mined here since the Qing Dynasty (1644-1911), and the area also has deposits of iron, antimony, phosphorus, graphite, quartz, limestone and oil shale.

Yanbian is also blessed with agricultural riches and is a major tobacco producer. It is famous for apples and pears, which have been exported since 1955.

The ancestors of the Korean Nationality migrated from the Korean peninsula from about the late 17th century, mostly peasants fleeing from their oppressive feudal landlords. Especially following a severe famine in the northern part of Korea in 1869, they settled down in large numbers in what is now the Yanbian area. Another wave of migration took place in the early years of this century when Japan annexed Korea and drove many peasants off the land. The Japanese seizure of the Manchurian provinces further served to drive landless Koreans to settle in Northeast China.

The Koreans have their own spoken and written language, which is thought to belong to the Altaic family. Their alphabet is a simple, ingenious one, and the Koreans are very proud of it.

Customs The traditional Korean dress is white, a symbol of simplicity and serenity. Men wear baggy trousers fastened at the ankles and a jacket which fastens on the right; sometimes they wear a high-crowned black horsehair hat. Women wear voluminous skirts and a tight jacket which reaches just below the armpits.

Their cuisine is very spicy and includes *kimchi* (pickled vegetables), cold noodles, sticky rice cakes and dog meat.

Yanbian is fairly evenly populated, with villages set a few miles apart from each other and ranging in size from about a dozen households to several scores. The houses are built of wood with low-eaved tile or thatched roofs. They are heated by flues running under a raised platform in the main rooms, which serves as a bed and also a place to sit on. Shoes are removed before entering the house.

The Koreans are very fond of music. They sometimes sing and dance to the accompaniment of drums and flutes in the fields or on construction sites. Traditional festivals are celebrated heartily, especially the Lunar New Year, and the Mid-Autumn Festival. Other occasions for merriment are the 100th day after a baby's birth and a person's 60th birthday.

In the old days, men laboured in the fields while women worked around the house. The eldest son became the head of the family upon the death or incapacitation of the father. Monogamy was practiced but early marriage and adoption of child brides and boys to carry on the family tree were common.

Liberation ended such abuses, which included a taboo against the remarriage of widows.

Struggle Against Oppression The Korean people put up continual resistance to their enslavement by the Japanese imperialists, both on the Korean peninsula itself and in Northeast China, where Japan set up the puppet Manchukuo government in 1932. Korean guerrilla bands roamed the region and the Japanese pursued a policy of ferocious suppression. Between 1933 and 1935, in Yanji County alone, more than 20,000 people fell victim to their butchery. Large numbers of villagers were rounded up and put in concentration camps.

Under the leadership of the Yanbian District Committee (founded in 1928) of the Chinese Communist Party the Koreans organized mass movements against the Japanese. Among their many exploits were the organizing of the "May 30 Uprising" in Yanbian in 1930 and the "August 1 Insurrection" at Jidun in 1933.

After Japan's surrender, the Kuomintang regime unleashed a civil war. More than 50,000 Koreans joined the struggle against Chiang Kai-shek and helped the Communist troops liberate the nation.

During the War of Resisting U.S. Aggression and Aiding Korea (the "Korean War", 1950-53) some 46,000 Koreans from the Yanbian region joined the Chinese People's Volunteers, along with some 5,000 interpreters, political workers, transport workers and nurses.

Reconstruction As the Northeast was one of the earliest areas to be liberated in China, socialist construction began rapidly following the end of the war against Japan.

On September 3, 1952, the Yanbian Korean Autonomous Prefecture was set up, and on September 5, 1958 the Changbai Korean Autonomous County was established, followed by the founding of various Korean autonomous townships in other parts of the Northeast.

Political work progressed rapidly, and large numbers of cadres of Korean origin were trained. By 1981, over 50 per cent of officials working at all levels of administration in these autonomous areas were of Korean origin.

Land reform started as early as March 1946, and various forms of aid were extended to help the Koreans develop their traditional agriculture. Along with the establishment of agricultural experiment, tractor and meteorological stations, some 11 million yuan in farm loans was issued and 4.2 million yuan in direct investment was made by the state in water-conservancy projects during the First Five-Year Plan period (1953-1957).

Farm mechanization got off to a good start in this agricultural region. By 1981, Yanbian had 3,697 large tractors and 7,500 hand tractors; all processing and threshing work is now done by machines. In that year, Yanbian achieved a grain output of 43,000 tons, more than double the figure of 1952.

Before liberation, industry was virtually non-existent in the area. But now, heavy and forest industries are well developed, including nonferrous-metal smelting and processing, coal mining, power generation, farm machinery manufacturing, paper making, and cement and chemical fertilizer production.

Cultural Progress Culturally, the Koreans suffered worst of all the peoples enslaved by the Japanese imperialists; they were forced to speak the Japanese language and adopt Japanese surnames. But Japan's attempt to destroy Korean culture came to naught in 1945, and there was a resurgence of cultural awareness among the Koreans.

Newspapers in the Korean language sprang up, including the Jilin Daily (later renamed the Yanbian Daily), Heilongjiang Daily and the Liaoning Daily. In 1947, the Yanbian Korean Publishing House was founded in Yanji, and the Yanbian People's Radio went on the air. Special Korean programmes are also aired by the Central People's Broadcasting Station and the Heilongjiang People's Broadcasting Station.

Particular attention was paid to education. In 1949, the Yanbian University was founded in Yanji. Other institutions of higher learning established during the early post-liberation period include the Yanbian Medical Institute, the Yanbian Amateur Agricultural University and a teachers college. Universal secondary education was realized as far back as 1958.

As a result, there are now large numbers of people of Korean origin at all levels of leadership in many areas of China, and at renowned educational institutions in China's major cities.

The Yanbian area is noted also for its culture and art troupes and cultural organizations. At the prefectural level, these include the United Association of Yanbian Culture and Art Workers and the Yanbian Branch of the Chinese Writers Association. The Yanbian song and dance, modern drama and theatrical companies are famous all over the country, and many Korean artists study at advanced institutes in other parts of China.

The Korean Nationality has set up an efficient network of health care centres and hospitals, including the Yanbian Hospital, a tuberculosis treatment centre, an anti-epidemic hospital and a psychiatric sanatorium. The Yanbian Korean Autonomous Prefecture boasts high standards of maternity, child care and family planning, as well as an enviable record in the fight against endemic diseases.

The Hezhes

The Hezhes are China's smallest minority nationality. In fact, poverty and oppression had reduced their numbers to a mere 300 at the time of liberation in 1949. Since then, however, they have made speedy advances in their economic life and health care, so that by 1982 the population had grown to 1,500.

They are a nomadic people who live mainly by hunting and fishing in the plain formed by the Heilong, Songhua and Wusoli rivers in Tongjiang, Fuyuan and Raohe counties in northeast China's Heilongjiang Province. Their language, which belongs to the Manchu-Tungusic group of the Altaic family, has no written form. For communication with outsiders they use the spoken and written Chinese language.

In winter they travel by sled and hunt on skis. They are also skilled at carpentry, tanning and iron-smelting; but these are still cottage industries.

Customs and Culture Traditional Hezhe clothing is made of fish skins and deer hides. The decorations of the clothes consist of buttons made of catfish bones and collars and cuffs dyed in cloud-shaped patterns. Women wear fish-skin and deer-hide dresses decorated with shells and coloured strips of dyed deer hide in cloud, plant and animal designs. Bear skins and birch bark are also used to make thick boots which everyone wears in winter.

Unmarried girls used to tie their hair in one braid, while married women wore two. Bracelets were common ornaments for all women, but only old women wore earrings.

Since liberation, these styles have fallen out of fashion to a great extent, along with the primitive shamanism which used to be the Hezhes' religion.

Monogamy is the normal practice, but polygamy was sometimes indulged in by the wealthier members of the tribe. Marriage partners had to be selected from among members of other clans, and early marriage, arranged by the parents, was normal. Though remarriage for widows was sanctioned, no marriage ceremony was performed.

The dead were buried in the wilderness, in log-lined pits covered with a mound. Dead infants were bundled in birch bark and suspended from the limbs of trees, in the hope that their souls would be freed into the air and promote the prosperity of the parents.

Story telling and ballad singing are favourite pastimes among the Hezhe nationality, who have a wealth of folktales. Some of the longer epics and ballads can last for days on end, as tales of ancient heroes are narrated in speech alternating with songs.

Short and lively *shuohuli* songs used to be sung by the elders to initiate the younger members of the tribe into the tribal lore. The Hezhes also sing songs with extempore words; typical are "jialing-kuo" and "henina."

Embroidery is a highly developed art among the Hezhes — probably perfected over the centuries of long winter nights. Geometrical and floral patterns decorate clothing, shoes and tobacco pouches.

They are also noted for their carved wooden furniture, birch-bark boxes and utensils, which sport images of Buddha, plants and animals.

Historical Background   The Hezhes trace their lineage back to the nomadic Nüzhens, a race of Tartar horsemen who ravaged the northern borders of several Chinese dynasties. The Hezhes of different regions call themselves by various names, prominent among which are Nanai, Nabei and Naniao — all meaning "natives" or "aborigines." They first came under Chinese sway during the Tang Dynasty (618-907) when the Heilong Military Region was set up to rule the area. In the early Qing Dynasty (1644-1911) the Hezhes were incorporated into the military "eight banner" system of the Manchu rulers.

The Qing government adopted divide-and-rule tactics by giving titles and administrative power to the local tribal chiefs, who then used their privileges to exploit the poorer Hezhes, thus creating a feudal hierarchy.

But it was when they fell under the rule of the Japanese puppet state of Manchukuo that the Hezhes reached the depths of minsery. A policy of genocide was practised, under which the Hezhes were herded into concentration camps. Their diet was inadequate, as they could no longer hunt and fish freely, and opium addiction was rife. The death toll under these conditions was high and the Hezhes dwindled rapidly in numbers, reaching the point of extinction as a separate nationality just before liberation.

Resurgence of the Hezhes With the end of the War of Resistance Against Japan in 1945, the Hezhes took an active part in the Chinese People's Liberation Army's mopping-up operations against remnant Kuomintang forces in their area.

They then returned to their old hunting grounds and rebuilt their homes with help from the central government. Loans and relief funds enabled them to resume their traditional way of life.

Farming was encouraged and many of the Hezhes went in for it, as others formed production teams to pursue hunting and fishing. With their initiative brought into full play, the Hezhes began to have a thriving economy. Electricity has transformed their once-gloomy dwellings with light, radios, TV sets and other conveniences of modern life. Textiles, leather and rubber have replaced the old animal skins they used to wrap themselves in, and up-to-date educational and medical facilities are available, even for the Hezhes who continue to lead a nomadic life.

The Hezhes run their own affairs in Fuyuan County's Xiabacha. Hezhe Autonomous Township, and send deputies to local, provincial and national People's Congresses.

The Mongolians

The Mongolians, numbering 3,411,700, live mostly in the Inner Mongolia Autonomous Region, with the rest residing in Liaoning, Jilin, Heilongjiang, Xinjiang, Qinghai, Gansu, Ningxia, Hebei, Henan, Sichuan, Yunnan and Beijing.

Having their own spoken and written language, which belongs to the Mongolian group of the Altaic language family, the Mongolians use three dialects: Inner Mongolian, Barag-Buryat and Uirad. The Mongolian script was created in the early 13th century on the basis of the script of Huihu or ancient Uygur, which was revised and developed a century later into the form used to this day.

The largest Mongolian area, the Inner Mongolia Autonomous Region with its capital at Huhhot, was founded on May 1, 1947, as the earliest such establishment in China. This vast and rich expanse of land is inhabited by 19,274,000 people, of whom 2,489,700 are Mongolians and the rest Hans, Huis, Manchus, Daurs, Ewenkis, Oroqens and Koreans.

The Inner Mongolia Autonomous Region is located in the northern part of China. Covering 1.2 million square kilometres and rising 900 to 1,300 metres above sea level, it has vast tracts of excellent natural pastureland with numerous herds of cattle, sheep, horses and camels. The Yellow River Bend and Tumochuan plains, known as a "Granary North of the Great Wall," are crisscrossed with streams and canals. Over southwestern Inner Mongolia flows the Yellow River, which is, among other things, famous for its carp and the well-developed irrigation and transport facilities it has provided for the area. Inner Mongolia also has several hundred richly endowed salt and alkali lakes and many large freshwater lakes, including Hulun Nur, Buir Nur, Ulansu Nur, Dai Hai and Huangqi Hai. More than 60 mineral resources such as coal, iron, chromium, manganese, copper, lead, zinc, gold, silver, tin, mica, graphite, rock crystal and asbestos have been found. The Greater Hinggan Mountain Range in the east part of the region boasts China's largest forests, which are also a fine habitat for a good many rare species of wildlife. This unique natural environment makes the region a famous producer of precious hides, pilose antler, bear gallbladder, musk, Chinese caterpillar fungus (Cordyceps sinensis), as well as 400 varieties of Chinese medicinal herbs, including licorice root, "dangshen" (Codonopsis pilosula), Chinese ephedra (Ephedra sinica), and the root of membranous milk vetch (Astragalus membranaceus). Specialities of the region known far and wide are mushrooms and day lily flowers, which enjoy brisk sales on both the domestic and world markets.

Following the founding of the Inner Mongolia Autonomous Region, autonomous prefectures and counties were established in other provinces where Mongolians live in large communities. These include the two Mongolian autonomous prefectures of Boertala and Bayinguoleng in Xinjiang, the Mongolian and Kazak Autonomous Prefecture in Qinghai, and the seven autonomous counties in Xinjiang, Qinghai, Gansu, Heilongjiang, Jilin and Liaoning. Enjoying the same rights as all other nationalities in China, the Mongolians are joining them in running the country as its true masters.

History Mongol was initially the name of a tribe roaming along the Erguna River. Moving to the grasslands of western Mongolia in the 7th century, the Mongols settled in the upper reaches of the Onon, Kerulen and Tula rivers and areas east of the Kentey Mountains in the 12th century. Later, their offshoots grew into many tribal groups, such as Qiyan, Zadalan and Taichiwu. The Mongolian grasslands and the forests around Lake Baikal were also home to many other tribes such as Tartar, Wongjiqa, Mierqi, Woyela, Kelie, Naiman and Wanggu, which varied in size and economic and cultural development.

Early in the 13th century, Temujin of the Mongol tribe unified all these tribes to form a new national community called Mongol. In 1206, he had a clan conference held on the bank of the Onon River, at which he was elected the Great Khan of all Mongols with the title of Genghis Khan. This was followed by the founding of a centralized feudal khanate under aristocratic rule, which promoted the development of Mongolian society. Military conquests ensued on a large scale soon after Temujin's accession to the throne. In 1211 and 1215, he launched massive attacks against the State of Jin (1115-1234) and captured Zhongdu (present-day Beijing). In 1219 he began his first Western expedition, extending his jurisdiction as far as Central Asia and southern Russia. He died in 1227.

In 1260, Kublai Khan (1215-1294) became the Great Khan and moved his capital from Helin north of the Gobi Desert to Yanjing, which was later renamed Dadu (Great Capital). In 1272 he founded the Yuan Dynasty (1206-1368), and in 1279 he subdued the Southern Song (1127-1279), bringing the whole of China under his centralized rule.

The subsequent Ming Dynasty (1368-1644) placed the areas where Mongols lived under the administration of more than 20 garrison posts commanded by Mongolian manorial lords. In the early 15th century the Wala (Woyela) and Tartar Mongols living west and north of the Gobi Desert pledged their allegiance to the Ming empire.

In the Qing Dynasty (1644-1911) more Mongol feudal lords dispatched emissaries to Beijing and presented tributes to the Qing court. Later, some Jungar feudal lords of the Elutes, incited by Tsarist Russia, staged rebellions against the central government. They were put down by the Qing court through repeated punitive expeditions and the Mongolian areas were reunified under the central authorities.

To tighten its control over the various Mongol tribes, the Qing government instituted in Mongolia a system of leagues and banners on the basis of the Manchu Eight-Banner Institution.

The Mongolians have a fine cultural tradition, and they have made indelible contributions to China in culture and science. They created their script in the 13th century and later produced many outstanding historical and literary works, including the *Inside History of Mongolia* of the mid-13th century and the *History of the Song Dynasty, History of the Liao Dynasty* and *History of the Jin Dynasty* edited by Tuo Tuo, a Mongolian historian during the Yuan Dynasty. The reign also enjoyed a galaxy of Mongolian calligraphers and authors like Quji Wosier who was credited with many works and translations done in the Han and Tibetan languages. *Da Yuan Yi Tong Zhi (China's Unification under the Great Yuan Dynasty)* was a famous work of geographical studies compiled under the auspices of the Yuan court. Mongolian architecture in the construction of cities and especially of palaces at that time was also unique.

Further advances in culture were made by Mongolians in the Ming Dynasty. Apart from such great literary and historical works as the *Golden History of Mongolia, An Outline of the Golden History of Mongolia* and *Stories of Heir Apparent Wubashehong*, Mongolian scholars produced many grammar books and dictionaries, as well as translations of the *Inside History of Mongolia* and the *Buddhist Scripture Kanjur* done into Chinese. These works enriched Mongolian culture and promoted cultural exchanges between the Mongolian, Han and Tibetan people.

The development of Mongolian culture in the subsequent Qing Dynasty was represented by a greater number of dictionaries and reference books like the *Principles of Mongolian, A Collection of Mongolian Words and Phrases, Exegesis of Mongolian Words, Mongolian-Tuote Dictionary, Mongolian-Tibetan Dictionary, Manchurian-Mongolian-Han-Tibetan Dictionary, Manchurian-Mongolian-Han-Tibetan-Uygur Dictionary, Manchurian-Mongolian-Han Tibetan-Uygur-Tuote Dictionary* and *A Concise Dictionary of Manchurian, Mongolian and Han*. Noted literary and historical works included *The Origin and Growth of Mongolia, Peace and Prosperity Under the Great Yuan Dynasty, Random Notes from the West Studio, Miscellanies from Fengcheng, A Guide to a Means of Life, A*

One Storey House, and *Weeping Scarlet Pavilion.* Mongolian scholars also translated such Chinese classics as *A Dream of Red Mansions, Outlaws of the Marsh, Romance of the Three Kingdoms* and *Pilgrimage of the West.*

The *Stories of Shageder,* also produced in this period, has been regarded as the most outstanding work in the treasure-house of Mongolian literature. Other great works of folk literature include the *Story of Gessar Khan* of the 11th century, the *Life Story of Jianggar,* an epic of the 15th century.

Mongolians owed their achievements in medical science, astronomy and calendar to the influence of the Hans and Tibetans. Mongolian medicine has been best known for its Lamaist therapy, which is most effective for traumatic surgery and the setting of fractured bones. To further develop their medical science, the Mongolians have translated into Mongolian many Han and Tibetan medical works, which include *Mongolian-Tibetan Medicine, A Compendium of Medical Science, Secret of Pulse Taking, Basic Theories on Medical Science in Four Volumes, Pharmaceutics* and *Five Canons of Pharmacology.* Outstanding contributions have also been made by the Mongolians in the veterinary science. In the field of mathematics and calendar, credit should be given to the Mongolian astronomist and mathematician Ming Antu. During the decades of his service in the Imperial Observatory, he participated in compiling and editing the *Origin and Development of Calendar, Sequel to a Study of Universal Phenomena* and *A Study of the Armillary Sphere.* His work *Quick Method for Determining Segment Areas and Evaluation of π* (completed by his son and students) is also a contribution to China's development in mathematics. He also made a name for himself in cartography. It was due to his geographical surveys in Xinjiang that the *Complete Atlas of the Empire,* the first atlas of China drawn with scientific methods, was finished.

Customs and Habits Mongolians grow up on horsebacks and horses thus play an important part in their life. Every Mongolian loves to prove his worth by showing good horsemanship and archery as well as wrestling.

"Nadam," meaning games in Mongolian, is the name of a traditional Mongolian fair, which is held in July and August each year. At the fair, people wearing their holiday best, participate in horse racing, archery, singing, dancing, chess playing and wrestling.

The life of the Mongolians is unique. Those in the pastoral areas wear fur coats lined with satin or cloth or nothing at all in winter and loose, long-sleeved cotton robes in summer. Mongolian costume is generally red, yellow or dark blue in colour. A red or green waistband, flint steel, snuffbox and knife in an ornate sheath for cutting meat are accessories common to all men and women. Knee-high felt boots are a type of common footwear. Mongolians, men and women, wear cone-shaped hats in winter; they also like to wear silk or cloth turbans. Girls wear their hair parted in the middle, embellished with two large beads and agate, coral and green jade ornaments.

In pastoral areas, beef, mutton and dairy products are the staple food, while in the farming areas, people like to eat grain. Tea is indispensable. Dried cow dung is a common cooking fuel.

Mongolian herdsmen used to live in felt yurts, which were usually seven to eight feet high and ten feet in diameter. With an opening in the top of the umbrella-shaped roof, they give ideal ventilation and good protection against wind and cold.

After liberation, as more and more herdsmen ended their nomadic life and settled down, they began to build yurt-like houses of mud and wood and one-storey houses, each with two or three rooms like those in other parts of the country.

The Mongolians are warm-hearted and straightforward. They welcome strangers travelling on the grasslands to stay for the night in their yurts and treat them to tea with milk, mutton and milk wine. Upon leaving, the guests will invariably be given a warm send-off by the hosts.

Culture   Mongolians believed in shamanism in ancient times. The red sect of Lamaism began to find its followers among the Mongolian rulers in the 13th century. In the 16th century, many feudal lords as well as herdsmen shifted to the yellow sect. Lamaism was later protected and encouraged by the imperial court of the Qing Dynasty, especially during the reign of Emperor Qian Long. Different titles, posts and privileges were granted to high-ranking lamas, who gradually formed a ruling feudal stratum existing side by side with the ruling feudal lords. These rulers not only rode roughshod over the people but took possession of numerous herds and large tracts of land. Their influence could be felt in every aspect of Mongolian life. The feudal rulers encouraged young people to become lamas, who neither got married nor took part in physical labour. As a result, the number of lamas increased to as many as one third of the Mongolian population during the Ming and Qing dynasties, seriously impeding the development of production and the growth of the population.

Mongolians practise monogamy. Before liberation, intermarriage between nobles and common people was permitted except that daughters of Zhasake lords were not allowed to marry common people. Marriage was generally arranged by parents, or local feudal lords as in the case of the western grasslands, with costly betrothal gifts demanded. Before weddings, Buddhist scriptures would be chanted and heavenly protection sought.

A Mongolian family usually consists of the parents and their children. When the son gets married he usually lives in a separate home close to his parents. There are also families formed of several married brothers and sisters-in-law in the farming and semi-farming areas.

The Mongolians have been known as "a people of music and poetry." Their singing, sonorous, bold, passionate and unconstrained, is the true reflection of the temperament of the Mongolian people.

"Haolibao" is a popular Mongolian form of singing to set melodies with the words improvised extemporaneously. Also very popular are many other forms of singing including "Mahatale" (paean), "Yurele" (congratulation), "Dairileqi" (antiphonal singing), riddles, proverbs, stories, legends, fairy tales and fables.

Mongolian dances are known far and wide. The best ones include the "Sabre" dance, "Ordos" dance, "Andai," "Buryat Wedding," "Horse Breaker" and "Little Black Horse." "Winecup" and "Chopsticks," widely recognized as the most lively Mongolian dances, are known for their brisk steps which are characteristic of the candour, warmth and stoutness of the Mongolian people.

Horse-head fiddle is a musical instrument favourite with the Mongolians. It provides fine accompaniment to solos with its low and deep, broad and melodious sounds.

Heroic Past   Following the Opium War of 1840, ruthless plunder and oppression by foreign and domestic reaction, colonialist rule of the Japanese in particular, plunged the Mongolians into dire poverty and brought about a sharp decrease in their population. In face of national extinction, the Mongolian people rose in heroic and persistent struggles. In 1607, Mongolians of the Eleute and Tartar tribes formed an armed force 5,000 strong and wiped out all the invading Tsarist Russian troops. Later, the Russians' tricks of deception, bribery and coercion were also frustrated by the tribal chieftains. Towards the end of the 17th century, Gardan, chieftain of the Jungar tribe, staged an armed rebellion at the instigation of the Russians, but it was soon put down by Mongolian soldiers and herdsmen.

In June 1859, when British and French troops attacked Dagu port in north China, 2,000 mounted Mongolian soldiers under Senggelinqin, in defiance of the Qing government's orders to surrender, put up a stubborn resistance, repulsing the enemy forces and inflicting on them a loss of four warships and 400 men.

In 1858, poor herdsmen in Uxin Banner of Ih Ju League in Inner Mongolia started an insurrection under the leadership of Pilejie against exorbitant taxes and levies, enforced military service and corvee.

Mongolians continued their struggle to protect their pastures and land and fought against the Northern Warlords during the Revolution of 1911.

The founding of the Chinese Communist Party in 1921 marked a new stage in the revolutionary struggle of the Mongolian people. Li Dazhao, then leader of the North China Political Committee of the Communist Party of China, was active among Mongolians.

During the War of Resistance Against Japan, guerrillas of Mongolian and other nationalities in Ih Ju League and the Daqing Mountains fought heroically against the Japanese occupation troops, while fighting against the Kuomintang policy of "opposing the Communists and subjugating the Mongolians."

Development After the war, a so-called provisional government of the "republic of Inner Mongolia" headed by Buying Dalai and other Mongolian traitors was set up in west Sonid Banner of Xilin. Ulanhu, a communist leader of Mongolian nationality, mobilised the masses and convened the People's Congress of Inner Mongolia, at which the "provisional government" was disbanded. The victory of the struggle was followed by the founding of the Federation of Autonomous Movement of Inner Mongolia in November 1945. On May 1, 1947, the Inner Mongolia Autonomous Region was formally inaugurated.

The Chinese Communist Party has always attached great importance to training minority cadres. It trained a good many outstanding Mongolian leaders in its early days. In the thirties, the Party founded a nationalities institute in Yan'an to train cadres of minority nationalities, including Mongolians.

A special effort has also been made to train women cadres.

The Mongolian economy in the old days was characterised by the polarisation of the rich and the poor. The rich included the nobility, high lamas and officials while the poor were the herdsmen and peasants.

Democratic and socialist reforms were carried out shortly after liberation, putting an end to the system of feudal exploitation. As a result, striking progress has been made in both animal husbandry and farming.

Animal husbandry is a traditional means of livelihood for the Mongolian people. But deterioration of pasturage seriously impeded its development in the old days. Huge efforts have been made to improve the situation since liberation. Along with the rational use of pastures, a network of veterinary and epidemic prevention stations was set up to improve the breeds of animals. Big progress has also been made in such chores as medicinal bathing, fodder gathering, shearing and animal by-product processing. As a result, the number of livestock of the region showed a sharp increase in recent years. In mid-1985, the region reported 38 million head of domestic animals, 410,000 more than a year before.

Since 1978, the "job responsibility system," under which the earnings of the herdsmen and peasants are linked with the amount of work they put in, has been implemented in the region. This has further fired the enthusiasm of the Mongolian people.

All this has brought tremendous changes to the life of the Mongolian people. In the old days, the majority of them lived in hunger, being deprived of the essential means of life such as an old yurt. Today they have well-furnished yurts with clean beds and new quilts. Sewing machines, radios, TV sets, telescopes and cream separators are no longer novelties to the ordinary Mongolian herdsmen. Many new houses with paned windows have been built in the Mongolian settlements.

Agriculture in Inner Mongolia was extremely backward before liberation. Crude cultivation with simple farm tools gave a low yield, averaging 525 to 600 kilogrammes per hectare in 1946. Since liberation, however, the irrigated area in the region has greatly expanded as a result of the many new water conservancy and other farmland projects. In Hangjin Rear Banner, one of the poorest counties in the region, people harvested 3,000 kilogrammes of grain per hectare in 1985, up from 1,500 kilogrammes in 1978. The annual income per person was 360 yuan in 1985, as against 50 yuan in the past.

In the old days, industry was almost non-existent in Inner Mongolia, let alone modern industries. It had only a few small power plants, tanneries and grain processing mills. Today the regoin boasts such modern industries as iron and steel making, nonferrous metals smelting, machine building, coal, power, chemical engineering, electronics, building materials, textiles, tanning, sugar refining, dairy processing, rubber processing, paper making and pharmaceutics. The iron and steel works in Baotou, the largest city in the region, has grown into one of the largest in the country. Light industry has also grown considerably to meet the needs of the Mongolian people. The region's total industrial output value for 1983 reached 7,530 million yuan (calculated according to the constant price of 1980). A wide range of food and light industrial products manufactured in the region, such as canned food, frozen meat, woollen fabrics and blankets, leather coats and shoes, and woollen yarn and rugs has found a ready market both at home and abroad.

The regional government has also developed the traditional industries to meet the needs of the Mongolian people for yurts, saddles, leather boots and brass teapots.

The past few decades have witnessed in Inner Mongolia a vigorous development of literature, music, dance and fine arts, with a wealth of cultural legacies collected, collated and developed and many new outstanding works produced. These include novels *On the Vast Grasslands, Spring Sunshine Over Uzhumqin Pasture, Golden Hinggan Mountains*, and *Son of the Grasslands*, the poems *The Courageous Cavalry* and *Happiness and Friendship*, the plays *Song of Bayinaola, Golden Eagle* and *On the Happy Road*, and the screenplays *People on the Grasslands, Blue Mountain Valley* and *Storm over Ordos*, all of which have won acclaim from the local people.

Today Inner Mongolia has 14 song and dance ensembles and theatrical companies and 44 opera troupes. Mongolian singers, dancers, musicians, theatrical, opera and film workers and artists have created many outstanding works including *Appointment at Aobao, On Our Grasslands, My Steed, The Sun Rises Over the Grasslands, The Song of Hunters, The Paean, Gadameilin, Spring Comes to the Grasslands* and *Rainbow*.

There was practically no higher education to speak of in Inner Mongolia before liberation. The number of school children accounted for only 2.6 per cent of the population while more than 90 per cent of the Mongolians were illiterate. In some places, people had to travel for days to find someone who could read and write letters for them. Speedy advances have been made in education, culture and science since liberation.

Stress has always been laid on the use and popularisation of the Mongolian language in the region. It is now widely used in schools and colleges, in publication and in the press. While encouraging people of Han and other nationalities in Inner Mongolia to study the Mongolian language, the local government has made an active effort to encourage the Mongolians to study the Han language, so as to further strengthen the unity and development of all the ethnic groups in the region.

Scientific experiments have been carried out on a large scale in Inner Mongolia. More than 450 academic societies with 118,000 scientific research workers have been formed at various levels. The membership includes 17,400 people of minority nationalities.

Advances have been made in theatrical writing and film production. Inner Mongolia now has several large theatrical troupes, including an experimental theatre, a drama troupe and a film studio, with Mongolian directors, actors, actresses, stage artists and playwrights credited with such popular works as *Golden Eagle, Aoligema, The Story of Three Mountains* and *Before Dawn.*

Also popular among the Mongolians is a type of theatrical troupe called Wulanmuqi, meaning "light cavalry." Members of such performing art troupes travel on horseback or by horse cart to give performances for herdsmen and peasants on the grasslands.

Before liberation, the Mongolians had no modern medical service, and the only treatment available came from a small number of lama doctors. Epidemic diseases were widespread, and the mortality rate was extremely high. Take Xilin Gol League. It had 84,000 Mongolians towards the end of the Qing Dynasty, but only 39,500 in 1936. The Mongolian population began to increase in 1953 thanks to the government's efforts to train more medical workers and eliminate such formerly widespread diseases as the plague, venereal disease and brucellosis. According to the 1984 statistics, Inner Mongolia had 4,600 hospitals and anti-epidemic stations with 4,800 beds and 100,000 medical workers, which were 83, 92 and 15 times the figures for 1947, when the autonomous region was founded.

Traditional Mongolian medicine has also developed rapidly, with 41 hospitals and clinics specially built to provide such medical service in Inner Mongolia. These institutions have, between them, 3,500 medical workers of the traditional school.

Improved medical work has promoted the growth of the Mongolian population, which reached 1.92 million in 1982 as against 1.23 million in 1964 and 0.8 million in 1952.

The Daurs

The Daurs, numbering 94,000, live mainly in the Inner Mongolia Autonomous Region and Heilongjiang Province. About 3,000 Daurs are found in the Tacheng area in the Xinjiang Uygur Autonomous Region in northwest China. They are descendents of Daurs who moved to China's western region in the early Qing Dynasty (1644-1911). The Daurs speak a language related to Mongolian and used Manchu during the Qing Dynasty as their written language. Since the 1911 Revolution, mandarin Chinese has replaced Manchu.

The biggest Daur community is in the Morin Dawa Daur Autonomous Banner, which was set up on August 15, 1958 on the left bank of the Nenjiang River in Heilongjiang Province. This 11,943 sq. km. area has lush pasture and farmland. The main crops are maize, sorghum, wheat, soybeans and rice. In the mountains which border the Daur community on the north are stands of valuable timber — such as oak, birch and elm — and medicinal herbs. Wildlife, including bears, deer, lynx and otters are found in the forests. Mineral deposits in the area include gold, mica, iron and coal.

History The Daur people are thought to be descended, along with the Ewenkis and Oroqens, from the Khitan nomads, who founded the Liao Dynasty (916-1125). They originally inhabited the lower reaches of the Heilong River.

In the early Qing Dynasty, the Daurs had a diversified economy which comprised fishing, hunting, farming and stock raising. They traded hides for metal implements, cloth and other articles from the more economically advanced Hans.

During the reign of Emperor Shun Zhi (1644-1662), the Daurs moved south and settled on the banks of the Nenjiang River, from where they were constantly conscripted to serve in the armies of the Qing emperors and in garrisons all over the Chinese empire. The Daurs helped to repel Cossack invaders from Tsarist Russia in 1643 and 1651. When the Japanese invaded Northeast China in 1931, the Daurs opposed them and helped the resistance forces until liberation in 1945.

Traditional Economy and Customs Before liberation, the Daurs had a well developed agriculture, with per-hectare yield of grain reaching 350 kg. They raised horses and oxen. Those living in the mountainous north of the area were also engaged in hunting, charcoal burning, edible plants gathering, tanning, and the manufacture of carts and wooden pipes. Distribution of land and animals was very uneven, with the big landlords exploiting the majority of the people.

Monogamy was the general rule, and marriages were arranged by the parents. A man from a different clan would go to live with his wife's family, but had no claim of their property. Closest ties are those between brothers-in-law. All important celebrations require the presence of the brothers-in-law and their families, who send gifts to new-born children.

The religion of the Daurs was shamanism, while a few were followers of lamaism. The biggest festival of the year was held in May, when pigs and oxen would be sacrificed to the gods to ensure prosperity for the coming year. At the Spring Festival, sacrifices were made to the ancestors and firecrackers set off in the evening. Everyone joined in a round of visits to their neighbours to partake of steamed New Year cakes and give presents of various delicacies.

Pipes are passed to visitors, men and women alike, as a sign of respect. Girls make elaborate tobacco pouches and slip them into the pockets of young men who take their fancy.

Wrestling, horse racing and archery are popular sports among the Daurs. They also play a kind of football with a ball made of ox hair.

Daur villages are neat, usually built on mountain slopes and facing streams, and the houses have courtyards surrounded by wickerwork fences.

The women have always been renowned for their needlework, decorating their clothing with fine patterns. Men wear straw hats in summer or simply tie a piece of white cloth around their foreheads. In winter they wear leather caps with ear flaps. Women wear white cloth socks and patterned shoes in summer, donning leather boots and long gowns in winter.

Typical of the daily diet of the Daurs is millet or buckwheat noodles mixed with milk, buckwheat cakes and oat porridge cooked with soybeans. Game figures high on the list of Daur delicacies, especially deer meat, pheasant and duck. They cultivate a variety of vegetables.

Inseparable from the Daur scene is the "leleche" — a small cart with large wheels drawn by an ox.

Cultural Life   The Daurs have a rich repertory of folk dances which they love to perform during festivals. Women participate in group singing and most women own a musical instrument called a "mukulian." Men play a similar instrument, but the women are the most accomplished players.

Daur folk literature is mostly based on observations of nature, but it also contains a wealth of legends and fables. One of their most popular stories is called "The Young Stalwart and Dai Fu." It tells of the struggles of the Daurs against national oppression and their feudal rulers in the latter part of the 19th century. Also famous among the Daurs are stories by Ahlabudan, a Qing Dynasty author, such as "Fringed Iris Pouch," "Song of the Four Seasons" and "Song of Refraining from Drinking." Also well known are tales adapted from classical Chinese novels. The best-read contemporary works are those by a Daur writer named Qin Tongpu, such as "A Farmer's Song," "Song of the Fishermen" and "Song of the Lumbermen."

The Daurs have a love for poetry, which they compose in several unique verse forms. Their long winter evenings are also enlivened by oral literature, riddles and proverbs, as well as handicrafts such as toy making, embroidery and paper cuts.

The dead are buried in graveyards arranged according to family lineage. Buried along with the deceased are ornaments, tobacco pipes, cooking utensils, and sometimes slaughtered horses.

Life Today Following liberation in 1945, land reform was carried out in the Daur areas and in 1947 pastures were put under public ownership, allowing free grazing to all the herdsmen.

Nirji Town is the seat of the People's Government of the Morin Dawa Daur Autonomous Banner (County). The town has a People's Cultural Palace, and thriving machine-building, repair, food-processing and chemical industries.

There are more than 100 settlements in the region and seven autonomous townships — all nowadays linked by roads and a railway. Local cadres have been trained to administer the banner.

Industry has come to the Daur community for the first time, with factories producing electric motors, transformers and chemical fertilizer. Farm machinery and power supply sources have also contributed greatly to the development of agriculture.

With the development of education, nearly all Daur children of school age now attend primary schools. An increasing number of young Daurs go to middle schools and colleges.

Epidemics, particularly "keshan" disease which affects the heart, are a thing of the past now that the banner has 26 medical centres.

The Ewenkis

This nationality has a population of 19,300 distributed across seven banners (counties) in the Inner Mongolia Autonomous Region and in Nahe County of Heilongjiang Province, where they live together with Mongolians, Daurs, Hans and Oroqens.

The Ewenki people have no written script but a spoken language composed of three dialects belonging to the Manchu-Tungusic group of the Altai language family. Mongolian is spoken in the pastoral areas while the Han language is used in agricultural regions. The Ewenki Autonomous Banner, nestled in the ranges of the Greater Hinggan Mountains, is where the Ewenkis live in compact communities. A total of 19,110 square kilometres in area, it is studded with more than 600 small and big lakes and 11 springs. The pastureland here totalling 9,200 square kilometres is watered by the Yimin and four other rivers, all rising in the Greater Hinggan Mountains.

Nantunzhen, the seat of the banner government, is a rising city on the grassland. A communication hub, it is the political, economic and cultural centre of the Ewenki Autonomous Banner.

Large numbers of livestock and great quantities of knitting wool, milk, wool-tops and casings are produced in the banner. Some 20-odd of these products are exported. The yellow oxen bred on the grassland have won a name for themselves in Southeast Asian countries. Pelts of a score or so of fur-bearing animals are also produced locally.

Reeds are in riot growth and in great abundance along the Huihe River in the banner. Some 35,000 tons are used annually for making paper. Lying beneath the grassland are rich deposits of coal, iron, gold, copper and rock crystal.

History The forefathers of the Ewenkis had originally been a people who earned their living by fishing, hunting and breeding reindeer in the forests northeast of Lake Baikal and along the Shileke River (upper reaches of the Heilong River), tracing their ancestry to the "Shiweis", particularly the "Northern Shiweis" and "Bo Shiweis" living at the time of Northern Wei (386-534) on the upper reaches of the Heilong River, and the "Ju" tribes that bred deer at the time of the Tang Dynasty (618-907) in the forests of Taiyuan to the northeast of Lake Baikal. Later, they moved east, with one section coming to live on the middle reaches of the Heilong River. In history, the Ewenkis and the Oroqens and Mongolians living in forests to the east of Lake Baikal and the Heilong River Valley in the Yuan Dynasty (1280-1368) were known as a "forest people," and a people "moving on deer's backs" by the time of the Ming (1368-1644). When it came to the Qing period (1644-1911) they were called the "Sulongs" or "Kemunikans" (another tribal people different from the Sulongs at the time) who knew how to use deer.

In 1635, the Kemunikans came under the domination of Manchu rulers after their conquest of the Lake Baikal area, to be followed around the years from 1639 to 1640 by their control of the Sulongs living to the east of Lake Baikal. From the mid-17th century onwards, aggression by Tsarist Russia had led the Qing government to remove the Ewenkis to the area along the Ganhe, Nuomin, Ahlun, Jiqin, Yalu and Namoer — tributaries of the Nenjiang River. In 1732, 1,600 Ewenkis were called up in the Buteha area and ordered together with their family dependents to perform garrison duties as frontier guards on the Hulunbuir Grassland. Their descendants are now the inhabitants of the Ewenki Autonomous Banner.

Economy and Life Style Imigrations in the past led to population dispersion which in turn resulted in great unevenness in the social development of the Ewenki people dwelling in different places with diverse natural conditions. As a result, some Ewenkis are no-mads; others are farmers or farmer-hunters. A small number of them are hunters.

The Ewenkis in the Ewenki Autonomous Banner and the Chen-baerfu Banner lead a nomadic life, wandering with their herds from place to place in search of grass and water. They live in yurts.

The Ewenkis excel in horsemanship. Boys and girls learn to ride on horseback at six or seven when they go out to pasture cattle with their parents. Girls are taught to milk cows and take part in horse-racing at around ten, and learn the difficult art of lassoing horses when they grow a little older.

A "Mikuole" festival is traditionally observed by Ewenki herds-men in May every year. At happy gatherings held everywhere on the grasslands, men, women and children in their holiday best go from yurt to yurt to partake wine, fine foods and other delicacies prepared for the occasion. It is a time for nomads to count new-born lambs and take stock of their wealth, and for young, sturdy lads to demon-strate their skills in lassoing horses and branding or castrating them.

With the institution of the "eight banner system" way back in the 17th century, Ewenki nomads were drafted into the army and had the obligation to pay leopard skins as tributes to the Qing rulers. This was at a time when they were at the transitional stage from primitivity to a class society. Helped by the Qing rulers, an upper stratum of Ewenkis invested with feudal rights then emerged. The expansion of agriculture and animal husbandry finally brought the Ewenki nomads to the threshold of a patriarchal feudal society.

A "nimoer" mutual-aid group consisting of a few to 10-odd families was usually formed by the Ewenkis to pasture their herds. People in the group were members of the same clan, and there was no exploitation of man by man at first. But in later years each "ni-moer" group came to be dominated by a feudal lord, who had far more cattle than the other nomads in the group. In name the pastures belonged to the "nimoer" group, but in fact it was owned by the feudal chief who had the biggest herd. The poor nomads in the "nimoer" were at the beck and call of the feudal chief for whom they had to perform corvee.

A concentration of land also took place in areas where the Ewenkis lived as farmers or farmer-hunters. In areas near mountains, they lived by hunting, lumbering and making charcoal, with a few going in for farming. There emerged landlords, some possessing as many as 300 hectares of land. Here poor Ewenkis became employed hunters of landlords who supplied guns, ammunition and hunting horses and took away the bulk of the game bagged.

In the forests of the Ergunazuo Banner were Ewenki hunters who, having no permanent homes, wandered from place to place with their reindeer in search of game. When they stopped in the hunt, these Ewenki hunters lived in make-shift, umbrella-shaped tents built on 25 to 30 larch poles. In summer these tents were roofed over with birch bark, and in winter with reindeer hides. When the hunters were on the move, their tents and belongings as well as their capture were carried by reindeer, which lived on moss.

The roving Ewenki hunters were still in the last stage of the primitive society on the eve of liberation. Five or six to a dozen families who were very closely related were grouped under a clan commune, the chief of which was elected. All in the commune took part in hunting, and the game bagged was divided equally among the families. However, changes were already taking place in the clan commune system at the time of liberation when shot-guns, reindeer and the much-prized squirrel pelts were coming into the possession of individual families.

Life Style The Ewenkis are an honest, warm-hearted and hospitable people. Guests in the pastoral areas are often treated to tobacco, milk tea and stewed meat by their Ewenki hosts. Such delicacies as reindeer meat, venison, elk-nose meat sausages are generously offered in the hunting areas.

When Ewenki hunters go out on long hunting trips, they leave whatever they cannot take along — foodstuffs, clothing and tools in unlocked stores in the forests. Other hunters who are in want, may help themselves to the things stored without the permission of their owners. The things borrowed would be returned to the store owners when the hunters happen to meet them at any time in future.

Monogamy is generally practised. In pre-liberation days exogamy was strictly observed. Members of the same clan were not permitted to marry one another, and those going against this unwritten law would be punished.

An Ewenki wedding is an occasion for dancing and merry-making. All Ewenki folk dances are simple and unconstrained. The dancers' foot movements, executed in a forceful and vigorous style and highly rhythmic, are characteristic of the honest, courage and optimistic traits of this ethnic minority.

Myths, fables, ballads and riddles form their oral literature. Embroidery, carving and painting are among the traditional lines of modelling arts as commonly seen on utensils decorated with various floral designs. An adept hand is also shown by the Ewenkis at birch bark carving and cutting in producing all kinds of fancy beasts and animals as toys for children.

Most Ewenkis are animists while those in the pastoral areas are followers of the Lamaist faith. A few living in the Chenbaerhu area are believers of the Eastern Orthodox Church.

While believing in animism, Ewenkis also worship their dead ancestors, and lingering influences of bear worship is still found among Ewenki hunters. After killing a bear, the Ewenkis would conduct a series of rituals at which the bear's head, bones and entrails are bundled in birch bark or dry grass and hung on a tree to give the beast a "wind burial." The hunters weep and kowtow while making offerings of tobacco to the dead animal. In the Chenbaerhu area every clan has its own totem — a swan or a duck — as an object of veneration. People would toss milk into the air upon seeing a real swan or duck flying overhead. No killing of these birds is permitted.

Wind burial was originally given to the dead. But it has now been replaced by burial in the ground, thanks to the influence of other ethnic groups living nearby, then and now.

Dispersed to live in different places and with many Ewenkis dragged into the army by the Qing rulers, the Ewenki nationality was threatened by extinction. Of a total number of 1,700 Ewenki troops sent to suppress a peasant army of other nationalities that rose against the Qing government in 1695, only some 300 survived the fighting. Following their occupation of northeast China in 1931, the Japanese imperialists not only intensified their exploitation of Ewenki people but drafted many of them into the Japanese army. They lured Ewenkis into the habit of opium-smoking and used some of them for bacteria experiments. All this, coupled with the spread of smallpox, typhoid fever and venereal diseases, brought about a sharp population decline. For example, there were upwards of 3,000 Ewenkis living along the Huihe River in 1931, but less than 1,000 remained in 1945.

Things took a turn for the better for this ethnic minority after the Japanese surrender in 1945. Two years later democratic reforms were carried out in both the pastoral and farming areas. As for Ewenki hunters roving in the forests, efforts were made to help them develop production and raise their cultural level. With the setting of cooperatives, these hunters, who were then at the transitional stage from primitivity to a class society, leap to socialism. Socialist reforms in most of the Ewenki area were completed towards the end of 1958.

The Ewenki Autonomous Banner was established on August 1, 1958, in the Hulun Beir League (Prefecture). Five Ewenki townships and an Ewenki district were set up later. A large number of Ewenkis were trained for administrative work.

A series of measures, including the introduction of fine breeds of cattle, the opening of fodder farms, improved veterinary services, building permanent housing for roving nomads and the use of machinery, have been taken to boost livestock production in the Ewenki Autonomous Banner since its inauguration in 1958. Hundreds of wells have been sunk to water livestock. Machinery is now used in cutting, bundling and transporting fodder as well as in fetching water, processing wool and making felt. As a result the livestock population in the Ewenki Autonomous Banner jumped from 66,000 head to 382,450 head in 1981.

Industry has also made headway in the autonomous banner, which has factories turning out farm and livestock machinery, iron tools, knitwear, garments, etc.

A speedy rise is also seen in people's living standards.

In the forested areas, Ewenki hunters, who used to be on the move after their game, now live in permanent homes. They still hunt, but they have also gone in for other occupations.

In the old days almost all the Ewenkis were illiterate. Today more than 90 per cent of all school-age children are at school. Some Ewenkis have been enrolled in the Central Nationalities Institute in Beijing, Inner Mongolia University in Huhhot and other institutions of higher learning.

With improved health care, TB, VD and other diseases that used to plague the Ewenki people have been put under control. Hospitals, maternity and child care centres, TB and VD prevention clinics are now at the service of the Ewenkis who knew no modern medical care formerly. As a result the population in the banner, which had dwindled for a century or more, has increased by many folds in the past four decades. The Ewenki nationality which was dying out is freed from the threat of extinction.

The Oropens

People of this enthnic group dwell in the forests of the Greater and Lesser Hinggan Mountains in Northeast China which abound in deer and other wild beasts the Oroqens hunt with shot-guns and dogs. The Oroqens, who lived in a primitive communal society four and a half decades ago, have leap-frogged several historical stages to socialism in the years following the founding of the People's Republic in 1949.

With no written script of their own, the Oroqens have a spoken language belonging to the Tungus branch of the Manchu-Tungusic group of the Altaic language family. Most of them have learned to read and write the language of the Hans, the biggest nationality in China.

The Oroqen population, which stood at 4,000 in 1917, dropped to 3,700 in 1943. A census taken in 1953 showed that their number had plummeted to 2,250. The population has started to grow slowly but steadily since, and the census in 1982 shows that their number has reached 4,100.

Most of the Oroqens live in the 55,000-square-kilometre Oroqen Autonomous Banner in the Greater Hinggan Mountains. Others have their home in several localities in Inner Mongolia and Heilongjiang Province. Situated in Inner Mongolia's Hulun Buir League, the Oroqen Autonomous Banner is 97 per cent forested land. The seat of the autonomous government is Alihe, a rising town with highways, railways, cinemas, hotels, department stores, restaurants, electric lighting and other modern amenities.

History For generations the Oroqens had lived a life of hunting and fishing in the forests. They went on hunting expeditions in groups, and the game bagged was distributed equally not only to those taking part in the hunt, but also to the aged and infirm. The heads, entrails and bones of the animals killed were not distributed but were cooked and eaten by all. Later, deer antlers, which fetched a good price, were not distributed but went to the hunters who killed the animals.

On the eve of liberation, polarization was quite marked in some localities where horses, on which Oroqens rode on hunting trips, belonged to individuals. The rich owned a large number of horses and the poor owned a few. Horses were hired out to those hunters who needed them, and payment took the form of game sent to horse-owners. Such a practice gradually developed into rent and exploitation of man by man.

The Oroqens are an honest and friendly people who always treat their guests well. People who lodge in an Oroqen home would often hear the housewife say to the husband early in the morning: "I'm going to hunt some breakfast for our guests and you go to fetch water." When the guests have washed, the woman with gun slung over her shoulders would return with a roe back. The Oroqens are expert hunters. Both the males and females are sharp shooters on horseback. Boys usually start to go out on hunting trips with their parents or brothers at the age of seven or eight. And they would be stalking wild beasts in the deep forest all on their own at 17. A good hunter is respected by all and young maidens like to marry him.

Horses are indispensable to the Oroqens on their hunting expeditions. Hunters ride on horses, which also carry their family belongings and provisions as well as the game they killed over mountains and across marshes and rivers. The Oroqen horse is a very sturdy breed with extra-large hooves that prevent the animal from sinking into marshland.

Oroqen women, who also hunt, show marvellous skill in embroidering patterns of deer, bears and horses on pelts and cloth that go into the making of headgears, gloves, boots and garments. Oroqen women also make basins, bowls, boxes and other objects from birch barks. Engraved with various designs and dyed in colour, these objects are artistic works that convey the idea of simplicity and beauty. Taught by their mothers while still very young to rub fur, dry meat and gather fruit in the forest, Oroqen girls start to do household work at 13 or 14. Pelts prepared by Oroqen women are soft, fluffy and light, and they are used in making garments, hats, gloves, socks and blankets as well as tents.

The Oroqens, who led a primitive life, used to have many taboos. One prohibited a woman from giving birth in the home. She had to do that in a little hut built outside the house in which she would be confined for a month before she could return home with her newborn.

Customs The Oroqens are a race of dancers and singers. Men, women and children often gather to sing and dance when the hunters return with their game or at festival times.

With a rich and varied repertory of folk songs, the Oroqens sing praises of nature and love, hunting and struggles in life in a lively rhythm. Among the most popular Oroqen dances are the "Black Bears Fight" and "Wood Cock Dance," at which the dancers execute movements like those of animals and birds. Also popular is a ritual in which members of a clan gather to perform dances depicting events in clan history.

"Pengnuhua" (a kind of harmonica) and "Wentuwen" (hand drum) are among the traditional instruments used. Played by Oroqen musicians, these instruments produce tunes that sound like the twittering of birds or the braying of deer. These instruments are sometimes used to lure wild beasts to within shooting range.

The Oroqens have many tales, fables, legends, proverbs and riddles that have been handed down from generation to generation.

Being Shamanists or animists, the Oroqens worship nature and their ancestors, and believe in the omnipresence of spirits. Their objects of worship are carefully kept in birch-bark boxes hung high on trees behind their tents.

The Oroqens have a long list of don'ts. For instance, they never call the tiger by its actual name but just "long tail," and the bear "granddad." Bears killed are generally honoured with a series of ceremonies; their bones are wrapped in straw placed high on trees and offerings are made for the souls of dead bears. Oroqens do not work out their hunting plans in advance, because they believe that the shoulder-blades of wild beasts have the power to see through a plan when one is made.

Wind burials are practised by the Oroqens. When a person dies his corpse is put into a hollowed-out tree trunk and placed with head pointing south on two-metre high supports in the forest. Sometimes the horse of the deceased is killed to accompany the departing soul to netherworld. Only the bodies of young people who die of contagious diseases are cremated.

Monogamy is practised by the Oroqens who are only permitted to marry with people outside their own clans. Proposals for marriage as a rule are made by go-betweens, sent to girls' families by boys' families.

The Oroqens originally peopled the region north of the Heilong River and south of the Outer Hinggan Mountains. But aggression and pillaging conducted by Tsarist Russia after the mid-17th century forced the Oroqens to migrate to the Greater and Lesser Hinggan Mountains. There were then seven tribes living in a clan commune society. Each clan commune called "Wulileng" consisted of five to a dozen families descended from a male ancestor. The commune head was elected. In the commune, which was then the basic economic unit of the Oroqens, all production tools were communally owned. The commune members hunted together, and the game bagged was equally distributed to all families.

The introduction of iron articles and guns and the use of horses during the Qing Dynasty (1644-1911) raised the productive forces of the Oroqens to a higher level. This gave rise to bartering on a bigger scale and the emergence of private ownership. That brought about profound social, economic changes. Individual families quit the clan commune and became basic economic units. The clan commune had disintegrated, though members of the same clan did live or hunt together in the same area. Organized under the Qing Dynasty's "eight banner system," the Oroqens were compelled to enlist in the armed forces and send fur to the Qing court as tributes. Most soldiers sent to fight in Xinjiang, Yunnan, Taiwan and other places lost their lives.

After the fall of the Qing Dynasty in 1911 came the rule of warlords who effected some changes in the administrative setup of the "eight banner system." Oroqen youths were dragged into "forest guerrilla units," and Oroqen hunters were forced to settle down to farm. Most of them later fled back to hunt in the forests. A few whom the warlords had made officers became landlords who hired Oroqen, Han, Manchu and Daur labourers to open up large tracts of land for crops.

The Japanese troops, who occupied northeast China in 1931, pulled down the cottages and smashed the farm implements of the remaining Oroqen farmers and drove them into the forests again. Oroqen youths were press-ganged into "forest detachments" officered by Japanese. The Japanese occupationists introduced opium-smoking to ruin the health of the Oroqen people, some of whom were used in bacteria experiments. All this, coupled with incidence of epidemic diseases, had so decimated the Oroqen population that only some 1,000 of them remained at the time of the Japanese surrender in 1945.

Over a long period of time, the Oroqens had fought alongside other nationalities in China against Tsarist Russian and Japanese aggression to safeguard national unity.

New Life After Liberation The Oroqen nationality was saved from extinction and a new life began to dawn for this ethnic minority in the years following the conclusion of the Anti-Japanese War in 1945. Shot-guns, cartridges and supplies of food-grain, cloth, cooking oil and salt were sent to the Oroqens by the People's Government in the early post-liberation days. People sent by the government helped them to raise production as well as to set up local People's Government.

Following the inception of the Oroqen Autonomous Banner

Manchu girls in modern wear.

Harvesting hop in Yanbian Korean Autonomous Prefecture.

A young Daur.

Raising deers.

A grassland in Inner Mongolia.

Mongolian girls.

A Bonan girl.

Hui bull fighters.

Bouyei girls.

Naxi girls

Yangshuo, a scenic area in the Guangxi Zhuang Autonomous Prefecture.

Cliff paintings on the banks of the Minjiang River—cultural relics of the Zhuang nationality

A Maonan woman.

A Jing woman.

A She girl.

Gaoshan residents in Beijing.

on October 1, 1951, several autonomous townships were set up in places where the Oroqens live in compact communities. Up to 1981, government allocation for construction in these places amounted to 46 million yuan. Working at leading bodies at various levels are Oroqen functionaries.

While helping the Oroqens to promote hunting, the government made efforts to help them switch over to a diversified economy and to lead a settled life.

The building of permanent housing for the Oroqens got started in 1952 with government allocations. A dozen villages were built in the Heihe Area for 300 families that used to lead a wandering life in 51 widely-scattered localities. Another three villages were built for 150 families in 1958.

Taught by Han and Daur farmers, the Oroqens began to grow crops in 1956. And by 1975, the people in the autonomous banner became self-supporting in food-grain for the first time in Oroqen history.

With no industry whatsoever in the past, the autonomous banner has now established 37 factories and workshops turning out farm machinery, electric appliances, flour, powdered milk, furniture, leather, fur and candies. The banner also has built schools, department stores, hospitals, banks and cinemas.

All school-age children are enrolled in primary and middle schools. Every year a number of youngsters enter institutions of higher learning. The Oroqen people also have their own song and dance troupes, film projection teams, broadcast stations and clubs.

Diseases took a heavy toll in the old days and 80 per cent of the women suffered from gynaecological troubles due to the lack of doctors and medicine and ignorance. They have been put under control with the help of mobile medical teams sent by the government, the launching of disease-prevention campaigns and the popularization of hygenic knowledge. As a result the Oroqen population increased to 4,100 in 1982.

NORTHWEST CHINA

The Huis

With a sizable population of 7.22 million, the Hui nationality is one of China's largest minority nationalities. People of Hui origin can be found in most of the counties and cities throughout the country, especially in the Ningxia Hui Autonomous Region and Gansu, Qinghai, Henan, Hebei, Shandong and Yunnan provinces and the Xinjiang Uygur Autonomous Region.

History The name Hui is an abbreviation for "Huihui," which first appeared in the literature of the Northern Song Dynasty (960-1127). It referred to the Huihe people (the Ouigurs) who lived in Anxi in the present-day Xinjiang and its vicinity since the Tang Dynasty (618-907). They were actually forerunners of the present-day Uygurs, who are totally different from today's Huis or Huihuis.

During the early years of the 13th century when Mongolian troops were making their western expeditions, group after group of Islamic-oriented people from Middle Asia, as well as Persians and Arabs, either were forced to move or voluntarily migrated into China. As artisans, tradesmen, scholars, officials and religious leaders, they spread to many parts of the country and settled down mainly to livestock breeding. These people, who were also called Huis or Huihuis because their religious beliefs were identical with people in Anxi, were part of the ancestors to today's Huis.

Earlier, about the middle of the 7th century, Islamic Arabs and Persians came to China to trade and later some became permanent residents of such cities as Guangzhou, Quanzhou, Hangzhou, Yangzhou and Chang'an (today's Xi'an). These people, referred to as "fanke" (guests from outlying regions), built mosques and public cemeteries for themselves. Some married and had children who came to be known as "tusheng fanke," meaning "native-born guests from outlying regions." During the Yuan Dynasty (1271-1368), these people became part of the Huihuis, who were coming in great numbers to China from Middle Asia.

The Huihuis of today are therefore a nationality that finds its origins mainly with the above-mentioned two categories, which in the course of development took in people from a number of other nationalities including the Hans, Mongolians and Uygurs.

It is generally acknowledged that Huihui culture began mainly during the Yuan Dynasty.

Warfare and farming were the two dominant factors of this period. During their westward invasion, the Mongols turned people from Middle Asia into scouts and sent them eastward on military missions. These civilians-turned-military scouts were expected to settle down at various locations and to breed livestock while maintaining combat readiness. They founded settlements in areas in today's Gansu, Henan, Shandong, Hebei and Yunnan provinces and the Ningxia Hui Autonomous Region. They later were joined by more scouts sent from the west. As time went by they became ordinary peasants and herdsmen. Among the expelled Islamic Middle Asians, there were a number of artisans and tradesmen. The majority of these people settled in cities and along vital communication lines, taking to handicrafts and commerce. Because of these activities a common economic life began to take shape among the Huihuis. Scattered as they were, they stuck together in relative concentration in settlements and around mosques which they built. This has been handed down as a specific feature of the distribution of Hui population in China.

The Huihui scouts and a good number of Huihui aristocrats, officials, scholars and merchants sent eastward by the Mongols were

quite active in China. They exercised influence on the establishment of the Yuan Dynasty and its military, political and economic
affairs. The involvement of Huihui upper-class elements in the
politics of Yuan Dynasty in turn helped to promote the development
of Huihuis in many fields.

Generally speaking, the social position of Huihuis during the
Yuan Dynasty was higher than that of the Hans. Nevertheless,
they were still subjected to the oppression of Yuan rulers. After
going through the hardships of their eastward exodus, they continued to be in the hands of various Mongolian officials, functioning
either as herdsmen or as government and army artisans. A fraction
of them even were allocated to Mongolian aristocrats to serve as
house slaves.

Being people who came to China from places where social
systems, customs and habits differed from those in the east, the Huihuis began to cultivate their own national consciousness. This was
caused also by their relative concentration with mosques as the
centre of their social activities, by their increasing economic contacts with each other, by their common political fate and their common belief in the Islamic religion.

It was during the Ming Dynasty (1368-1644) that the Huihuis
began to emerge as a nationality.

Along with the nationwide restoration and development of
the social economy in the early Ming Dynasty years, the distribution
and economic status of the Huihui population underwent a drastic
change. The number of Huihuis in Shaanxi and Gansu provinces
increased as more and more Huihuis from other parts of the country
submitted themselves to the Ming court and joined their people in
farming.

Other factors contributed to their dispersion: industrial and
commercial exchanges, assignment of Huihui garrison troops to
various areas to open up wasteland and grow food grain, nationwide
tours by Huihui officials and scholars, and especially the migration
of Huihuis during peasant uprisings. They still managed, however,
to maintain their tradition of concentration by setting up their own
villages in the countryside or sticking together in suburban areas

or along particular streets and lanes in cities. The dislocation of military scouts dating from the Yuan Dynasty had enabled the Hui-huis to extricate themselves gradually from military involvement and to settle down to farming, breeding livestock, handicrafts and small-scale trading. Thus they established a new common economic life among themselves, characterized by an agricultural economy.

During the initial stage of their eastward exodus, the Huihuis used the Arab, Persian and Han languages. However, in the course of their long years living with the Hans, and especially due to the increasing number of Hans joining their ranks, they gradually spoke the Han language only, while maintaining certain Arab and Persian phrases. Huihui culture originally had been characterized by influences from the traditional culture of Western Asia and assimilation from the Han culture. However, due to the introduction of the Han language as a common language, the tendency to assimilate the Han culture became more obvious. The Huihuis began to wear clothing like the Hans. Huihui names were still used, but Han names and surnames became accepted and gradually became dominant.

Islamic Religion The Islamic religion had a deep influence on the life style of the Hui people. For instance, soon after birth, an infant was to be given a Huihui name by an ahung (imam); wedding ceremonies must be witnessed by ahungs; a deceased person must be cleaned with water, wrapped with white cloth and buried coffinless and promptly in the presence of an ahung who serves as the presider. Men were accustomed to wearing white or black brimless hats, specially during religious services, while women were seen with black, white or green scarves on their head — a habit which also derived from religious practices. The Huis never eat pork nor the blood of any animal or creature that died of itself, and they refuse to take alcohol. These taboos originated in the Koran of the Moslems. The Huis are very particular about sanitation and hygiene. Likewise, before attending religious services, they have to observe either a "minor cleaning," i.e. wash their face, mouth, nose, hands and feet, or a "major cleaning," which requires a thorough bath of the whole body.

Islamism also had great impact on the political and economic systems of Hui society. "Jiaofang" or "religious community," as once practised among the Huis, was a religious system as well as an economic system. According to the system, a mosque was to be built at each location inhabited by Huis, ranging from a dozen to several hundred households. An imam was to be invited to preside over the religious affairs of the community as well as to take responsibility over all aspects of the livelihood of its members and to collect religious levies and other taxes from them. A mosque functioned not only as a place for religious activities but also as a rendezvous where the public met to discuss matters of common interest. Religious communities, operating quite independently from each other, had thus become the basic social units for the widely dispersed Hui people. Following the development of the Hui's agricultural economy and the increase of religious taxes levied on them, some chief imams began to build up their personal wealth. They used this to invest in land properties and engage in exploitation through land rents. The imams gradually changed themselves into landlords. Working in collaboration with secular landlords, they enjoyed comprehensive power in the religious communities, which they held tightly under their control. They left routine religious affairs of the mosques to low-rank ahungs.

The last stage of the Ming Dynasty and the early years of the Qing Dynasty (1644-1911) saw the emergence of a new system of religious aristocracy among the Huis in Hezhou (today's Linxia in Gansu Province). It came into existence as a result of intensified land concentration which exceeded the boundaries of one single religious community. This made certain imams rulers of a whole series of religious communities, turning them into Islamic aristocrats. They were deified. Kiosks were erected in their cemeteries for Moslems under their jurisdiction to worship. Their position was seen as hereditary. They enjoyed a series of feudalistic privileges as well as absolute authority over their people. The system had been in existence, however, only in some of the Hui areas in Gansu, Ningxia and Qinghai. The Huis in hinterland China had always functioned under the religious community system.

Contribution to Chinese Civilisation The Huis are an industrious people. Their development and progress have been facilitat-ed, however, by adopting the Han language and living with the Hans. Since the Yuan and Ming dynasties, large numbers of Hui peasants joined the Hans and people of other nationalities in reclaiming wasteland, farming and grazing in the hinterland and along border regions. Hui artisans were famous for their craftsmanship in making incense, medicine, leather and cannons, as well as in mining and smelting of ore. Hui merchants played a positive role in the economic exchanges between the hinterland and border regions and in trade contacts between China and other Asian countries. Hui scholars and scientists made outstanding contributions to China in introducing and spreading the achievements of Western Asia in astronomy, calendars, medicine and a number of other academic and cultural developments. These helped to promote the wellbeing and productive activities of the people of China as a whole. Chinese history has seen not a few outstanding Huis representing their people in the fields of politics, economy and culture.

During the Yuan Dynasty, the astronomist Jamaluddin compiled a perpetual calendar and produced seven kinds of astroscopes including the armillary sphere, the celestial globe, the terrestrial globe and the planetarium; Alaowadin and Yisimayin led the development of a mechanized way of shooting stone balls from cannons, which exercised an important bearing on military affairs in general; the architect Yehdardin learned from Han architecture and designed and led the construction of the capital of the Yuan Dynasty, which laid the foundation for the development of the city of Beijing.

During the Ming Dynasty, the Hui navigator Zheng He led massive fleets in making as many as seven visits to more than 30 Asian and African countries in 29 years. This unparalleled feat served to promote the friendship as well as economic and cultural exchanges between China and these countries. Zheng He was accompanied by Ma Huan and Ha San, also of Hui origin, who acted as his interpreters. Ma Huan gave a true account of Zheng He's visits in his book "Magnificent Tours of Lands Beyond the Ocean," which is of major significance in the study of the history of communication between China and the West. Hui scholar Li Zhi (1527-1602) of Quanzhou in Fujian Province was a well-known progressive thinker in Chinese ideology history.

A number of outstanding politicians emerged among the Huis. Sayyid Ajall Sham Suddin (1211-1279) of early Yuan Dynasty was one of them. During his late years when he was serving as governor of Yunnan Province, he laid stress on agriculture, setting up special areas for peasants to reclaim wasteland and grow food grain. He advocated the harnessing of six rivers in Kunming, capital of the province; established communication posts extensively for couriers to change horses and rest; initiated teaching in Confucianism and made strong efforts in harmonizing relations among various nationalities. All these benefitted political, economic and cultural developments in Yunnan, helping to bring closer relations between the province and the central government.

Hai Rui (1514-1587), a politician of the Ming Dynasty, was upright throughout his life. He had the courage to remonstrate with Emperor Jiajing about his fatuousness and arbitrariness that brought the nation and the people to calamity. Hai also lashed out at what he considered to be the evils of the court and inept ministers. Later during his term of office as roving inspector directly responsible to the emperor and as chief procurator of Nanjing, Hai enforced discipline, redressed mishandled cases and checked local despots in a successful attempt to boost public morale.

Since the Yuan and Ming dynasties, a great number of established Hui poets, scholars, painters and dramatists emerged. These included Sadul, Gao Kegong, Ding Henian, Ma Jin, Ding Peng and Gai Qi.

Revolutionary Tradition The Hui people have a long tradition of fighting against oppression. As far back as the Yuan Dynasty and during the Ming Dynasty they supported a number of revolts and uprisings.

During a massive peasant uprising towards the end of the Ming Dynasty, the Hui people in northern Shaanxi Province and eastern Gansu Province were one of the main forces leading the revolt. Intensification of class and national contradictions after the

Opium War and during the Taiping Revolution led to large-scale people's uprisings in Yunnan Province and Northwest China. Revolts were launched by the Huis in Yunnan Province and the northwest in collaboration with other local people. They persisted in their warfare for nearly 20 years, dealing a heavy blow to the feudal rulers of the Qing Dynasty. Their struggle actually became a powerful factor in the anti-Qing upsurge that took place then on a nationwide scale.

Huis in the cities of Wuhan, Xi'an, Chengdu, Chongqing and Shanghai took part in many local struggles that conformed with the general course of the Revolution of 1911 — the Chinese bourgeois democratic revolution led by Dr. Sun Yat-sen, which finally led to the overthrow of the Qing Dynasty.

The Hui people also engaged in various struggles against imperialist aggression by such countries as Britain, Tsarist Russia and Japan.

The May 4th Movement of 1919 — an anti-imperialist, anti-feudal, political and cultural movement influenced by the October Revolution of Russia and led by intellectuals having the rudiments of Communist ideology — pointed out the orientation for the total liberation of the Hui people. Huis of various social strata took an active part in the movement. The Huis of Jinan, capital of Shandong Province, for instance, organized themselves into a number of patriotic groups. These included the Hui Society for the Support of Diplomatic Struggles and they participated in the destruction of the newspaper "Changyan", which was a mouthpiece of pro-Japanese elements.

Huis were active during the periods of the 1st and 2nd Revolutionary Civil Wars and Communist Party-led workers' and peasants' movements throughout the country. These included the Great Strike of February 7, 1923[16] — an anti-imperialist, anti-warlord strike of the Beijing-Hankou Railway workers, and the Great Strike of Canton and Hong Kong[17] that took place in June 1925.

The 1934-1935 Long March — a major strategic move of the Red Army which succeeded in reaching the revolutionary base in northern Shaanxi after traversing 11 provinces and covering

12,500 kilometres — sowed seeds of revolution among a broad section of the Hui population. In the course of the Long March, many Hui people volunteered to send information to the Red Army and serve as its guides. Quite a number of young Huis joined the Red Army and went with it to northern China to fight the Japanese aggressors. A mounted division consisting of Hui cavalrymen was formed in the Shaanxi-Gansu-Ningxia Border Region.

During the War of Resistance Against Japan (1937-1945), the Huis of the Shaanxi-Gansu-Ningxia Border Region and in all of the anti-Japanese base areas set up various forms of anti-Japanese national salvation organizations under the leadership of the Chinese Communist Party. In places mostly populated by Huis, the Party helped them in establishing self-government on a township basis. These Hui organizations played a significant role. They mobilized people into resistance against Japanese aggression, organized anti-Japanese armed forces and solved problems related to production and livelihood. Several dozens of anti-Japanese armed forces of varying sizes were founded among the Huis in the Shaanxi-Gansu-Ningxia Border Region and in Hebei, Shandong, Shanxi and Anhui provinces under the leadership of the Party and the New Fourth Army. The Hui detachment led by Ma Benzhai contributed to uniting the broad masses of Hui and Han peoples behind the enemy lines in central Hebei Province. They waged a joint and persistent guerrilla warfare against the Japanese. Later during the War of Liberation, most of these Hui armed forces were organized into field armies which fought for the defeat of Chiang Kai-shek and the liberation of China.

Economy The Hui economic status before 1949 was characterized by a rising feudal landlord economy mixed with certain capitalist economic elements. Generally speaking, it was about the same as that of the Hans. But since the Huis were located throughout the country, their economic conditions differed from place to place. Those living in the countryside were mostly landless peasants, small landholders or owners of hilly, sandy, alkaline or flood land. A striking feature of rural Huis was that in addition to agriculture, they diversified their efforts on many sideline occupations. These included commerce and animal husbandry or animal-slaughtering, hide-processing, oil-extracting and transportation services.

As exploitation by feudal landlords reigned in Hui areas, the land issue among the Huis was quite acute. It had become a common phenomenon during the old society for Huis to flee their villages as a result of bankruptcy. Feudal concentration of land in Hui-populated areas of Northwest China was even more serious. Most of the good farmlands had been occupied by feudal bureaucrats, landlords and imams. Their exploitation of the ordinary Huis was often ruthless, either in the case of exploitation through land rent and usurious loans, or extraeconomic exploitation. In Qinghai Province, feudal land taxes were being supplemented by incidental levies that increased year by year. By 1943, they had added up to 10 times of the original tax. Such heavy taxation, coupled with continuous drafting, corvée and fund collecting, had forced many peasants and herdsmen from the Hui and other nationalities to sell their children and go into exile. As Moslems, the Huis had also had to shoulder the heavy burden of exploitation as exercised within their religious circles. The great numbers of imam aristocrats and Islamic sects in Northwest China vied with one another in using religion as a cover to usurp and enforce free labour services on their religious subjects under various deceptive pretexts.

Prior to the founding of the People's Republic, most of the industry and commerce as managed by the Huis were linked wtih their specific lifestyle and customs. They were limited to such fields as catering, leather tanning and selling of fish, vegetable, fur, spice, plaster and jewelry.

Cultural and educational developments among the Huis had long been slow and backward. In the case of Ningxia, the entire province had only one primary school and two middle schools before 1949. There was not even one institution of higher learning. In remote mountainous areas it was quite common for Hui villages not to have anyone who could read or write. The Huis in Linxia of Gansu Province and in a number of other places were even denied the right to cultural recreation. Imams could have them whipped or fined cooking oil or flour if they were heard singing or found watching opera performances. The fetters imposed on Hui women were even heavier. Public health facilities in these areas were exceedingly poor. The lack of doctors and medicine was quite common. The sick were subjected to superstitious treatment by ahungs whose prescription was writing quotations from Islamic scriptures on the inside of a bowl and having the patient gulp down water from the container.

Life After Liberation Since liberation in 1949, the People's Government has carried out a policy of regional national autonomy in Hui-populated areas. Because Huis differ from place to place, such self-autonomy has taken on various forms. Along with the Ningxia Hui Autonomous Region, the Linxia and Changji Hui Autonomous prefectures in Gansu Province and the Xinjiang Uygur Autonomous Region came into existence. Also six Hui autonomous counties were established in Zhangjiachuan of Gansu Province, Menyuan and Hualong of Qinghai Province, Yanqi of Xinjiang Uygur Autonomous Region and Dachang and Mengcun of Hebei Province. In addition, there are three other autonomous counties jointly set up by Huis with people of other nationalities. The right to national equality and national autonomy has thus been realized among the Hui people.

Cadres from the Hui nationality occupy an appropriate percentage in the organs of autonomy at all levels. Most leading positions in the power organs as well as leading positions in various executive departments and professional bodies are taken up by outstanding Huis. Emphasis has been laid on the training of Hui office executives, professionals and technical personnel who are competent in their work and politically progressive. Efforts have been made to recruit members of the Chinese Communist Party and of the Chinese Communist Youth League from among the Huis. All Hui cadres, executives and professionals are expected to work for the advancement of industry, agriculture, animal husbandry, culture and education in accordance with local conditions. Considerable attention has been paid by the State to the various Hui autonomous areas in terms of investment in capital construction and of manpower, material resources and technology.

Huis that live scattered across the country have the similar right to enjoy national equality and to direct their own affairs. Their identity as members of an established nationality is respected. The political status of the Hui people has been greatly raised. An appropriate number of representatives have been elected from the Huis to take part in National People's Congresses. People's Congresses held at lower levels also have Hui representation. Hui cadres work in government departments at central and local levels.

The majority of Huis believe in Islamism. Their religious freedom, customs and habits are respected and guaranteed. Since 1979, the policies on nationalities and religion have continued in Ningxia Hui Autonomous Region and elsewhere in the country after disruptions caused by the Cultural Revolution (1966-76). By May 1984, 1,400 mosques had been restored in Ningxia. This has made it possible for Moslems throughout the autonomous region to normalize their religious activities. An institute for the study of Islamic scriptures was established in 1982. It takes in students from among the ahungs every year. An Islamism research society also was set up to conduct academic and research activities on Islamism. In recent years, many young Huis have made efforts to learn Islamic classics in Arabic. Patriotic figures from Islamic circles have attended Chinese People's Political Consultative Conferences and People's Congresses at various levels. Many of them have taken up leading positions in government organs.

The social and economic situation among the Hui nationality has undergone fundamental changes during the last three decades. The Democratic Reform and the subsequent socialist transformation put an end to the system of class oppression within the ranks of the Huis. This made it possible for them to join hands with the other nationalities of China in embarking on the road of socialism.

The Ningxia Hui Autonomous Region has established a number of modern industries, covering such fields as coal, power, machinery, metallurgy, chemicals, light industry, petroleum and electronics. Industrial and agricultural production in the region has risen continuously since 1979.

The production and livelihood of the Huis in the countryside have improved continuously. Considerable progress has been made by the Huis in farmland capital construction, construction of water conservancy works and mechanized farming. They also have made efforts to fight drought, waterlogging, soil salinization and erosion and sand encroachment of farmland as well as natural calamities. In Ningxia Hui Autonomous Region and Linxia Hui Autonomous Prefecture of Gansu Province, irrigated farmland has been increasing year by year as a result of the construction of large-scale key water control projects at Qingtong and Liujia Gorges on the upper reaches of the Yellow River and a series of reservoirs and irrigation canals. Stripe-shaped fields suitable for tractor-ploughing, irrigation and drainage have appeared in quite a few places. The fields will serve as a foundation for the construction of commodity grain production bases.

To improve the situation in the Liupan Mountain area plagued by serious water shortage almost every year, the State has allocated funds for the construction of pumping projects. These are in Tongxin, Guyuan and Haiyuan and will extract water from the Yellow River and life it step by step onto the age-old dry lands. The projects are expected to solve the problem of drinking water and irrigation water among the broad masses of Hui and Han peoples.

Mechanization of farming has progressed in Hui villages. Farming methods and cultivation techniques, too, have undergone marked improvements.

The Hui people as well as people of other nationalities in Ningxia have accumulated rich experience in checking sand erosion by means of afforestation in the course of their protracted struggle against desertization. In 1978, the State decided to build a large-scale shelter-forest that would run across the length of the autonomous region. The forest belt, when completed, will help control the sand and thus change the climate and other natural conditions of Ningxia. This in turn will speed the modernization of the region's agriculture.

Since the founding of the People's Republic in 1949, elementary education has on the whole been made universal among the Huis. In Hui-populated areas, the Hui people have set up their own primary and secondary schools in their communities. Their children are able to attend schools close to their homes. They also have their own professors, engineers, doctors, scientists, writers, artists and specialists. In 1958 the first college was founded in the autonomous region. Today, specialized personnel of Hui and other nationalities are being trained at Ningxia University, Ningxia Medical College and Ningxia Institute of Agronomy. Ending 1982, the autonomous region had more than 5,000 schools at various levels with a student population of about 800,000.

Numerous fetters that had been forced upon Hui women over the years have been gradually removed as a result of improved education. Secondary and primary schools for female students have been established in some of the Hui-populated areas. An increasing number of Hui women are attending evening schools and schools arranged during slack winter seasons. Having acquired education at varying degrees, many of them are now skilled workers, and more are cadres of various levels, as well as actresses, doctors, teachers and engineers.

Mass literary, artistic and sports activities have been spreading among the Huis, resulting in the emergence of outstanding artists and sportsmen. The skills of veteran Hui artisans in producing such traditional special handicrafts as carved ivory, cloisonné, Suzhou embroidery, carved bricks and carpets have been carried on and developed.

Medical and public health establishments have been widely set up in Hui-populated areas. Hui nationality medical workers have been trained in large numbers. In major cities like Beijing and Tianjin, where the concentration of Huis is relatively larger, special hospitals have been provided for them. Mobile medical teams have been organized in some places to tour the countryside and mountainous areas where the Huis live. Many of the local epidemic diseases either have been put under control or eliminated. This, coupled with the improvement of economic and cultural life among the Huis, has greatly raised the general level of their health.

The Dongxiangs

People of the Dongxiang nationality, numbering 279,400, live in that part of the Linxia Hui Autonomous Prefecture situated south of the Yellow River and southwest of Lanzhou, capital city of the northwest province of Gansu. Half of them dwell in the Dongxiang Autonomous County, and the rest are scattered in Hezheng and Linxia counties, the city of Lanzhou, the Xinjiang Uygur Autonomous Region and some other places.

The Dongxiang nationality got its name from the place it lives — Dongxiang. However, this ethnic group was not recognized as a minority nationality prior to the founding of the People's Republic in 1949. The Dongxiangs were then called "Dongxiang Huis" or "Mongolian Huis."

The Dongxiang language is basically similar to Mongolian, both belonging to the Mongolian branch of the Altaic language family. It contains quite a number of words borrowed from the Chinese language. Most of the Dongxiang people also speak Chinese, which is accepted as their common written language. Quite a few of them can use Arabic alphabet to spell out and write Dongxiang or Chinese words.

The Dongxiangs are an agricultural people who grow potatoes, wheat, maize and broad beans as well as hemp, rapeseed and other industrial crops.

History   Historians are divided in their views about the origin of the Dongxiang nationality. Some hold that they are descendants of Mongolian troops posted in the Hezhou area by Genghis Khan (1162-1227) during his march to the west. Other historians say they are a mixture of many races — Hui, Mongolian, Han and Tibetan nationalities.

However, according to legends and historical data, the Dongxiangs probably originated from the Mongolian Nationality. As far back as the 13th century, Mongolian garrison units were stationed in the Dongxiang area. In these units were Mongols and military scouts and artisans Genghis Khan brought from West Asia. In time of war, the military scouts would fight as soldiers on the battlefield. And they farmed and raised cattle and sheep in time of peace. These garrison troops later took local women as wives, and their offspring at the beginning were called "military households" which became "civilian households" with the passage of time.

During the early years of the Ming Dynasty (1368-1644), they were offered amnesty by the Ming rulers, and they settled down permanently in the Dongxiang area.

The Dongxiang people had been groaning under national and class oppression throughout the ages. This had driven them to take up arms against their oppressors many times.

For several decades before the founding of the People's Republic in 1949, the Dongxiang people were suffering under the oppressive rule of the feudal Hui warlords, Ma Anliang, Ma Qi and Ma Bufang, and Kuomintang warlord Liu Yufen.

What infuriated the Dongxiangs most was the pressganging of their young men into the armed forces by the Kuomintang and Hui warlords. At one swoop in 1948, the pressgangs rounded up a total of more than 3,000 young men. Even the ahungs in some mosques were not spared. They were thrown into the army after their beards were shaved. Pressganging operations that were carried out time and again had made the Dongxiang villages and towns devoid of young men.

Religion   The Dongxiangs are Moslems, and at one time there were 595 mosques and 79 other places of worship in the Dongxiang area. This gave every 30 Dongxiang households a place of worship. Apart from the 12 imams, there were more than 2,000 full-time religious workers. That means every 18 households had to provide for one religious worker. And there were 34 different kinds of religious expenses which had to be borne by the ordinary people.

The Moslems in the Dongxiang area were then divided into three sects — the Old, the New and the Emerging sects. Carrying out a "divide and rule" policy, the ruling class sowed dissension among these sects. As a result, the Moslems were at feud among themselves. At times there were armed clashes.

Since the early post-liberation days, the People's Government has pursued a policy of freedom of religious beliefs in the Dongxiang area and taken measures to restore unity among the Moslem population. In 1958, the Dongxiang people carried out the struggle against religious and feudal privileges and the system of oppression and exploitation. This resulted in a further liberation of the productive forces.

"Flowers" in Bloom   There are in the Dongxiang area many folk songs which the local people have dubbed "flowers" and were sung in the past by people to express their hopes for a better life and to pour out their wrath against oppression. The "flowers," which had been ruthlessly trampled down in the old days, began to blossom anew following the emancipation of the Dongxiang people.

There are quite a number of popular narrative poems and folktales in the Dongxiang area. The long poem "Meilagahei and Miss Machenglong" sings the praise of the heroism of a young couple who pitted themselves against out-moded ethics and the feudal marriage system. The folklore "Green Widow Kills the Boa" depicts the courage, wisdom and self-sacrificing spirit of Dongxiang women.

Historical Changes   Many changes took place in the Dongxiang area after the arrival of the People's Liberation Army in the autumn of 1949. On September 25, 1950, the Dongxiang Autonomous County was founded to be followed by the establishment of many ethnic minority townships in other localities. "Solidarity Committees" were set up everywhere to eliminate disunity then still existing between the Dongxiangs and other ethnic groups. Many Dongxiangs were trained to be government functionaries at various levels.

Trees and grass were and are being planted on barren hills to check erosion which had plagued the Dongxiang area for ages. Large tracts of farmland on hillslopes have been transformed into terraced plots. All this, coupled with the construction of irrigation facilities, has greatly raised annual foodgrain production.

A power station and factories turning out farm implements, cement, flour, bricks and tiles have made their appearance in the area, one of the most under-developed localities in China a few decades ago. Transport and travelling have been made easier with the arrival of trucks and buses, and with the construction of a highway network that links together all the townships, and the Dongxiang area with the provincial capital of Lanzhou.

Diseases such as kala-azar and leprosy in the area have, in the main, been stamped out, thanks to improved health care and health education conducted among the people.

The Tus

The Tu nationality, with a population of 159,400 known for their simplicity and industriousness, lives in the northwestern part of China — to the east of Qinghai Lake and south of Qilian Mountain Range and along the banks of the Huangshui and Datong rivers. It is concentrated mainly in the Huzhu Tu Autonomous County in Qinghai Province, and also in the counties of Minhe and Datong. Others are scattered in Ledu, Menyuan and the Tianzhu Tibetan Autonomous County in Gansu Province.

The language of the Tu nationality belongs to the Mongolian branch of the Altaic language family. Its basic vocabulary is either the same as or similar to that of the Mongolian language, but it is much closer to the languages of the Dongxiang and Bonan Nationalities. Quite a number of religious terms are borrowed from the Tibetan language, while a good portion of everyday words, as well as new terms and phrases, come from the Han language, which has long been the medium of communication among the Tus of Datong County. The Tu people do not have a written language of their own; they use that of the Hans instead.

The costumes and personal adornments of the Tu people are strikingly unique. Men and women alike wear shirts with delicately-designed embroidered collars whose colours are bright and well blended. Men like to dress in cloth robes, putting on high-collared fur gowns with waist belts in winter. They often dress up in felt hats with brocade brims. For women, jackets are tilted in the front with sleeves made up of five different kinds of cloth. Sometimes they slip on a sleeveless garment done in black, indicating formal attire. They used to be very particular about hair styles, which numbered seven or eight different varieties. But this custom was suppressed under the Kuomintang regime before liberation in 1949. Nowadays, simple hair style topped by a brocaded felt hat has become fashionable among Tu women.

Historical Origins The fact that the Tus claim to be "Mongguer" (Mongolians) or "Chahan Mongguer" (White Mongolians) gives expression to the close relations that existed between the early Tus and the Mongolian nationality. Popular legends among the Tus of Huzhu Autonomous County have it that their ancestors were Mongolian soldiers under one of Genghis Khan's generals by the name of Gerilite (Geretai). They intermarried with the indigenous Houers of what is now Huzhu County.

Chinese records also tell of Mongolian troops under Genghis Khan making their appearance in Xining (now capital of Qinghai Province), which exercised jurisdiction over Huzhu County during the Yuan Dynasty (1271-1368) founded by Genghis Khan. All historical records have accounts of Mongolian troops having either been stationed in Xining during the Mongolian western expeditions or moved into the place at some point in history.

Especially worth mentioning is the account of Yuan imperial clansman Buyan Tiemuer's troops being attacked and defeated in Andingwei during the reign of Ming Emperor Zhengde (1506-1521). The survivors settled down to the east of Weiyuan City near Xining. The area is now under the administration of the Huzhu Tu Autonomous County. This shows that a portion of the Tu people in Huzhu County are descendants of Mongolians that moved in from Andingwei during the Ming Dynasty.

"Huoer" was long ago a Tibetan name for the nomadic herdsmen who lived in northern Tibet and vast areas north of Tibet (or north of the Yellow River, according to a different interpretation).

In modern times the term refers specifically to the Tu people.

Herders and Farmers Economically, the people of the Tu nationality started off as lifestock breeders, especially of goats and sheep. This was due to the abundance of water and grass in the fertile mountainous area that they inhabited. The Tus used to be well known among the locals for their expertise in animal husbandry. According to historical documents, they began to familiarize themselves with farming at least from the early period of the Ming Dynasty.

Also starting from that period, the Tu area fell under the rule of 16 hereditary headmen, whose titles and territories were granted by the Ming Emperor. Since the land tilled by the Tu people belonged to the headmen, the former had to shoulder a multitude of labour services and extortions enforced by the landlords, apart from taxes of various descriptions. The headmen made full use of their "inspection tours" once every three years to exploit their people. It was only in 1931 that the Kuomintang government formally abolished the headman system. The displaced headmen were, however, appointed as deputy county heads, district heads or township heads to continue their function as tools of the regime. Economically, most of them retained their positions as rich landlords and continued to dominate the means of production.

Like elsewhere in China, the Tu area was gradually being reduced to a semi-colonial and semi-feudal society when history entered its modern stage. The only difference was that, due to lack of modern means of transportation and the existence of serious feudal separatist tendencies, the Tu society had then more of a feudalistic nature. Nevertheless, the imperialists did manage to rob the Tu people of their wealth by plundering their raw materials and local produce while dumping foreign products on the Tu market. The penetration of foreign influence was also manifested in missionary activities. In the period from 1915 through to the eve of liberation in 1949, seven churches and four church-run primary schools were set up in the area.

Feudal oppression and exploitation in the Tu area was extremely ruthless in the first half of this century. For 38 years, the Tu people toiled under the barbarous rule of the warlords of the Ma family (Ma Qi, Ma Lin and Ma Bufang). Just ordinary taxes and corvee in the form of grain as enforced by the Ma family could be of more than 40 different kinds. About half of the peasants' annual income was grabbed by the Ma family. This, coupled with forced labour and military service, brought the Tu people to a state of real disaster. In addition to ruthless exploitation through land rent and non-economic extortions in various forms, the practice of usury functioned as another major means of economic plunder. Many poor peasants were heavily in debt as much as several generations on end.

The Ma warlords were also bureaucrat capitalists marked by a strong feudalistic tendency. A commercial enterprise owned by the Ma family, for example, not only had the power to requisition labourers and means of transportation from the people, but also the right to set up its own court and carry out inquisitions by means of torture. It had its own squad of bodyguards and hired roughnecks equipped with guns and horses. The Mas also ran a number of workshops in the Tu areas, whose workers were mostly poor peasants either requisitioned or arrested by the reactionary regime for not having been able to repay loans. The interest on loans was around 150 per cent and could be as high as 400 per cent.

Liberation   The Tu people did not, however, submit tamely to such oppression. On many occasions they rose in resistance, along with people of the Han and other nationalities.

In September 1949 the Tu people ushered in their liberation with great jubilation. With the help of the central government in Beijing, they smashed the reactionary social system and set up an administration of their own.   This was followed by a struggle to eliminate bandits and bring down local despots, which paved the way for the final successful drive for land reform.

The Huzhu Tu Autonomous County was established in February 1954, in spite of the fact that the Tu people account for only 13.5 per cent of the population of the county. Autonomous townships have also been set up in areas where there are concentrated populations of the Tus. The Tu people have their representatives in the People's Congresses at both the Qinghai provincial and the national levels.

Religious Reform The Yellow Sect of Lamaism used to have a wide-spread following among the Tu people. To strengthen their domination over the ordinary people, the ruling classes of previous regimes had, without exception, collaborated with the upper clerical elements. The latter enjoyed the support of the authorities as well as all kinds of privileges.

After 1949 the Tu people carried out a religious reform under the leadership of the People's Government. They burned the feudal deeds and loan receipts of the Lama landlords and abolished all religious privileges, forced apportions and labour services.

These struggles helped further emancipate the minds of the Tu people, who threw themselves actively into the drive for socialist construction. Whereas superstition forbade the disturbing of "sacred" mountains and springs, the Tu people began transforming mountain slopes into farmlands and digging irrigation canals. Women, who began enjoying unprecedented political rights, took an active part in all these constructive endeavours.

The traditional practice of cremating the dead persists in most parts of the Tu-populated areas.

Birth of Industry Prior to 1949 no modern industry of any kind had been developed in the Tu areas. Agricultural production and transportation were backward. Since the founding of the People's Republic, the Huzhu Tu Autonomous County has set up over 30 industrial and mining enterprises turning out more than 200 kinds of products including farm machinery, chemical fertilizers, wine, ores and coal. Whereas the entire county did not have a single motor vehicle or farm machine before 1949, it now has a substantial number of trucks, cars and buses, tractors, harvesters, threshers and processing machines. The opening of roads to motor traffic throughout the county has helped bring about a big change in its agricultural production. Over 1,100 hectares of irrigated farmland has been newly developed, along with the construction of 60 reservoirs and ponds for draining waterlogged areas. The building of seven hydro-electric power stations has made electricity available throughout the county.

Cultural, educational and public health facilities have been gradually developed. By 1981 the county had founded more than 500 schools of various kinds with a combined Tu student population of over 10,000. College graduates, engineers, artists, journalists, teachers and doctors of Tu origin are playing active roles on all fronts. Quite a few cadres from the nationality have been promoted to leading positions at the provincial, prefectural and county levels.

People of the Tu nationality are renowned for their talent for singing and dancing. Ballads with beautiful melodies, as well as oral literature with stirring plots can be heard everywhere in the Tu-populated areas. A traditional ballad-singing festival is held once a year, when thousands upon thousands of singers and young people gather from all over the area to get together and sing to their hearts' content.

The Salars

The Salar nationality has a population of 69,100, of whom 90 per cent live in the Xunhua Salar Autonomous County in eastern Qinghai Province. The rest are mainly located in neighbouring Hualong County and Gansu Province's Linxia County. Others are found scattered in a number of other places in Qinghai and Gansu, as well as in the Xinjiang Uygur Autonomous Region.

Past Socio-economic Conditions There have been different theories put forward on the origin of the Salars. The prevalent view held at the moment is that the ancestors of the Salars came from the region of Samarkand in Central Asia during the Yuan Dynasty (1271-1368).

Xunhua County is a mountainous area situated along the banks of the Yellow River in southeastern Qinghai Province. Although it has a mild climate and fertile land crisscrossed by canals, it is handicapped by insufficient rainfall. In pre-liberation days, the peasants did not have the capability of harnessing the Yellow River, and the county was often referred to as "arid Xunhua." The Salars are mainly farmers, going in for such crops as wheat, Tibetan barley, buckwheat and potatoes. As sideline occupations, they engage in stock breeding, lumbering, salt-producing and wool-weaving.

During the Yuan Dynasty, a Salar headman bearing the surname of Han was made hereditary chief of the nationality. With the rise of the Ming Dynasty (1368-1644), he submitted to the new rulers and continued to hold his position. He had under him a basic bureaucracy which looked after such things as military affairs, punishments, revenue and provisions. Following the development of the economy and the expansion of the population, the region inhabited by the Salars was divided into two administrative areas, i.e. the "inner eight gongs" of Xunhua and the "outer five gongs" of Hualong, during the reign of Emperor Yongzheng of the Qing Dynasty (1644-1911). A "gong" included a number of villages, equivalent to the later administrative unit of "xiang" (township).

New organisational setups were introduced during the reigns of the Qing Emperors Yongzheng and Qianlong to step up the control and exploitation of the Salars. During both the Ming and Qing periods Salar men were constantly subjected to conscription, which was an extremely heavy burden on the Salar people.

As the Salars are devout Muslims, the villages were dominated by the mosques and the Muslim clergy. Along with the development of the feudal economy, land became concentrated in the hands of the ruling minority — the headman, community chiefs and imams.

Prior to liberation in 1949, the landlord economy was dominant. Relying on their political power, and feudal and religious privileges, the Salar landlords maintained ownership over most of the land and farm animals, as well as water sources and oil mills. The broad masses of the Salar poor peasants, on the other hand, were either landless or owned only a very insignificant portion of barren land. They were subjected to crippling land rents and usury, in addition to all kinds of heavy unpaid labour services including building houses, felling trees and doing transportation work for the landlords. As a result, at times there were large-scale exoduses of Salars from their villages, leaving the farmlands lying waste and production at a standstill.

The Salar people were constantly engaged in struggles against such ruthless exploitation.

Culture   The language of the Salars, which belongs to the Tujue (Turkic) branch of the Altaic language family, is almost identical with the languages of the Uygurs and Uzbeks, with whom they share the Muslim religion. It contains quite a number of words taken from the Chinese and Tibetan languages as a result of long years of mutual contacts. Nowadays, most young and middle-aged Salars know how to speak Chinese, which is also accepted as the written language of the Salar nationality.

The Salar nationality has a rich and colourful tradition of folklore. Many of the legends, stories and fairy tales sing the praises of the courage and wisdom of the labouring people, and lament the hard lives of the Salar women in the past, as well as their struggle against feudal oppression.   The typical folk tune genre is the "Hua'er (flower)," a kind of folk song sung sonorously and unrestrainedly in the Chinese language.   However, in most cases it is presented with a sweet, trilling tone due to the influence of Tibetan folk songs. The singers are all able to fill in impromptu words according to whatever happens to strike a chord in their hearts. Significant reforms have been introduced to this form of art since 1949.   The Salars now sing to express their rejoicing over their new life. Amateur theatrical troupes, and song and dance groups are flourishing among the Salar people.

Customs   Deeply influenced by Islam, the customs and habits as practised among the Salars are roughly the same as those of the Huis that live nearby.   Women like to wear kerchiefs on their heads and black sleeveless jackets over clothes in striking red colours. They are good at embroidery and often stitch flowers in five different colours onto their pillow cases, shoes and socks.   Men wear flat-topped brimless hats of either black or white colours, and wear sheepskin coats without linings and woolen clothing in winter. Young men living along the banks of the Yellow River love to swim.   Some of the customs and habits of the Salars have changed since liberation as a result of social and economic development.   Polygamy, for instance, has been abolished, and cases of child marriage have been greatly reduced.   The extravagant practice of slaughtering cattle in large numbers for weddings, funerals and festivals has been changed.

Women of the Salar nationality in the past suffered tremendously under religious strictures and feudal ethics. Unmarried girls were not allowed to appear in public, while married women had to hide their faces in front of strange men. They had to turn their faces sideways when answering an inquiry and make a detour should they meet a strange man coming their way. But, since liberation, Salar women have broken away from such practices and the traditional concept of men being superior to women is slowly disappearing. Salar women are now taking an active part in all local production endeavours.

Post-liberation Life Xunhua was liberated in September 1949. The feudal system of land ownership was abolished following a land reform carried out after bandits were eliminated and local despots brought down. On Marh 1, 1954, the Xunhua Salar Autonomous County was established (Salars living in other places, too, have been given a certain degree of autonomy).

Since then, the nationality has produced a number of cadres after many years of training through practical work with the help of Han cadres as well as through attending various kinds of training courses. Quite a number of them have been promoted to leading posts at the county and township levels.

The year 1958 saw the abolition of religious and feudal privileges, sweeping away the oppression and exploitation of the Salar people. Policy guidelines of unity, education and transformation were adopted towards the upper strata and religious hierarchy. The majority of these have been won over to the side of the people.

Since liberation, the Salar people of Xunhua have fought relentlessly to improve the irrigation of their lands. They have worked under difficult conditions to build a system of major and minor canals, and a reservoir in the Mengda Mountains. This has greatly changed the general appearance of Xunhua, which used to be so dry that people could die of thirst and crop seedlings could wither through lack of water in spite of the fact that the county is situated right on the banks of the Yellow River. With the help of the State, the all-round level of mechanization has been raised. Farm machinery of all types has been increasingly introduced. The county has a well-developed fruit-growing sector, turning out pears, apricots, grapes, jujubes and apples. The area is quite famous for its Chinese prickly ash, known for size and strong flavour, and its various kinds of walnuts and red peppers. The county produces such Chinese medicines as dangshen (codonopsis pilosula), Chinese ephedra and musk. There is also an abundance of forestry and mineral resources.

Agriculture, forestry, animal husbandry and side-line occupations are doing well; and so are industry and transportation. Initial results have been achieved in the establishment of a number of small industries in such fields as power-generating, the repair and manufacture of farm machinery, building materials, and the processing of farm produce and by-products. All of the townships are now accessible by highway.

Before 1949, over 97 per cent of the Salars were illiterate. Some of the children, having reached school age, studied the Islamic scriptures in the mosques, but very few attended proper schools. Now primary school education is universal among the Salars. A normal school has been set up in the area to train primary school teachers of Salar and other nationalities, and the Salars have produced their first university students. Cultural establishments such as bookstores, cultural centres and cinemas have been built. Film projection teams have been organized to tour and show movies to those living in remote mountainous areas.

Public health facilities used to be almost unknown among the Salars in the old society. But with the setting up of a county hospital and a number of clinics, and the training of Salar medical workers, the situation has been greatly improved.

The Bonans

The Bonan nationality is one of China's smallest minority nationalities, with only 9,000 people. Its language belongs to the Mongolian branch of the Altaic language family and is close to that of the Tu and Dongxiang nationalities. Due to long years of contacts and exchanges with the neighbouring Hans and Huis, the Bonan people have borrowed quite a number of words from the Han language. The Han language is accepted as the common written language among the Bonans.

Judging from their legends, language features and customs, many of which were identical with those of the Mongolians, the Bonan nationality seems to have taken shape after many years of interchanges during the Yuan and Ming (1271-1644) periods between Islamic Mongolians who settled down as garrison troops in Qinghai's Tongren County, and the neighbouring Huis, Hans, Tibetans and Tus. The Bonans used to live in three major villages in the Baoan region, situated along the banks of the Longwu River within the boundaries of Tongren County.

During the early years of the reign of Qing Emperor Tongzhi (1862-1874), they fled from the oppression of the feudal serf owners of the local lamaist Longwu Monastery. After staying for a few years in Xunhua, they moved on into Gansu Province and finally settled down at the foot of Jishi Mountain in Dahejia and Liuji, Linxia County. Incidentally, they again formed themselves into three villages — Dadun, Ganmei and Gaoli — which they referred to as the "tripartite village of Baoan" in remembrance of their roots.

Dahejia is the place where the Bonans mainly concentrated. It is located in the western part of Linxia County, with the towering Jishi Mountain lying to the west and the surging Yellow River to the north. The area is thickly wooded and enjoys a moderate temperature supported by plenty of water and lush grass, which make it suitable for farming and stock breeding. However, prior to 1949, under the heavy burden of feudal oppression and exploitation, the place was bleak and desolate. In Dahejia, Bonan and Hui bureaucrats, landlords and religious leaders owned large tracts of farmland, forests and orchards. They also monopolized the river transport and owned 20 of the 27 water mills. The majority of the people were reduced to tenants toiling under the severe exploitation of land rents and usury. Rent in kind was a form of exploitation widely practised in the area. In most cases, rentals were as high as 50 per cent. Exploitation by the landlords also took on other forms such as hiring farm labourers on a long-term basis and trading in slave girls.

The Bonan people are mainly Muslims, but are divided into two different sects — the Old and the New. Religion was used by members of the reactionary ruling class as a cover to exercise complete power over the local people. The mullahs even had private jails to imprison and torture at random those who broke religious laws or showed any sign of resistance against oppression. Exploitation carried out in the name of religion accounted for as much as 20 to 30 per cent of the total revenues of the peasants.

As a result of such brutal oppression and exploitation, agricultural production in the area was quite backward. The per-hectare yield of grain never exceeded 750 kg. The poor peasants had to eke out a living by peddling, making charcoal, selling medicinal herbs or running rafts on the Yellow River during slack seasons to subsidize their meagre existence.

During the rule of the Kuomintang, the Chiang (Kai-shek)-Ma (Bufang) clique imposed conscription and other hardships on the Bonans and made their lives even harder. Most of the able-bodied male peasants were forced to flee the area to avoid being drafted into the army or to seek a better living elsewhere. The heavy farm labour fell onto the shoulders of the women.

A sideline occupation for which Bonans are particularly noted is the making of knives. A cottage industry, the Bonan knives are famous all over China for their beauty and sturdiness.

After the founding of New China in 1949, the Bonan people, like the other local people of the Hui, Han and Salar nationalities, achieved national equality and the right to run their own affairs. A new kind of atmosphere in which people of various nationalities help each other and live in harmonious unity prevails in Dahejia. In 1951, the Jishishan, Bonan, Dongxiang and Salar Autonomous County was established in Gansu Province, and a series of social reforms have enabled the Bonan people to emancipate themselves gradually in the political, economic and ideological fields. In 1958, they joined hands with the people of the local Hui, Dongxiang and Salar nationalities in Dahejia in abolishing the feudal privileges of the local Islamic clergy and the entire traditional system of oppression and exploitation. In the course of the struggle, they exposed the crimes of a handful of leading religious elements in sabotaging the reform and sowing discord among the various nationalities as well as in beating and abusing the peasants, infringing on the freedom of marriage and enforcing unpaid labour services in the name of religion. Together with the abolition of all irrational systems and the lessening of religious burdens on the people, the government has taken steps to ensure an all-round implementation of the Party's policy on freedom of religion.

The economic and cultural life of the Bonans is improving year by year. A 102 km highway between Linxia and the Dahejia area was constructed in the early years following liberation. Post and tele-communications offices were set up in Dahejia, which, together with the establishment of a rediffusion network, have brought about an increasingly closer link between the Bonan people and other nationalities throughout the country. A number of township-run and village-run factories and workshops have also been set up in the Dahejia area. The traditional knife-making handicraft of the Bonan people has been developed and improved.

It had been the aspiration of the Bonans and people of other nationalities in Dahejia for generations to build canals to irrigate their arid lands. Their joint efforts since 1949 have seen a continuous development of water conservancy projects. A network of canals cover the mountain slopes and the arable lands. Desolate mountains are now covered with economic stands of timber such as elms, willows, Chinese prickly ash trees, apple trees and walnut trees.

In recent years, the Bonan people have taken measures to develop their traditional skills in making knives and repairing farm tools and to establish a number of small enterprises for the processing of agricultural produce and by-products. This has greatly helped to increase their incomes.

Prior to 1949, the whole of the Bonan settlement had only one single dilapidated primary school with just over 30 pupils. Now they have a number of primary schools and middle schools. Quite a few young people have been sent for advanced studies to the Northwest Institute of Nationalities, the Central Institute of Nationalities and other institutes of higher learning. Work to wipe out illiteracy has made significant progress following the establishment of various kinds of winter schools, night schools and literacy classes.

Especially worth mentioning is the emancipation of Bonan women. They have won the right to take part in political, social, cultural and recreational activities on the same level of equality as men.

In the past, the Baoan area was ravaged by epidemics, and medical care was primitive. But now, clinics and health centres have been set up and local medical workers have been trained. Mobile medical teams are regularly sent to the area by provincial, prefectural and county medical authorities to provide free medical care. Epidemic diseases that had long plagued the area have now been brought under control. Gone are the days when women had to give birth to their children on the mountains or in the fields simply because they could not afford to leave their work or have the opportunity to consult doctors.

The Bonan culture is deeply influenced by Islam, which still dictates their forms of marriage, funerals and festive ceremonies, as well as their family life and social customs. These are similar to those of the neighbouring Hui, Dongxiang and Salar peoples, as are their costumes and personal adornments. The Bonans have also maintained a number of customs which are characteristic of nomadic tribes and identical with those of the Mongols. For example, they are fond of wrestling, horsemanship and shooting.

After 1949, the Bonan people voluntarily abolished a number of irrational customs and habits that were left over from the feudal system, as well as a series of outmoded conventions and practices discriminating against women. These included polygamy.

The Bonans like to sing and dance. They are good at playing traditional string and woodwind instruments, and, like the Huis, Dongxiangs and Salars, their ballads are known as "Hua'er" (flower). Impromptu singing during feasts is a typical form of entertainment.

The Yugurs

Nearly 90 per cent of the Yugur nationality's 10,000 people live in the Sunan Yugur Autonomous County, and the rest in Huangnibao area near the city of Jiuquan in western Gansu Province.

Due to historical reasons, the nationality uses three languages: a Turkic branch of the Altaic language family (Raohul) used by the Yugurs in the western part of the autonomous county; a Mongolian branch of the same language family (Engle) by those in the eastern part of the county; and the Chinese language by those in Huangnibao. Chinese is also a common medium of communication among all Yugurs.

Origins The Yugur nationality can trace its origins to the nomadic ancient Ouigurs in the Erhun River valley during the Tang Dynasty (618-907). In the mid-9th century, the ancient Ouigurs, beset by snowstorms, feuding within the ruling group and attacks from the Turkic Kirgiz, had to move westward in separate groups. One of the groups emigrated to Guazhou (present-day Dunhuang), Ganzhou (present-day Zhangye) and Liangzhou (present-day Wuwei) in the Hexi Corridor — the most fertile area in central-western Gansu Province — and came under the rule of Tufan, a Tibetan kingdom. They were thus called the Hexi Ouigurs. Later, they captured the city of Ganzhou and set up a khanate — thus they were also called

Ganzhou Ouigurs.

The Hexi Ouigurs had all along maintained very close ties with the central empire and regarded these ties as relations of "nephew to uncle." During the Northern Song Dynasty (960-1126), the Khan of the Ganzhou Ouigurs often sent special envoys to the imperial capital to present tribute to the emperor, and, in return, the Song court gave "the nephew Ouigur Khan in Ganzhou" special products from central China. The Khan's emissaries went to the capital of the Song Dynasty on several missions to offer camels, horses, coral and amber as tribute to the imperial court in the fifth year (980) of the reign of Emperor Tai Zong and the third year (1010) of the reign of Emperor Zhen Zong.

In the mid-11th century, the Western Xia Kingdom conquered Ganzhou and toppled the Ouigur regime. The Hexi Ouigurs then became dependants of the former and moved to pastoral areas outside the Jiayu Pass. However, their links with the Song court were still maintained. Ouigur envoys came to the Song capital with tribute again during the first year of the reign of Emperor Shen Zong (1068) and requested a copy of a Buddhist scripture. According to an envoy in 1073, there were more than 300,000 Ouigurs at that time. In 1227 the Mongols conquered Western Xia Kingdom and put the Hexi Ouigurs under their direct rule.

Part of the Hexi Ouigurs were assimilated with neighbouring ethnic groups over a long period of co-existence from the mid-11th to the 16th century, and developed into a community — the present-day Yugurs. They lived around Dunhuang in western Gansu and Hami in eastern Xinjiang.

The Ming (1368-1644) rulers moved many of the Yugurs farther east as the frontier became unsettled.

The Yugurs underwent changes in the mode of economic production after their eastward move. Those in the Huangnibao area, availing themselves of exchanges with the Hans, learned farming and gradually substituted it for animal husbandry, while those in the Sunan area still engaged in livestock breeding and hunting. Thanks to the introduction of iron implements from the Hans, the Yugurs' skills in farming, animal husbandry and hunting all improved.

The Qing government (1644-1911), in an attempt to strengthen its rule, divided the Yugurs into "seven tribes" and appointed a headman for each and a powerful chieftain — the "Huangfan Superintendent of the Seven Tribes" — over them all.

The Qing government made it a law for the Yugur tribes to offer 113 horses every year in exchange for tea. At first, they got some tea, but later, virtually none. The horses thus contributed were tribute pure and simple. The tribute demanded by the central government also included stag antlers, musk and furs. The Suzhou Yugurs had to deliver grain or silver.

After 1911, the Yugur areas came under the rule of Warlords Ma Lin and Ma Bufang.

Feudal System The tribal feudal system of the Yugurs before liberation had remnants of the primitive tribal organization as well as feudal class exploitation and rule.

The posts of chieftain, chief and deputy chief of the nine tribes were hereditary. The tribal chiefs were all surnamed An — hence the saying: "All bosses are Ans." The chieftain of all the tribes presided over conferences of tribal chiefs and handled affairs of common interest. Tribal chiefs took care of the affairs of their own tribes, and all money and property levied by them had to be shared with the chieftain. The division of tribes was approved and the power of the tribal chiefs defined by the Ming and Qing courts.

The lower-level superintendents were designated by the tribal chief. The appointments were decided after consultations with the upper elements of the Lamaist monasteries and big households (big owners of livestock and pastures, and rich herdsmen), representatives of whom invariably occupied the posts. The term of office, renewable, was generally one to three years.

Each tribe held several meetings a year for levying of taxes, etc. Such meetings were called by the chief, with each household participating. Superficially they claimed to make decisions in a democratic way, but everything was decided by the chief and the superintendents.

Before liberation, there were also two special posts called "Qian Hu" (thousand families) and a number of "Venerated Elders" among the tribes. The title of "Qian Hu" was bestowed by the Taer Monastery in Qinghai and, later, by warlord Ma Bufang for the expansion of their influence. The "Qian Hus" were very influential and had to be consulted on important tribal matters. The "Venerated Elders" were responsible for collecting various taxes on behalf of the tribe chiefs and giving assistance to the chiefs in settling disputes.

The chiefs, availing themselves of this tribal system and feudal privileges, plundered the herdsmen. When there were cases of theft, robbery, fighting, disputes over pastures or family quarrels that had to be handled by the chiefs, the accuser and the accused had to present gifts to them and were held responsible for the tea and meals of the judges and the fodder for their animals. The penalties so exacted went more often than not into the pockets of the chiefs, so the handling of lawsuits was an important means of revenue for the chiefs.

The pastures were owned by the tribe as a unit. There were three modes of ownership within the tribe: tribal, monastery and private ownership. The majority of the pastures and livestock were in the hands of tribal chiefs, powerful lamas and big herd owners. Their exploitation of the herdsmen was through severe corvee. pasture leasing and usury.

The Kuomintang regime worked to maintain and make use of this backward and exploitative system, and exerted its rule through the feudal upper classes.

Religion was once another pillar of reactionary rule. The Yugurs, before their eastward migration, believed in Lamaism, and at the same time kept their ancient native religion — "Han Dian Gel" (worship of the Heavenly Khan). This was possibly a legacy of primitive shamanism and the liturgy was in a language called "Raohul" still being spoken by part of the Yugurs.

Lamaism began to get the upper hand in the Yugur area in the Ming and Qing dynasties. Each tribe had its own monastery. The lamas worked hand-in-glove with the chiefs in important tribal matters; some tribes practised integration of religion and politics. The Lamaist monasteries had their own feudal system of oppression and exploitation: courts, prisons and instruments of torture. They could order compulsory donations and gratuitous forced labour, and compel children join the clergy. Some lamas extorted large amounts of money and property out of the common people by way of fortune-telling and exorcism. Donations for religious purposes accounted approximately for 30 per cent of the annual income of a middle-class family.

All these hardships reduced the ethnic group virtually to extinction. At the time of the nationwide liberation in 1949, its population was less than 3,000.

Socio-economic Development In February and April of 1954, the Sunan Yugur Autonomous County and Jiuquan Huangnibao Yugur Autonomous Township were established.

In the light of the different socio-economic conditions in the localities, special steps and methods were adopted in democratic reform and socialist transformation. In Huangnibao which had similar socio-economic conditions to the areas inhabited by the Hans, land reform was carried out as in the rest of the country, while reform in the Sunan area was carried out through peaceful consultation. The years of 1955 and 1956 saw a reform in the ownership of pastures. The feudal ownership of pastureland by tribes, monasteries and individuals was abolished and a committee set up to exercise unified management, overall planning and rational utilization of pastures. A mass cooperative movement followed, to solve the shortage of labour and raise productivity. Animals were herded in separate groups instead of in a mass. The cattle barons' economy was step by step transformed into joint state-private ownership.

The cooperative movement gave a new lease of life to the herdsmen, and many began to settle down. Hospitals were established, education was brought within the reach of all children and the elderly were taken care of. The herdsmen replaced their traditional crude woolen tents with wooden huts.

On the basis of the cooperative movement, the religious feudal privileges and the system of oppression and exploitation had been eliminated by 1958.

With the progress of the socialist revolution, the Yugurs tried to reform their backward customs and habits. Before liberation, mercenary and arranged marriages were prevalent, and involved expensive betrothal gifts. Child brides or bridegrooms were in vogue in some areas and rich herdowners without sons bought "brides" and had them marry strangers who would thus become their house servants. This practice of "brides for non-existent sons" meant humiliation and oppression for the Yugur women. After liberation, a new marriage law was promulgated, giving both sexes freedom of choice in marriage.

In the past, there were three types of funeral; cremation, burial and sky burial (whereby bodies were exposed to birds of prey). These funeral ceremonies always involved immense expense for prayers by lamas and donations to the monasteries. This had been done away with and cremation had been generally accepted by 1958.

Culture   The Yugurs have a rich literary tradition handed down orally, such as legends, folk tales, proverbs and ballads. The folk songs feature uniquely simple yet graceful tunes, and vivid content.

They are skilled at the plastic arts, weaving beautiful patterns on bags, carpets and harnesses. Vivid patterns in harmonious colours of flowers, grass, insects, birds and domestic animals are woven on women's collars, sleeves and cloth boots. Geometrical patterns made of coral beads, sea shells and green and blue stone chips, and silk threads in bright colours are used as hair decorations.

The Yugurs have their own peculiar way of dressing. A typical well-dressed man sports a felt hat, a high-collared long gown buttoned on the left, a red-blue waist band and high boots. A woman of marriageable age combs her hair into many small pigtails which are tied up into three big ones, with two thrown over the chest and one over the back after marriage. The women usually wear a trumpet-shaped white felt hat with two black lines in front, topped by red tassels.

Post-liberation Development   Thanks to hard efforts, the Yugurs have made much headway in all fields since liberation.

Wool shearing has been mechanized, animal stocks improved and steps taken to have the herdsmen settle down and pastures grazed by rotation. Reservoirs have been built, ponds dug and underground water tapped to irrigate 46,700 hectares of dry pastures and provide drinking water for animals. The situation of "worried herdsmen having sheep but no water, wandering from place to place" has been fundamentally changed.

The Yugurs used to hunt wild animals without trying to domesticate any, but in 1958 they began to set up farms to domesticate wild deer.

In industry, the area now has farm and livestock-breeding machinery factories, carpet, fur, and food processing industries, and coal mining. Electricity reaches all townships and most Yugur homes. Wool shearing, threshing and fodder-crushing machines are now in extensive use.

There is a developed network of highways now. Before liberation there was "not a meter of smooth ground and not a single bridge across the rivers" as the saying went. Merchants made use of this backwardness to exploit the local Yugurs: a mere five or six pieces of brick tea could buy a horse.

Before liberation there were only four primary schools with a total student body of 70, mostly children of tribal chiefs, herd owners and landlords. Sunan County now has two senior middle schools, eight junior middle schools and 76 primary schools. Many young Yugurs are able to finish secondary technical or college education. The nationality now has its own teachers as well as technicians.

Medical care has markedly improved, whereas, in the old society, people's only recourse was to pray to Buddha when they suffered from illnesses.

The Uygurs

The Xinjiang Uygur Autonomous Region covers more than 1,709,400 square kilometres or approximately one sixth of China's total landmass, and is by far the biggest of the country's regions and provinces. It occupies much of the sparsely-populated Northwest.

Besides the Uygur ethnic group, Han, Kazak, Hui, Mongolian, Kirgiz, Tajik, Xibe, Uzbek, Manchu, Daur, Tatar and Russian people live in Xinjiang. The Uygurs, numbering 5,957,100, account for three-fifths of the total. They believe in Islam.

The region is bounded by the Altay Mountains in the North, the Pamirs in the West, the Karakoram Mountains, Altun Mountains and Kunlun Mountains in the South. The Tianshan Mountains bisect Xinjiang into northern and southern parts with very different climates and landscapes. Southern Xinjiang includes the Tarim Basin and the Taklimakan Desert, China's largest, while northern Xinjiang contains the Junggar Basin, where the Karamay Oilfields and the fertile Ili River valley are situated. The Turpan Basin, the hottest and lowest point in China, lies at the eastern end of the Tianshan Mountains. The Tarim, Yarkant, Yurunkax and Qarran rivers irrigate land around the Tarim Basin, while the Ili, Irtish, Ulungur and Manas rivers flow through arable and pastoral areas in northern Xinjiang. Many of the rivers spill into lakes. The Lop Nur, Bosten (Bagrax),

Uliungur and Ebinur lakes teem with fish.

Xinjiang's climate is dry and warm in the south, and cold in the north with plenty rainfall and snow. The Uygurs farm areas around the Tarim Basin and the Gobi Desert. Wheat, maize and paddy rice are the region's main grain crops, and cotton is a major cash crop. Since China's liberation in 1949, cotton has been grown in the Manas River valley north of 40 degrees latitude. The Tianshan Mountains are rich in coal and iron, the Altay in gold, and the Kunlun in jade. The region also has big deposits of non-ferrous and rare metals and oil, and rich reserves of forests and land open to reclamation.

Xinjiang History Xinjiang has been part of China since ancient times. The Uygurs, together with other ethnic groups, have opened up the region and have had very close economic and cultural ties with people in other parts of the country, particularly central China.

Xinjiang experienced a New Stone Age Culture with an economy based on animal husbandry and hunting. It shared common features with those in other parts of northern China. Ruins discovered at Aktla and Wengulok in Shufu County are the westernmost ones of the New Stone Age Culture to have been found so far in China. Utensils unearthed are mostly stone knives and sickles quite similar to those found in central China dating from the New Stone Age to the Shang Dynasty (16th-11th century B.C.). They provided valuable material for the study of primitive culture in the region, and indicated that it began to forge ties with central China in the far distant past.

Xinjiang was called simply "Western Region" in ancient times. The Jiaohe ruins, Gaochang ruins, Yangqi Mansion of "A Thousand Houses," Baicheng (Bay) Kizil Thousand Buddha Grottoes, Bozklik Grottoes in Turpan, Kumtula Grottoes in Kuqa and Astana Tombs in Turpan all contain a great wealth of relics from the Western and Eastern Han dynasties (206 B.C. — A.D.220). They bear witness to the efforts of the Uygurs and other ethnic groups in Xinjiang in developing China and its culture. "The Book of Shang," one of the Confucian classics, "Shan Hai Jing" (Book of Mountains and Seas, an ancient geographical work) and "Spring and Autumn of Lü" (an anthology of pre-Qin thinkers compiled by Lü Buwei) all mentioned the Western Region. "Yu Gong," a chapter from the "Book of Shang," refers to the "jade of Kun Mountains," suggesting that jade was already being sent to central China from southern Xinjiang.

Zhang Qian, who lived in the second century B.C., went to the Western Region as an official envoy in 138 and 119 B.C., further strengthening ties between China and central Asia via the "Silk Road." In 60 B.C., Emperor Xuan Di of the Western Han Dynasty established the Office of Governor of the Western Region to supervise the "36 states" north and south of the Tianshan Mountains with the westernmost border running through areas east and south of Lake Balkhash and the Pamirs.

During the Wei, Jin, Northern and Southern dynasties (220-581 A.D.) the Western Reigon was a political dependent of the government in central China. The Wei, Western Jin, Earlier Liang (317-376), Earlier Qin (352-394) and Later Liang (386-403) dynasties all stationed troops and set up administrative bodies there. In 327, Zhang Jun of the Earlier Liang Dynasty set up in Turpan the Gao Chang Prefecture, the first of its kind in the region.

In the mid-seventh century, the Tang Dynasty established the Anxi Governor's Office in Xizhou (present-day Turpan, it later moved to Guizi, present-day Kuqa) to rule areas south and north of the Tianshan Mountains. The superintendent's offices in the Pamirs were all under the jurisdiction of the Anxi Governor's Office. In the meantime, four Anxi towns of important military significance — Guizi, Yutian (present-day Hotan), Shule (present-day Kaxgar) and Suiye (on the southern bank of the Chu River) — were established.

In the early eighth century, the Tang Dynasty added Beiting Governor's Office in Tingzhou (present-day Jimsar). The Beiting and Anxi offices, with an administrative and military system under them, implemented effectively the Tang government's orders.

In the early 13th century, Genghis Khan (1162-1227) appointed a senior official in the region. The Yuan Dynasty (1271-1368) established Bieshibali (present-day areas north of Jimsar) and Alimali (present-day Korgas) provinces. The Hami Military Command was set up during the Ming Dynasty (1368-1644). During the Qing Dynasty (1644-1911) the northern part of the Western Region, namely, north of Irtish River and Zaysan Lake, was under Zuo Fu General's Office in Wuliyasu. The General's Office in Ili exercised power over areas north and south of the Tianshan Mountains, east and south of Lake Balkhash and the Pamirs. Xinjiang was made a province in 1884, the 10th year of the reign of Emperor Guang Xu.

Uygur History   Uygur means "unity" or "alliance." The origin of the ethnic group can be traced back to the Ding Ling nomads in northern and northwestern China and in areas south of Lake Baikal and between the Irtish River and Lake Balkhash in the third century B.C. Some people maintain that the forefathers of the Uygurs were related to the Hans. The Ding Ling were later called the Tie Le, Tie Li, Chi Le or Gao Che (high wheel). The Yuan He tribe reigned supreme among the Gao Che tribes during the fifth century A.D., and the Wei He among the Tie Le during the seventh century. Several tribes rallied behind the Wei He to resist Turkic oppression.

These ancient Uighur people were finally conquered by Turkic Kirghiz in the mid-ninth century. The majority of the Uighurs, who were scattered over many areas, moved to the Western Region under the Anxi Governor's Office, and areas west of Yutian. Some went to the Tufan principality in western Gansu Province. The Uighurs who settled in the Western Region lived commingled with Turkic nomads in areas north of the Tianshan Mountains and western pasturelands as well as with Hans, who had emigrated there after the Western and Eastern Han dynasties. They inter-married with people in southern Xinjiang and Tibetan, Qidan (Khitan) and Mongol tribes, and evolved into the group now known as the Uygurs.

The Uighurs made rapid socio-economic and cultural progress between the ninth and the 12th centuries. Nomadism gave way to settled farming. Commercial and trade ties with central China began to thrive better than ever before. Through markets, they exchanged horses, jade, frankincense and medicines for iron implements, tea, silk and money. With the feudal system further established, a land and animal owners' class came into being, comprising Uighur khans and Bokes (officials) at all levels. After Islam was introduced to Kaxgar in the late 10th century, it gradually extended its influence to Shache (Yarkant) and Yutian, and later in the 12th century to Kuya and Yanqi, where it replaced Shamanism, Manichae, Jingism (Nestorianism, introduced to China during the Tang Dynasty), Ao'ism (Mazdaism) and Buddhism, which had been popular for hundreds of years. Western Region culture developed quickly, with Uighur, Han, Sanskrit, Cuili and Poluomi languages, calendars and painting styles being used. Two major centres of Uygur culture and literature — Turpan in the north and Kaxgar in the south — came into being. The large number of government documents, religious books and folk stories of this period are important works for students of the Uygur history, language and culture.

In the early 12th century, part of the Qidan tribe moved westward from north-east China under the command of Yeludashi. They toppled the Hala Khanate established by the Uighurs, Geluolu and other Turkic tribes in the 10th century, and founded the Hala Khanate of Qidan (Black Qidan), or Western Liao as it is now referred to by historians. The state of Gao Chang became its vassal state. After the rise of the Mongols, most of Xinjiang became the territory of the Jagatai Khanate. In the meantime, when many Hans were sent to areas either south or north of the Tianshan Mountains to open up waste land, many Uygurs moved to central China. The forefathers of the Uygurs and Huis in Changde and Taoyuan counties in Hunan Province today moved in that exodus. The Uygurs exercised important influence over politics, economy, culture and military affairs. Many were appointed officials by the Yuan court and, under the impacts of the Han culture, some became outstanding politicians, military strategists, writers, historians and translators.

The Uygur areas from Hami in the east to Hotan in the south were unified into a greater feudal separatist Kaxgar Khanate after more than two centuries of separatism and feuding from the late 14th century. As the capital was moved to Yarkant, it was also known as the Yarkant Khanate. Its rulers were still the offspring of Jagatai. During the early Qing period, the Khanate was a tributary of the imperial court and had commercial ties with central China. After periods of unsteady relations with the Ming Dynasty, the links between the Uygurs and ethnic groups in central China became stronger. Gerdan, chief of Dzungaria in northern Xinjiang, toppled the Yarkant Khanate in 1678 and ruled the Uygur area. The Qing army repelled in 1757 (the 22nd year of the reign of Emperor Qian Long) the separatist rebellion by the Dzungarian nobles instigated by the Russian Tsar, and in 1759 smashed the "Batu Khanate" founded by Poluonidu and Huojishan, the Senior and Junior Khawaja, in a separatist attempt.

The Qing government introduced a system of local military-command offices in Xinjiang. It appointed the General in Ili as the highest Western Regional Governor of administrative and military affairs over northern and southern Xinjiang and the parts of Central Asia under Qing influence and the Kazak and Blut (Kirgiz) tribes. For local government, a system of prefectures and counties was introduced.

The imperial court began to appoint and remove local officials rather than allowing them to pass on their titles to their children. This weakened to some degree the local feudal system. The court also encouraged the opening up of waste land by garrison troops and local peasants, the promotion of commerce and the reduction of taxation, which were important steps in the social development of Uygur areas.

Xinjiang was completely under Qing Dynasty rule after the mid-18th century. Although political reforms had limited the political and economic privileges of the feudal Bokes (lords), and taxation was slightly lower, the common ethnic people's living standards did not change significantly for the better. The Qing officials, through local Bokes, exacted taxes even on "garden trees." The Bokes expanded ownership on land and serfs, controlled water resources and manipulated food grain prices for profit.

Harsh feudal rule and exploitation gave rise to the six-month-long Wushi (Uqturpan) uprising in 1765, the first armed rebellion by the Uygur people against feudalism. With the aim of preserving their rule and getting rid of Qing control, Uygur feudal owners made use of struggles between religious factions to whip up nationalism and cover up the worsening class contradictions. Zhangger, grandson of the Senior Khawaja, a representative of those owners, under the banner of religion and armed with British-supplied weapons, harassed southern Xinjiang many times from 1820 to 1828, but failed to win military victory.

Uprisings and Foreign Intervention   Not long after the outbreak of the Opium War, the Uygurs and Huis in Kuqa, influenced by rebellions of the Tai Ping Heavenly Kingdom and the Nian Army uprisings by ethnic minority peasants in Yunnan, Shaanxi and Gansu provinces, launched an armed uprising in 1864.   People in Urumqi, Shache (Yarkant), Ili, Barkol, Qitai, Hami, Mori, Jimsar and Changji responded.   Uprisings against the Qing court swept Xinjiang, and several separatist regimes came into being.   However, a handful of national and religious upper elements usurped the fruits of the uprisings under the cloak of "nationality interest" and "religion," and became self-styled kings or khans.   The warfare that ensued among them brought still greater catastrophes to the local people.

Britain fostered Yukub Beg, the General Commander of the Kokand Khanate in 1865, who invaded Xinjiang and established the Zhedsar Khanate (Seven-City Khanate). Yukub Beg was a tool in the hands of Britain and Tsarist Russia, who wanted to split Xinjiang. He exercised cruel rule and, in the name of Allah, killed 40,000 non-Muslims in southern Xinjiang. His persecution was also extended to Islamic believers, who were tried at unfair "religious courts." The local people had to shoulder the war burdens, supplying warring factions with food grain, fuel, vehicles and draught animals, and the local economy suffered catastrophic damage. Bankrupt peasants fled, and some had to sell their children for a living. The slave trade boomed at local bazaars.

To preserve Russia's vested interest and maintain an equilibrium in influence with Britain in Central Asia, the Tsar, behind the back of the Qing Court, signed illegal commercial and trade treaties with Yukub Beg. Russia claimed that it could not "sit idle" while there were uprisings in the provinces in western China, and in the name of "recovery and defence upon request," it sent troops to occupy Ili in 1871 and started a 10-year period of colonial rule. The Russian troops forced people of the Uygur, Kazak, Hui, Mongolian and Xibe tribes into designated zones in a "divide and rule" policy. Many Uygurs had to flee their home towns, and moved to Huicheng and Dongshan.

It was in the interest of all ethnic groups to smash the Yukub Beg regime and recover Ili. So many local people supported the Qing troops when they overthrew Yukub Beg and recovered Xingjiang in 1877. However, not long after the Qing government had signed the "Sino-Russian Treaty of Peking" and the "Tahcheng Protocol on the Delimitation of the Sino-Russian Border," whereby China was compelled to cede 440,000 square kilometres of land to Russia, the Qing Court again concluded the "Ili Treaty" with Russia in 1881. Although China recovered Ili, it lost another 70,000 square kilometres of territory west of the Korgas River, and was charged nine million roubles compensation. On the eve of its withdrawal from Ili, Tsarist Russia coerced more than 10,000 Uygur, Hui, Mongolian, Kazak and Kirgiz people to move to Russia. Farmland, irrigation facilities, houses and orchards were devastated and food grain and animals looted. Five of nine cities in Ili became virtually ruins, and the Uygurs in the nine townships on the right bank of the Ili River were reduced to poverty.

The Qing government decided to make the Western Region — formerly ruled by the General in Ili — a province named Xinjiang, a step of important significance for local development and the strengthening of the north-west border defence against imperialist aggression. Ties between the area and central China became closer, and there was greater unity between the Uygurs and other ethnic groups in the common struggle against imperialism and feudalism.

After the 1911 Revolution, Qing rule was replaced by feudal warlords. Sheng Shicai, who claimed to be progressive, usurped power in Xinjiang in the "April 12" coup of 1933.

In the same year, Britain encouraged Mohamed Imin, who dreamed of a greater Turkey, to found the Hotan Islamic Republic, and Maula Shabitida, an advocate of greater Islam, to set up the

East Turkistan Islamic Republic. Japanese imperialism in 1937 masterminded the plots by Mamti and Raolebas to form an "independent" Islamic State, and Mamti, in collaboration with Mahushan, rebelled. However, all these separatist efforts failed.

Contemporary History In 1933, when China was at a crucial point in history, the Chinese Communist Party began revolutionary activities in Xinjiang aimed at peace, democracy and progress. Sheng Shicai had to take some progressive steps, and declared six major policies — anti-imperialism, amity with the Soviet Union, national equality, honest government, peace and national reconstruction. In the same year, the "Anti-Imperialist Association of the People of Xinjiang" was formed, and the journal, "Anti-Imperialist Front," was published. Part of the Chinese Workers' and Peasants' Red Army, that left its base in Jiangxi Province to go north to resist Japanese aggression, went to Xinjiang in 1937. Chen Tanqiu, Mao Zemin and Li Jilu, Chinese Communists, then came to work in Xinjiang, galvanizing efforts in resisting Japanese aggression. Sheng Shicai then openly turned to the Kuomintang, persecuting the Communists, progressive people, patriotic youth and workers.

The Kuomintang began to rule Xinjiang in 1944, forcing sharper national and class contradictions on the Uygurs and other ethnic groups. It exacted dozens of taxes under all kinds of pretexts. One example was the taxation on land. An average peasant had to pay well over 15 per cent of annual income for it. The amount of taxes in terms of money was eight times the sum in 1937. Local industry and commerce virtually went bankrupt, and the situation for rural Uygurs was even worse.

Uprisings took place in Ili, Tacheng and Altay to oppose Kuomintang rule. They served to accelerate the liberation of the region in the national liberation war.

Tao Zhiyue, the Commandant of the Kuomintang Xinjiang Garrison, and Burhan Shahidi, Chairman of the Kuomintang Xinjiang Provincial Government, accepted Chinese Communist Party's peace terms, and revolted against the Nanjing Government, and Xinjiang was peacefully liberated in October, 1949.

Post-liberation Development The Chinese People's Liberation

Army stationed in Xinjiang began their efforts to reclaim waste land. They built a number of modern industries with money saved from the military budget, and trained Uygurs in new industrial skills.

By the end of 1953, land reform in rural Xinjiang had been completed, the landlord class eliminated, and the feudal land ownership abolished. The Xinjiang Uygur Autonomous Region was formally established on October 1, 1955. Five autonomous prefectures and six autonomous counties were set up in the following months. National autonomy became a reality.

The 1966-1976 "cultural revolution" brought disastrous upheaval to Xinjiang. The Communist Party made great efforts to put things right after the Third Plenary Session of the 11th Central Committee of the Party in 1978. It marked a new period of development for the region.

Wang Enmao, first secretary of the Party's Xinjiang regional committee, who was a political commissar with the army that marched to Xinjiang in 1949 under the command of General Wang Zhen, said: "We have achieved a long-standing stable political situation and a sound economic and cultural basis.

"These, together with our rich natural resources, will ensure Xinjiang's economic and cultural boom in the near future."

The region's power industry now provides 3.4 billion kilowatt hours of electricity a year. This has enabled Xinjiang to build up a full range of industries, including iron and steel, coal mining, petroleum, machine-building, chemicals, building materials, textiles, sugar-refining and cigarette-making.

There are now more than 4,000 factories and mines manufacturing 2,000 types of products. Industrial output was worth nearly six billion yuan in 1984, compared with 91 million yuan in 1949, and 380 million yuan in 1955 when the autonomous region was founded.

The region now has 22,000 kilometres of roads, including 8,200 kilometres of asphalt roads, compared with only 3,000 kilometres of dirt roads in 1949.

Urumqi, the regional capital, is now connected with Lanzhou, a hub of northwest China, by rail. It is now possible to reach Korla in southern Xinjiang by rail, and the Urumqi-Usu railway is under construction.

There is a network of air transport in the region, boasting 11 airports, more than any other provinces or autonomous regions. The region's airlines cover 11,500 kilometres, carrying 100,000 passengers a year. The Urumqi terminal is connected by air with Beijing, Shanghai, Guangzhou, Xi'an and Lanzhou, and is also an important international airport.

Intensive capital construction has been carried out in Urumqi, Kaxgar, Yining (Gulja), Hami, Turpan, Changji, Tacheng, Bole (Bortala), Altay, Korla, Aksu, Artux and Hotan over the past 30 years. Retail sales in 1984 were 8.1 times the 1955 figure, and foreign trade increased 3.7 times in the period. Business was conducted with more than 30 countries. Foreign trade in 1984 was worth 151 million U.S. dollars.

By the end of 1984, Xinjiang had already formed economic or technical ties of co-operation with 26 provinces, autonomous regions and municipalities, involving a total of 2,840 development projects. These schemes had helped add 100 million yuan to the region's annual industrial and agricultural output value, and 10 million yuan in profits. More than 300 types of new products had been developed.

Since 1955, output of grain has risen by 3.3 times, cotton 7.64 times and oil-bearing seeds 3.16 times. Xinjiang harvested 615,500 tons of sugar beet in 1984, making it more than self-sufficient in sugar.

Ten per cent or 150,000 of Xinjiang's rural households now specialize in crop cultivation, livestock breeding, food processing and service trades. Of these, 60,000 families are engaged solely in growing crops, and their per-hectare output is double that of ordinary farmers on average.

A significant improvement has also been made in the living standards of the ethnic people. The per-capita income of the peasants and herders averaged 363 yuan in 1984.

The State Council decided in November 1978, to build a 7,000-kilometre forest belt running across northern China, through Heilongjiang, Jilin, Liaoning, Hebei, Beijing, Shanxi, Inner Mongolia, Shaanxi, Gansu, Ningxia, Qinghai and Xinjiang. In the six years from 1978 to 1983, a total of seven million hectares of land had been planted with trees. About 75,000 hectares of trees were planted in Xinjiang in the spring of 1985, equivalent to the total for two previous years.

Following 30 years of sustained efforts, local livestock experts have bred fine-wool sheep, whose wool compares favourably with that of Australian sheep.

The number of animals in stock at the end of 1984 totalled more than 30 million — nearly triple the 1949 figure, and 84 per cent more than in 1955.

The central government provided 14.14 billion yuan in subsidies to Xinjiang between 1950 and 1984, and spent another 14.77 billion yuan on Xinjiang's capital construction.

Xinjiang now has 144,000 family businesses, 36 times the 1978 figure, employing more than 208,000 people.

A four-year scientific survey of Xinjiang's natural resources, production capabilities and development potential is now under way to prepare the region for an economic upsurge at the turn of the century.

The survey, being carried out by a task force of 315 scientists and technicians, is expected to produce an overall strategic development plan for the region, which, along with other parts of China's West, has been designated to receive top priority in economic development around the year 2000.

In its scope and importance, the current survey, which began in May 1985, is the greatest ever undertaken in Xinjiang. It was sponsored by the regional government and the Chinese Academy of Sciences, and is divided into 47 programmes, covering industry, agriculture, energy, transport, water and environmental protection.

Xinjiang has plentiful resources of water, land and sunshine, which make it an ideal place for agriculture and pastoral production.

People tend to think of Xinjiang as arid, but the region's glaciers have 500 billion cubic metres of water, in addition to 20 billion cubic metres of subterranean water and 90 billion cubic metres of lake and river water. This means 7,700 cubic metres for every local inhabitant — five times the figure in some coastal areas.

Xinjiang's oil reserves have been verified at almost five billion barrels, and high-yield wells have been sunk in the Tarim and Junggar basins. Coal reserves are estimated at about 18.3 billion tons, about one third of the nation's total.

Xinjiang has been found to have reserves of 118 types of minerals, and leads the nation in reserves of beryllium, lithium, white mica and albite. Twenty-seven deposits of gold have been discovered.

Successful application of regional autonomy can be seen in the fact that 64 per cent of the representatives on the region's People's Congress are from ethnic minorities, while minority cadres make up 69 per cent of the region's officials, and hold all leading administrative posts.

According to Amudun Niyaz, Chairman of the Xinjiang Uygur Autonomous Region's People's Congress Standing Committee, there are now 192,000 minority cadres, 4.2 times more than in 1955, while the number of minority technical personnel increased from 2,400 in 1955 to 115,000 in 1984.

Education has made much headway. There are now about 3 million students in the region — in 14 universities, 2,325 middle and secondary technical schools and 8,252 primary schools.

Public health facilities in the region have increased by 7.6 times, and the number of hospital beds has risen by 9.4 times over the past 30 years. There are 9.4 times as many health workers as in 1955. Traditional Uygur medicine has been developed. Hospitals or health clinics specializing in the ethnic group's special medicine have been built in Hotan, Kashi, Urumqi, Yecheng, Kuqa and Yining. Many books of traditional Uygur medicine have been published.

Customs and Habits In the past, many poor Uygur peasants lived on a diet of narrow-leaved oleaster and dried apricot and peach, mulberry and grain porridge. Now, wheat flour, rice and maize are the staple foods. Uygurs in some areas like milk tea with baked maize or wheat cakes. Some are made by mixing flour with sugar, eggs, butter or meat and are delicious. Paluo (sweet rice), cooked with mutton, sheep fat, carrots, raisins, onions and rice, is an important festival food for guests.

The Uygurs' cotton growing and cotton yarn spinning industry has a long history. Working people usually wear cotton cloth garments. Men sport a long gown called a qiapan, which opens on the right and has a slanted collar. It is buttonless and is bound by a long square cloth band around the waist. Women wear broad-sleeved dresses and black waist coats with buttons sewn on the front. Some now like to wear Western-style suits and skirts. The Uygurs, old and young, men and women, like to wear a small cap with four pointed corners, embroidered with black and white or coloured silk threads in traditional Uygur designs. The women's favourite decorations include earrings, bracelets and necklaces. Some paint their eyebrows and fingernails on grand festive occasions. Girls in the past combed their hair into a dozen pigtails, and regarded long hair as part of female beauty. After marriage, they usually wear two pigtails with loose ends, decorated on the head with a crescent-shaped comb. Some tuck up their pigtails into a bun.

Over the centuries, many mosques, mazas (Uygur complexes, nobles' tombs), theological seminaries and religious courts were set upt in Uygur areas. Over the past few hundred years, religion has greatly influenced economic, judicial and educational affairs and the Uygur family and matrimonial system. Exploiters made use of religious rules to marry more than one wife, and had the right to divorce them at any time. The marriage of the ordinary Uygurs was mostly arranged by the parents. Male chauvinism was practised in the family, and Uygur women, humiliated and with nobody to turn to, often retreated into prayer.

After liberation, feudal religious privileges were abolished, and religion was taken out of the control of the reactionary ruling class, and became a matter of individual conscience. As science and knowledge spread, many of the old feudalistic religious habits lost popularity. People can now decide for themselves whether the Sawm should be observed during Ramadan, how many naimazi (services) should be performed in a day and whether women in the street should wear veils.

As these matters do not affect normal religious belief, the Uygurs are beginning to enjoy a more genuine religious freedom. The family, marriage and property are under the protection of the law, and Uygur women enjoy equality with men. Many are now working alongside men in modern industries.

There are now 13 million Moslems in the country, compared with eight million in the early post-liberation period. In 1953, the Chinese Islamic Association was established with Burhan Shahidi as its chairman. Seven million people in Xinjiang believe in Islam, accounting for well over half of the national total. There are 15,800 religious professionals, about 2,000 of whom are either deputies to the People's Congress or the Chinese People's Political Consultative Conference at various levels, or work in the regional or county branches of the Chinese Islamic Association. The region now boasts a total of 15,500 mosques or prayer centres, or one for almost every Moslem village.

Culture Since liberation, Uygur culture and art, which have a long and rich tradition, has flourished. Uygur literature is very rich in style and subject matter. Many folk tales, parables, comedies, poems and proverbs praise the courage, wisdom and kindness of the ordinary people, while satirizing the greed, cruelty and foolishness of the exploiting classes. For instance, "The Tales of Afandi" contain stinging satire about the Bayis and Imams who bully the people.

Much of the written Uygur literature has been passed down from the 11th century, such as the epic "Kutadolu Biliq" ("Blessings and Wisdom") by Yusuf Hass Hajib, and "The Turkic Dictionary" by Mohamu Kashgar, which are important works for students of ancient Uygur history, culture and language. More modern works include Maulabilalibin Maulayusuf's "Wars on the Chinese Land," an epic describing the 1864 struggle of the Uygurs in Ili against the Qing government. Mutalifu, the patriotic and revolutionary poet, composed poems such as "Chinese Guerrillas," "Militant Girls" and "Love and Hatred" during the Anti-Japanese War. After liberation, much work has been done to collect, compile and publish classic and folk Uygur literature.

The Uygurs are excellent at dancing. The "12 Mukams" (opera) is an epic comprising more than 340 classic songs and folk dances. After liberation, this musical treasure, which was on the verge of being lost, was collected, studied and recorded. The "Daolang Mukams," popular in Korla, Bachu (Maralwexi), Markit and Ruoqiang (Qarkilik), is another suite with distinct Uygur flavour.

There are a wide variety of plucked, wind and percussion Uygur musical instruments, including the dutar, strummed rawap and dap. The first two are instruments with a clear and crisp tone for solo and orchestral performances. The dap is a sheep-skin tambourine with many small iron rings attached to the rim. It is used to accompany dancing.

The Uygur dances, such as the "Bowls-on-Head Dance," "Drum Dance," "Iron Ring Dance" and "Puta Dance," feature light, graceful and quick-swinging choreographical movements. The "Sainaim Dance" is the most popular, while the "Duolang Dance," sometimes referred to as a flower of Uygur folk culture, brims over with vitality. It depicts the hunting activities of the ancient people of Markit. The movements portray strength, wildness and enthusiasm. The "Nazilkum," popular in Turpan, Shanshan and Hami, fully reflects the Uygurs' optimism and gift for humour.

The Kazaks

The Kazak nationality, with a population of 907,582, mainly lives in the Ili Kazak Autonomous Prefecture, Mori Kazak Autonomous County and Barkol Kazak Autonomous County in the Xinjiang Uygur Autonomous Region. Some are also located in the Haixi Mongolian, Tibetan and Kazak Autonomous Prefecture in Qinghai Province and the Aksay Kazak Autonomous County in Gansu Province.

The Kazak language belongs to the Turkic branch of the Altaic language family. As the Kazaks live in mixed communities with the Hans, Uygurs and Mongolians, the Kazaks have assimilated many words from these languages. The nationality had a written language based on the Arabic alphabet, which is still in use, but a new Latinized written form was evolved after liberation.

Ethnic Identity Except for a few settled farmers, most of the Kazaks live by animal husbandry. They migrate to look for pasturage as the seasons change. In spring, summer and autumn, they live in collapsible round yurts called "yu," and in winter build flat-roofed earthen huts in the pastures. In the yurt, living and storage spaces are separated. The yurt door usually opens to the east, the two flanks are for sleeping berths and the centre is for storing goods and saddles; in front are placed cushions for visitors. Riding and hunting gear, cooking utensils, provisions and baby animals are kept on both sides of the door.

The pastoral Kazaks live off their animals. They produce a great variety of dairy products. For instance, Nai Ge Da (milk dough) Nai Pi Zi (milk skin) and cheese. The butter is made from cow's and sheep's milk. They usually eat mutton stewed in water without salt — locally called Zhua Rou (meat eaten with the hands). By custom, hey slaughter animals in late autumn and cure the meat by smoking it for the winter. The Kazak sausage, made of horse meat, can be kept for quite a long time and has a special flavour. In spring and summer, when the animals are putting on weight and producing lots of milk, the Kazak herdsmen put fresh horse milk in shaba (barrels made of horse hide) and mix it regularly until it ferments into the cloudy, sour Ma Nai Zi Qiu (horse milk wine), a favourite summer beverage for the local people. The richer herdsmen drink tea boiled with cow's or camel's milk, salt and butter. Rice and wheat flour confections also come in a great variety: Nang (baked cake), Zhua Fan (rice cooked with minced mutton and eaten with the hands), dough fried in sheep's fat, and flour sheets cooked with mutton. Their diet contains few vegetables.

The horse-riding Kazak herdsmen are traditionally clad in loose, long-sleeved furs and garments made of animal skins. The garments vary among different localities and tribes. In winter, the men usually wear sheepskin shawls, and some wear overcoats padded with camel hair, with a belt decorated with metal patterns at the waist and a sword hanging at the right side. The trousers are mostly made of sheepskin. Women wear red dresses and in winter they don cotton-padded coats, buttoned down the front. Girls like to sport embroidered cloth leggings bedecked with silver coins and other silver ornaments, which jangle as they walk. Herdsmen in the Altay area wear square caps of baby-lamb skin or fox skin covered with bright-coloured brocade, while those in Ili sport round animal-skin caps. Girls used to decorate their flower-patterned hats with owl feathers, which waved in the breeze. All the women wear white-cloth shawls, embroidered with red-and-yellow designs, hanging down to their ings.

The Kazak family and marriage before liberation fully showed the characteristics of the patriarchal feudal system. The male patriarch enjoyed absolute authority at home; the wife was subordinate to the husband, and the children to the father. The women had no right to property. The marriage of the children and the distribution of property were all decided by the patriarch. When the man came of age and got married he received some property from his parents and began to live independently in his own yurt. Only the youngest brother eventually stayed with the family. Herdsmen with close blood relations formed an "Awul" (a nomadic clan). Rich herd owners or venerated elders were considered the "Awulbas" (chiefs of the community).

The Kazak nationality usually practised monogamy, but in the old society, polygamy was quite common among the feudal lords and tribal chiefs, in accordance with their Islamic faith.

The feudal mercenary marriage system deprived young men and women of their independence in matrimonial affairs and high bride-prices were charged. Hence richer people married up to four wives each and poor herdsmen were unable economically to establish a family. Among the latter, a system of "barter marriage" was practised. Two families, for example, could exchange their daughters as each other's daughter-in-law without asking for betrothal gifts. This often gave rise to a large disparity in age of the matrimonial partners, let alone mutual affection.

The Kazaks are warm-hearted, sincere and hospitable. They entertain all guests, invited and uninvited alike, with the best things they have — usually a prize sheep. At dinner, the host presents a dish of mutton with the sheep's head to the guest, who cuts a slice off the right cheek and puts it back on the plate as a gesture of appreciation. He then cuts off an ear and offers it to the youngest among those sitting round the dinner table. He then gives the sheep's head back to the host.

The Kazaks are Muslims. Though there are not many mosques in the pastures, Islam exercises a great influence upon their social life in all aspects.

heels. Kazak men and women alike wear long boots over felt stock-
Their religious burdens used to be heavy. They had to deliver
religious food grain and animal taxes in accordance with Islamic
rules. If they wanted to invite mullahs for prayers on occasions of
festivals, wedding, burial ceremonies or illnesses, they had to present
given amounts of money or property. The religious leaders, in collaboration with the local government, even set up their own religious
courts.

The Kazaks' festivals and ceremonies are related to religion.
The Corban and Id El-fitr festivals are occasions for feasts of mutton
and mutual greetings. The Nawuruz Festival in the first month of
the lunar calendar is a grand occasion to say good-bye to the old,
usher in the new, and hope for a better year in stock breeding. Every
family entertains with "kuji," a food made of mutton, milk dough,
barley, wheat and other delicacies. They give feasts when there are
births, engagements or weddings.

The Kazaks, men and women alike, are good horse riders.
Young men like wrestling and Diao Yang (a game in which horsemen compete for a sheep's carcass). There are horsemanship displays
on the grasslands during festivals. The young people like to play a
"girl-running-after-boy" game. The boys and girls ride their horses
to an appointed place; the boys can flirt with the girls on the way.
However, on the way back, the girls chase the boys and are entitled
to whip them if they can as a way of "vengeance." Such merry-making more often than not terminates with love and marriage.

The Kazak funeral ceremony is an occasion for great solemnity.
Following Islamic custom, they dress the body in white linen and
bury it three days after death. Sacrifices of animals are offered on
the seventh and 40th day. The tail of the horse of the deceased is
cut off and nobody else is allowed to ride it. Whenever the family
moves, the dead man's clothing is put on the horse's back and moved
too. The women sing songs of sorrow and condolence as the family
moves, and one year later the horse is killed as a sacrifice to the dead.

The nationality has its own rich literary heritage. As there were
many illiterates, folk literature handed down orally was quite developed. After liberation, ballad singers, or "Akens," made great ef-

forts to collect, study and re-create old verses, tales, proverbs, parables and maxims. Many outstanding Kazak classic and contemporary works have been published in the Kazak language.

Kazak music and dance also have their own unique features and are very popular. The Kazaks like summer the best, terming it "gazri" (merry-making) time. They often sing and dance throughout summer nights on the pastures. The "Dombra" (a two-stringed instrument) is their favourite.

Tribal Life All Kazaks belonged to definite clans before liberation. They and their area were divided into three hordes (ordas): the Great Horde, Middle Horde and Little Horde — or the Right, Left and Western branches as the Qing government documents referred to them. The Middle Horde was the most powerful, with the largest number of people and most complete clan lineage. The Kazaks in China mostly belong to the Great and Middle Hordes.

The clans were formally blood groups of different sizes. The smallest productive organization and nomadic community within the clan was the "Awul," people with the same grandfather or father; sometimes they included people without any blood ties, mostly dependent poor herdsmen from without. So, there was a sharp contrast of wealth in the "Awul" of three, five, a dozen or more families. Owing to wars, migration or other causes, such internal blood relations became very loose.

The ruling group was composed of the nobility, tribal chiefs, herd owners and "Bis." The Bis generally came from a rich herdsman's family, were well-versed in the laws, customs and eloquence, and were generally regarded as qualified mediators. The ethnic group did not have any written law, but each clan had its own common law which protected private property, the privileges of the tribal chiefs, and tribal solidarity and unity. Whenever there were disputes over property, marriage or other matters, the "Bi" mediated and handled them in accordance with the clan law, generally practising "punishment by nine," i.e., compensation of nine head of animals paid by the loser to the winner of the lawsuit.

The Kazak clan organization before liberation was a combination of the feudal system of exploitation and the clan patriarchy.

The ruling class plundered the people economically and enjoyed political privileges. The broad masses of the poor herdsmen were deprived of all rights whatsoever.

Economic Life Owing to damage to stock breeding from natural and social disasters before liberation, some of the Kazaks had to forsake animal husbandry and turn to farming, which accounts now for a fairly large percentage of the nationality's economic life.

The Kazaks have accumulated much experience in stock raising over a long period of history. However, under the feudal system, their production level was very low and, being conservative in technical matters, the nomads made little effort to improve their expertise and depended entirely on the natural growth of the stock. As they had no means to resist natural disasters, great numbers of animals died in snowstorms in winter and spring. Disease also took its toll of the herds.

Kazak handicrafts were basically a family undertaking. Blacksmiths and carpenters were not specialized, they were herdsmen with expertise in these fields. The making of buttered tea, milk products and felt, tanning animal skins and tailoring furs were all done by women. Though Kazak animal husbandry provided wool, hides and skins and livestock, the commodity economy was not developed. In the pastures barter trade was in vogue, with sheep as the standard of the price. The herdsmen exchanged their stock for food grain, tea, cloth, daily utensils and handicrafts. In remote Altay, they bartered a sheep skin for only 100 to 150 grams of tea.

A handful of rich Kazaks before liberation owned thousands of head of cattle, sheep, horses and camels, while the majority of herdsmen kept very little stock and that was for subsistence. Though the pastures were owned by the whole tribe, they were in fact the property of clan chieftains and big herd-owners, the winter pasture-lands in particular.

The clan chiefs, religious leaders and herd-owners, especially the former, enjoyed feudal privileges and practised all kinds of economic exploitation. The poor herdsmen were dependent in different degrees on them. Under the name of "clan mutual assistance," tribal chiefs ordered herdsmen and even their families to toil for them without pay. This included herding, delivery of lambs, milking, wool shearing, grass cutting, felt making, displacement of homes and household chores. Those herdsmen were mostly short of stock and unable to herd and move their small groups of animals independently. They had to be subject to exploitation by herd-owners for a living. Tribal chiefs and herd-owners occupied the so-called "communal" pastures, and outside herds had to pay rents if they wanted to graze there.

As commerce developed in Xinjiang after the 19th century, Kazak animal husbandry economy grew closer ties with markets. The merchants, the privileged Russian merchants in particular, plundered the herdsmen through unfair exchange of commodities. Usury came into being, too. Such ruthless exploitation made the head of animals drop drastically and Kazak stock breeding virtually struggled on the brink of bankruptcy on the eve of liberation.

The Kazaks began farming in the late Qing Dynasty (1644-1911). The main farm implements include katuman (a kind of mattock), sickles, ploughs and grinding stones. In some localities, seeds were sown from horseback before ploughing. Flood irrigation was used, weeding was never done and fertilizers were not applied. As they were short of production means, the poor Kazaks who switched to farming had to be hired hands. In the Kazak rural and semi-rural areas, the herd-owners and herd-owner-landlords monopolized the farmland, irrigation facilities, draught animals and farm implements.

Of all the feudal practices, "partnership farming" was the most common. "Partnership farming" was a form that incorporated labour rent and rent in kind. The landlords or rich peasants offered land, seeds and farm implements, and the tenants sold their labour, sometimes bringing with them some of the seeds and farm implements. The harvest was divided up 50 to 50, or two-thirds for the landlords. Exploitation through hiring of labour was also a very common practice. The pay was either in cash or in kind, all very low. Water and farm implements were leased by the landlords. The landlord class made use of feudal privileges to force peasants to toil for them without pay or exercised political persecution, sometimes even to the extent of enslaving the peasants, for the purpose.

History of the Kazaks There are many records on the origin of the Kazak nationality in Chinese history. In the more than 500 years since Zhang Qian of the Western Han Dynasty (206 B.C.-A.D. 25) went as a special envoy to Wusun in 119 B.C., the inhabitants of the Ili River valley and round the Issyk Kul were mainly Wusun people and part of the Saizhong and Yueshi ethnic people, the forefathers of the Kazaks. As early as the reign of Emperor Wu Di (140-88 B.C.) of the Western Han Dynasty, Wusun established tributary relations of alliance with the Han court through the marriage of Xijun and Xieyou princesses and woman official Feng Liao with the Wusun King of Kunmo and senior generals. In the mid-sixth century, the Turkomans founded a Turkic khanate in the Altay Mountains. As a result, they mixed with the Wusun people, and the forefathers of the Kazaks later mixed with the nomadic or semi-nomadic Uighurs, Geluolus, Qidans (Khitans), Kelies, Naimans and Mongols of the Kipchak and Jagatai khanates. The fact that some of the Kazak tribes still retained the names of Wusun, Kelie and Naiman into later centuries sufficiently proves that the Kazak nationality is an old ethnic group in China.

In the early 13th century, as Genghis Khan marched westward, the Wusun, Kelie and Naiman tribes had to move likewise. Part of the Kipchak, Jagatai and Wuokuotai khanates of the Mongol Empire were Kazak pastures. In the 1460s, some of the herdsmen in the lower reaches of the Syr-Darya, under the leadership of Jilai and Zanibek, returned to the Chu River valley south of Lake Balkhash. As they went eastward to escape the rule of the Uzbek Khanate, they were named "Kazak," meaning "refugees" or "runaways." They then mixed with southward-moving Uzbeks and the settled Mongols of the Jagatai Khanate. As the population grew, they extended their pastures to northwest of Lake Balkhash, the Chu River valley and to Tashkent, Andizan and Samarkand in Central Asia, gradually evolving into the Kazak nationality.

From the mid-18th century, Tsarist Russia began to invade Central Asia and eat up Kazak grasslands and areas east and south of Lake Balkhash — part of China's territory. After the mid-19th century, owing to aggression by the Tsar, the Middle and Little hordes and the western branch of the Great Horde were cut off from China. Russian Cossacks infiltrated the area, driving the Kazaks into the deserts where men and animals could hardly survive. From 1864 to 1883, the Tsarist government compelled the Qing court to sign a number of unequal treaties, forcing the principle of "people go with the land" on the "Tacheng Protocol on the Delimitation of Sino-Russian Boundary." This met with strong opposition from the local minority nationalities. Many Mongolians, Kazaks and Kirgiz migrated back to Chinese-controlled territory. Twelve Kazak Kelie clans grazing near Zhaysang Lake moved their animals south of the Altay Mountains in 1864. More than 3,000 families of the Kazak Heizai clan moved to Ili and Bortala in 1883. Many others followed suit after the delimitation of the border.

The Ili Uprising during the 1911 Revolution overthrew Qing rule in Xinjiang. However, it did not shake the foundation of feudal system, as warlords Yang Zengxin, Jin Shuren and Sheng Shicai gained control of the region. The Chinese Communist Party began to carry out revolutionary activities among the Kazaks in 1933. Fearful that their feudal privileges might be encroached upon, the feudal rulers within the nationality boycotted the establishment of schools and the development of farming, and other economic and cultural undertakings. Under warlord Sheng Shicai's rule, some Kazaks had to flee their homes, and others, because of threats and cheating by chieftains, moved to Gansu and Qinghai provinces from 1936 to 1939. There, they were plundered and massacred by warlord Ma Bufang. Ma also sowed dissension among the Kazaks, Mongolians and Tibetans, and instigated them to fight each other. As a result, the Kazaks launched an uprising in Golmud in 1939. Those in Gansu and Qinghai had to lead a vagrant life until the liberation in 1949.

A revolution against Kuomintang rule took place in Ili, Tacheng and Altay in 1944. Kazaks, who constituted the majority, and the Uygurs of Nilka County formed three armed guerrilla units to start it. During the period of the Liberation War, the Kuomintang tore to shreds the "Eleven Articles on Peace" it had signed with the revolutionary government of the three districts. It instigated Usman, a Kazak political turncoat, to start an armed uprising to smash the revolution. He attacked Altay twice, in October of 1946 and in September of 1947, looting and burning the houses of the local people. The Kazaks and people of other ethnic groups beat him off in the end.

Kazak Life Today Xinjiang was liberated peacefully in September 1949, and the new government helped settle the Kazaks roaming about in Gansu, Qinghai and Xinjiang. Some 25,000 poor Kazaks returned to their homes in Altay and began to live in Qinghe (Qinggil), Fuyun and Fuhai (Burultokay) counties. In 1954 the Haixi Mongolian-Tibetan-Kazak Autonomous County in Gansu, and the Mori Kazak Autonomous County, Barkol Kazak Autonomous County and Ili Kazak Autonomous Prefecture in Xinjiang were set up. Regional national autonomy promoted unity within the Kazak nationality and among all ethnic groups.

Democratic reform and socialist transformation were then carried out in the Kazak area. Farming and stock breeding were integrated and the herdsmen were settled. Medium-sized and small tanning, woolen fabrics, oil pressing, chemical fertilizer and coking industries were built. They played a significant role in promoting local economic development and improving the ethnic people's livelihood. The Xinyuan Iron and Steel Plant on the Kunes Grassland attracted many Kazak herdsmen to become industrial workers. As capital construction developed in the pasturelands, the Kazaks worked out a series of measures — pastoral planning, fodder growing, improvement in animal raising skills, and prevention and treatment of epidemic diseases of domestic animals — to transform the old practice of sole dependence on nature. Much of the Gobi Desert has been converted into grazing and farming areas, the stocks of domestic animals have been improved and their quality raised. As a consequence, the output of animal by-products has risen.

The Kazaks were struggling in poverty before liberation. Some 2,000 people died of starvation in the Altay Prefecture from 1944 to 1945, and 40 per cent of the Kazak herdsmen in Altay County alone were homeless in 1946. The grasslands of Fuyun and Qinghe were deserted. There had been more than 10,000 Kazaks in Qinghai, but at the time of liberation in 1949 only one-tenth had survived.

The population was drastically dropping every year owing to natural disasters, social catastrophes and lack of medical care. The drop was curtailed after liberation and the population is growing again.

Education is now universal in Ili, Tacheng and Altay, where Kazaks live in concentrated communities. In the pastures, two types of schools, mobile yurt primary schools and settled primary schools, have been set up for the convenience of herdsmen's children. The recent spread of the new Kazak script has helped pave the way for raising the local cultural level and making scientific and technical knowledge accessible to more people.

The Kirgizs

The Kirgiz nationality has a population of 114,000, 80 per cent of whom live in the Kizilsu Kirgiz Autonomous Prefecture in the southwestern part of the Xinjiang Uygur Autonomous Region. The rest live in the neighbouring Wushi (Uqturpan), Aksu, Shache (Yarkant), Yingisar, Taxkorgan and Pishan (Guma), and in Tekes, Zhaosu (Monggolkure), Emin (Dorbiljin), Bole (Bortala), Jinghe (Jing) and Gonliu in northern Xinjiang. Several hundred Kirgiz whose forefathers emigrated to Northeast China more than 200 years ago now live in Wujiazi Village in Fuyu County, Heilongjiang Province.

Origins and History   The Kirgiz language belongs to the Turkic subdivision of the Altaic family of languages. It borrowed many words from the Chinese language after liberation, and a new alphabet was then devised, discarding the old Arabic script and adopting a Roman alphabet-based script.   The Uygur and Kazak languages are also used by the Kirgiz in some localities.

The forefathers of the Kirgiz lived on the upper reaches of the Yenisey River. In the mid-sixth century A.D., the Kirgiz tribe was under the rule of the Turkic Khanate. After the Tang Dynasty (618-907) defeated the Eastern Turkic Khanate, the Kirgiz came into contact with the dynasty and in the 7th century the Kirgiz land was officially included in China's territory.

From the 7th to the 10th century, the Kirgiz had very frequent communications with the Hans. Their musical instruments — the drum, sheng (a reed pipe), bili (a bamboo instrument with a reed mouthpiece) and panling (a group of bells attached to a tambourine) — showed that the Kirgiz had attained quite a high level of culture. According to ancient Yenisey inscriptions on stone tablets, after the Kirgiz developed a class society, there was a sharp polarization and class antagonism. Garments, food and housing showed marked differences in wealth and there were already words for "property," "occupant," "owner" and "slave."

During the Liao and Song dynasties (916-1279), the Kirgiz were recorded as "Xiajias" or "Xiajiaz". The Liao government established an office in the Xiajias area. In the late 12th century when Genghis Khan rose, Xiajias was recorded in Han books of history as "Qirjis" or "Jilijis," still living in the Yenisey River valley. From the Yuan Dynasty (1206-1368) to the Ming Dynasty (1368-1644), the Jilijis, though still mainly living by nomadic animal husbandry, had emigrated from the upper Yenisey to the Tianshan Mountains and become one of the most populous Turkic-speaking tribal groups. After the 15th century, though there were still tribal distinctions, the Jilijis tribes in the Tianshan Mountains had become a unified entity.

In the early Qing Dynasty (1644-1911), the Kirgiz, who had remained in the upper Yenisey River reaches, emigrated to the Tianshan Mountains to live together with their kinfolk. Many then moved to the Hindukush and Karakorum Mountains. At this time, some Kirgiz left their homeland and emigrated to Northeast China. In 1758 and 1759, the Sayak and Sarbagex tribes of Eastern Blut and the Edegena tribe of Western Blut, and 13 other tribes — a total of 200,000 — entered the Issyk Kul pastoral area and asked to be subjected to the Qing.

The Kirgiz played a major role with their courage, bravery and patriotism in the defence of modern China against foreign aggression.

The Kirgiz and Kazaks assisted the Qing government in its efforts to crush the rebellion by the nobility of Dzungaria and the Senior and Junior Khawaja.

They resisted assaults by the rebellious Yukub Beg in 1864, and when the Qing troops came to southern Xinjiang to fight Yukub Beg's army, they gave them assistance.

However, under the pretext of "border security," the Kuomintang regime in 1944 ordered the closing of many pasture lands, depriving the Kirgiz herdsmen of their livelihood. As a result, the Puli Revolution broke out in what is now Taxkorgan Tajik Autonomous County and part of the Akto area, and formed a revolutionary government. This revolution, together with uprisings in Ili, Tacheng and Altay, shook the Kuomintang rule in Xinjiang. More than 7,000 people took part in the Puli Revolution, the majority being Kirgiz, Tajiks and Uygurs.

Past Socio-economic Conditions Before liberation, the Kirgiz derived their main revenue from livestock breeding, which was entirely at the mercy of nature. About 15 per cent of the population engaged in farming, which was done in a very primitive way: a slash-and-burn method, without deep ploughing and fertilizer application. The handicraft industry was undeveloped and remained but a household undertaking. There were workshops making horse gear, carpets, felt cloth, fur hats and knitting wool. Cooking utensils, knives, tea, tobacco and needles had to be bought with animals or animal by-products. Hunting was another important side-line occupation.

The long-standing feudal patriarchal system left a deep impact upon Kirgiz economic life. Before liberation, 10 per cent of the population owned 70 per cent of the livestock. The masses of herdsmen owned very few or none of the domestic animals and had to work for the herd owners and farm landlords.

Once a man was hired, his whole family had to graze domestic animals, milk cows, shear wool, weave and cook for the herd owner in return for only two or three sheep a year plus food and clothing.

In the farming area, the landlord class plundered the poor peasants through labour hiring, land and water rent, and usury. Exploitation by religious leaders was also severe. The land owned by the Islamic clergy had to be tilled by peasants without pay and the taxes exacted by them accounted for 20 per cent of an average peasant's annual income.

The Kirgiz tribal organization before liberation was as follows: a major tribe had a number of sub-tribes, not necessarily herding in the same locality; each subtribe was composed of a number of "Ayinle," or clans; an "Ayinle" of five to ten families was a production unit as well as a traditional social organization; within the "Ayinle" there were customary relations of exploitation under the cover of "mutual clan assistance."

The ties between tribes were very loose, and there were generally no relations of dependence. The tribal chiefs, mostly big herd owners, wielded a certain degree of political power. The rulers of the Chinese dynasties throughout history invariably tried to accelerate and worsen the contradictions among the tribes so that they could "divide and rule."

Life Style   In the first half of the 18th century, most of the Kirgiz in Xinjiang believed in Islam. Those in Emin (Dorbiljin) County in Xinjiang and Fuyu County in Heilongjiang, influenced by the Mongols, upheld Lamaism while retaining some shamanistic legacies: shamanistic "gods" were invited on occasions of sacrificial ceremonies or illnesses and the shamanistic Snake God was worshipped.

The Kirgiz material life is still closely related to animal husbandry; garments, food and dwellings all distinctively feature nomadism.

Men wear white round-collared shirts trimmed with lace and covered by a sheepskin jacket or a blue collarless, long cloth gown. Some wear camel wool fabrics with the sleeves in fringed black cloth. Normally, a rawhide belt is worn at the waist, attached to which is a knife and a flint for making fire. Some sport jackets with a standing collar and front buttons. They wear loose trousers and high boots. A characteristic Kirgiz shoe is the "qiaokaoyi" shoe, made of rawhide. Throughout the year, all men, old or young, wear round corduroy caps in green, purple, blue or black and covered by a high, square-topped animal skin or felt hat with a rolled-up brim. The inside of the animal skin hat is bordered with black velvet,

Kirgiz women wear loose collarless jackets with silver buttons down the front. The long, pleated skirt is bordered with fur. Some wear dresses with the skirt pleated in the lower part, and covered with a black vest. Young women like red dresses and skirts, red velvet round caps or red otter skin hats decorated with pearls, tassels and feathers. While young women prefer red or green scarves, the elderly ones like white kerchiefs. Some of women's high boots are embroidered. Unmarried girls wear their hair in many small plaits, reduced to two after marriage. The pigtails are decorated with silver chains, coins or keys interlinked with a chain of pearls. Bracelets, earrings, necklaces and rings are made of silver. Girls in some areas wear on their chests round silver pieces carved with patterns.

The diet of the Kirgiz herdsmen mainly consists of animal by-products, with some cabbages, onions and potatoes. They drink goat's milk, yoghurt and tea with milk and salt. Rich herdsmen mainly drink cow's milk and eat beef, mutton, horse and camel meat, wheat flour and rice. They store butter in dried sheep or cattle stomachs. All tableware is made of wood.

The tents are made of felt, generally square in shape, fenced around with red willow stakes. The tent frame is first covered with a mat of grass and then a felt covering with a one-metre-square skylight, to which a movable felt cover is attached. The tent is tied down with thick ropes to keep it steady in strong winds and snow-storms.

The nomad Kirgiz live on the plains near rivers in summer and move to mountain slopes with a sunny exposure in winter. The settled Kirgiz mostly live in flat-roofed square mud houses with windows and skylights.

The Kirgiz family is generally composed of three generations, with married sons living with their parents. Marriage used to be arranged by the parents, sometimes even before birth — this was called "marriage arrangement at pregnancy." Traditional courtship starts when the bridegroom calls on the bride's family with a roasted sheep. The relatives of the bride then tie the couple to posts in front of the tent. They will be released only after the father and brothers of the bridegroom ask for "mercy" and present gifts. The wedding is presided over by an imam who cuts a baked cake into two, dips the pieces in salt water and puts them into the mouths of the newly-weds as a wish for the couple to share weal and woe and be together for ever. The bridegroom then takes the bride and her betrothal gifts back to his home.

There is distinct division of labour at home: the men herd horses and cattle, cut grass and wood and do other heavy household chores, while the women graze, milk and shear the sheep, deliver lambs, process animal by-products and do household chores. Before liberation, the male was predominant and decided all matters of inheritance and property distribution. When the son got married, he was entitled to a portion of the family property which was usually inherited by the youngest son. Women did not have the right to inherit. The property of a childless male was inherited by his close relatives. When there is a funeral, all relatives and friends attend, wearing black clothing and black kerchiefs.

The Kirgiz are very hospitable and ceremonial. Any visitor, whether a friend or stranger, is invariably entertained with the best — mutton, sweet rice with cream and noodles with sliced mutton. Offering mutton from the sheep's head shows the highest respect for the guest. At the table, the guest is first offered the sheep tail fat, shoulder blade mutton and then the mutton from the head. The guest should in the meantime give some of what is offered back to the women and children at the dinner table as a sign of respect on the part of the visitor. Anyone who moves his tent is entertained by his old and new neighbours as tokens of farewell and welcome.

In the Kirgiz calendar, similar to that of the Hans, the years are designated as years of the rat, ox, tiger, rabbit, fish, snake, horse, sheep, fox, chicken, dog and pig. The appearance of the new moon marks the beginning of a month, 12 months form a year and 12 years is a cycle. At the beginning of the first month of the year, the Kirgiz celebrate the "Nuolaoz" Festival, similar to the Han Spring Festival. There are also Islamic festivals. On major festivals and summer nights, old and young, men and women, gather on the pasturelands for celebrations: singing, dancing, ballad-singing, story-telling and games which include Diao Yang (competing to snatch up a headless sheep from horseback), wrestling, horse racing, wrestling on horseback, catching objects from racing horses, horseback shooting, tug-of-war and swinging.

The Kirgiz are renowned singers and dancers. The songs with rich content include lyrics, epics and folk songs. There are many kinds of musical instrument. A three-stringed instrument called a "kaomuz" is uniquely Kirgiz and the nationality's favourite.

Many poems, legends, proverbs and fables have been handed down among the Kirgiz for centuries. The epic, "Manas," is virtually an encyclopaedia for the study of the ancient Kirgiz. It has 200,000 verses describing, through the deeds of several generations of the Manas family, the bravery and courage of the Kirgiz in resisting plunder by the nobles of Dzungaria and their aspirations for freedom. It is also a mirror of the habits, customs and ideas of the Kirgiz of the time.

Kirgiz paintings and carvings feature animal horn patterns for decoration on yurts, horse gear, gravestones and buildings. The Kirgizs like bright red, white and blue colours. So their decorative art is always brightly coloured and eye-pleasing, and full of freshness and vitality.

Life After Liberation After liberation the Kirgiz began a new life. They smashed the feudal shackles and embarked on the socialist road. In the early post-liberation period, a People's Government was established in the Kirgiz area. The year of 1954 saw the establishment of the Kizilsu Kirgiz Autonomous Prefecture which includes Artux, Wuqia (Ulugqat), Akqi and Akto counties in southern Xinjiang, with Artux as the prefectural seat.

Since liberation, the life of the Kirgiz has improved in all respects. In the pasturelands, animal husbandry is the focus of attention. Efforts have been made to integrate it with farming and encourage a diversified economy. The survival rate of new-born domestic animals has risen markedly and the quality of breeds has improved. In the farming area, wasteland has been reclaimed and water conservancy projects built on a large scale. The Kirgiz are no longer dependent on other parts of the country for grain and animal feed supplies. In the meantime, local industry has been expanded to cover machine-building, cement, power, non-ferrous metals, food, fur-processing and mining. The Kangsu area, where there was only one small coal mine in the past, has become a comprehensive industrial base of coal, iron, cement and refractory materials.

The Kirgizs living in the mountains had never seen a truck before liberation. They were cut off from the outside world by floods in summer and by blizzards in winter. Now there is a network of 6,000 km of roads with Artux as the centre.

Before liberation, there was not a single middle school in the prefecture, and the illiteracy rate in the pasturelands amounted to about 90 per cent. But by 1981 there were 40 middle schools, and spare-time education was booming.

There were no doctors in the past. When a person fell ill, all he could do was resort to the prayers of the imams. Typhoid and cholera wrought havoc among the population, the natural increase of which long remained at a very low level. Now there are clinics in every township.

Since the founding of the People's Republic in 1949, the Kirgizs have undergone a fundamental change in their way of life. The majority of them have settled down. New villages and towns have mushroomed all over the area and herdsmen have moved to bright and warm houses. The settled herdsmen grow vegetables and melons in plots around their houses and their diet has greatly improved.

The Xibes

The Xibe nationality, with a population of 83,600, is widely distributed over northern China from the Ili area in the Xinjiang Uygur Autonomous Region in the west to the northeast.

Custom Owing to historical reasons, the Xibe people in northeast and northwest China have each formed their own characteristics in the course of development. The language and eating, dressing and living habits of the Xibes in the northeast are close to those of the local Han and Manchu nationalities. Living in more compact communities, those in Xinjiang have preserved more of the characteristics of their language script and life styles. The Xibe language belongs to the Manchu-Tungusic branch of the Altaic Language Family. Legend has it that the Xibe nationality once had its own script but has lost it after the Qing Dynasty (1644-1911) was founded. A growing number of Xibe people came to learn the Manchu and Han languages, the latter being more widely used. In Xinjiang, however, some Xibe people know both the Uygur and Kazak languages. In 1947, certain Xibe intellectuals reformed the Manchu language they were using by dropping some phonetic symbols and adding new letters of the Xibe language. This Xibe script has been used as an official language by the organs of power in the autonomous areas.

The Xibe nationality in Xinjiang believed in Polytheism before

Liberation in 1949. In addition to the gods of insect, dragon, land and smallpox, the Xibes also worshipped divine protectors of homes and animals. Besides, some Xibe people believe in shamanism and Buddhism. The Xibe people are pious worshippers of ancestors, to whom they offer fish every March and melons every July.

In clothing, the Xibe women in Xinjiang like close-fitting long gowns reaching the instep. Their front, lower hem and sleeves are trimmed with laces. Men wear short jackets with buttons down the front, with the trousers tightly tied around the ankle. They wear long robes in winter. The Xibe costume in northeastern China is basically the same as that of the Hán nationality. Rice and flour are staples for the Xibes. Those in Xinjiang who raise cattle and sheep like tea with milk, butter, cream, cheese and other dairy products. April 18 on the lunar calendar is the national festival of the Xibes, who would make flour or bean sauce on this day to mark the successful conclusion of their ancestors' westward move. In autumn, they would pickle cabbage, leek, carrot, celery and hot pepper. The Xibes enjoy hunting and fishing during the slack farming season. They also cure fish for winter use.

There are usually 100 to 200 households in each Xibe village, which is enclosed with a wall two or three miles long. A Xibe house usually consists of three to five rooms with a courtyard, in which flowers and fruit trees are planted. The gates of the houses mostly face south. Xibe women are good at paper cutting, and windows are often decorated with beautiful scissor cuts.

In the past, each Xibe family used to consist of three generations, sometimes as many as four or five generations, being influenced by the feudal system. Marriage was, in most cases, decided by parents. Women held a very low status and had no right to inherit property. The family was governed by the most senior member who had great authority. When the father was living, the sons were not allowed to break up the family and live apart. In family life, the old and the young each had his position according to a strict order of importance, and they paid attention to etiquette. "Hala," a council formed by male clan heads, handled major issues within the clans and enforced clan rules.

History The Xibes think they are descendants of the ancient Xianbei people, and there are many versions of the origin of this nationality. Xianbei was a branch of the ancient Donghu nationality in northern China, roving as nomads over vast areas between the eastern slopes of the Great Xinggan Mountains in northeast China. In A.D. 89, the northern Xiongnus, defeated by the Han Dynasty general Dou Xian, moved westward, abandoning their land to the Xianbeis. Between A.D. 158 and 167, the Xianbei people formed a powerful tribal alliance under chieftain Tan Shihuai. Between the third and sixth centuries, the Murong, Tuoba, Yuwen and other powerful tribes of Xianbei established political regimes in the Yellow River valley, where they mixed with Han people. But a small number of Xianbeis never strayed very far from their native land along the Chuoer, Nenjiang and Songhua rivers. They were probably the ancestors of the Xibe nationality.

Before the Ming Dynasty (1368-1644), the Xibe nationality lived in a vast area centring around the present-day Fuyu County in Jilin Province and reaching as far as Jilin in the east, Hulunbuir in the west, the Nenjiang River in the north and the Liaohe River in the south. In the late 16th century, the Manchu nobility rose to power. In order to expand their territory and consolidate their rule, the Manchu rulers repeatedly tried to conquer neighbouring tribes by offering them money, high position and marriage, and more often by armed force. Various Xibe tribes submitted themselves one after another to the authority of the Manchu rulers. By the end of the 17th century, the Xibe tribes in different areas had all been incorporated into the "eight banners" of Mongolia and Manchu. According to the "eight-banner system," soldiers in the banners worked the land in time of peace and went to battles during war time, shouldering heavy military and labour services. In less than 150 years after the Qing Dynasty (1644-1911) was founded, the Xibe people were removed from their native land in northeast China to various other places as far as Yunnan and Xinjiang. The Qing court also gave different treatment to various Xibe tribes according to the time and way of their submission to show varying degrees of favour and create differences in classification among them.

In the mid-18th century, the Qing government quelled the rebellions in Junggar and other localities of Xinjiang, and moved Xibes and people of some other ethnic minorities from northeast China to Xinjiang to consolidate and reinforce the northwestern border defences. For this garrisoning assignment which was to last 60 years, 1,016 Xibe officers and soldiers were despatched, and they took along more than 2,000 family members. In one year and five months, the poorly-equipped Xibes scaled mountains and forded rivers, eating in the wind and sleeping in the dew, trekking across deserts and grasslands in Mongolia to the faraway northwestern border. With striking stamina and tenacity, they endured starvation, drought, diseases and difficulties brought about by Qing officials, big and small, who embezzled army provisions and goaded them on. This was how the Xibes came to live far apart in northeast and northwest China. The heavy toll taken by the trip sharply reduced the originally small Xibe population.

The ancient Xibe people lived by fishing and hunting generation after generation. By the mid-16th century, the social organizations of the Xibe nationality had shifted from blood relationship to geographical relationship. The internal links in the paternal consanguineous groups became very loose. In each Xibe village lived members with different surnames. Because of the low productivity, collective efforts were required in hunting and fishing. Members of the same village maintained relatively close links in productive labour, and basically abided by the principle of joint labour and equal distribution. By the mid-17th century, the "eight-banner system" had not only brought the Xibe nationality under the reign of the Qing Court, but also caused drastic changes in their economic life and social structure.

The Xibes are a hard-working and courageous people. Although geographical isolation has given rise to certain differences between the Xibes in northeast and northwest China in the course of history, they have all made contributions to developing and defending China's border areas. The Xibes in Xinjiang in particular have made great contribution to the development of farming and water conservancy in the Ili and Tacheng areas. Since the Qing court stopped supplying provisions to the Xibes after they reached Xinjiang, they had to reclaim wasteland and cut irrigation ditches without the help of the government. They first repaired an old canal and reclaimed 667 hectares of land. With the increase of population, the land became insufficient. Despite such difficulties as lack of grain and seeds and repeated natural disasters, the Xibe people were determined to turn the wasteland on the south bank of the Ili River into farmland to support themselves and benefit future generations. After many failures and setbacks, they succeeded in 1802 after six years of hard work in cutting on mountain cliffs a 200-km irrigation channel to draw water from the Ili River. With the completion of this project, several Xibe communities settled along the channel.

Later, the Xibe people constructed another canal to draw water from the upper reaches of the Ili River in the mid-19th century. In the 1870s, they cut two more irrigation channels, obtaining enough water for large-scale reclamation and farming. The local Kazak and Mongolian people learned a lot of farming techniques from the Xibes.

While building irrigation channels and opening up wasteland, the Xibes also joined soldiers from other ethnic groups in guarding the northwestern border. In the 1820s, more than 800 Xibe officers and soldiers fought alongside Qing government troops on a punitive expedition against rebels backed by British colonialists. In a decisive battle they wiped out the enemy forces and captured the rebel chief.

In 1876, the Qing government decided to recover Xinjiang from the Tsarist Russian invaders. The Xibes stored up army provisions in preparation for the expedition despite difficulties in life and production inflicted by the marauders and cooperated with the Qing troops in mopping up the Russian colonialists south of the Tianshan Mountain and recapturing Ili.

The Xibe people in Xinjiang staged an uprising in support of the 1911 Revolution soon after it broke out. Those in northeast China joined the Han and Manchu people in anti-Japanese activities after that part of the country fell under Japanese rule in 1931. Many Xibes joined such patriotic forces as the Anti-Japanese Allied Forces, the Army of Volunteers and the Broad Sword Society. Quite a few Xibes joined the Chinese Communist Party and the Communist Youth League. In September 1944, struggle against Kuomintang rule broke out in the Ili, Tacheng, Altaic areas in Xinjiang. The Xibes there formed their own armed forces and fought along with other insurgents.

Before liberation, the feudal relations of production in Xibe society emerged and developed with the incorporation of the Xibes into the "Eight Banners" of the Manchus, under which the banner's land was owned "publicly" and managed by the banner office. Irrigated land was mostly distributed among Banner officers and soldiers in armour according to their ranks as their emolument. The rest was leased to peasants. This system of distribution from the very beginning deprived the Xibe people of the irrigated land which they had opened up with blood and sweat.

In the 1880s, the "banner land system" for the Xibe people in northeast China began to collapse, and the banner land quickly fell under the control of a few landlords. Although the banner system stipulated that the banner land could not be bought or sold, cruel feudal exploitation gradually reduced the Xibe people to dire proverty and deprived them of their land, and an increasing number of them became farmhands and tenants, leading a very miserable life.

Life After Liberation The founding of New China in 1949 ushered in a bright future for the Xibe people, who have since enjoyed political equality as one of the smaller minority nationalities in China. In March 1954, the Qapqal Xibe Autonomous County was established on the site of Ningxi County in Xinjiang, where the Xibe nationality live in compact communities.

Since liberation, a series of social reforms have been carried out in the Xibe areas. Industrial and agricultural production has grown tremendously and people's living standards have gone up accordingly. The economic and cultural leaps in the Qapqal Autonomous County are a measure of the great success the Xibe people have achieved. As a result of their hard work, grain output in the county in 1981 was nearly four times the pre-liberation average, and the number of cattle three times as big. Small industrial enterprises including coal mines, farm machinery works, fur and food processing mills, which were non-existent before, have been built for the benefit of people's life. There are in the county 12 middle schools and 62 primary schools enrolling 91.3 per cent of the children. The Xibe nationality have always been more developed educationally. Many Xibe intellectuals know several languages and work as teachers, translators and publishers. Horse riding and archery are two favourite sports among the Xibe people. Since liberation, endemic diseases with a high mortality rate such as the Qapqal disease have been stamped out, and the population of the Xibe nationality has been on the increase.

The Tajiks

Standing at China's west gate in the eastern part of the Pamirs on the "roof of the world" is the Taxkorgan Tajik Autonomous County in Xinjiang, a town built up since liberation. It is the place where the ancient Tajik nationality has lived generation after generation. Most of the 26,500 Tajiks live in compact communities in Taxkorgan, and the rest are scattered over areas in southern Xinjiang, including Shache, Zepu, Yecheng and Pishan. The Tajiks in Taxkorgan live alongside Uygurs, Kirgizs, Xibes and Hans.

Taxkorgan is perched at the highest part of the Pamirs. The world's second highest peak, Mount Qogir, towers in the south, and in the north stands Mount Muztagata, "the father of ice peaks." In addition, several dozen perennially snow-capped mountains, 5,000 to 6,000 metres above sea level, dot the 25,000-square-kilometre county. For centuries, the Tajiks have been engaged in animal husbandry and farming by making use of the luxuriant pasturage and abundant water resources. Every spring, they sow highland barley, pea, wheat and other cold-resistant crops. They drive their herds to highland grazing grounds in early summer, return to harvest the crops in autumn and then spend winter at home, leading a semi-nomadic life.

Custom   Over the centuries, the Tajiks have adapted their dressing, eating and living habits to the highland conditions. Men wear collarless long jackets with belts, on top of which they add sheepskin overcoats in cold weather. They wear tall lambskin hats lined with black velvet and decorated with lines of embroidery. The flaps can be turned down to protect ears and cheeks from wind and snow. Women wear dresses. Married women wear back aprons, and their embroidered cotton-padded hats also have back flaps. Women usually tie a white square towel on top of their hats when they go out, but brides like red ones. Both men and women wear felt stockings, long soft sheepskin boots with yakskin soles, which, light and durable, are suitable for walking mountain paths. The Tajik herdsmen enjoy butter, sour milk, and other dairy products, and regard meat as a delicacy. It is a taboo to eat pork and the flesh of animals which died of natural causes.

Most Tajik houses are square and flat-roofed structures of wood and stone with solid and thick walls of rock and sod. Ceilings, with skylights in the centre for light and ventilation, are built with twigs on which clay mixed with straw is plastered. Doors, usually at corners, face east. Since the high plateau is often assailed by snowstorms, the rooms are spacious but low. Adobe beds that can be heated are built along the walls and covered with felt. Senior family members, guests and juniors sleep on different sides of the same room. When herdsmen graze their herds in the mountains, they usually live in felt tents or mud huts.

In most cases, three generations of a Tajik family live under the same roof. The male parent is the master of the family. Women have no right to inherit property and are under the strict conrol of their father-in-law and husband. In the past, the Tajiks seldom had intermarriages with other nationalities. Such marriages, if any, were confined to those with Uygurs and Kirgizs. Marriages were completely decided by the parents. Except for siblings, people could marry anyone regardless of seniority and kinship. Therefore marriages between cousins were very common. After the young couple were engaged, the boy's family had to present betrothal gifts such as gold, silver, animals and clothes to the girl's family. All relatives and friends were invited to the wedding ceremony. Accompanied by his friends, the groom went to the bride's home, where a religious priest presided over the nuptial ceremony. He first sprayed some flour on the groom and bride, and then asked them to exchange rings tied with strips of red and white cloth, eat some meat and pancake from the same bowl and drink water from the same cup, an indication that they would from that time on live together all their lives. The following day, escorted by a band, the newlyweds rode on horseback to the groom's home, where further celebrations were held. The festivities would last three days until the bride removed her veil.

Childbirth is a major event for the Tajiks. When a boy is born, three shots will be fired or three loud cheers shouted to wish him good health and a promising future; a broom will be placed under the pillow of a newborn girl in the hope that she will become a good housewife. Relatives and friends will come to offer congratulations and spray flour on the baby to express their auspicious wishes.

The Tajik people pay great attention to etiquette. Juniors must greet seniors and, when relatives and friends meet, they will shake hands and the men will pat each other's beard. Even when strangers meet on the road, they will greet each by putting the thumbs together and saying "May I help you?" For saluting, men will bow with the right hand on the chest and women will bow with both hands on the bosom. Guests visiting a Tajik family must not stamp on salt or food, nor drive through the host's flocks on horseback, or get near to his sheep pens, or kick his sheep, all of which are considered to be very impolite. When dining at the host's, the guests must not drop left-overs on the ground and must remain in their seats until the table is cleaned. It would be a breach of etiquette to take off the hat while talking to others, unless an extremely grave problem is being discussed.

The funeral service is conducted in accordance with Islamic rules: the body is first "cleansed", then shrouded with white cloth and covered with the dead person's own clothes, but the feet and head must be exposed to indicate that everything is all right. On the night of vigil and day of interment, relatives, friends and fellow villagers will all come to offer their condolences or escort the hearse to the graveyard where women are not allowed to go. According to tradition, the body of a Tajik who dies away from home must be shipped back for interment.

The Tajik spring festival, which falls in March, marks the beginning of a new year, which is the most important occasion for the Tajik people. Every family will clean up their home and paint beautiful patterns on the walls as a symbol of good luck for both people and heads. Early on the morning of the festival, members of the family will lead a yak into the main room of the house, make it walk in a circle, spray some flour on it, give it some pancake and then lead it out. After that, the head of the village will go around to bring greetings to each household and wish them a bumper harvest. Then families will exchange visits and festival greetings. Women in their holiday best, standing at the door, will spray flour on the left shoulder of guests to wish them happiness. The beginning of the Fasting Month marks the end of a year. On this day, every family will make torches coated with butter. At dusk, the family members will get together, have a roll call and each will light a torch. The whole family will sit around the torches and enjoy their festive dinner after saying their prayers. At night, every household will light a big torch tied to a long pole and planted on the roof. Men and women, young and old, will dance and sing through the night under the bright light of the torches. The Islamic Corban festival is another important occasion for the Tajik nationality.

As a result of frequent exchanges with other nationalities, many Tajiks also speak the Uygur and Kirgiz languages and generally use the Uygur script for writing.

History The origin of the Tajik nationality can be traced to tribes speaking eastern Iranian who had settled in the eastern part of the Pamirs several centuries before Christ. In the 11th century, the nomadic Turkic tribes called those people "Tajiks" who lived in Central Asia, spoke Iranian and beleived in Islam. That is how "Tajik" came to be the name of the nationality inhabiting this area. So, the Tajik people who had lived in various areas of Xinjiang and those who had moved from the western Pamirs to settle in Taxkorgan at different times were ancestors of the present-day Tajik nationality in China.

The ancient tomb of Xiang Bao Bao, found through archaeological excavation in recent years in Taxkorgan, is a cultural relic ever discovered in the westernmost part of the country. Many burial objects found in this 3,000-year-old tomb and funeral rites they revealed show that the Tajik nationality has been a member of the big family of nationalities in China since ancient times.

In the late 18th century, Tsarist Russia took advantage of the turmoil in southern Xinjiang to occupy Ili and intensified its scheme to grab the Pamirs of China by repeatedly sending in "expeditions" to pave the way for armed expansion there. In 1895, Britain and Russia made a private deal to dismember the Pamirs and attempted to capture Puli. Together with the garrison troops, the Tajik people defended the border and fought for the territorial integrity of the country. At the same time, Tajik herdsmen volunteered to move to areas south of Puli, where they settled for land reclamation and animal husbandry while guarding the frontiers.

Social System   Before liberation, the Tajik people were mainly engaged in animal husbandry and farming, but productivity was very low, unable to provide enough animal by-products in exchange for grain, tea, cloth and other necessities. The economic polarization resulting from heavy feudal oppression was best illustrated by the distribution of the means of production. The majority of the Tajik herdsmen owned very small herds, so that they were unable to maintain even the lowest standard of living, and still others had none at all. A small number of rich herdsmen not only owned numerous yaks, camels, horses and sheep, but held by force vast tracts of pasturage and fertile farmland.

In the Tajik areas, the chief means of exploitation used by rich herdowners was hiring labourers, who received only one sheep and one lamb as pay for tending 100 sheep over a period of six months. The pay for tending 200 sheep for the herdowner for one year was just the wool and milk from 20 ewes. Herdowners also extorted free service from poor herdsmen through the tradition of "mutual assistance within the clan."

Tajik peasants in Shache, Zepu, Yecheng and other farming areas were cruelly exploited by the landlords. In those areas, "gang farming" was a major way of exploitation. Besides paying rent in kind that took up two-thirds of their total output, tenants had to work without pay on plots managed by the landlords themselves every year, and even the peasants' wives and daughters had to work for the landlords. There was practically no difference between tenants and serfs except that the former had a bit of personal freedom.

Islam was introduced to southern Xinjiang in the late 10th century, and the Tajik nationality was one of the first to espouse the religion. The feudal rulers among the Tajiks also used their religious privileges to exploit the labouring people. Levies in the name of religious expenses exceeded one-third of the total income of a herdsman's family.

There were all kinds of taxes and levies in both pastoral and rural areas. Especially during the 1947-1949 period, the Tajik herdsmen in Taxkorgan were forced to hand in more than 3,000 sheep and 500 tons of forage and firewood a year to the reactionary government. Poverty-stricken under heavy exploitation, the Tajik people were unable to make a decent living, and widespread diseases reduced their population to just about 7,000 when Xinjiang was liberated in December 1949.

Post-liberation Development In 1954, the Taxkorgan Tajik Autonomous County was founded on the basis of the former Puli County where the Tajik nationality lived in compact communities.

At the time of liberation, Taxkorgan had only 27,000 animals, two per capita of the total population in the county; total grain output was 850 tons, 55 kg per capita. Since 1959, the county has been self-sufficient in grain and fodder and able to deliver a large number of animals and quantities of furs and wool to the state each year. Several hundred hectares of new pasture and grassland have been added in recent years. There was no factory or workshop in Taxkorgan before liberation, and even horseshoes had to come from other places. Now more than 10 small factories and handicraft workshops have been built, such as farm and animal husbandry machine factories, hydroelectric power stations and fur-processing mills. Mechanization of farming and animal husbandry has expanded. Veterinary stations have been built in most communities. Tajiks have been trained as veterinarians and agrotech-nicians. Tractors are being used in more than half of the land in the county. One breed of sheep developed by the Tajik herdsmen is among the best in Xinjiang.

Taxkorgan was a backward, out-of-the-way area before libera-tion, when it would take a fortnight by riding a camel or a week on horseback to reach Kashi, the biggest city in southern Xinjiang. In 1958, the Kashi-Taxkorgan Highway was completed, shortening the trip between the two places to one day.

In the town of Taxkorgan, the county seat, which is perched right on top of the Pamirs, wide streets link shops, the hospital, schools, the post office, bank, bookstore, meteorological station and other new buildings in traditional architectural style and factories under construction. Great changes have also taken place in many mountain hamlets, where shops and clinics have been built. The herdsmen and peasants are enjoying good health with the improve-ment of living conditions and medical care. Since 1959, schools have been set up in all villages, and roaming tent schools have been run for herdsmen's children. Many young Tajiks have been trained as workers, technicians, doctors and teachers.

The Tajik people's living standards have improved considerably with the steady growth of the local economy. A growing number of herdsman households have bought radios and TV sets.

The Uzbeks

The Uzbek nationality has a population of 12,500 scattered over wide areas of the Xinjiang Uygur Autonomous Region. Most of them being city dwellers, the Uzbeks live in compact communities in Yining, Tacheng, Kashi, Urumqi, Shache, and Yecheng.

History The name Uzbek first originated from the Uzbek Khan, one of the local rulers under the Mongol Empire in the 14th century. Himself a Moslem, the Uzbek Khan spread Islam in his Khanate. In the 15th century, a number of Uzbeks moved to the Chuhe River valley, where they were called Kazaks. Those who remained in the area of the Khanate continued to be known as Uzbcks, who later formed the Uzbek alliance.

The ancestors of the Uzbek nationality moved to China's Xinjiang from Central Asia in ancient times. In the Yuan Dynasty (1271-1368), Uzbek merchants often travelled along "the Silk Road" through Xinjiang to do bussiness in inland areas. In the 16th and 17th centuries, Uzbek trading cavarans from Buhara and Samar Khan used Yarkant in Xinjiang as an entrepot for business deals in silk, tea, chinaware, fur, rhubarb and other such products. Some Uzbek merchants moved goods to inland areas via Aksu, Turfan and Suzhou (present-day Jiuquan of Gansu Province). During this period, Uzbeks from Central Asia began to settle in certain cities in Xinjiang, and the number grew with each passing year. Later on Uzbeks also settled in Kashi, Aksu, Yarkant and other cities in southern Xinjiang and a number of places in northern Xinjiang.

Pre-liberation Economy   After the Opium War, Xinjiang fell prey to foreign imperialists as China was reduced to a semi-colonial and semi-feudal state.   Britain and Russia started a fierce battle for Xinjiang's rich resources and vast market.   Under a series of unequal treaties, Tsarist Russia not only annexed large chunks of land from China's Xinjiang but grabbed political and economic privileges there.   This enabled Russia to monopolize northern Xinjiang's foreign trade and thus control Xinjiang's economic lifeline. A great number of Russian merchants came to plunder cheap raw materials and dominate the market.   From the 1880s to the early 20th century, Russian merchants were found in major cities in Xinjiang and the markets were flooded with low-quality Russian goods. The British imperialists were anxious to plunder southern Xinjiang. All this directly affected the Uzbeks' longstanding domestic and foreign businesses in various parts of Xinjiang and brought drastic changes to the Uzbek economy.

After the late 19th century, Uzbek merchants, big and small, who were mainly engaged in import and export trade, were either dependent on or attached to foreign capital.   A few big Uzbek merchants, colluding with foreign interests and relying on foreign markets and foreign economic power, formed foreign trading firms. Possessing enormous financial resources and operating on a large sale, these trading firms had direct contacts with capitalists in Britain, Russia, India and Afghanistan.   But most middle and small Uzbek merchants, who were short of fund and unable to compete with the foreign trading firms, went bankrupt and gradually became agents or salesmen for the big firms.   Some had to work in processing mills affiliated to the foreign trading firms, and others were compelled to earn a living in rural areas as farm labourers.

The Uzbeks' handicraft shops, mainly silk mills, were relatively concentrated and developed in Shache.   The larger handicraft shops later became embryonic capitalist businesses.   Since the purchase of raw materials and sale of products in the silk industry were directly controlled by foreign monopoly capital and suppressed by the local feudal system, the once booming Uzbek handicraft industry quickly declined before it was fully developed. Only some special crafts were preserved such as hand-embroidered skull caps, laces, bed sheets and pillow cases, which were in most cases made by women as household sidelines. Even these were almost reduced to naught, because the supply of raw materials and sales of products were under the control of the foreign trading firms.

A very small number of Uzbeks in northern Xinjiang were engaged in animal husbandry as a major or secondary operation, working for herdowners.

The Uzbek farming population was mainly distributed in Kashi, Shache, Bachu and Aksu in southern Xinjiang and around some cities like Ining in northern Xinjiang. Except for a few landlords, most of the Uzbeks were poor peasants who had no or little land, living from hand to mouth by working for the landlords.

Custom The Uzbek people have frequent exchanges with various other nationalities in Xinjiang, and have particularly close relations with the Uygurs and Kazaks. The Uzbek, Uygur and Tatar languages all belong to the Tuskic branch of the Altaic language family and are very close to each other. The Uzbek script is an alphabetic writing based on the Arabic letters. The Uzbeks believe in Islam, and their customs, dressing and eating habits are basically the same as those of the Uygurs.

Both men and women wear skull caps with bright coloured embroidery in unique patterns, and some are made of corduroy or black velvet. Women sometimes wear scarfs on top of their caps. Men wear buttonless robes reaching the knee, with oblique collars and the right side of the front on top of the other. The robe is tied with a triangular embroidered girdle. Women wear broad and pleated dresses without girdles. Uzbek men usually wear leather boots and overshoes with low-cut uppers. Women's embroidered boots are very beautiful and unique in design. The collars, front openings and sleeves of men's shirts are trimmed with colourful, patterned lace, which is typical of the handicraft art of the nationality.

Like other nationalities in Xinjiang who believe in Islam, the Uzbek people do not drink alcohol and eat pork. They like mutton, beef and horse meat and dairy products. Crusty pancake and tea with milk are standard fare for all three meals of the day, and they enjoy stewed meat with potatoes, honey and syrup. "Naren," a mixture of minced cooked meat, onion and sour milk, dressed with gravy and pepper, is a table delicacy reserved for guests. The Uzbeks eat it with their fingers.

The Uzbeks build their houses in different designs. Some have round attics, and most are rectangular adobe houses with flat roofs. These wood and mud structures have thick walls with beautifully patterned niches, in which odd things can be placed. Patterns are also carved on wooden pillars.

Most Uzbek families are nuclear families with parents and children living separate, and brothers living apart from one another. There are also families in which three generations live together. Marriage between siblings or between people of different generations is strictly forbidden. The Uzbeks have traditional marital ties with the Uygurs and Tatars. In the past, marriages were completely arranged by parents. The boy's family had to present betrothal gifts to the girl's family and cover the cost of wedding feasts. The nuptial ceremony is as a rule held at the bride's home. The bride's parents would treat guests to fried rice and sweets during the day, and the newly-weds will go to the groom's home in the evening after the ceremony is held according to Islamic rules. Sometimes, relatives and friends of the bride would "carry the bride off" after the wedding ceremony, and the groom has to offer gifts to "redeem" her. When the "carried-away" bride is "redeemed," she has to make a circle round a fire in the courtyard before entering the house. This is perhaps a legacy of ancient nuptial ceremonies. Funerals are conducted according to Islamic rules. People who attend funerals tie a strip of white cloth around the waist, and women wear a piece of white cloth on their heads. The dead person's children stay in mourning for seven days. On the 40th, 70th and 100th day of the person's death, imams will be invited to chant scriptures.

Since liberation, old feudal customs that hampered production and national development have been changed, and mercenary marriage and polygamy have been abolished. Women who previously had to live in seclusion and wear veils when they went out and whose social status was very low have freed themselves from these restrictions and are taking part in social activities.

The Uzbek nationality is one of those in Xinjiang that are good at singing and dancing and their folk music is melodious and appealing. The Uzbeks have a great variety of musical instruments. Most of them are plucked and percussion instruments. One string instrument with a triangular sound box is known for its sweet and appealing tone. Uzbek dances are famous for their vivacity, grace and variety. Most dances are solos, with the dancer waving her arms while turning round and round. The traditional tambourine dance is unique in style and very entertaining.

Since liberation, the Uzbek nationality has been enjoying the right of national equality. Although no administrative area of national autonomy has been established for the Uzbek nationality because its population is small and widely distributed over different areas, it is represented in the National People's Congress and local people's congresses at all levels where Uzbeks live in large communities, and many Uzbeks have become cadres. The Uzbek people have scored successes in democratic reform, socialist transformation and socialist construction.

For more than 30 years, with cultural and economic development in the Xinjiang Uygur Autonomous Region, many Uzbeks who live in cities have become industrial workers, employees in commercial, financial and transport departments, or cadres in state institutions and enterprises. Many women skilled in embroidery have joined handicraft cooperatives and contributed to the development of the traditional art of Uzbek embroidery. Since most Uzbeks live in cities, they have good access to education and many Uzbek intellectuals are working as teachers.

The Russians

There are 3,900 ethnic Russians living in Ili, Tacheng, Altay and Urumqi in the Xinjiang Uygur Autonomous Region and in the Inner Mongolia Autonomous Region.

They first began moving to China from Tsarist Russia after the 18th century. More entered various parts of Xinjiang after the 19th century, and even after the October Revolution in 1917.

They speak Russian, their customs and clothing are almost identical to those of the Russians in the Soviet Union, and most of them believe in the Orthodox Eastern Church.

Before China's liberation in 1949, the Russians living in towns were mostly employed in various repairing businesses, transport, handicrafts, horticulture, animal husbandry and beekeeping. In rural areas, groups of about 10 Russian families lived together in small villages. They reclaimed and cultivated the wasteland on the banks of the Ili and Tekes river.

They had achieved a fairly high level of development in production and culture. But under reactionary rule, they were exploited and oppressed.

Since liberation, the Russians have carried out a series of social reforms and have taken an active part in socialist revolution and construction. The Russians living in urban areas now work mainly in industry, transport, finance, trade and medicine. Some Russians in the Hulun Buir League, Inner Mongolia, have become agricultural workers on state farms.

Although the Russian ethnic group in China has a small population, it has deputies to the National People's Congress and the regional People's Congress. They take an active part in running state and regional affairs.

The Tatars

There are about 4,100 Tatars in China, most of whom live in Ining, Tacheng and Urumqi in the Xinjiang Uygur Autonomous Region.

History Their history in China dates from the Tang Dynasty (618-907), when the Tatar tribe was ruled by the nomadic Turkic Khanate in northern China. As this state fell into decline, the Tatars grew in strength, and their name was used to refer to several tribes in the north after the Tang Dynasty. Their homeland was later annexed by Mongols, and when the Mongols pushed west, many Central Asians and Europeans called them Tatars.

In the mid 13th century, Batu, the grandson of Genghis Khan, established the Golden Horde Khanate in Central Asia. It began to decline in the 15th century, and the Kashan Khanate began to rise on the middle reaches of the Volga River and in areas along the Kama River. The rulers of the Kashan Khanate, to boast their strength, began calling themselves Tatars, the sons of the Mongols.

Tatar gradually became the recognised name for the inhabitants of Kashan Khanate. Today's Tatar ethnic group was formed through a mixture of the Baojiaer people, Kipchacks and Mongolians over a long period.

After the 19th century, the serfdom crisis in Tsarist Russia

The Bogeda Guesthouse in downtown Urumqi.

The Duku Highway winding its way in the Tianshan Mountain Range, which opened to traffic in September, 1983.

Lhasa under construction.

A dagoba in the Tar Monastery in Qinghai Province.

Lhoba man.

"Ahsi Tiaoyue," a Yi dance.

Fishing in the Erhai Lake.

Head-gear of the Hani nationality.

Celebrating the "Gan Ba" Festival.

Costume of a Lisu girl.

Carrying water in bamboo tubes.

A pair of Lahu lovers

Taking part in "Mu Niao Ge," a Jingpo game

A wedding ceremony of the Miao nationality

Costume of a Miao youth.

A Dong weaver.

The Huangguoshu Waterfall in the Zhenning Bouyei-Miao Autonomous County in Guizhou Province.

worsened, and serf owners intensified their plundering of land. Most of the Tatars' land along the Volga and Kama was grabbed, and the inhabitants forced to flee. Some went south to Central Asia and then on to southern Xinjiang.

In the late 19th century, Tsarist Russia expanded aggressively into Xinjiang, and won trade privileges there. For a time, Russian merchants travelled to Xinjiang, and were followed by Tatar merchants from Kashan. Many stayed in Xinjiang to trade. During this period, many Tatar intellectuals and clerics moved to Xinjiang. Up to the early 20th century, a continuous stream of Tatars came to Xinjiang from Russia.

The Tatar language belongs to the Turkic language family of the Altaic language system. Because the Tatars mix freely in Xinjiang with the Uygurs and the Kazaks, the three languages have had strong effects on one another, and have produced various local dialects. The Tatars' written language is based on Arabic letters.

In the late 19th and early 20th centuries, some wealthy Tatar merchants netted great profits and forced smaller traders to the brink of bankruptcy. Of the few Tatars engaged in animal husbandry, most were poor herdsmen who had few animals and no pastures.

As a result of exploitation by Tatar and Kazak feudal masters, some poor Tatar herdsmen were forced to become hired hands, whose families suffered great hardship, and others were taken on by feudal masters as "adopted sons," who had to work as hired herdsmen but without pay.

In addition, there were also a smaller minority of Tatars engaged in handicrafts, chiefly in leather-making, tailoring and embroidery. These trades were carried out as household sidelines.

Since liberation in 1949, the Tatar people have enjoyed equal political rights in Xinjiang, where many ethnic groups live in tightly-knit communities. They have representatives on the National People's Congress and various tiers of regional and local government. A series of social reforms has extricated the poor Tatar peasants from feudal exploitation and oppression. Some have now become industrial workers.

The Tatars' educational development began in the late 19th century when Tatar clerics opened schools in several areas. Besides the Koran, Islamic history and Islamic law, these schools taught arithmetic and Chinese language. The Ining Tatar School, set up in 1942, was one of the earliest modern schools for ethnic minorities in Xinjiang. It played an active role in reforming the old religious education and teaching science and culture.

Many Tatar intellectuals earlier this century worked hard to set up and run schools. Some went deep into rural areas, and played a big part in establishing Xinjiang's educational cause. Their efforts benefited not only the Tatars, but also the Uygur, Huis, Kazaks, Xibes and Uzbeks.

The Tatars believe in Islam. In the past, the feudal ruling class used the religion as a means to levy all sorts of taxes on the Tatars and to set up religious courts to suppress the working people. Tatar women, in particular, were subject to oppression before liberation, but now, many of them are educated and take part in productive work.

Custom   Most Tatars in cities live in flat-roofed mud houses equipped with flues for heating. They like to hang tapestry inside their homes, which are usually very clean and tidy. Courtyards planted with flowers and trees have the appearance of small gardens. The Tatars in pastoral areas have adapted to a nomadic life, and live in tents.

Tatar cuisine, popular in Xinjiang, includes various kinds of pastries. At festivals, they serve pastries called "Gubaidiai" and "Yitebailixi," the former being cured with cheese, dried apricots and rice, and the latter with pumpkin, meat and rice. Both kinds have crisp crusts and soft contents. Tatar drinks include beer-like "keerxima," made of fermented honey, and "Kesaile" wine brewed from wild grapes.

Tatar men usually wear embroidered white shirts under short black vests or long gowns. Their trousers are also black. They often wear small black-and-white embroidered caps, and black fur caps in winter. Women wear small flowery caps inlaid with pearls, and long white, yellow or purplish red shirts with pleats. Their jewellery includes earrings, bracelets and necklaces of red pearls. Since liberation, more modern styles have influenced both men's and women's clothing, and a growing number of Tatars are now wearing Western-style clothes.

Most of Tatars in cities belong to small monogamous families. Sons and daughters live apart from their parents after they get married, but they still support their parents until they die, showing great respect for their elders. Intermarriages between Tatars and other ethnic groups believing in Islam are quite common. Marriages between cousins occur but are uncommon.

A wedding is held at the bride's home in accordance with religious rules. The newlyweds must drink sugar water from the same cup, symbolizing a long sweet life together. Usually, the groom must live for some time at his parents-in-law's home, and in some families, must not go to his own home until the first child is born.

Babies are christened three days after birth, and their names are usually taken from the Islamic classics. A child usually takes the surname of father or grandfather. The cradle rites are held seven weeks later, with the cradle and clothes provided by a grandmother. Forty days after the child's birth, he or she is bathed in water fetched from 40 places, a custom intended to bring about healthy growth. When a person dies, the body is shrouded with white cloth in conformity with Islamic practice.

The cultural life of the Tatars is rich and colourful. Their music has a lively rhythm, and several musical instruments are used, including the "Kunie" (a wooden flute), the "Kebisi" (a kind of harmonica) and a two-stringed violin. Tatar dances are lively and cheerful. Men use many leg movements, such as squatting, kicking and leaping. Women move their waists and arms more. Their dance styles incorporate features of the Uygur, Russian and Uzbek dances, but also have their own unique characteristics.

At festivals, the Tatars often hold mass dancing contests. "The Plough Head Festival" every spring is an annual grand gathering, held usually at beautiful scenic spots, and includes such collective games as singing, dancing, wrestling, horse racing and tug-of-war. The game they enjoy most is the "jumping walk" contest. All contestants hold an egg on a spoon in their mouths. The first to reach the finishing line without dropping the egg is the winner. Tatar drama began developing earlier than those of most other ethnic groups in Xinjiang. By the early 1930s, a Tatar drama troupe had been set up and began giving performances in Ining, Tacheng and Urumqi.

SOUTHWEST CHINA

The Tibetans

The Tibetan nationality has a population of 3,870,100, most of whom live in the Tibet Autonomous Region. There are also Tibetan communities in Qinghai, Gansu, Sichuan and Yunnan provinces.

The Tibetan language belongs to the Tibetan sub-branch of the Tibetan-Burmese language branch of the Chinese-Tibetan language family. According to geographical divisions, it has three major local dialects: Weizang, Kang and Amdo. The Tibetan script, an alphabetic system of writing, was created in the early 7th century. With four vowels and 30 consonants, it is used in all areas inhabited by Tibetans.

The areas where Tibetans live in compact community are mostly highlands and mountainous country studded with snow-capped peaks, one rising higher than the other. The Qinghai-Tibet Plateau rising about 4,000 metres above sea level is run through from west to east by the Qilian, Kunlun, Tanggula, Gangdise and Himalaya mountain ranges. The Hengduan Mountains, descending from north to south, runs across the western part of Sichuan and Yunnan provinces. Mt. Qomolangma on the Sino-Nepalese border is 8,848 metres above sea level, the highest in the world. The Tibetan areas are crisscrossed by rivers and dotted with lakes.

Animal husbandry is the main occupation in Tibet where there are vast expanses of grasslands and rich sources of water. The Tibetan sheep, goat, yak and Pien cattle are native to the Qinghai-Tibet Plateau. The yak is a big and long-haired animal, capable of withstanding harsh weather and carrying heavy loads. Known as the "Boat on the Plateau," the yak is a major means of transport as well as a source of meat. The Pien cattle, a cross breed of bull and yak, is the best draught animal and milk producer. In farming, the fast ripening and cold- and drought-resistant Qingke, a kind of highland barley, is the main crop. Other crops include wheat, pea, buckwheat and broad bean. In the warmer places in the river valleys, there are rape, potato, turnip, apple and wallnut. People also grow rice and cotton in river valleys in southern Tibet where the weather is very warm.

The dense forests in the Tibetan areas provide shelter for many precious animals such as sunbird, vulture, giant panda, golden-haired monkey, black leaf monkey, bear and ermine. The forests also produce precious medicines such as bear's gallbladder, musk, pilose antler, caterpillar fungus, snow lotus and glossy ganoderma.

These areas are also richly endowed with water power and mineral resources. There are enormous amounts of hydropower and terrestrial heat for generating electricity, and huge reserves of natural gas, copper, iron, coal, mica and sulphur. The landlocked lakes abound in borax, salt, mirabilite and natural soda. Oilfields have been found in recent years in the Qaidam basin in Qinghai and the northern Tibet Plateau.

History The Tibetans first settled along the middle reaches of the Yarlung Zangbo River in Tibet. Evidence of the new and old stone age culture was found in archaeological excavations at Nyalam, Nagqu, Nyingchi and Qamdo. According to ancient historical documents, members of the earliest clans formed tribes known as "Bos" in the Shannan area. In the 6th century, the chief of the Yarlung tribe in the area became leader of the local tribal alliance and declared himself the "Zambo" (king). This marked the beginning of Tibetan slavery society and its direct contacts with the Han people and other nationalities and tribes in northwest China.

At the beginning of the 7th century, King Songzan Gambo began to rule the whole of Tibet and made "Losha" (today's Lhasa) the capital. He designated official posts, defined military and administrative areas, created the Tibetan script, formulated laws and unified weights and measures, thus establishing the slavery kingdom known as "Bo," which was called "Tubo" in Chinese historical documents.

After the Tubo regime was established, the Tibetans increased their political, economic and cultural exchanges with the Han and other nationalities in China. The Kingdom of Tibet began to have frequent contacts with the Tang Dynasty (618-907) and the Tibetan and Han peoples got on well with each other. In 641, King Songzan Gambo married Princess Wen Cheng of the Tang Dynasty. In 710, King Chide Zuzain married another Tang princess, Jin Cheng. The two princesses brought with them the culture and advanced production techniques of Central China to Tibet. From that time on, emissaries travelled frequently between the Tang Dynasty and Tibet. The Tibetans sent students to Changan, capital of the Tang Dynasty, and invited Tang scholars and craftsmen to Tibet. These exchanges helped promote relations between the Tibetans and other nationalities in China and stimulated social development in Tibet.

From the 10th to 12th century, Tibet fell apart into several independent regimes and began to move towards serfdom. It was at this time that Buddhism was adapted to local circumstances by assimilating certain aspects of the indigenous religion, won increasing numbers of followers and gradually turned into Lamaism. Consisting of many different sects and spread across the land, Lamaism penetrated into all spheres of Tibetan life. The upper strata of the clergy often collaborated with the rich and powerful, giving rise to a feudal hierarchy combining religious and political power and controlled by the rising local forces.

The Yuan Dynasty (1279-1368) founded by the Mongols in the 13th century brought the divided Tibet under the unified rule of the central government. It set up an institution called Xuanzhengyuan (or political council) and put it in charge of the nation's Buddhist affairs and Tibet's military, governmental and religious affairs. Phagsba, a Tibetan lama, was given the title of imperial tutor and appointed head of the council. The Yuan court also set up three gov-

ernment offices to govern the Tibetan areas in northwest and southwest China and Tibet itself. The central government set up 13 Wanhu offices (each governing 10,000 households) in Inner and Outer
Tibet east of Ngari. It also sent officials to administer civil and military affairs, conduct census, set up courier stations and collect taxes
and levies. Certificates for the ownership of manors were issued
to the serfowners and documents given to local officials to define
their authority. This marked the beginning of the central authorities' overall control of Tibet by appointing officials and instituting
the administrative system there.

The ensuing Ming Dynasty (1368-1644) carried over the Tusi
(headmen) system·in the Tibetan areas in northwest and southwest
China. In Tibet proper, three sect leaders and five secular princes
were named. These measures ensured peace and stability in the
Tibetan areas during the Yuan and Ming dynasties, and the feudal
economy there developed and culture and art flourished. Tibet's
contacts with other parts of the country became more frequent and
extensive.

The Qing Dynasty (1644-1911), the last monarchy in China,
set up a government department called Lifanyuan to administer affairs in Tibet and Mongolia. In Tibet, the Qing emperor conferred
the titles of the "Dalai Lama" (1653) and "Bainqen Erdini" (1713)
on two living Buddhas of the Gelugba sect of Lamaism. The Qing
court began to appoint a high resident commissioner to help with
local administration in 1728, and set up the Kasha as the local government in 1751. In 1793, the Qing army drove the Gurkhas invaders out of Tibet and formulated regulations concerning its administration. The regulations specified the civil and military official appointment systems and institutions governing justice, border defence,
finance, census, corvee service and foreign affairs, establishing the
high commissioners' terms of reference in supervising Tibetan affairs. In other areas inhabited by Tibetans in northwest and southwest China, the Qing court continued the Tusi (headmen) system established by the Yuan and Ming dynasties, and put them under the
administration of the Xining Commissioner's office (established
in 1725) and the Sichuan governor (later the Sichuan-Yunnan bord-

er affairs minister).

After the Republic of China was founded in 1911, the central government set up a special department to administer Mongolian and Tibetan affairs. In 1929, the Kuomintang government set up a commission for Mongolian and Tibetan affairs in Nanjing and established Qinghai Province. In 1939, Xikang Province was set up. The Tibetan areas in northwest and southwest China, except Tibet, were placed under the administration of Qinghai, Gansu, Sichuan, Xikang and Yunnan provinces respectively.

After the Chinese Communist Party was founded in 1921, its central committee clearly stated in its Agrarian Revolution Programme that the feudal privileges of Tibetan princes and Lamas would be abolished. During its Long March northward to fight the Japanese invaders, the Chinese Worker and Peasant Red Army passed through Tibetan areas in Sichuan, Xikang, Yunnan, Gansu and Qinghai, where they mobilised the poor Tibetans to carry out land reform and establish democratic political power of the labouring people. Areas inhabited by Tibetans were liberated one after another after the founding of the People's Republic of China in 1949. Tibet proper was liberated peacefully in 1951.

Serf System Before the democratic reform was carried out, the Tibetan areas were dominated by the serf system that integrated political and religious powers.

The local government set up by the Qing Dynasty in Tibet, which was called Kasha, was run by four Kaloons (ministers), three laymen and one lama. The local government consisted of two offices. One was called Zikang (auditor's office), which was formed by four lay officials who administered all affairs about lay officials and audited local revenue, corvee and taxes. The other was called Yicang, a secretarial office formed by four lamas who administered all affairs about religious officials. The Tibetan local government accepted, in name, the leadership of the Dalai Lama or a regent.

The Dalai Lama was served by several Kampos or lama officials who took care of the Dalai Lama's office and affairs about his residence — the Potala Palace.

Owing to historical developments, there were some regional regimes beyond the control of the local government. In Outer Tibet, an internal affairs office called Nangmakang was formed by Bainqen's important Kampos, which was later called Bainqen Kampo Lija (changed into a committee after liberation). It accepted, in name, the leadership of Bainqen. Similarly, several other areas were governed by the local sect leaders or headmen. These were the legacies of the Tusi and Wanhu systems.

The basic administrative unit, equivalent to a county, was called Zong in Tibetan and the unit under it, equivalent to a district, was called Si, short for Sika or manor. Some large Sikas had the status of the Zong. Certain tribal organizations still existed on a few pastoral areas, which were subject to the leadership of the Tibet local government.

In Qinghai, Gansu, Sichuan and Yunnan provinces, some Tibetan areas came under the administration of the provincial governments in the Qing Dynasty. But most of the areas were still under the jurisdiction of Tusi officials and big monasteries.

The local regimes established on the basis of feudal serfdom that integrated political and religious powers were in the hands of feudal manorial lords, who were either lamas or laymen. They expanded the Tibetan army or formed local retainer forces to protect their reactionary rule. They formulated laws and regulations, set up prisons and used instruments of torture. Even the manors and monasteries had their own private prisons. They seized serfs' property by hook or by crook, punished them at will and executed serfs trying to run away or accused of violating the law. They used such shocking tortures as gouging out the eyes, cutting off the nose or hands, hamstringing or breaking the kneecap.

Tibetan society was rigidly stratified. The people were divided into three strata in nine grades, according to the size of the land they possessed. The social ladder extended from senior officials, hereditary aristocracy and higher lamas all the way down to herdsmen, serfs and craftsmen. But, generally speaking, these people fell into two major opposing classes — the serfowners and the serfs.

The Tibet local government was legally the owner of all the

land and pasture. It in turn parceled out the land to the aristocrats and monasteries as their manors. The officialdom, the nobility and the clergy thus became the three major categories of feudal lords.

The manors held by the officialdom, called Zhungchi, were directly managed by the local government and contracted out to serfs for rent. Part of the rent was used as remuneration for senior officials and the rest portioned out to government offices as their operating expenses.

Noble titles in Tibet were hereditary or granted for meritorious services. Ranking was commensurate with the amount of property possessed. There were about 200 to 300 noble families in Tibet. About 20 of them owned scores of manors each.

The manors of monasteries were bestowed by the local government or donated by the nobles. Some of them were the property of the monasteries and the rest belonged to higher lamas. A number of manors owned by monasteries were totally controlled by the top living Buddhas or lamas there.

The three major categories of feudal lords and their henchmen accounted for about five per cent of the Tibetan population. The nobles and the monasteries each owned about 30 per cent of the land in Tibet and the remaining 40 per cent belonged to the local government. The land and pasture in the Tibetan areas other than Tibet were controlled by headmen, local officials and other members of the ruling clique and monasteries.

The serfs included Thralpas and Dudchhong, who accounted for over 90 per cent of the Tibetan population. With no land or personal freedom, they were chattels of their lords.

Thralpas were persons doing unpaid labour. In Tibet, a thralpa tilled a small piece of land rented from the manorial lord, which was called thralkang land. To obtain such a piece of land, a thralpa had to perform all kinds of services for the local government and do unpaid labour on the manor.

Dudchhong, meaning small household, is a lower rank among the serfs made up of bankrupt thralpas. Dudchhongs were not allowed to till thralkang land. Instead, they had to depend on manorial lords or richer thralpas, doing hard work for them while tilling a tiny piece of land to feed themselves.

Five per cent of the Tibetans were house slaves, called Nangzan. With no means of production or personal freedom, they were the most heavily oppressed class in Tibet and had to do the hardest jobs all their lives.

Besides, some remnants of clan society still lingered on in the nomadic tribes in remote areas. On the other hand, in villages close to the Han people's farming areas, a landlord economy had emerged.

Serfs in all Tibetan areas were overburdened with exorbitant rents in cash or in kind. More than 70 per cent of their annual proceeds were taken away by manorial lords, plunging them into dire poverty.

Apart from paying exorbitant rents, serfs had to do all kinds of corvee labour, which was called Ulag.

Taxes and levies in Tibetan areas were innumerable. Some levies had been temporary at first and were later made regular. In certain places, scores or even more than 100 different kinds of tax were recorded.

All the manorial lords, especially the monasteries, were usurers. They cruelly exploited the serfs by forcing them to accept loans at usurious rates of interest or exchange of unequal values. Usurious loans often ruined the serfs and their families or reduced them to beggary or slavery.

The serfs and slaves, who accounted for over 95 per cent of the population, were bound for life to the land of the manorial lords, ordered about and enslaved from generation to generation. They were freely given away as gifts, donations or dowries, sold or exchanged for goods. Long shackled by feudal serfdom, the population of the Tibetan nationality showed little growth and production stagnated.

Culture   Under the rule of feudal serfdom, which combined political and religious powers, the Tibetans' social life and customs and habits bore obvious marks of their historical traditions and distinctive culture.

As a rule, a Tibetan goes only by his given name and not family name, and the name generally tells the sex. As the names are mostly taken from the Buddhist scripture, namesakes are common, and differentiations are made by adding "senior," "junior" or the outstanding features of the person or by mentioning the birthplace, residence or profession before the names. Nobles and Living Buddhas often add the names of their houses, official ranks or honorific titles before their names.

All Tibetans, men and women, like to wear ornaments. Men usually wear a queue coiled on top of the head. Some cut their hair short, like a canopy. Women, when coming of age, begin to plait their hair into two queues or many tiny queues which are adorned with ornaments. Both men and women wear felt or fine fur hats. They wear long-sleeved silk or cloth jackets topped with loose gowns which are tied with a band on the right. Women in some farming areas wear sleeveless gowns or home-spun wool. Herdsmen and women do not wear jackets, but are clad in sheepskin robes, with sleeves, collars and fronts edged with fine fur or dyed cloth laces. Men wear trousers and women wear skirts. All men and women wear woollen or leather boots. Men have long waistbands while women in farming areas wear aprons with beautiful patterns. They use woollen blankets as matresses or cushions and their quilts are made of sheepskin or wool. Poor peasants and herdsmen have neither matresses nor quilts. They often leave one or both arms uncovered while tying the sleeves around the waist, making it convenient for working. The Tibetan gown which is very big also serves as both matress and quilt at night. Lamas wear the kasaya, a patchwork outer vestment of purplish red felt. They wrap their bodies with long pieces of cloth and wear aprons, tall boots and monks' hats.

Zamba, roasted Qingko barley or pea meal mixed with tea, is the staple food of Tibetan peasants. Tea with butter or milk is the favourite of all Tibetans. Buttered tea is made in a wooden tub. In pastoral areas, the staple foods are beef and mutton. They eat out of wooden bowls and with shorthandled knives which they always carry with them. The Tibetans take five or six light meals a day and have a liking for Qingko wine. Sour milk and cheese are also standard fare. In some areas, people also eat rice and noodles. Women in pastoral areas use butter as ointment to protect their skin. Lamas may eat meat.

People in the farming areas live in stone houses while those in pastoral areas camp in tents. The Tibetan house has a flat roof and many windows, being simple in structure and colour. Of a distinctive national style, Tibetan houses are often built on elevated sunny sites facing the south.

In the monasteries, the main hall also serves as the prayer hall, with dagobas of different sizes built in front of the main entrance for burning pine and cypress twigs. There are numerous prayer wheels, which are to be turned clockwise in praying for happiness and hoping to avert disaster.

Communications were poor in the old days, with yaks and mules as the chief means of transport. Riding horses were reserved for the manorial lords, who decorated the saddles according to their ranks and positions. Cattle hide rafts, wooden boats and canoes hewed out of logs were used in water transportation. Suspension, cable and simple wooden bridges were seen occasionally.

In some big towns and monasteries, there were a few carpenters, blacksmiths, stone carvers and weavers. They, too, had to perform services and pay taxes to manorial lords and were looked down upon by other people.

Farmers used crude implements such as iron plough shares, hoes, sickles and rakes and wooden tools. Cultivation was extensive, with crop rotation and fallow. Weeding and manuring were done very rarely, resulting in low output. In livestock breeding areas, the tools were even more primitive. Herds were moved about with the seasons, and the herdsmen never laid aside fodder nor built sheds for the winter. Farmers and livestock breeders had no way of resisting natural calamities and pests, but praying to gods for protection. Natural disasters usually devastated large tracts of land and took heavy tolls of animals.

The Tibetan family is male-centred and marriage is a strictly inner-class affair. Marriage relationships vary from place to place. In some areas, cousins on the male line are forbidden to marry while cousins on the female line who are several times removed are allowed to marry each other. In other areas, cousins on the male line who are several times removed may marry each other, with no restrictions on intermarriages between relatives on the female line. Monogamy is the principal form of marriage. There is no inhibition on social intercourse between young men and women before marriage. The husband controls and inherits the property of the family and the wife is subordinate to the husband, even if he is married into a woman's family. The proportion of polygamy is small. Marriages between serfs had to be approved by their manorial lords. When serfs on different manors got married, one party had to pay a certain amount of ransom to the manorial lord of the other party or the manorial lord of one party had to give a serf to the other lord as compensation. Without the permission of their manorial lords, the serfs could not get married all their lives.

The commandments of the yellow sect Lama, which holds a predominant position in Lamaism, forbid the monks to marry. Monks belonging to the other sects are free to marry and the weddings are held at religious services in their lamaseries.

The most common form of burial in Tibet is sky burial, called Jator, meaning "feeding the birds." The bodies are taken to the Jator site in the mountains and fed to vultures. Upon the death of a reincarnate living Buddha, a grand ceremony is held. Having been embalmed with spices and antiseptics, the body is wrapped in five-coloured silk, and enshrined in a dagoba. The bodies of ordinary living Buddhas and higher lamas are usually cremated after being rubbed with butter, and the ashes are kept in a designated place as the last dedication to the monastery. But cremation is forbidden in the harvest season. All these forms of burial indicate that the deceased have gone to the next world.

In the old days, ceremonies and religious rites were held for weddings, burials or births in the homes of manorial lords. For the serfs, however, these meant nothing but extra services. Women had to give births outside their houses and women serfs had to work only a few days after delivery. Lack of proper medical care and nutrition resulted in a very high infant mortality rate.

The strict social caste system was manifested even in the use of language. The Tibetan language has three major forms of expression: the most respectful, the respectful and the everyday speech, to be used respectively to one's superiors, one's peers and one's inferiors. The social distinctions were also reflected in people's dresses, houses, horses and Hadas — silk scarfs presented on all social occasions to show respect.

Lamaism belongs to the Mahayana School of Buddhism, which was introduced into Tibet in the seventh century and developed into Lamaism by assimilating some of the beliefs and rites of the local religion called "Bon." Lamaism is divided into many different sects, each claiming to be the orthodox. Apart from the Red sect, all the others, including the White sect, the Sakya sect and the Yellow sect, established at different times local regimes that integrated political and religious powers.

The Yellow sect practises the institution of reincarnation of living Buddhas. The Dalai Lama and Bainqen Erdini are supposed to be the reincarnations of two Grand Living Buddhas of the Yellow sect. It was stipulated during the Qing Dynasty that the reincarnation of the Dalai Lama, the Bainqen Lama and other Grand Living Buddhas of the Yellow sect had to be approved by the Qing court or determined by drawing lots from a gold urn. When a Grand Living Buddha dies, his disciples are required to choose a child, in most cases from a noble family, to be his reincarnation. Monasteries of the Yellow sect are scattered all over the Tibetan areas. The most famous of them are the Sera, Drepung, Zhashi Lumpo and Qamdo, as well as Lapuleng in Gansu and Ta'er in Qinghai.

In the western part of Tibet and the pastoral areas of Qinghai and Sichuan provinces, the early Tibetan native religion, the Bon, known locally as the Black sect, is still active. There are also Daoist temples built by the Han people, mosques built by the Huis and some Christian and Catholic churches built by foreign missioneries in a few places.

A large amount of cultural relics, including ancient scripts, woodblocks, metal and stone carvings, have been preserved in the Tibetan areas. The engraved block printing technique was introduced from other parts of China. Some books were written in Sanskrist on loose leaves. Apart from the two well-known collections of Buddhist scriptures known as the Kanjur and the Tanjur, there are works on prosody, language, philosophy, history, geography, astronomy, mathematics and medicine as well as novels, operas, biographies, poetry, stories and fables, which are all distinguished for their unique styles. Many of the early works, such as the "Thirty Rules of Tibetan Grammar," the four-part "Ancient Encyclopaedia of Tibetan Medicine," "Feast of the Wise," the epic "Princess Wen Cheng", world's longest epic poem "Gesser Khan," the biographical novels "Milariba" and "Boluonai," the "Sakya Maxims" and the "Love Songs of Cangyang Gyacuo" (the Sixth Dalai Lama), are very popular and have been translated into many languages and distributed in China and abroad.

Education in the Tibetan areas used to be monopolized by the monasteries. Some of the lamas in big lamaseries, who had learned to read and write and recite Buddhist scriptures and who had passed the test of catechism in the Buddhist doctrine, would be given the degree of Gexi, the equivalent of the doctoral degree in theology. Others, after a period of training, would be qualified to serve as religious officials or preside over religious rites.

Tibetan medicine has a long history. Doctors of this school of medicine pay great attention to practical skills. They diagnose illnesses by observation, auscultation, smelling, interrogation and pulse feeling. They also know how to collect medicinal herbs and prepare drugs and are skilled in acupuncture, moxibustion and surgery. Tibetan doctors are especially outstanding in veterinary medicine.

The Tibetans have their own calendar. They designate the years by using the five elements (metal, wood, water, fire and earth), yin and yang, and the 12 animals representing the 12 Earthly Branches. A year is divided into four seasons and 12 months, which have 29 or 30 days. There is an intercalary month every three years. The calculation is accurate, able to predict solar and lunar eclipses. Pebbles and twigs are used in computing, and counting is done in threes.

The technique of Tibetan sculpture is superb. The portraits of the Grand Living Buddhas are the very images of the persons depicted. Tibetan painting features fine lines, well-knitted composition, vivid expressions of figures and bright colours. Tibetan architecture is unique in style, with buildings neatly arranged or rising like magnificent towers and castles. The Potala Palace in Lhasa was built on the sunny side of a mountain slope. With golden roofs and white-washed walls, the building rises naturally with the slope, looking extremely imposing. It is a masterpiece of Tibetan architecture.

Maxims and proverbs are very popular among the Tibetans. The metaphors are lively and pregnant with meaning. Tibetans are also good dancers and singers. Their songs and music are well modulated in tone and the words fit well with the tunes. They often dance while they sing. Their dancing is beautiful with movements executed either with the arms and waist or with legs and feet, and the tap dance is most typically Tibetan. Most of the musical instruments were introduced from the interior of China. Long-handled drums and trumpets are the main musical instruments used by the lamas. They can depict natural sounds, the cries of animals and the singing of birds that can be heard at a great distance. Religious dances are often performed by people wearing masks of deities, humans or animals. The Tibetan opera is one of the famous opera forms in China. It is performed without curtain or stage. In the past, all performers were men. Wearing masks, they danced and sang to the accompaniment of musical instruments. Sometimes the orchestra would chime in with the singers, creating a lively atmosphere.

There are many taboos and activities that bear a strong mark of religion. Buddhists are forbidden to kill. Many wild animals, including fish, field vole, Mongolian gazelle and vulture, are under protection. The Tibetans, rich or poor, all have family niches for keeping Buddha statues. Most people wear a metal amulet box, about the size of a cigarette case, on the breast, and turn prayer wheels. It is forbidden to turn prayer wheels counter-clockwise and stride over ritual objects and braziers.

The Tibetan New Year is the most important festival in Tibet. People in their holiday best extend greetings to each other and go to the monasteries to receive blessings. On the 15th day of the first moon, all major monasteries hold religious rites and all families light up butter lamps when night falls. It is also the occasion for lamas in the Ta'er (Ghumbum) monastery in Qinghai and the Qoikang monastery in Lhasa to display their exquisite and beautifully decorated butter carvings.

Post-liberation Life With the founding of the People's Republic of China on October 1, 1949, the Tibetan areas in the western part of the country was liberated one after another and the Tibetans there entered a new period of historical development.

In 1951, representatives of the Central People's Government and the Tibet local government held negotiations in Beijing and signed on May 23 a 17-article agreement on the peaceful liberation of Tibet. Soon afterwards, the central government representative Zhang Jingwu arrived in Lhasa and Chinese People's Liberation Army units marched into Tibet from Xinjiang, Qinghai, Sichuan and Yunnan in accordance with the agreement.

China's First National People's Congress was held in Beijing in 1954. The Dalai Lama, Bainqen Erdini and representatives of the Tibetan people attended the congress and later visited various places in the country. The State Council then called a meeting at which representatives of the Tibet local government, the Bainqen Kampo Lija and the Qamdo People's Liberation Committee formed a preparatory group for the establishment of the Tibet Autonomous Region after repeated consultations and discussions. In April 1956, a preparatory committee for the purpose was officially set up.

Regional autonomy and social reforms were introduced cautiously and steadily in one Tibetan area after another according to their specific circumstances arising from the lopsided development in these areas due to historical reasons.

A number of autonomous administrations have been established in Tibetan areas since liberation. They include the Tibet Autonomous Region, the Yushu, Hainan, Huangnan, Haibei and Golog Tibetan autonomous prefectures and the Haixi Mongolian, Tibetan and Kazak Autonomous Prefecture in Qinghai Province; the Gannan Tibet Autonomous Prefecture and the Tianzhu Tibetan Autonomous

County in Gansu Province; the Garze and Aba Tibetan autonomous prefectures and the Muli Tibetan Autonomous County in Sichuan Province; and the Diqing Tibetan Autonomous Prefecture in Yunnan Province.

In light of the historical and social development of the Tibetan people, the central government introduced democratic reforms in various places according to local conditions and through patient explanation and persuasion. Experiments were first carried out to gain experience.

A campaign against local despots and for the reduction of rent and interest was unfolded in the Tibetan areas of Northwest China in 1951 and 1952. In farming areas, people were mobilised to abolish rent in labour service and extra-economic coercion in the struggle to eliminate bandits and enemy agents. Sublet of land was banned. But rent for land owned by the monasteries was either intact or reduced or remitted after consultation. In pastoral areas, aid was given to herdsmen to develop production and experience was accumulated for democratic reforms and socialist transformation there.

In the Tibetan areas of Southwest China, peaceful reforms were introduced between 1955 and 1957 in the farming areas. Feudal land ownership and all feudal privileges were abolished after consultation between the labouring people and members of the upper strata. Usury was also abolished and slaves were freed and given jobs. The arms and weapons of manorial lords were confiscated. The government bought out the surplus houses, farm implements, livestock and grain of the landlords and serfowners.

It was clearly laid down in the agreement on the peaceful liberation of Tibet that democratic reforms would be carried out to satisfy the common desire of the peasants, herdsmen and slaves. But, in light of the special circumstances in Tibet, the central government declared that democratic reforms would not be introduced before 1962. However, the reactionary manorial lords, including monks and aristocrats, tried in every way to oppose the reforms.

In March 1959, the former Tibetan local government and the reactionary clique in the upper strata tore up the 17-article agreement under the pretext of "safeguarding national interests" and "defending religion" and staged an armed rebellion in Lhasa. They instigated rebel forces in different places to attack Communist Party and government offices and kill people, while abducting the Dalai Lama and compelling people to flee the country.

The State Council, acting upon the request of the Tibetan people and patriots in the upper strata, disbanded the Tibet local government (Kasha) and empowered the Preparatory Committee for the Tibet Autonomous Region to exercise the functions and powers of the local government. With the active support of the Tibetan labouring people and patriots of all strata, the People's Liberation Army soon put down the rebellion.

The Preparatory Committee began carrying out democratic reforms while fighting the rebels. In the farming areas, a campaign was launched against rebellion, unpaid corvee service and slavery and for the reduction of rent and interest. In the pastoral areas, a similar campaign against the three evils was coupled with the implementation of the policy of mutual benefit to herdsmen and herdowners. All the means of production belonging to those serfowners and their agents who participated in the rebellion were confiscated, and the serfs who rented land from them were entitled to keep all their harvests for that particular year. All the debts labouring people owed to them were abolished. The means of production belonging to those serfowners and their agents who did not participate in the rebellion was not confiscated but bought over by the state. Rent for their land was reduced and all old debts owed by serfs were abolished. In the monasteries, the feudal system of exploitation and oppression was abolished and democratic management was instituted. Land and other means of production including animals, farm implements and houses confiscated or bought by the state were redistributed fairly and reasonably among the poor serfs, serfowners and their agents, with priority given to the first group. In livestock breeding areas, while the animals owned by manorial lords and herdowners who participated in the rebellion were confiscated and distributed among the herdsmen, no struggle was waged against those who did not participate, their stock was not redistributed, and no class differentiation was made. Instead, the policy of mutual benefit to both herdowners and herdsmen was implemented.

Under the leadership of the Communist Party, the million serfs overthrew the cruel system of feudal serfdom and abolished the regulations and contracts that had condemned them to exploitation and oppression for generations. They received land, domestic animals, farm implements and houses and were emancipated politically. In September 1965, the Tibet Autonomous Region was officially established.

The Tibetans have since embarked on a road of socialist transformation, cautiously but steadily.

The great victory in the democratic revolution and the ensuing socialist transformation brought about tremendous changes to the whole Tibetan community. Since 1980, the central government has introduced a set of special policies to enable the Tibetan people to recoup their strength and make up for the damage they had suffered during the "cultural revolution" (1966-1976). The policies include remission of taxation on collective and individual producers for a long time to come; authorisation of private use of land and livestock by households for a long time while public ownership of land, forests and grassland is upheld; protection of the peasants' and herdsmen's right of determination in production and encouragement of a diversified economy based principally on household operations; free disposal of farm and animal by-products on the market, and encouragement of individual and collective industrial and commercial enterprises. All these have brought forth the initiative of the Tibetan people and stimulated the growth of the local economy. Tibet has also received support and aid from the central government and other areas of China. From 1952 to 1984, the central government gave a total of 7.9 billion yuan to Tibet in the form of financial grants. To celebrate the 20th anniversary of the founding of the Tibet Autonomous Region, some provinces and cities and the state economic departments built 43 major construction projects in the region. These included a geothermal power station at Yangbajan, auxiliary facilities for the Qinghai-Tibet highway, the premises of Tibet University, a hotel, a theatre, a training centre with audio-visual teaching aids and a stadium in Lhasa, a solar energy power station at Xigaze, and a hospital and an art gallery at Zetang.

Rapid developments have been reported by all trades and services in Tibet. Starting from scratch, Tibet's industry boasted more than 300 factories and mines by the end of 1984, covering power generating, metallurgy, woollen textiles, machinery, chemical engineering, pharmaceuticals, paper making and printing. They turned out more than 80 products, with a total value of 168 million yuan a year. The bleak and desolate Bangon, Markam and Qaidam areas have become major industrial centres. Good harvests have been reaped consecutively. In 1984, total grain output reached 494,000 tons and the animals in stock by the end of the year numbered 21.68 million, nearly double the 1965 figure.

Communications facilities also grew rapidly. There was no highway in Tibet before liberation. Since the People's Liberation Army marched into Tibet, several major trunk roads were built, including the Qinghai-Tibet highway (1954), the Sichuan-Tibet highway (1954), the Yunnan-Tibet highway (1976) and the Xinjiang-Tibet highway (1957) which linked up the Tibetan areas. A network of motor roads fanning out from Lhasa has been formed, extending to almost all counties. In 1984, the total length of roads open to traffic in Tibet reached 21,500 kilometres. The people's air force made the first successful flight from Beijing to Lhasa in 1956 and since then regular air services have linked Lhasa with Xining, Chengdu, Lanzhou and Xi'an. Roads also connect Tibet with the Kingdom of Nepal. The Longhai Railway runs through the Tianzhu Tibetan Prefecture in Gansu and the Qinghai-Tibet Railway starting from Xining has already reached Golmud in Qinghai. An oil pipeline extending from Golmud to Lhasa — a significant project for strengthening the defence of the southwest China borders and developing the local economy — has been completed. A postal and telecommunications network linking Tibet with other parts of the country has been built. The Lhasa post and telecommunications office constructed in 1979 was a further step towards modernisation.

Radical changes have also taken place in culture and education.   The one million serfs who were deprived of education before liberation are attending schools in Tibet or nationalities institutes in other parts of the country.   With no institution of higher learning before, Tibet had three such institutions by the end of 1985 as well as 2,600 middle and primary schools, with a total enrolment 87 per cent more than in 1965.   Many Tibetan professors, engineers, doctors, veterinarians, agronomists, accountants, journalists, writers and artists have been trained.   The Tibetan language and customs and habits are enjoying respect and the outstanding heritage of Tibetan culture has been carried forward.   Medical and health organizations have been established in all parts of the region, which had more than 500 hospitals by the end of 1984.   A special team of medical personnel are making a systematic study of Tibetan medicine and pharmacology.

The living standards of the Tibetan people have been rising steadily.   The peasants, who lived in rickety sheds and never had enough food, have moved into bright and spacious houses with glass windows and stored up more grain and meat than they can consume. Brightly decorated furniture, television sets and cassette recorders have also made their way into the home of former serfs.   However, about ten per cent of the peasants and herdsmen have not yet shaken off poverty, although their living conditions are better than in the old days.

Religious activities are protected by the government.   Fifty temples have been renovated and 120 more are under repair.   Buddhist statues, volumes of scriptures, ancient porcelain articles and other precious relics lost during the ten-year turmoil of the "cultural revolution" have been returned to the monasteries.   Among them was a bronze statue of Sakyamuni brought to Tibet by Princess Brikuthi from Nepal in the 7th century.   It is now kept in the Qoikang Monastery in Lhasa.   An institute of Buddhist theology has been set up and preparations are being made to restore the scripture printing house.   Tibet now has 3,000 lamas, and the government sets no limit to the number of monks in the monasteries.

Tibetan officials and government functionaries are increasing rapidly.   By the end of 1985, there were 31,900 officials and government functionaries of Tibetan and other minority nationalities, accounting for 62 per cent of the total. The principal positions in the governments at all levels are now held by members of these minority ethnic groups. Their ability and educational standards have been improving steadily.

The Moinbas

The Moinbas are scattered in the southern part of Tibet Autonomous Region. Most of them, numbering 6,200, live in Medog, Nyingch and Cona counties.

They have forged close links with the Tibetan people through political, economic and cultural exchanges and intermarriage over the years. They share with the Tibetans the common belief in Lamaism and have similar customs and lifestyles.

Their language, which has many dialects, belongs to the Tibetan-Burmese language family, and many of them can speak Tibetan.

Customs and Habits In Menyu area, men and women prefer to wear robes with aprons and black yak hair hats or caps. They wear soft-soled leather boots, which are decorated with red or black striped designs. Women usually wear white aprons, earrings, rings and bracelets. People in the subtropical Medog County dress differently. Women as well as men wear short or long jackets, and the women wear long striped skirts and various jewellery.

The Moinba's staple food includes rice, maize, millet and buckwheat. Maize and millet are ground and prepared to make porridge. Like the Tibetans, the Moinbas also eat zhamba (roasted qingke barley), butter tea and pepper.

Their homes are two- or three-storey, herringbone-shaped houses of wood with bamboo or straw roofs. The second and third floors are used for living quarters and the first for livestock. They observe monogamy in marriage. Some are believers of primitive shamanism, while others are followers of Lamaism. Water burial, ground burial, sky burial and cremation are all used for their dead. They follow the Tibetan calendar and observe the same festivals as the Tibetans.

The Moinbas have composed many beautiful tunes and ballads over the centuries. Among their most popular folk songs are the "sama" and "dongsanba," which are similar to many Tibetan songs. Their dances are simple and dynamic.

Menyu area, at the foot of the Himalayas, enjoys abundant rainfall, swift rivers, beautiful landscape and fertile land, which bears rice, maize, buckwheat, qingke barley, winter wheat, soybeans and sesame. Virgin pine forests are inhabited by wild boards, bears, foxes and golden monkeys.

History Various actions had been taken by Tibetan authorities over the centuries to consolidate their rule over Menyu area. The area became the hereditary manor of Tibetans' Zhuba Geju (faction) during the mid 14th and early 15th centuries. In the mid-17th century, the Fifth Dalai Lama united the whole of Tibet and established the yellow sect of Buddhism as the dominant religion. He sent two of his disciples to Menyu to set up an office there. They enlarged the Dawang Monastery and began the integrated rule of religion and politics over the area.

In the mid-19th century, the Resident Minister of the Qing court in Tibet and the Tibet local government also posted two officials in Menyu to administer their rule and to give the monastery special administrative powers. Each year, the Tibet local government would send officials to the area to levy taxes, purchase rice and administer trading of salt and rice. Local officials appointed by the government were responsible for passing on orders, settling local disputes, and running village and township affairs.

The Moinbas became poverty-stricken under a system of feudal serfdom following the establishment of the rule of the Zhuba Geju (faction) over them in the 14th century. Traces of this primitive system remained until the liberation of Tibet.

They used the simple slash-and-burn method of agriculture. Fields were left to nature's mercy, and productivity was very low.

Hunting was an important part of survival. Game was distributed among villagers, with the hunters getting double portions. Some game was bartered for grain and other necessities.

The three types of manorial lords — the Tibet local government, the nobility and the monastery — each possessed large areas of land, forests, pastures and other means of production, while the Moinbas were made serfs and slaves.

There were two categories of serfs — the tralpa and the dudchhung. The tralpa rented small plots of land from the manorial lords, and paid rent in cash and kind, such as butter tea, timber, dyes and charcoal, in addition to doing unpaid labour. The dudchhung were mostly immigrants from central Tibet and border areas, and were at the bottom of the social ladder. They were the poorest and most-cruelly oppressed of all. They had to pay heavy taxes and do heavy unpaid labour. Some had to rent land from the tralpa.

Today, vestiges of this old society can still be found in certain clans and villages, where part of the land, pastures, hills and forests are communally owned. Villagers can reclaim wasteland and chop wood and bamboo free of charge at the consent of their headman. Outsiders who want to do the same must also have the headman's permission.

The Moinbas lived like beasts of burden under the cruel oppression and exploitation of the three manorial lords. They were forced to do unpaid labour for as many as 110 days a year. Many died as a result, and some hid deep in forests to escape.

On many occasions they revolted against this criminal rule. They sabotaged communication links and refused to do unpaid labour or pay taxes.

New Life Tibet was peacefully liberated in 1951, and democratic reforms were introduced in 1959 after a counter-revolutionary armed rebellion was put down. During the action, the Moinbas joined the Tibetan people in support of the People's Liberation Army. Since then, they have shaken off their yoke and begun a new life.

The days of having to survive on wild fruits and nuts, wearing animal skins and banana leaves and living in caves and forests have gone forever. Agricultural output has risen considerably through the development of hillsides, introduction of irrigation systems and superior crop strains, and ending of the traditional slash-and-burn farming method.

Now the Moinbas have moved into bright, new electric-lit houses. Narrow footpaths and single log bridges have been replaced by roads and suspension bridges.

The Moinba people now have many schools for both children and adults, and have trained their first generation of teachers, accountants and other professionals. Some young people are studying at the Tibet Minorities' Institute in Lhasa and the Central Minorities' Institute in Beijing. Men and women of Moinba origin are working as administrators at various levels of government.

The Lhobas

The 2,100 people of the Lhoba nationality have their homes mainly in Mainling, Medog, Lhunze and Nangxian counties in southeastern Tibet. Additionally, a small number live in Luoyu, southern Tibet.

The Lhobas speak a distinctive language belonging to the Tibetan-Burmese language family, Chinese-Tibetan language system. Few of them know the Tibetan language. Having no written script, Lhoba people used to keep records by notching wood or tying knots.

People of this ethnic group were oppressed, bullied and discriminated against by the Tibetan local government, manorial lords and monasteries under feudal serfdom in Tibet. Being considered inferior and "wild," some were expelled and forced to live in forests and mountains. They were not allowed to leave their areas without permission and were forbidden to do business with other nationalities. Intermarriage with Tibetans was banned. They had to make their living by gathering food, hunting and fishing because of low grain yields in the region.

Life in the Past Largely farmers, Lhoba men and women are skilled at making bamboo objects and other crafts. They bartered such objects and animal hides, musk, bear paws, dye and captured game for farm tools, salt, wool, clothing, grain and tea from Tibetan traders. Their pilgrimages to monasteries were good opportunities for bartering.

Hunting is essential to the Lhobas. Young boys start early to join adults on hunting trips. Upon reaching manhood they tracked animals in deep forests either collectively or alone. The game they caught was partly distributed among villagers, partly used for bartering and some was extorted from them by the manorial lords.

There were essentially two classes — "maide" and "nieba" — within Lhoba society before Tibet's liberation. The "maides" considered themselves as nobles, while regarding the "niebas" as inferior people who should be at their disposal. The descendants of this latter class of people could not become "maides" even if they became wealthy and owned slaves. They could only become "wubus" — a group of people having a slightly higher position than the "niebas." Young men and women of these different groups could not marry due to strict class distinctions. The "niebas," who were slaves to "maide" owners, had no means of production. They were beaten, jailed or even executed if they were caught running away or stealing.

Women's status in their families, as well as in society, was particularly low, and they had no inheritary rights.

Life Style Customs, habits and dress of different clan members vary. Men in northern Luoyu wear sleeveless, buttonless, knee-length black jackets of sheep's wool. They wear helmetlike hats either made from bear skin or woven from bamboo stripes or ratten laced with bear skin. Barefooted, they wear bamboo earrings, necklaces and carry bows and arrows or wear swords at their side. Women have narrow-sleeved blouses and skirts of sheep's wool. They also go barefooted. Apart from their silver or brass earrings, bracelets and necklaces, the women wear a variety of waist ornaments such as shells, silver coins, iron chains and bells. Heavy ornaments are considered a symbol of wealth.

Diets also vary in different localities. Staple foods are dumplings made of maize or millet flour, rice or buckwheat. In places near Tibetan communities people have zhamba, potatoes, buttered tea and spicy food. Being heavy drinkers and smokers, at celebrations the Lhobas enjoy wine and singing to observe good harvests and good luck.

Many suffered from goitre, an endemic disease caused by lack of salt. Some were undernourished and some were born deaf and mute. Epidemic diseases were rampant due to the poor living conditions. The population of this ethnic group kept declining before liberation.

Conditions improved for the Lhoba people after the liberation of Tibet in 1951. Production was boosted and people's living standards and general health improved with loans and relief extended by the government. The Lhobas, who previously were serfs, got land, farm implements and draught animals. They began a new life since the democratic reform carried out in Tibet after 1959 when the central government put down an armed rebellion launched by the reactionary elements of the upper stratum of Tibet. For the first time they were treated as equals by society. Now they are well represented in government at regional, county, district and township levels.

With the help of their Han and Tibet neighbours, they have adopted advanced, intensive farming methods. They opened up land on hills and began cultivation of new areas. Hunting, handicrafts and other sideline businesses developed at the same time. Farming has been further improved as more capital construction projects have been completed, improved animal and crop strains adopted and scientific farming methods popularized.

Before liberation, most of the Lhobas were illiterate. Some elderly people could not count. Now children attend day schools while adults learn at evening classes. A few young people are studying in institutions of higher learning in the cities of Beijing, Nanjing and Lhasa.

People see films shown by film projection teams sent by government or army units. Trained doctors and other medical personnel have replaced the witch doctors who in the past were invited to cast spells to chase ghosts and demons from the sick, a practice that cost many lives. There are clinics and health centres in Lhoba villages.

Transportation and communication have been improved in the rocky areas inhabited by the Lhobas, with newly built roads and bridges opening up more of the region.

The Qiangs

The Qiang nationality has a population of 102,000. They mostly dwell in hilly areas, criss-crossed by rivers and streams, in the Mao-wen Qiang Autonomous Prefecture in Sichuan Province. A small number live with Tibetan, Han and Hui nationalities in such localities as Wenchuan, Dali, Heishui and Songpan.

They occupy a fertile land of mild climate and adequate rain. The mountain slopes are natural pastures. The area abounds in precious Chinese caterpillar fungus, bulb of fritillary, antlers, musk and bear's gallbladers, which are used for medicine. Deep in the forests are such rare animals as giant pandas, golden monkeys and flying foxes. The region is also rich in iron, coal, crystal, mica and plaster stone deposits.

History "Qiang" was a name given by ancient Hans to the nomadic people in west China. The Qiangs were not a single distinctive nationality then. According to historical records, a clan group made their homes in what is today's Sichuan Province. The Han Dynasty (206 B.C.-A.D. 220) court in the 2nd century had set up an administrative prefecture for the area. During A.D. 600 to 900 when the Tibetan Regime gradually expanded its rule over the region, some Qiangs were assimilated by the Tibetans and others

by the Hans, leaving a small number unassimilated.   These developed into the distinctive nationality of today.

The Qiangs do not have a written script of their own.   They
speak a language belonging to the Tibetan-Burmese language family
of the Chinese-Tibetan system.   Owing to their close contact with
the Han people, many Qiang people speak Chinese, which is also the
written form for this ethnic group.

The Qiang and Han peoples have had time-honoured close political, economic and cultural ties.   Administratively, Han courts from
the Qin, Han, Sui and Tang dynasties down to the Ming Dynasty
all had political units in the Qiang-occupied areas.   In the early
Qing Dynasty (1644-1911), the system of appointing local hereditary
headmen by the central authority to rule over the Qiangs gave way
to officials dispatched from the court.   The central administrative
system helped enhance the ties between the Qiang and Han nationalities.   With their horses, medicinal herbs and other native produce,
the Qiangs used to barter farm implements and daily necessities from
the Hans.   Mutual support and help stimulated the social and economic development of Qiang society.

For a long period before liberation, the Qiangs lived in primitive
conditions marked by slash and burn farming.   A feudal landlord
economy dominated production.   Landlords and rich peasants, who
accounted for only 8 per cent of the population, were in possession
of 43 per cent of the cultivated land.   Poor peasants and hired farm
hands, accounting for 43 per cent of the population, had only 16
per cent of the land.   Many poor peasants lost their land due to
heavy rent coupled with usury.   They became hired labourers,
wandering from place to place to make a living.

Life Style   The Qiangs dress themselves simply but beautifully.
Men and women alike wear gowns made of gunny cloth, cotton and
silk with sleeveless sheep's wool jackets.   They like to bind their hair
and legs.   Women's clothing is laced and the collars are decorated
with plum-shaped silver ornaments.   They wear sharp-pointed and
embroidered shoes, embroidered girdles and earrings, neck rings, hairpins and silver badges.

Millet, highland barley, potatoes, winter wheat and buckwheat make up their main staple foods. The Qiangs drink a great deal of wine and smoke orchid leaves.

They live in blockhouses made of piled up stones of different sizes. Unique in style, solid and practical, these houses are two or three stories high. The first floor is for livestock and poultry, the second retained as bedrooms and the third for grain storage. The Qiang people are skilled in opening up roads on rocky cliffs and erecting bamboo bridges over swift rivers. The bamboo chain bridges they built, laid with boards, stretch up to 100 metres with no nails and piers being used. Some of the Qiangs are excellent masons and are good at digging wells. During slack farming seasons they go to neighbouring places to do chiseling and digging. Their skills are highly acclaimed.

Marriages, mainly monogamous, were arranged by parents in the past. Usually, the wives were several years older than their husbands. It was common for cousins to marry and for bridegrooms to live with their wives' families. And it still is not unusual for brides to live in their parents' houses within a year or so after marriage. In Qiang society, younger brothers could make their widowed sister-in-laws their wives and elder brothers could marry the widows of their younger brothers. Such habits have been gradually discarded since liberation.

Most Qiangs were believers of Animism, except for those who lived near Tibetan communities and were followers of Lamaism. The Qiangs worshipped white stones placed on roofs as the "Heavenly God."

The Qiang people have created a unique culture and arts and crafts. The clever and deft Qiang women can do embroidery and drawnwork extemporaneously without designs. The Qiangs are good singers and dancers. "Wine song," "plate song," "mountain song" and "guozhuang" and "leather drum" dances with accompaniment of gongs, tambourines, sonas and bamboo flutes are popular.

New Life The Qiang area was liberated in January, 1950. In July, 1958 the Maowen Qiang Autonomous County was established. By relying on collective efforts, they carried out large-scale capital construction projects in their rocky region, where productivity used to be low because of backward local conditions and the shortage of men. Among the projects are tractor stations, reservoirs, hydroelectric power stations and pumping and drainage facilities. Now more farm machinery is used and scientific farming methods have been introduced. Grain output increases every year.

In the Qiang area, which had no industry and highways before, enterprises have sprung up and two concrete and 28 steel-chain bridges have been built over the Minjiang River. The area's total highway mileage has reached 260 kilometres. A postal route network covers every corner of the area.

The 210 primary and nine middle schools that have been built after liberation enroll over 82 per cent of school-age children. Thanks to the efforts of medical workers, mass screening and treatment has brought black fever and hook worm, two major epidemic diseases, under control. New delivery methods have greatly raised the infant survival rate and the Qiang population has risen markedly.

The Qiang area is dotted with small hydroelectric power stations. Electricity has reached to 97 per cent of the households and is used in processing farm and sideline produce and in mining and industry. People's life has been enriched by village film projection teams and a broadcasting network.

The Yis

The Yi nationality, with a population of 5,453,400, is mainly distributed over the provinces of Sichuan, Yunnan and Guizhou, and the Guangxi Zhuang Autonomous Region. There are about 1,500,000 Yis in Sichuan Province, and most of them live in an area south of the Dadu River and along the Anning River. Traditionally, this area is subdivided into the Greater Liangshan Mountain area, which lies east of the Anning River and south of the Huangmao Dyke, and the Lesser Liangshan Mountain area, which covers the Jinsha River valley and the south bank of the Dadu River. There are about 1,300,000 Yis in the Liangshan Yi Autonomous Prefecture, which holds the single largest Yi community in China. Yunnan Province has more than three million Yis, most of whom are concentrated in an area hemmed in by the Jinsha and Yuanjiang rivers, and the Ailao and Wuliang mountains. Huaping, Ninglang and Yongsheng in western Yunnan form what is known as the Yunnan Lesser Liangshan Mountain area. In Guizhou, 560,000 Yis live in compact communities in Anshun and Bijie. Some 4,600 Yis live in Longlin and Mubian counties in the Guangxi Zhuang Autonomous Region.

Most Yis are scattered in mountain areas, some in frigid mountain areas at high altitudes, and a small number live on flat land or

232

in valleys. The altitudinal differences of the Yi areas directly affect their climate and precipitation. Their striking differences have given rise to the old saying that "the weather is different a few miles away" in the Yi area. This is the primary reason why the Yis in various areas are so different from one another in the ways they make a living.

The Yi areas are rich in natural resources. The Jinsha River running through Sichuan and Yunnan and its tributaries surging through the Yi areas in northern and northeastern Yunnan are enormous sources of water power. The Yi areas are not only rich in coal and iron, but are also among China's major producers of non-ferrous metals. Gejiu, China's famous tin centre, reared the first generation of Yi industrial workers. Various Yi areas in the Greater and Lesser Liangshan Mountains, western Guizhou, and eastern and southern Yunnan abound in dozens of mineral resources, including gold, silver, aluminium, manganese, antimony and zinc. Vast forests stretch across the Yi areas, where Yunnan pine, masson pine, dragon spruce, Chinese pine and other timber trees, lacquer, tea, camphor, kapok and other trees of economic value grow in great numbers. The forests teem with wild animals and plants as well as pilose antler, musk, bear gallbladers and medicinal herbs such as fuling (Poris cocos) and pseudoginseng.

History   The Yi language belongs to the Tibetan-Burmese Language Group of the Chinese-Tibetan Language Family, and the Yis speak six dialects. Many Yis in Yunnan, Guizhou and Guangxi know the Han (main Chinese) language. The Yis used to have a syllabic script called the old Yi language, which was formed in the 13th century. It is estimated that the extant old Yi script has about 10,000 words, of which 1,000 are words of everyday use. A number of works of history, literature and medicine as well as genealogies of the ruling families written in the old Yi script are still seen in most Yi areas. Many stone tablets and steles carved in the old Yi script remain intact. Since the old Yi language is not consistent in word form and pronunciation, it was reformed after liberation for use in books and newspapers.

Historical records written in the Han and the old Yi languages show that the ancestors of the Yi, Bai, Naxi, Lahu and Lisu nationalities were closely related with ancient Di and Qiang people in west China. In the period between the 2nd century B.C. and the early Christian era, the activities of the ancient Yis centred around the areas of Dianchi in Yunnan and Qiongdou in Sichuan. After the 3rd century, the ancient Yis extended their activities from the Anning River valley, the Jinsha River, the Dianchi Lake and the Ailao Mountains to northeastern Yunnan, southern Yunnan, northwestern Guizhou and northwestern Guangxi.

In the Eastern Han (25-220), Wei (220-265) and Jin (265-420) dynasties, inhabitants in these areas came to be known as "Yi," the character for which meant "barbarian." After the Jin Dynasty, the Yis of the clan named Cuan became rulers of the Dianchi area, northeastern Yunnan and the Honghe (Red) River area. Later those places were called "Cuan areas" which fell into the east and west parts. The inhabitants there belonged to tribes speaking the Yi language. In the Tang and Song dynasties, the Yis living in "East Cuan" were called "Wumans." In different historical periods, "Cuan" changed from the surname of a clan to the name of a place, and further to the name of a tribe. In the Yuan and Ming dynasties, "Cuan" was often used to refer to the Yis. After the Yuan Dynasty, part of "Cuan" acquired the name "Luoluo" (Ngolok), which probably originated from "Luluman," one of the seven "Wuman" tribes in the Tang Dynasty. From that time on, most Yis called themselves "Luoluo," although many different appellations existed. This name lasted from the Ming and Qing dynasties till liberation.

Ancient Yis experienced a long primitive society in the stone age. Legends and records written in the old Yi script show that the Yis went through a matriarchal age in ancient times. *"Annals of the Yis in the Southwest"* records that the Yi people in ancient times "only knew mothers and not fathers," and that "women ruled for six generations in a row." Patriarchy came into being at least 2,000 years ago.

Roughly in the 2nd and 3rd centuries B.C., the Yis living around the Dianchi Lake in Yunnan entered class society. In the early Han Dynasty, prefectures were set up in this area, and the chief of the Yi people was granted the title "King of Dian" with a seal. Around the 8th century, a slave state named "Nanzhao" was established in the northern Ailao Mountain and the Erhai areas, with the Yis as the main body and the Bai and Naxi nationalities included. The head of the state was granted the title "King of Yunnan." In the same period, "Luodian" and other groups of slave owners and regimes appeared in the Yi areas in Guizhou. In 937, the state of "Dali" superseded "Nanzhao," when it collapsed under the blows of slave and peasant uprisings. From then on, the slave system of the Yis in Yunnan gradually distintegrated.

After the 13th century, "Dali" and "Luodian" were conquered one after the other by the Yuan Dynasty, which set up regional, prefectural and county governments and military and civil administrations in the Yi areas in Yunnan, Guizhou and Sichuan, appointing hereditary headmen to rule the local inhabitants. By the end of the Yuan Dynasty, the feudal economy of the Yi landlords in Yunnan had developed rapidly, but remnants of the manorial economy and slavery still existed to varying extents in the secluded areas. The Ming Dynasty used both administrative officials from elsewhere and local hereditary headmen, and some of the governments consisted of both types of administrators, expanding the influence of the feudal landlord economy. The large number of Han immigrants also promoted economic growth in the Li areas. The Qing Dynasty abolished the system of appointing hereditary headmen and confirmed the appointment of administrative officials. This enhanced its direct rule over the Yi areas, hastened the disintegration of the manorial economy and firmly established the feudal landlord economy.

Tradition The Yi nationality has a glorious tradition of revolutionary struggle. In the recent 100 years or more the Yis waged powerful anti-imperialist and anti-feudal struggles as well as those against slaveowners. Influenced by the Taiping Revolution (1851-1864), the struggles waged by the Yis and other nationalities against the Qing government lasted more than a decade.

In 1935, the Chinese Red Army pushed north to resist the Japanese invaders. The troops on the historic Long March passed through the Yi areas, leaving a good and deep impression on the Yis wherever they went. On their way through northwestern Guizhou and northeastern Yunnan, the Red Army cracked down on local tyrants, wicked gentry and corrupt officials, and opened their barns to relieve the starving Yis. The Red Army distributed confiscated grain, salt, ham, clothes and other such goods among the Yis and people of other nationalities, who in return gave enthusiastic assistance to it. Many young Yis joined the Army.

After crossing the Jinsha River, the Red Army pushed towards the Dadu River in two prongs from Yuexi and Mianning. Supported by the Army, the Yis and Hans in Mianning established the Worker-Peasant-Soldier Democratic Government of the county, formed revolutionary troops, abolished the "hostage system" imposed by the Kuomintang government, and set free several hundred Yi headmen and their relatives held as hostages. The Red Army strictly observed discipline, firmly implemented the Chinese Communist Party's policy for minority nationalities, declared that it aimed to emancipate the minority nationalities, and proclaimed that all poor Yis and Hans were kith and kin. It called on the Yi people to unite with the Red Army and overthrow the warlords and fight for national equality. Inspired by the Red Army's policies, Yuedan the Junior, the chieftain of a Yi clan in Mianning County, entered into alliance with the Red Army General Liu Bocheng. Helped by the Yis and the chieftain, the Red Army troops passed through the Yi areas without a hitch and won the victory of capturing the Luding Bridge and forcing the Dadu River. Luo Binghui, the fine son of the Yi people and a former serf, became a devoted revolutionary fighter and an outstanding commander of the Red Army and later the Chinese People's Liberation Army through countless battles.

Socio-economic Conditions in the Past Socio-economic development in the Yi areas was lopsided before liberation, due to oppression and exploitation by the reactionary ruling class, as well as historical and geographical differences. The socio-economic structure fell by and large into two types — feudalism and slavery. Most of the Yis in Yunnan, Guizhou and Guangxi had entered feudal society earlier on, and a developed landlord economy had emerged in most areas except for remnants of the manorial economy in some areas of northeastern Yunnan and northwestern Guizhou. Certain elements of capitalism had appeared in the Yi areas along the Yunnan-Vietnam Railway and the Gejiu-Bisezhai-Shiping Railway. Slavery remained intact for a long time in the Greater Liangshan Mountain area in Sichuan and the Lesser Liangshan Mountain area in Yunnan.

The Yi people in Yunnan, Guizhou and Guangxi, who were under feudal rule, were mainly engaged in agriculture and animal husbandry. The growth of handicraft industries and commerce varied from place to place. Generally speaking, the production level of Yis living near cities and towns was approximate to that of local Hans, but was much lower in mountain areas.

Landlords accounted for 5 per cent of the population in those areas, and poor peasants and farmhands 60 to 80 per cent. The land possessed by landlords was on the average 10 times or several dozen times the amount owned by poor peasants, who were subjected to cruel feudal exploitation. Land rent paid in kind reached 60 to 70 per cent of the harvest and tenants had to bear heavy corvee and miscellaneous levies.

Though the system of appointing hereditary headmen in northeastern Yunnan and northwestern Guizhou was abolished in the Qing Dynasty, some local tyrants, until liberation in 1949, used political power and influence in their hands to bully and exploit peasants as slaveowners did, treating poor peasants as serfs.

Slavery kept production at an extremely low level for a long time in the Greater and Lesser Liangshan Mountain areas in Sichuan and Yunnan. While agriculture was the main line of production, land lay waste and production declined strikingly. Slash-and-burn cultivation was still practised in some mountain areas. The lack of irrigation facilities and adequate manure, coupled with heavy soil erosion, lowered average grain output to less than a ton per hectare. Animal husbandry was a major sideline with sheep making up a large part of the livestock. The rate of propagation was very low due to extensive grazing and management.

For many centuries, barter was the form of trading among the Yis in the Liangshan Mountain areas. Goods for exchange mainly included livestock and grain. Salt, cloth, hardware, needles and threads and other daily necessities were available only in places where Yis and Hans lived together. Occasionally, some Han merchants, guaranteed safe-conduct by Yi headmen, carried goods into the Liangshan Mountain areas. At the risk of being captured and turned into slaves, they went and often made a net profit of more than 100 per cent. Suffering from a severe shortage of means of production and of subsistence, the Yis had to endure heavy exploitation in order to get a little essential goods. One hen was worth only a needle, and a sheepskin only a handful of salt. Many slaves had to go without salt all the year round.

Due to complex historical reasons, the slave system of the Yis in the Liangshan Mountains lasted till 1949.

Before liberation, the Yis in the Liangshan Mountain areas were stratified into four different ranks — "Nuohuo," "Qunuo," "Ajia" and "Xiaxi." The demarcation between the masters and the slaves was insurmountable. The rank of "Nuohuo" was determined by blood lineage and remained permanent, the other ranks could never move up to the position of rulers.

"Nuohuo," meaning "black Yi," was the highest rank of society. Being the slave-owning class, Nuohuo made up 7 per cent of the total population. The black Yis controlled people of the other three ranks to varying degrees, and owned 60 to 70 per cent of the arable land and a large amount of other means of production. The black Yis were born aristocrats, claiming their blood to be "noble" and "pure," and forbidding marriages with people of the other three ranks. They despised physical labour, lived by exploiting the other ranks and ruled the slaves by force.

"Qunuo," meaning "white Yi," was the highest rank of the ruled and made up 50 per cent of the population. This rank was an appendage to the black Yis personally and, as subjects under the slave system, they enjoyed relative independence economically and could control "Ajia" and "Xiaxi" who were inferior to them. "Qunuo" lived within the areas governed by the black Yi slaveowners, had no freedom of migration, nor could they leave the areas without the permission of their masters. They had no complete right of ownership when disposing of their own property, but were subjected to restrictions by their masters. They had to pay some fees to their masters when they wanted to sell their land. The property of a dead person who had no offspring went to his master. Though the black Yi slaveowners could not kill, sell or buy Qunuo at will, they could transfer or present as a gift the power of control over Qunuo. They could even give away Qunuo as the compensation for persons they had killed and use Qunuo as stakes. So, Qunuo had no complete personality of their own, though they were not slaves.

"Ajia" made up one third of the population, being rigidly bound to black Yi or Qunuo slaveowners, who could freely sell, buy and kill them.

"Xiaxi" was the lowest rank, accounting for 10 per cent of the population. They had no property, personal rights or freedom, and were regarded as "talking tools." They lived in damp and dark corners in their masters' houses, and at night had to curl up with domestic animal to keep warm. Supervised by masters, Xiaxi did heavy housework and farmwork all the year round. They wore rags and tattered sheepskins, and lived on wild roots and leftovers. Slaveowners inflicted all sorts of torture on those who were rebellious, and fettered them with iron chains and wooden shackles to prevent them from escaping. Like domestic animals, Xiaxi could be freely disposed of as chattels, ordered about, insulted, beaten up, bought and sold, or killed as sacrifices to gods.

Corvee was the basic form of exploitation by the slaveowners. Qunuo and Ajia must use their own cattle and tools to cultivate their masters' land. Qunuo had to perform five, six or more than 10 days of corvee each year. They could send their slaves to do it or pay a sum of money instead. Corvee performed by Ajia took up one third to one half of their total working time. They often had to neglect their own land because of cultivating the land of their masters. Besides corvee, Qunuo and Ajia had to take usurious loans imposed by their black Yi masters.

Ordered about to toil like beasts of burden, the slaves had no interest in production at all. To win freedom, slaves in the Liangshan Mountain areas resorted to measures like going slow, destroying tools, maltreating animal, burning their masters' property and even committing suicidal attacks on their masters. Though it was hard for slaves in remote mountain areas to run away, they still tried to escape at the risk of their lives. Spontaneous and sporadic rebellions staged by slaves against slaveowners never ceased. Organized and collective struggle for personal rights also grew, and collective anathema often turned into small armed insurgences.

Customs Rigid rules were stipulated for marriages within the same rank but outside the same clan among the black Yis, who relied on the "mystery" of blood lineage as a spiritual pillar. Some 70,000 black Yis in the Liangshan Mountains formed nearly 100 clans, big or small, of which there were less than 10 big clans each with a male population of more than 1,000. Each clan's territory was clearly demarcated by mountain ridges or rivers, and no tresspass was tolerated. There were no regular administrative bodies in the clans, but each had some headmen called "Suyi" (seniors in charge of public affairs) and "Degu" (seniors gifted with a silver tongue), who were representatives of the black Yi slaveowners in excercising class dictatorship. They upheld the interests of the black Yis as a rank, were experienced and knowledgeable about customary law and capable of shooting trouble. "Degu," in particular, enjoyed high prestige inside and outside their clans. Headmen did not enjoy privileges over and above ordinary clansmen, nor were their positions hereditary. Important issues in the clans, such as settling blood feud and suppressing rebellious slaves, must be discussed at the "Jierjitie" (consultation among the headmen) or "Mengge" (general conference of the clan membership).

While preserving some of their original characteristics, the clans under the slave system mainly functioned as institutions to enforce rank enslavement and exploitation, splitting and cracking down on slave rebellions internally and plundering other clans or resisting their pillage externally. When subordinate ranks staged a rebellion, the black Yi clans would take collective action against it, or several clans would join hands to suppress it. Under such circumstances, the unanimity of interests among the black Yi slaveowners fully manifested itself. Strictly controlled by the black Yi clans, the slaves could hardly run away from the areas administered by the clans. On the other hand, black Yis often fought among themselves in order to obtain more slaves, land or property. It follows that the clan, as an institution, was a force safeguarding and supporting the privileges of the black Yi slaveowning class.

The white Yi clans, among the Qunuos and part of the Ajias, while being similar to the black Yi clans in form, were actually subordinate to various black Yi clans. Only a few white Yi clans were not subject to black Yi rule and they formed what was known as the independent white Yi area. The white Yi clans succeeded to some extent in protecting their own members, and at times they would unite in "legitimate" struggles to defend their own interests and win temporary concessions from black Yi slaveowners. But, under the rule of the black Yi clans, they became an auxiliary tool of the slaveowners to oppress the slaves. Some clan chieftains of the Qunuo rank were fostered by slaveowners as proxies, called "Jiemoke" in the Yi language, who collected rents, dunned for repayment of debts and served as hatchet men, mouthpieces and lackeys for slaveowners.

There was no written law for the Yis in the Liangshan Mountains, but there was an unwritten customary law which was almost the same in various places. Apart from certain remnants of the customary law of clan society, this customary law reflected the characteristics of morality and the social rank system. It explicitly upheld the rank privileges and ruling position of the black Yis, claiming that the rule of slaveowners was a "perfectly justified principle." The legal viewpoint of the customary law was clear-cut. Any personal attacks against black Yis, encroachment on their private property, violation of the marriage system of the rank and infringement on the privileges of the black Yis were regarded as "crimes," and the offenders would be severely punished.

In most Yi areas, maize, buckwheat, oat and potato were staples. Rice production was limited. Most poor Yi peasants lived on acorns, banana roots, celery, flowers and wild herbs all the year round. Salt was scarce. In the Yi areas, potatoes cooked in plain water, pickled leaf soup, buckwheat bread and cornmeal were considered good foods, which only the well-to-to Yis could afford. At festivals, boiled meat with salt was the best food, which only slaveowners could enjoy.

Cooking utensils of a distinct ethnic colour, made of wood or leather, have been preserved in some of the Yi areas. Tubs, plates, bowls and cups, hollowed out of blocks of wood, are painted in three colours — black, red and yellow — inside and outside, and with patterns of thunderclouds, water waves, bull eyes and horse teeth. Wine cups are hollowed out of horns or hoofs.

Yi costume is great in variety, with different designs for different places. In the Liangshan Mountains and west Guizhou, men wear black jackets with tight sleeves and right-side askew fronts, and pleated wide-bottomed trousers. Men in some other areas wear tight-bottomed trousers. They grow a small patch of hair three or four inches long on the pate, and wear a turban made of a long piece of bluish cloth. The end of the cloth is tied into the shape of a thin, long awl jutting out from the right-hand side of the forehead. They also wear on the left ear a big yellow and red pearl with a pendant of red silk thread. Beardless men are considered handsome. Women wear laced or embroidered jackets and pleated long skirts hemmed with colourful multi-layer laces. Black Yi women used to wear long skirts reaching to the ground, and women of other social ranks wore skirts reaching only to the knee. Some women wear black turbans, while middleaged and young women prefer embroidered square kerchiefs with the front covering the forehead like a rim. They also wear earrings and like to pin silver flowers on the collar. Men and women, when going outdoors, wear a kind of dark cape made of wool and hemmed with long tassels reaching to the knee. In wintertime, they lined their capes with felt. But few slaves could afford clothes of cotton cloth, and most of them wore tattered home-spun linen.

Most Yi houses were low mud-and-wood structures without windows, which were dark and damp. Ordinary Yi houses had double-bevelled roofs covered with small wooden planks on which stones were laid. Interior decoration was simple and crude, with little furniture and very few utensils, except for a fireplace consisting of three stones. In the Liangshan Mountains, slaveowners' houses and slaves' dwellings formed a sharp contrast. Slaves lived with livestock in the same huts that could hardly shelter them from wind and rain.

Slaveowners' houses had spacious courtyards surrounded by high walls, and some of them were protected by several or a dozen pillboxes.

The Yis are monogamous, living in nuclear families. Before liberation, marriages were generally arranged by parents, and the bride's family often asked for heavy betrothal gifts. In many places, married women stayed at their own parents' home till their first children were born. In some other places, feigned "kidnapping of the bride" was practised to add to the joyous atmosphere. The groom's family would send people to the bride's home at a pre-arranged time to snatch the girl and carry her home on horseback. The girl was supposed to cry aloud for help, and her family members and relatives would pretend to chase after the kidnappers. In other cases, when people from the groom's side went to fetch the bride, her people would first "attack" them with water, cudgels and stove ashes, then treat them to wine and meat after a frolic scuffle, and finally let them take the bride away on horseback. On the wedding night, there would also be frolic fighting between the bride and the groom as part of the ceremony. These were obviously legacies of primitive marriage conventions.

Patriarchal and monogamous families were the basic units of the clans in the Liangshan Mountains. When a young man got married, he built his own family by receiving part of his parents' property. Young sons who lived with their parents could get a larger portion of the property. There were rigid differences between sons by the wife and those by concubines in sharing legacies. Property handed down from the ancestors usually went to sons by the wife. The Yis traditionally associated the father's name with the son's. When a boy was named, the last one or two syllables of his father's name would be added to his own. Such a practice made it possible to trace the family tree back for many generations. In the Yi families, women were in a subordinate position with no right to inherit property, but the remnants of matriarchal society could still be seen clearly sometimes. The Yis much respected the power of uncles on the mother's side, and relations between such uncles and nephews were close. Slaves' marriages and homemaking were in the hands of slaveholders. The fate of slave girls was even more wretched, and they were forced to marry just to meet the needs of slaveowners for more slaves.

The Yis in the Greater and Lesser Liangshan Mountains practised cremation, burning dead bodies in mountains and burying the ashes in the ground or placing them in caves. After the funeral, the mourners used bamboo strips wrapped with white wool to make memorial tablets, which were wound with red thread and placed in the trough carved in a wooden stick. Again, the stick was wrapped with white cloth or linen. Some memorial tablets were made of bamboo or wood and carved in the shape of figurines, which were placed at the young sons' homes. Three years later, such memorial tablets were either burned or placed in secluded mountain caves.

The Yis in Yunnan, Guizhou and Guangxi believed in polytheism before liberation, combining worship for ancestors with the influence of Taoism and Buddhism. The Yis in the Liangshan Mountains worshipped gods and ghosts and believed in idolatry, and offered sacrifices to forefathers frequently. Their religious activities were presided over by sorcerers.

The earliest Yi calendar divided the year into 10 months, each with 36 days. The tenth month was the period of the annual festival. Influenced by the Han Lunar Calendar, the Yis later divided the year into 12 months, using the 12 animals representing the 12 Earthly Branches to calculate the year, month and date. There was a leap year every two years in the Yi calendar. The new year festival was not fixed but generally fell between the 11th and 12th lunar months. In celebrating the new year, the Yis would slanghter cattle, sheep and pigs to offer sacrifices to ancestors. In the Liangshan Mountains, people of the subordinate ranks had to present half a pig's head to their masters to confirm their affiliation. The Yis in Yunnan and Guizhou now celebrate the spring festival as the Hans do. "The Torch Festival," held around 24th of the sixth lunar month, is a common tradition for the Yis in all areas. During the festival, the Yis in all villages would carry torches and walk around their houses and fields, and plant pine torches on field ridges in the hope of driving away insect pests. After making their rounds, the Yis of the whole village would gather around bonfires, playing moon guitars (a four-stringed plucked instrument with a moon-shaped sound box) and mouth organs, dancing and drinking wine through the night to pray for a good harvest. The Yis in some places stage horse races, bull fighting, playing on the swing, archery and wrestling.

New Life The founding of the People's Republic of China in 1949 ended the bitter history of enslavement and oppression of the Yis and people of other nationalities in China. From 1952 to 1980, the Liangshan Yi Autonomous Prefecture of Sichuan, the Chuxiong Yi Autonomous Prefecture and the Honghe Hani and Yi Autonomous Prefecture of Yunnan were established one after another. Autonomous counties for the Yi nationality or for several minority nationalities including Yi were founded in Eshan, Lunan, Ninglang, Weishan, Jiangcheng, Nanjian, Xundian, Xinping and Yuanjiang of Yunnan, Weining of Guizhou and Longlin of Guangxi.

Transformation of the only existing slave society in the contemporary world over the past 30 years or more has been a matter of profound significance in the Yi people's history. In response to the aspirations of the Yi slaves and other poor people, the people's government, after consulting with Yis from the upper stratum who had close relations with the common people, decided to carry out democratic reforms in the Yi areas of Sichuan and in the Ninglang Autonomous County of Yunnan in 1956. The basic objective of the democratic reforms was to abolish slavery and let the labouring people enjoy personal freedom and political equality; to abrogate the land ownership of the slaveowning class and introduce the land ownership of the labouring people to release the rural productive force and promote agricultural production so as to create conditions for the socialist transformation of agriculture and the movement of co-operation.

In accordance with the principle of peaceful consultation, the people's government granted an appropriate political status and commensurate material benefits to those upperstratum people who actively assisted with democratic reforms. In this way, many slaveowners were won over, while the few unlawful and intransigent slaveowners were isolated. Thus, democratic reforms went on smoothly.

In the spring of 1958, democratic reforms concluded in the Yi areas in the Greater and Lesser Liangshan Mountains in Sichuan and Yunnan. The reforms destroyed slavery, abolished all privileges of the slaveowners, confiscated or requisitioned land, cattle, farm tools, houses and grain from the slaveowners, and distributed them among the slaves and other poor people. In the Liangshan Yi Autonomous Prefecture and the Xichang Yi areas, 120,000 hectares of land were confiscated, and 280,00 head of cattle, 34,000 farm tools, houses composed of 880,000 rooms and 8,000 tons of grain were either requisitioned or purchased and given to the poor and needy along with 4,700,000 yuan paid as damages by unlawful slaveowners. The reforms emancipated 690,000 slaves and other poor people, making them masters of the new society.

The people's government also built houses and provided farm tools, grain, clothes, furniture and money for the slaves and other poor people and helped them build their own homes. In the Liangshan Mountains, the government set up homes for 1,400 old and feeble slaves who had lost the ability to work under slavery. Many former slaves got married and started their own families, and many families were reunited.

The emancipated slaves took the socialist road most firmly and shortly after the democratic reforms formed advanced cooperatives in agricultural production.

The democratic reforms inspired the emancipated slaves and poor peasants to reshape their land and expand agricultural production steadily. The Chuxiong Yi Autonomous Prefecture of Yunnan achieved a great success in increasing output of hemp, tobacco, cotton, peanut and other cash crops. The autonomous counties of Ninglang, Weishan and Eshan in the Honghe Yi Autonomous Prefecture built water conservancy projects, which have played a big role in farming.

There was no industry at all in the Yi areas in the pre-liberation days except for the Gejiu Tin Mine in Yunnan and a few blacksmiths, masons and carpenters taken from the Han areas to the

Liangshan Mountains. Now people in the Liangshan, Chuxiong and Honghe autonomous prefectures have built farm machinery, fertilizer and cement factories, small hydroelectric stations and copper, iron and coal mines.

Lack of transportation facilities was one of the factors contri buting to the seclusion of the Liangshan Mountains. Construction of roads started right after liberation. In 1952, the highway connecting Sichuan and western Yunnan was reconstructed and opened to traffic. At the same time, trunk highways linking the Liangshan Autonomous Prefecture with other parts of the country were constructed. The Yixi Highway was opened to traffic in 1957, linking up the Greater and Lesser Liangshan Mountains for the first time in history. A highway network extending in all directions within the prefecture had been formed by 1961. By the end of 1981, the total length of highways in the prefecture had increased from seven km. before 1949 to 7,368 km. While there were only 18 push carts in the whole area before liberation, the number of vehicles in 1981 reached 11,000, of which 5,000 were motor vehicles. The local transportation department employed a total of 10,000 people. The Chengdu-Kunming Railway crosses six counties in the Liangshan Yi Autonomous Prefecture over a distance of 337 km., with 45 stations on the line.

With the development of the local economy, people in the prefecture had built 1,480 hydroelectric stations with a total generating capacity of 97,000 kw. by 1981, providing electric power and lighting for 80 per cent of the area.

Being extremely backward in education in the old days, the Yi people now have primary schools in all villages. The autonomous prefecture began setting up middle schools, secondary technical schools and schools for training ethnic teachers in the late 1950s. In 1981, there were 180 middle schools with 220 minority teachers and 12,000 students, 3,780 elementary schools with 3,700 minority teachers and 66,900 pupils. Children of emancipated slaves and poor peasants now have access to education. A new generation of Yi intellectuals with socialist consciousness is coming to the fore, and many Yi cadres hold leading positions at all levels of government in the prefecture.

In the past, there were no professional doctors, and the only way to avert and cure diseases was to pray. Now there are hospitals and clinics in all counties. Serious epidemic diseases such as smallpox, typhoid, leprosy, malaria, cholera have either been brought under control or wiped out by and large. A lot of traditional medical experience of the Yis has been collected, summed up and improved. The world famous Yunnan *baiyao* (a white medicinal powder with special efficacy for treating haemorrhage, wounds, bruises, etc.) is said to have been prepared according to a folk prescription handed down for generations by Yi people in Yunnan.

The colourful literature and art of the Yis are flourishing. The Yi people have created a great deal of historical and literary works written in the old Yi language and folk literary works handed down orally. The oral folk literary works, numerous and in a great variety, include poems, tales, fables, proverbs, riddles, etc. *History of the Yis in the Southwest* and *Lebuteyi,* two encyclopaedic works written in the old Yi language and involving philosophy, history and religion have been translated into the Han (main Chinese) language. The epics *Ashima, The Song of the Axi People* and *Meige* are popular throughout Yunnan.

Since liberation, many Yi folk tales, epics and songs have been published after being collected and collated. Also published are some new works reflecting the present life of the Yi people, such as *The Merry Jinsha River* and *Daji and His Father.* Yi songs and dances are rich in ethnic colour. The new folk song *The Stars and the Moon Are Together* expresses through beautiful melodies the happiness and warmth felt by the Yis in the great family of nationalities in China. *The Happy Nuosu,* another new song with cheerful and lively melodies, reflects the joyous and energetic life of the Yi people.

The Bais

Of the 1,130,000 Bai people, 80 per cent live in concentrated communities in the Dali Bai Autonomous Prefecture in Yunnan Province, southwest China. The rest are scattered in Xichang and Bijie in neighbouring Sichuan and Guizhou provinces respectively.

The Bais speak a language related to the Yi branch of the Tibetan-Burmese Group of the Chinese-Tibetan language family. The language contains a large number of Chinese words due to the Bais' long contact with the majority Chinese nationality.

Situated on the Yunnan-Guizhou Plateau, the Bai area is criss-crossed with rivers, of which the major ones are the Lancang, the Nujiang and the Jinsha. The river valleys, dense forests and vast tracts of land form a beautiful landscape and provide an abundance of crops and fruits. The area round Lake Erhai in the autonomous prefecture is blessed with a mild climate and fertile land yielding two crops a year. Here, the main crops are rice, winter wheat, beans, millet, cotton, rape, sugar-cane and tobacco. The forests have valuable stocks of timber, herbs of medicinal value and rare animals. Mt. Diancang by Lake Erhai contains a rich deposit of the famous Yunnan marble, which is basically pure white with veins of red, light blue, green and milky yellow. It is treasured as building material as well as for carving.

Origins and History Archaeological finds from Canger and Haimenkou show that the Erhai area was inhabited as early as the Neolithic Age, and artifacts of that period indicate that the people of the region used stone tools, engaged in farming, livestock rearing, fishing and hunting, and dwelt in caves. Possibly, they began to use bronze knives and swords and other metal tools about 2,000 years ago.

The people in the Erhai area developed closer ties with the Han majority in inland provinces in the Qin (221-207 B.C.) and Han (206 B.C.-A.D. 220) dynasties. In 109 B.C. the Western Han Dynasty set up county administrations and moved a large number of Han people to this border area. These people brought more advanced production techniques and iron tools, contributing to the economic development of the area. During the Sui (581-618) and Tang (618-907) dynasties, the farming there had reached a level close to that of the central plains.

Bai aristocrats backed by the Tang court unified the people of the Erhai area and established the Nanzhao regime of Yis and Bais. Its first chief, Piluoge, was granted the title of King of Yunnan by a Tang emperor.

Slaves were used to do heavy labour, while "free" peasants were subject to heavy taxation and forced to render various services including conscription into the army. Some of them, who lost their land, were made slaves.

The Nanzhao regime lasted for 250 years. During that period of time, while maintaining a good relationship with the central government, the rulers cruelly oppressed the slaves and mercilessly plundered other ethnic nationalities through warfare. Productivity was thus seriously harmed. This caused slave rebellions and uprisings. Nanzhao's power came to an end in the year 902. Then a regime based on a feudal lord system, known as the Kingdom of Dali, was established. The kingdom adopted a series of measures such as abolishing exorbitant taxes and removing conservative ministers. As a result, social productivity was restored.

The kingdom lasted for over 300 years (937-1253) as a tributary to the Song Dynasty (960-1279) court. It sent battle steads, handicrafts and precious medicines to the court, and in return received science and technology, as well as books in the Han language. Economic and cultural exchanges with the Hans contributed greatly to the development of this border area.

The kingdom was conquered by the Mongols in the 13th century, and Yuan Dynasty (1206-1368) rule was established there. The Mongols designated Yunnan a province while establishing Dali and Heqing as prefectures. In ordre to strengthen their control over Dali, the Yuan rulers offered former chieftains official posts and granted their families hereditary privileges. Though land was mainly concentrated in the hands of the local aristocracy at that time, the feudal lord system began to give way to a landlord system.

The Ming Dynasty (1368-1644) took power from the Yuan rulers in 1381. The Ming court removed local chieftains and replaced them with court officials. This kind of reform resulted in the weakening of the political and economic privileges of the local lords, brought freedom to the slaves and raised the enthusiasm of the peasants for farming. Those Bais and Hans who had emigrated were encouraged to return, while Hans from other areas were persuaded to settle there. This measure accelerated the development of the landlord economy of Bai society.

In addition to the continuation of the Ming policy of dispatching officials from the central government, the Qing (1644-1911) court also appointed local officials and chieftains to rule over the Bais.

Some Bai people in remote areas still suffered feudal exploitation and oppression at the time of liberation.

Culture and Folklore   Over the centuries, the Bais have created a science and culture of their own. Agriculture was dominant in the Erhai area as early as the Neolithic Age. People then knew how to dig ditches for irrigation. During the Nanzhao regime, they began the cultivation of rice, wheat, broomcorn, millet and several other crops, and built the Cangshan water-conservancy project which could bring water to tens of thousands of hectares of land. To their credit are inventions and advances in meteorology, astronomy, calendar, architecture, medical science, literature, music, dancing, carving and painting. Among the representative works of the Bai people are "Transit Star Catalogue for Time Determination" by the Ming Dynasty scholar Zhou Silian, "Collection of Secret Prescriptions" by Chen Dongtian and "Tested Prescriptions" by Li Xingwei. These classics recorded and summarized in detail the valuable experience of the Bai people in astronomy and medicine.

The superb architectural skill of the Bai people is represented by the three pagodas at the Chongsheng Temple in Dali. Built during the Tang Dynasty, the 16-storey main tower is 60 metres high and still stands erect after more than 1,000 years. It bears a resemblance to the Dayan Pagoda (Wild Goose) in Xi'an, an ancient Chinese capital city in today's Shaanxi Province. Figurines in the Shibaoshan Grottoes in Jianchuan County are lifelike, possessing both the common features of figure creation in China and the unique features of the Bai artists. The architectural group in the Jizushan Temple, with bow-shaped crossbeams, bracket-inserted columns, and gargoyles representing people, flowers and birds created with the open carving method, shows the excellent workmanship of the Bai people. The Bais also have high attainments in lacquerwares.

They have created a wealth of literary works reflecting their life, work, and struggles against nature and oppression. The epic, "Genesis," sings the praises of the communal life of Bai primitive society. Some poems by Bai poets have been included in the "Complete Poems of Tang Dynasty."

The "History of the Bais," "Anecdotes of Nanzhao" and "Kingdoms of Southwest China" are among the best historical works written by Bai historians. They provide important data for the study of the history of the Erhai area.

The Bai people are good singers and dancers. The "Lion Dance," created during the Nanzhao regime, was appreciated in the central plains during the Tang Dynasty. Bai opera, known as chuichui, is an art form combining folk music and dancing. It has also absorbed some of the characteristics of Han operas.

The famous painting depicting the Resurgence of the Nanzhao was created in 899 A.D. by Bai painters Zhang Shun and Wang Fengzong. This masterpiece was stolen by foreign imperialists in 1900 from Beijing.

Customs and Habits The Bais are Buddhists and worshippers of "communal god." Dotted with monasteries and temples, Dali has been known as a "Scented Wonderland." Abbots who held huge amount of land and other property in the past were big landlords and usurers. The ordinary people were heavily burdened by this caste and by religious activities which required sacrifices of cattle and other valuables.

Monogamous families have been the basic social cells of the Bais, with a very few people who practised polygamy. Parents live with their unmarried children, but only in big landlord families did four generations live together. Before liberation, matches between young men and young women of the same surname or clan were not permitted, while marriages between cousins were encouraged, and were arranged by the parents. High bride prices caused many poor families to fall into debt. Women were discriminated against, and only men had the right to inherit family property. But all such feudal practices and customs have been fading away since liberation. Young people now enjoy the freedom to choose their lovers.

Cremation was practised before the Yuan Dynasty. Later, due to the influence of the Han nationality, this was changed to burial. Funerals were very elaborate.

The "March Fair," which falls between March 15 and 20 of the lunar calendar, is a grand festival of the Bais. It is celebrated every year at the foot of the Diancang Hill to the west of Dali city. It is a fair and an occasion for sporting contests and theatrical performances. People gather there to enjoy dances, horse racing and other games. June 25 is the "Torch Festival." On that day, torches are lit everywhere to usher in a bumper harvest and to bless the people with good health and fortune. Streamers bearing auspicious words are hung in doorways and at village entrances alongside the flaming torches. Villagers, holding aloft torches, walk around in the fields to drive insects away.

Economy Before liberation, the feudal landlord economy was dominant in most Bai areas. Incipient capitalism had developed in a few cities and towns, while vestiges of the primitive communalism and remnants of the slave system were still in existence.

About 90 per cent of the people were farmers who possessed only 20 per cent of the arable land.

In areas where the lord system prevailed, peasants were all serfs, who owned neither land nor personal freedom.

In the communal setup in Bijiang and Fugong areas, class distinctions were not clear. There was land which was tilled collectively and the harvest distributed equally among the people. Private ownership of land also was practised on a small scale. There were also land sales and leasing.

Commercial capitalism found its way into some Bai areas at the beginning of the modern times. Trading companies owned by bureaucrat landlords emerged, shipped in commodities such as yarns and cloth from the United States, Britain and France via India, Burma and Vietnam, and exported gold, silver, and farm and sideline produce.

The Bai people had staged numerous uprisings against the Qing rulers and foreign imperialists. In one of these uprisings, which took place in the mid-19th century, they set up their own political power, the Dali Administration. The new government adopted measures to promote industrial and agricultural production, reduce land taxation and stamp out discrimination against the various nationalities.

Democratic revolutionary ideas spread to the Bai areas after the birth of the Chinese Communist Party in 1921.

The Bai people supported the Red Army on their Long March (1934-1935) and took an active part in the Anti-Japanese War. An armed uprising in April 1949, under the leadership of local Communists, liberated the city of Jianchuan, a move which facilitated the march into the southwest of the Chinese People's Liberation Army.

New Life Democratic reform and socialist transformation proceeded in the Bai areas in much the same way as in the Han-inhabited areas, but the reforms were carried out in a more gradual manner in those areas with vestiges of pre-capitalist economic organization. Cooperatives were set up to boost production on the basis of abolishing class exploitation and the remnants of primitive communalism.

The Dali Bai Autonomous Prefecture was founded in November 1956 after the completion of the democratic reform and socialist transformation. The prefecture now boasts 540 mining and industrial enterprises with 33,150 workers. Xiaguan, the prefectural capital, has become an important industrial city. Its total industrial output value is 19 times that of 1949. The prefecture has 186 hydroelectric power stations supplying electricity to most of the area.

It also has constructed 400 reservoirs, 8,470 dykes and 540 pumping stations, providing water for 93,000 hectares of land.

Some 3,100 km of highway, built since liberation, connect all the counties in the prefecture. Almost all school-age children are attending schools. The number of middle and vocational school children is constantly increasing. Many professors, scientists and writers of Bai origin are serving their own people. A total of 1,600 agro-technicians have been trained since liberation. They play an active role in promoting scientific farming.

Doctors and medicines were almost unknown in the past, and snail fever, especially, used to take a heavy toll in the Bai areas. But, thanks to sustained efforts, the prefecture has in the main brought the disease under control. Many of the local hospitals in the Bai areas are equipped with advanced facilities and apparatus.

The Hanis

Most of the 1,059,000 Hanis live in the valleys between the Yuanjiang and Lancang rivers, that is, the vast area between the Ailao and Mengle mountains in southern Yunnan Province. They are under the jurisdiction of the Honghe Hani-Yi Autonomous Prefecture, which includes Honghe, Yuanyang, Luchun and Jinping counties. Others dwell in Mojiang, Jiangcheng, Pu'er, Lancang and Zhenyuan counties in Simao Prefecture; in Xishuangbanna's Menghai, Jinghong and Mengla counties; in Yuanjiang and Xinping, Yuxi Prefecture, and (a small number) in Eshan, Jianshui, Jingdong and Jinggu counties.

Customs and Culture Their language belongs to the Yi branch of the Tibetan-Burmese language group of the Chinese-Tibetan language family. Having no script of their own before liberation, they kept records by carving notches on sticks. In 1957 the people's government helped them to create a script based on the Roman alphabet.

The areas inhabited by the Hanis have rich natural resources. Beneath the ground are deposits of tin, copper, iron, nickel and other minerals. Growing on the rolling Ailao Mountains are pine, cypress, palm, tung oil and camphor trees, and the forests abound in animals such as tigers, leopards, bears, monkeys, peacocks, parrots and pheasants. Being subtropical, the land is fertile and the rainfall plentiful — ideal for growing rice, millet, cotton, peanuts, indigo and tea. Xishuangbanna's Nanru Hills are one of the country's major producers of the famous Pu'er tea.

The Hanis are monogamous. Before liberation, a man was allowed to have a concubine if the wife had born him no son after some years of marriage. However, he was not supposed to forsake his original wife to remarry. Marriages are mostly arranged by the parents.

The Hanis in Mojiang and Biyue have a very interesting custom for settling an engagement. The parents of both the girl and boy involved should walk some distance together, and so long as they meet no animals the engagement can go ahead.

The brides usually return to live with their parents only two or three days after the wedding ceremony and join their husbands again at rice-transplanting time. But this is not practised in the Honghe area.

A son's name begins with the last one or two words of his father's name in order to keep the family line going. This practice has been handed down for as many as 55 generations in some families.

The Hanis prefer clothing made of home-spun dark blue cloth. Men wear front-buttoned jackets and trousers, and black or white cloth turbans. Women have collarless, front-buttoned blouses with the cuffs and trouser legs laced. Hanis in Xishuangbanna wear jackets buttoned on the right side and decorated with silver ornaments. They wear black turbans. Women there, as well as in the Lancang area, wear skirts, round caps, and strings of silver ornaments. Both men and women wear leggings. In Mojiang, Yuanjiang and Jiangcheng, some women wear long, pleated or narrow skirts, while others have knee-length trousers with embroidered girdles. Women in general like to wear earrings, silver rings and necklaces. Married and unmarried women wear different hairstyles.

The Hanis build their two- and three-storey houses of bamboo, mud, stone and wood on hill slopes. A village comprises from ten to as many as 400 households. In places like Honghe, Yuanyang and Luchun, houses have mud walls and thatched roofs, supported by wooden pillars placed on stone foundations, while in Xishuangbanna, houses are built of bamboo.

They are polytheists and ancestor worshippers. Rituals are regularly held to worship the Gods of Heaven, Earth, the Dragon Tree and their village, as well as their family patron gods. Believing they are protected by the God of the village gate, the Hanis in Xishuangbanna also hold ceremonies to pay respects to this deity. A shaman presides over the rites, at which sacrifices of cattle are offered.

There are days devoted to animals, such as Sheep Day, on which sacrifices are made. On days when someone dies, a wild animal comes into the village, a dog climbs onto the roof of a house, or a fire breaks out, people would be called to stop working and hold ceremonies to avert misfortune.

The Hani people celebrate their New Year in October, as their lunar calendar begins in that month. During the week-long festivities, pigs are slaughtered and special glutinous rice balls are prepared. Relatives and friends visit each other, go-betweens are busy making matches, and married women go to see their parents. They also celebrate the June Festival, which falls on the 24th of that month. This is a happy occasion especially for the young people. They sing, dance, play on swings and hold wrestling contests. At night, people in some places light pine torches while beating drums and gongs to expel evil spirits and disease. Like their Han neighbours, the Hanis who live in the Honghe area celebrate the Spring, Dragon Boat and Moon festivals.

Legends, fairy tales, poetry, stories, fables, ballads, proverbs, mythology and riddles form their oral literature. "Genesis" is a legend describing the origin of all things on earth. "An Account of Floods" tells how men conquered floods. "Labare" and "Ahjigu" are songs sung on solemn occasions such as weddings, funerals, festivals and religious rituals.

The Hanis are good singers and dancers. They use three- and four-stringed instruments, flutes and gourd-shaped wind instruments. Popular are the "Hand Clapping" and "Fan" dances. The "Dongpocuo" dance popular in Xishuangbanna is a typical Hani dance; it is vigorous, graceful and rhythmic.

Origins and History Historical records indicate that a tribal people called the "Heyis" was active south of the Dadu River in the 3rd century B.C. These were possibly the ancestors of the Hanis of today. According to the records, some of them had moved to the area of the Lancang River between the 4th and 8th centuries. Local chieftains then paid tribute to the Tang court and in return they were included on the list of officials and subjects of that dynasty. The Yuan Dynasty (1271-1368) established a prefecture to rule the Hanis and other minorities in Yunnan. The Ming Dynasty (1368-1644) exercised its rule through local chieftains, who were granted official posts. During the Qing Dynasty (1644-1911) court officials replaced the chieftains.

The social development of the Hanis was uneven in different areas before liberation in 1949. Those in contact with the Hans were more developed economically and culturally. The feudal landlord economy was dominant during the Ming and Qing dynasties. Productivity was more or less on the Han level but the peasants were exploited harshly by the landlords who seized large tracts of fertile land.

The situation in Jinghong, Menglong and Xiding was different. Vestiges of primitive communal land ownership still remained. There, the majority of land was public property. Commune members owned paddy fields and tea plantations, and could reclaim and cultivate communal land. However, private land ownership was fairly developed in Menghai, Mengsong and Mengla counties. Landlords and rich peasants possessed most of the arable land there, as well as the tea plantations, forests and waste land. Poor peasants were subjected to exploitation in various forms.

In counties like Honghe, Yuanyang, Luchun, Jinping and Jiangcheng, the economy was in a sort of transition from primitive economy to the feudal landlord economy. Peasants were burdened by exorbitant taxes and levies enforced by the chieftains, who were both land owers and political rulers.

In the Ailao mountains, the Hanis were impoverished and suffered under various forms of exploitation. In one village, which had some 150 households 50 years ago, only 17 families were left at the time of liberation due to famine and disease.

A New and Prosperous Life   The Hani-inhabited areas were liberated in 1949. In the early post-liberation days, local governments at different levels enthusiastically worked for the unity of different nationalities while mopping up the Kuomintang remnants, bandits and local tyrants. Between 1950 and 1957 the state allocated to the Hanis large quantities of relief grain, clothing, seeds and cattle, coupled with agricultural loans, to help them overcome their difficulties and develop production.

The Honghe Hani-Yi Autonomous Prefecture was set up in 1957 as a merger of the earlier Honghe Hani Autonomous Prefecture and Mongzi Prefecture. Meanwhile, a number of autonomous counties were established. Democratic reforms, with land reform as the central task, were started in 1952 and completed within five years. Land reform brought about profound changes in the relations of production: The peasants became the masters of their own land, their living standards improved, unity among different nationalities was further strengthened, and social order in this border area was enhanced. Land reform was followed by the socialist transformation of agriculture.

Many farmland capital construction works have been carried out since liberation. These include opening up terraced land, changing dry land into paddy fields, building reservoirs and expanding irrigated acreage. More than 700 small hydroelectric power stations have been put up throughout the Hani areas, supplying electricity to 70 per cent of the townships, and farm mechanization is on the rise. The post-liberation years have also seen marked development in forestry, livestock breeding, side-line occupations and fishing.

Industrial enterprises which have sprung up after liberation cover metallurgy, mining, machine-building, chemicals, cement, textiles, plastics, cigarettes and food processing. In Honghe Prefecture alone, 400 state- and collective-run factories are in operation. A highway network, with Kunming to Daluo, Gejiu to Jingping, and Simao to Jiangcheng as the trunk lines, links all the counties within the area and facilitates communications with neighbouring places. De-

Manchu women's costume and ornaments.

Girls of Korean nationality love to play on balancing board.

Hezhen fishermen at work.

In her Mongolian holiday best.

An Ewenki **woman**.

Daur women rejoice in Yinkumai, their folk dance.

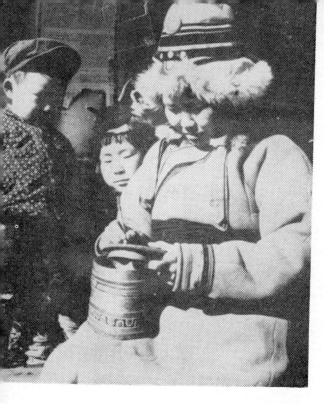

An Oroqen woman painting
a box made of birch bark.

Hui farmers busy
harvesting rice.

Two Dongxiang embroide-
resses comparing notes.

Salar farmers gathering
apples.

A discussion on embroidery
by embroideresses of the Tu
nationality.

...pical Bonan
...nives.

Skilled Yugurs knitting a sweater with home-spun wool.

Two skilled Uygur tailoresses.

A Kazak shepherd.

Brave Kirgiz out hunting with hawk.

A Xibe dance.

A Tajik woman in her best.

Uzbek girls.

A new couple of the Russian nationality.

An elderly Tatar with his grand children.

A Tibetan family preparing buttered tea.

Moinbas reading a local newspaper.

A Lhoba husking rice.

A Qiang woman making tapestry.

A Bai player of tree leaves.

Yi women
making new
wear.

Hani women
harvesting
pineapples

partment stores now supply cheap salt, which used to be in short supply, and other daily necessities, bringing most of the comforts of modern life to the Hani people.

The Dais

The Dai nationality lives in the southern part of Yunnan Province, mainly in the Xishuangbanna region. The area is subtropical, with plentiful rainfall and fertile land.

Local products include rice, sugar cane, coffee, hemp, rubber, camphor and a wide variety of fruits. Xishuangbanna is the home of China's famous Pu'er tea. The dense forests produce large amounts of teak, sandalwood and medicinal plants, and are home to wild animals including elephants, tigers and peacocks.

The Dai language belongs to the Chinese-Tibetan language family and has three major dialects. It is written in an alphabetic script.

History The history of contact between the Dai and Han peoples dates back to 109 B.C., when Emperor Wu Di of the Han Dynasty set up Yizhou Prefecture in southwestern Yi (the name used to signify the minority areas of what are now Sichuan, Yunnan and Guizhou provinces). The Dais in subsequent years sent tribute to the Han court in Luoyang, and among the emissaries were musicians and acrobats. The Han court gave gold seals to the Dai ambassadors and their chieftain was given the title "Great Captain."

According to Chinese documents of the ninth century, the Dais had a fairly well developed agriculture. They used oxen and elephants to till the land, grew large quantities of rice and had built an extensive irrigation system. They used kapok for weaving, panned salt and made weapons of metal. They plated their teeth with gold and silver.

In the 12th century a Dai chieftain named Bazhen unified all the tribes and established the Mengle local regime with Jinghong as the capital, and called it the "Jinglong Golden Hall Kingdom." According to local records, the kingdom had a population of more than one million, and was famous for white elephants and fine-breed horses. It recognized the Chinese imperial court as its sovereign. When Bazhen ascended the throne, he was given a "tiger-head gold seal" by the Emperor, and the title "Lord of the Region."

Previously, the Dais in the Dehong region had established the Mengmao Kingdom, with Ruilijiang as the capital.

During the Yuan Dynasty (1271-1368), the Dai area was subordinate to Yunnan Province and the system of appointing hereditary headmen from among the ethnic minorities was instituted; this system was consolidated during the Ming Dynasty (1368-1644).

Past Socio-Economic Conditions The increasing economic and cultural interflow between the Han and Dai peoples, as well as the migration of many Han people to the frontiers, taking with them advanced production skills and culture and science, promoted the economic development of Dai society. The feudal lord system established in the Dai areas at the end of the Yuan Dynasty and the beginning of the Ming Dynasty further promoted social production. The use of iron implements was widespread, new strains of crops were cultivated, and cotton was grown extensively. A number of fairly large commercial townships such as Cheli were established.

The Qing Dynasty (1644-1911), on the whole, carried on the practice of the Yuan and Ming system in the minority areas. However, it placed the Dai areas with more advanced economy under its jurisdiction and sent officials to practise direct control. During the Kuomintang rule, a county was set up in the Dai area close to the frontier and the policy of national oppression was carried out through the county administration.

The historical conditions of the Dai communities were not the same, nor were the stages of their social development. So each had its own characteristics as to the form of land ownership, class structure and political system. Such areas as Jingdong, Xinping and Yuanjiang, where the Dais mingled with the Hans, had entered the feudal landlord economy stage earlier because the Dais absorbed the Han's more advanced tools and techniques of production. Social progress was slower in Xishuangbanna and Dehong on the border, particularly Xishuangbanna, which still retained a fairly complete feudal manorial economy.

Since the Yuan, Ming and Qing regimes practised the system of appointing national-minority hereditary headmen, the "Cheli Official" had for generations been the highest manorial lord and ruler until liberation. All the land, forests and water belonged to him, and he subdivided his domain to be hereditarily ruled by his clan members and trusted followers. Under such a system, part of the land owned directly by the manorial lords became their private manors or served as pay for their household officials. The remaining part was alloted to the serfs and came under the common ownership of the whole village.

The manorial lords established a set of political institutions, and had their own troops, courts and prisons to facilitate their plunder and strengthen their rule.

The frontier Dai areas such as Dehong, Menglian and Gengma were nearly the same as Xishuangbanna, basically having a feudal manorial economy. However, their social economy underwent new changes. The land alloted to the peasants became more stabilized and hereditary, and land rent in kind was widely practised. In Mangshi and Yingjiang, the landlord economy developed faster and the rich peasant economy also grew, because of the Dai people's frequent contact with the Hans.

For a long time the Dais had grown rice as their main crop, and they had developed a rather complete, intensive farming system and gained rich experience in irrigation. However, under the shackles of feudalism, yields were low. The reckless exploitation by the luxury-loving ruling class and the Han landlords and merchants forced many peasants to flee their villages.

Religion The religious beliefs of the Dai people were closely related to their economic development. Residents on the borders generally were followers of Hinayana, a sect of Buddhism, while retaining remnants of shamanism. There were many Buddhist temples in the countryside, and it was a common practice, especially in Xishuangbanna, to send young boys to the temples to learn to read and write and chant scriptures, as a form of schooling. Some of them became monks, while most of them returned to secular life. While staying in the temple, the boys had to do all kinds of hard work, and the Dai people had to bear all the financial burden of the temples.

Customs and Habits   The marriage of the Dais was characterized by intermarriage on strictly equal social and economic status. Polygamy was common among chieftains, who also humiliated the wives and daughters of peasants at will. The patriarchal monogamous nuclear family was the common form among peasants. Pre-marital social contact between young men and women was quite free, especially during festivals. It was common for the groom to move into the bride's home after the wedding.

The graveyards of aristocrats and poor people were strictly separated. When a monk or a Buddhist leader died, he was cremated and his ashes placed in a pottery urn to be buried behind a temple.

Men wore collarless tight-sleeved short jackets, with the opening at the front or along the right side, and long baggy trousers. In winter they drape a blanket over their shoulders. They wore black or white turbans. Tattooing was common. When a boy reached the age of 11 or 12, a tattoo artist was invited to tattoo his body and limbs with designs of animals, flowers, geometric patterns or the Dai written script. Traditionally, women wore tight-sleeved short dresses and sarongs.

Rice is the staple food. The Dais in Dehong prefer dry rice, while those in Xishuangbanna like sticky rice. All love sour and hot flavours. In addition to beef, chicken and duck, they enjoy fish and shrimp. Cabbages, carrots, bamboo shoots and beans are among the popular vegetables. The Dais also love wine, liquor, and betel nuts.

The villages of the Dais in Dehong and Xishuangbanna are found on the plains, near rivers or streams, and among clusters of bamboo. The buildings generally are built on stilts. Some of the houses are square, with two storeys. The upper storey serves as the living place, while the lower space, without walls, is used as a storehouse and for keeping livestock.

Dai festivals, closely related to religious activities, included the "Door-Closing" festival in mid-June by the lunar calendar, the "Door-Opening" festival in mid-September, and the "Water-Splashing" festival in spring. "Door-Closing" started three months of intensive religious activities. "Door-Opening" marked the beginning of normal life. "Water-Splashing," still held every year, is the most important festival, during which the Dais splash water on one another, and hold dragon boat races in the hope of chasing away all the illnesses and bad fortune of the past year and bringing about good weather and bumper harvests.

The Dais have a rich, colourful culture. They have their own calendar, which started in 638 A.D. There are books in Dai script for calculating solar and lunar eclipses. Dai historical documents carry a rich variety of literary works covering poetry, legends, stories, fables and children's tales. They love to sing and dance, accompanied by their native musical instruments.

Regional Autonomy   The Dai people were liberated in 1950, and national regional autonomy was set up between 1953 and 1955 in all the places where the Dais live in compact communities. These include the Xishuangbanna Dai Autonomous Prefecture, the Dehong Dai-Jingpo Autonomous Prefecture, the Menglian Dai-Lahu-Va Autonomous County and the Gengma Dai-Va Autonomous County. Implementation of national regional autonomy has helped the Dais to achieve the right to run their own affairs, consolidate national unity and create favourable conditions for democratic reform and socialist transformation.

In order to abolish the feudal system, the people's government led the Dai people in carrying out democratic reforms in accordance with specific local conditions. Land reform in the hinterland Dai areas was carried out in the same way as in the Han areas. In the border Dai region it was carried out through peaceful negotiations with the upper strata of the Dais. Following the complete abolition of feudal land ownership, feudal exploitation and privileges were abolished, and the forces of production liberated. Later, mutual-aid teams and agricultural cooperatives were set up. By the end of 1956 all the Dai villages in the hinterland had gone cooperative. The Dai areas on the border region had become cooperative by 1959.

Economic Development   Capital construction on farmland, centring round the building of water conservancy projects, has been carried out smoothly in the Dai areas. Wasteland was reclaimed. New agro-techniques, scientific ways of farming and agricultural mechanization were introduced. These resulted in higher yields.

The production of grains, sugar cane and tea has all reached a record high in recent years. The Xishuangbanna area has become China's second largest natural rubber production base, after Hainan Island.

Before 1949, Dai handicrafts, covering weaving, wine-making, oil pressing and bamboo work, were on a very small scale. There are now many enterprises for mining, machine building, electric power generation, tanning, food and tea processing, sugar refining and rubber manufacture.

Electric generation has developed especially rapidly. To date, three power stations with a capacity of 24,000 kw have been built on the section of Liusha River in Xishuangbanna. The prefecture also has 70 small power stations. In Dehong 175 small stations generate electricity for industrial and home use.

Before liberation, communications were primitive in the Dai areas. Except for the China-Burma Highway, which passed through the Dehong area, most Dai areas were accessible only by unpaved tracks and on horseback. It took 25 to 30 days to walk from Yunjinghong to Kunming, capital of the province, and the road was infested with bandits and wild animals. Xishuangbanna itself was divided into two by the Lancang River, and there were neither bridges nor ferries.

In 1951, a highway between Kunming and the important border township of Daluo was built by the People's Government, and by April 1979 all the townships in the prefecture were connected by motor road, the total length of which reached 1,621 kilometres. A big reinforced concrete bridge was put across the Lancang River, linking the hinterland with the border regions. Now there is a land and waterway transport network with Yunjinghong as the centre. There are regular plane flights between Kunming and Simao, and between Kunming and Baoshan.

There was little commerce before liberation, and the scanty manufactured goods were sold at high prices. An urban-rural socialist commercial network has now been set up in the Dai areas, consisting of general stores and companies dealing in minority trade, foreign trade, farm implements, grocery, medicine and food. Every township has a state-owned central shop, and every village has a purchase and supply agency.

Large amounts of funds have been allocated by the state to promote education. Primary schools have been set up to replace Buddhist temples as education centres for children, and textbooks have taken the place of scriptures.

Both Xishuangbanna and Dehong run newspapers printed in Dai script. Many books translated into Dai have been published and news is broadcast in both the Chinese and Dai languages over the radio.

In the past, malaria, cholera, typhoid, bubonic plague and other epidemic diseases were rampant in the Dai areas, especially malaria. Medical teams were sent by the People's Government to the Dai areas soon after liberation to set up medical organizations, train Dai health workers and give free medical care. Plague, cholera and typhoid were soon under control. All the Dai prefectures and counties now have their own hospitals, health and epidemic prevention stations, malaria prevention and treatment stations, and maternity and child care clinics.

The Lisus

The Lisu nationality numbers 481,000 people, and most of them live in concentrated communities in Bijiang, Fugong, Gongshan and Lushui counties of the Nujiang Lisu Autonomous Prefecture in northwestern Yunnan Province. The rest are scattered in Lijiang, Baoshan, Diqing, Dehong, Dali, Chuxiong prefectures or counties in Yunnan Province as well as in Xichang and Yanbian counties in Sichuan Province, living in small communities with the Han, Bai, Yi and Naxi peoples.

The Lisu language belongs to the Chinese-Tibetan language family. In 1957, a new alphabetic script was created for the Lisu people.

Geography The Lisus inhabit a mountainous area slashed by rivers. It is flanked by Gaoligong Mountain on the west and Biluo Mountain on the east, both over 4,000 metres above sea level. The Nu River and the Lancang River flow through the area, forming two big valleys. The average annual temperature along the river basins ranges between 17 and 26 degrees Centigrade, and the annual rainfall averages 2,500 millimetres. Main farm crops are maize, rice, wheat, buckwheat, sorghum and beans. Cash crops include ramie, lacquer trees and sugarcane. Many parts of the mountains are covered with dense forests, famous for their China firs. In addition to rare animals, the forests yield many medicinal herbs including the rhizome of Chinese goldthread and the bulb of fritillary. The Lisu area also has abundant mineral and water resourses.

History According to historical records and folk legend, the forbears of the Lisu nationality lived along the banks of the Jinsha River and were once ruled by "Wudeng" and "Lianglin," two powerful tribes. After the 12th century, the Lisu people came under the rule of the Lijiang Prefectural Administration of the Yuan Dynasty, and in the succeeding Ming Dynasty, under the rule of the Lijiang district magistrate with the family surname of Mu.

During the 1820s, the Qing government sent officials to Lijiang, Yongsheng and Huaping, areas where the Lisus lived in compact communities, to replace Naxi and Bai hereditary chieftains. This practice speeded up the transformation of the feudal manorial economy to a landlord economy, and tightened up the rule of the Qing court over Lisu and other ethnic groups. In the years preceding and following the turn of the 20th century, large numbers of Han, Bai and Naxi peoples moved to the Nu River valleys, taking with them iron farm tools and more advanced production techniques, giving an impetus to local production.

For a long time the Lisus, under reckless oppression and exploitation by landlords, chieftains and headmen, as well as the Kuomintang and foreign imperialists, led a miserable life. In Eduoluo Village of Bijiang County alone, 237 peasants out of the village's 1,000 population were tortured to death in the 10 years prior to liberation by local officials, chieftains, headmen or landlords. The Lisus also suffered exorbitant taxes and levies. The household tax, for example, was 21 kilogrammes of maize per capita, accounting for 21 per cent of the annual grain harvest. Moreover, there were unscrupulous merchants and usurers. The arrival of imperialist influence at the turn of the 20th century put the Lisus in a far worse plight.

During the period between the 18th and 19th century, the Lisus waged many struggles against oppression. From 1941 to 1943, together with the Hans, Dais and Jingpos, they heroically resisted the Japanese troops invading western Yunnan Province and succeeded in preventing the aggressors from crossing the Nu River, contributing to the defence of China's frontier.

Socio-economic Conditions Before Liberation The social economy in the various Lisu areas was at different levels before liberation. In Lijiang, Dali, Baoshan, Weixi, Lanping and Xichang, areas closer to China's interior, a feudal landlord economy was prevalent, with productivity approaching the level in neighbourging Han and Bai areas. Some medium and small slave-owners had appeared from among the Lisus living around the Greater and Lesser Liangshan Mountains, taking up agriculture or part-agriculture and part-hunting, and using ploughs in farming.

As for the Lisus living in Bijiang, Fugong, Gongshan and Lushui, the four counties around the Nu River valley, their productivity was comparatively low. They had to make up for their scanty agricultural output by collecting fruits and wild vegetables and hunting. Their simple production tools consisted of iron and bamboo implements. Slash-and-burn was practised. The division of social labour was not distinct, and handicrafts and commerce had not yet been separated from agriculture. Bartering was in practice. Some primitive markets began to appear in Bijiang and Fugong counties.

Improvement in productivity brought about changes in ownership. Prior to liberation, private ownership of land had been established in the four counties around the Nu River valley, though landholding was generally small. The rural population had split up into classes, but the remnants of primitive public ownership and patriarchal slavery still existed. Land ownership was in three main forms: private ownership by individual peasants, ownership by the clan, and public ownership by the clan or village. Among the three, the first was dominant, while the second was a transitional form from the primitive public ownership of land to private ownership. Only a small portion of land was publicly owned.

As a result of the penetration of landlord economic factors and the instability of the small peasant economy, more and better land came under the ownership by some clans, village chieftains or rich households. An increasing number of poor peasants became landless. They lived on rented land or as hired farmhands.

Patriarchal slavery existed in the Nu River area in the period between the 16th century and the beginning of the 20th century. The slaves were generally regarded as family members or "adopted children." They lived, ate and worked with their masters, and some of the slaves could buy back their freedom. The masters could buy and sell slaves, but had no power over their lives. The slaves were not stratified. All these reflected the characteristics of exploitation under the early slavery system.

In post-liberation days, the remnant of the clan system could still be found among the Lisus in the Nu River valley. There were more than a dozen clans there, each with a different name. They included Tiger, Bear, Monkey, Snake, Sheep, Chicken, Bird, Fish, Mouse, Bee, Buckwheat, Bamboo, Teak, Frost and Fire. The names also served as their totems. Within each clan, except for a feeling of kinship, individual households had little economic links with one another.

The clan and village commune played an important part in practical life. The "ka," or village, meant a place where a group of close relatives lived together. Some villages were composed of families of different clans. Every village had a commonly acknowledged headman, generally an influential elderly man. His job was to settle disputes within the clan, give leadership in production, preside over sacrificial ceremonies, declare clan warfare externally, sign alliances with other villages, collect tributes for the imperial court, and arrange corvée. Under the rule of a chieftain, such headmen were appointed his assistants. When the Kuomintang came, they became the heads of districts, townships or "bao" (10 households). When there was a war, the various communal villages might form a temporary alliance; when the war was over, the alliance ended.

Apart from common ownership of land and working on it together, clan members helped one another in daily life. When there was wine or pork, they shared it. When a girl got married, they shared the betrothal gifts given to her parents; and when a young man took in a wife, the betrothal gifts for the bride's family were borne by all. Debts too, were to be paid by all. These collective rights and obligations in production and daily life made it possible for clan relations to continue for a long time.

Religion In the past the Lisu people worshipped many gods, nature and a multitude of other things. This appeared to be a remnant of totemism. Religious professionals made a living by offering sacrifices to ghosts and fortune-telling. During the religious activities, animals were slaughtered and a large sum of money spent. In the middle of the 19th century, Christianity and Catholicism were spread into the area by Western missionaries.

Customs and Habits The monogamous family was the basic unit of Lisu society. Sons left their parents and supported their own families after getting married. The youngest or only son remained with the parents to take care of them and inherit property. The daughter had no right of inheritance but could take her husband into her parents' home instead of being married off. Marriages were arranged by parents, with enormous betrothal gifts.

The dead were buried. Generally the village or the clan had its own common graveyard. For a man, the cutting knives, bows and quivers he had used when alive were buried with him. For a woman, burial objects were her weaving tools, hemp-woven bags and cooking utensils, to be hung by her grave. When an elderly man or woman died, the whole village stopped working for two or three days. People tendered condolences to the bereaved family, bringing along wine and meat. Generally the mound on the burial ground was piled one year after the burial, and respects to the dead were paid three years after the burial, and offerings ended.

In most areas the Lisu people wear home-spun hemp clothes. Women put on short dresses and long skirts. Their heads are decorated with red and white glass beads and their chests with necklaces formed by strings of coloured beads. Men wear short dresses and pants reaching the knee. Some of them wear black turban. A cutting knife dangles at a man's left waist, and a quiver hangs at his right waist.

Their main staple foods are maize and buckwheat. Hunting yields abundant meat. During their major festivals, they slaughter oxen and pigs. Both men and women are heavy drinkers.

The Lisu people live in two types of house. One is of wooden structure, with the four sides formed with 12-foot-long pieces of timber, and on top of them is a cover of wooden planks. It looks like a wooden box. The other is of bamboo-wooden structure, supported by 20 to 30 wooden stakes and surrounded with bamboo fences, with a thatched or wooden roof. In the centre of the house is a big fire-place.

The festivals of the Lisus living closer to the hinterland are nearly the same as those of the Han, Bai, Naxi and other peoples around. During the Lunar New Year, the first thing they do is to feed their cattle with salt to show respect for their labour. They have the Torch Festival in the sixth month of the year, and the Mid-Autumn Festival in the eighth month. The Lisus in the Nu River and Weixi areas enjoy their "Harvest Festival" in the 10th month, during which people exchange gifts of wine and pork. They sing and dance till dawn.

Life After Liberation   The Chinese People's Liberation Army liberated the vast area in northwestern Yunnan Province in early 1950, bringing a new life to the Lisu people.

In August 1954 the Nujiang Lisu Autonomous District was es-tablished, covering Lushui, Bijiang, Fugong and Gongshan counties. The autonomous district was changed into an autonomous prefecture in January 1957, and Lanping County, too, was placed under its jurisdiction.

To promote production and help improve livelihood of the Lisus in the area the People's Government, between 1956 and 1959, sent in 200,000 pieces of iron farm tools, 200,000 metres of cotton cloth, 240 tons of tea, 1,500 tons of salt and 150,000 tons of grain.

Democratic reform and socialist transformation were carried out in different ways in different areas.   A land reform such as that adopted in the Han area was carried out in Lijiang, Yongping, Yongsheng and Yunlong counties where a landlord economy had been developed, to eliminate feudal exploitation.   A milder land re-form was carried out in Yunnan's Zhongdian, Ninglang, Luxi and Baoshan counties, in Sichuan's Xichang and Yanbian counties, and in the areas where the Lisus mixed with the Tibetans, Dais and Yis. In the four counties around the Nu River valley and among the Lisus inhabiting the hilly regions of the Dehong Autonomous Prefecture, production was promoted through mutual aid and cooperative farming, in combination with necessary reforms, so as to enable the Lisus to gradually pass into socialism.

The reforms promoted production. Farming area, including paddy fields, in the Nujiang Autonomous Prefecture has been greatly expanded. And per-hectare yield has gone up.

Local industries have developed. They cover farm tools, rare metals, pharmaceuticals, building materials, car repair, and salt and sugar refining. Every county in the prefecture has its own electric power station.

The Nu River area was not accessible by highway in the past, and there were few post roads. The only means of transport was a man's shoulders or horseback. Now the four counties in the prefecture are linked to the hinterland by highway, and the total length of post roads comes to 2,200 kilometres. Over the rivers including the turbulent Nu, 28 steel suspension bridges and more than 200 of other types have been built. Highways lead to most parts of the prefecture. The people are served by a post and tele-communications network.

In the past, the four counties in the Nu River area had only five primary schools, attended by less than 200 pupils, and there were only two middle school students. The practice of keeping records by tying knots or wood engraving was common. To change the backwardness, the people's government allocated special funds for education and sent many teachers to the prefecture. Now almost all school-age children attend school. Hundreds of Lisu youth have been enrolled in colleges and universities. They are provided with stipend, free food, textbooks and even clothing.

Hospitals and health and epidemic-prevention stations at the prefectural or county levels have been set up.

A state trade network, consisting of shops for ethnic groups and purchasing and selling agencies, serves the Lisu people. State purchasing prices for local products have been repeatedly raised to activize rural economy.

The Vas

The Va nationality, with a population of 298,600, lives in Ximeng, Cangyuan, Menglian, Gengma, Lancang, Shuangjiang, Zhenkang and Yongde counties in southwestern Yunnan Province. Some are found scattered in the Xishuangbanna Dai Autonomous Prefecture and the Dehong Dai-Jingpo Autonomous Prefecture. Ximeng and Cangyuan counties are the main places where the Va people live in compact communities. In the areas where the Va people live, there are also Hans, Yis, Dais, Hanis, Lahus, Jingpos, Blangs, De'angs and Lisus.

Ximeng, Cangyuan, Menglian and Langcang are situated between the Lancang and Nu rivers, blocked by undulating mountain ridges some 2,000 metres above sea level. Traditionally this area was called the Ava hilly region.

With a subtropical climate, the fertile Ava region has plentiful rainfall and only 40 frost-free days a year. It is suitable for the growth of dry rice, paddy, maize, millet, buckwheat, potatoes, cotton, hemp, tobacco and sugarcane, as well as such subtropical fruits as bananas, pineapples, mangoes, papayas and oranges.

The Va language belongs to the Austroasiatic family. Before liberation, except for some parts of the area where an alphabetic script was used, the Va people had no written language, and they kept records and accounting or passed messages with material objects or by engraving bamboo strips. Each strip ranged from half an inch to an inch in width. Objects used implied specific meaning or feelings. For instance, sugarcane, banana or salt meant friendship, hot pepper anger, feathers urgency, and gunpowder and bullets the intention of clan warfare. An alphabetic script was created for the Va people in 1957.

Customs and Habits The monogamous family was the basic unit of the Va society. Family property generally was inherited by the youngest son, while daughters were denied the right to inherit. A man was allowed to have more than one wife.

Men and women had sex freedom before marriage. Small groups of young men and women met and sang love songs. After giving their chosen partners betal nuts or tobacco leaves as a token of love, they could go to sleep together. Such freedom ended upon marriage. Marriages were arranged by parents, and the bridegrooms had to pay several cattle as betrothal gifts. Eloping used to take place as a result of forced marriages.

Most of the Va villages were built on hilltops or slopes. Some villages in the Ximeng area have a history of several hundred years and embrace 300 to 400 households. When a family built a new house, others came to help and presented timber and straw as gifts. Generally the house was completed in one day by collective effort. The "big house" of a big chieftain or a rich person was marked by a special woodcut on top. The walls were decorated with many cattle skulls still carrying horns. The other sections were the same as commoners' houses, built on stilts, and the space below was used for breeding domestic livestock. Before iron cauldrons were introduced into the area, the Vas used big bamboo tubes to cook rice, and the cooked rice was divided into equal shares by the hostess at the meal. They loved to chew betal nuts and drink liquor.

The Va people dress differently according to different areas. Men's garments consist of a collarless jacket and very wide trousers. Their turbans are usually black or red and their ears are pierced, through which red and black tassels are threaded. Young men like decorating their shins with circular ornaments woven with bamboo strips or rattan. A Va woman wears a black short dress and a straight long skirt with folds. She has a silver (or rattan) hoop round her head and silver necklets and chains of coloured beads round her neck. Round her hips are many circular hoops of rattan. Va women are fond of bracelets round their wrists and earrings.

Religion   In the past the Va people living in the central area of Ava Mountain were worshippers of nature, believing that all the mountains and rivers and natural phenomena had their deities. They were believed to bring good or bad fortune to people. The loftiest god for the Vas was "Mujij," whose five sons were believed to be the deities in charge of the creation of heaven, the creation of earth, lightening, earthquake and the bringing up of the Va people, respectively. There were also deities of water, trees and so on. Even stomach ache and skin itching were believed to be caused by gods.

Frequent religious activities were held to obtain protection from deities and ghosts. Every year the activities started with making sacrifices to the deity of water, praying for good weather and good harvests. Cattle were carved up and their tails cut off as offerings. "Latou," or the hunting of human head, remnant of the primitive customs, had been abolished with the influence of the more advanced neighbouring ethnic minorities.

Apart from sacrificial ceremonies held by the whole village, many families also held their own sacrificial offerings. These involved chickens, pigs or oxen and cost a lot of wealth and time. It was estimated that the Vas in this area spent one-third of their yearly income on religion and superstition, and the amount of labour wasted averaged 60 days per capita annually.

In Cangyuan and Shuangjiang counties, some of the Va residents, influenced by the Dais, became followers of Lesser Vehicle of Buddhism. Christianity had spread into a part of the area.

Social Economy   In 109 B.C., Emperor Wu Di of the Han Dynasty set up Yizhou Prefecture which covered an area extending to the east of Gaoligong Mountain. As a result, the forbears of today's Vas, Blangs and De'angs came under the rule of the Han Dynasty. Thereafter, through the Tang, Song, Yuan, Ming and Qing dynasties, the Va people had had inseparable ties with other peoples in the hinterland.

Between the Tang and Ming dynasties, the Vas mainly engaged in hunting, fruit collecting and livestock breeding — the preliminary stage of agricultural economy. After the Ming Dynasty, agriculture became their main occupation, and they had passed out of the primitive clan communes into village communes. However, development in various areas was not balanced. Over a long time in the past, the Vas living with the Hans, Dais and Lahus had had their culture and economy develop faster through interchanges.

As a whole, however, development of the Va society was rather slow before liberation. This was due mainly to long-term oppression by reactionary ruling classes and imperialist aggression. There were three areas in terms of social development:

The Ava mountainous area with Ximeng as the centre and including part of Lancang and Menglian counties, inhabited by one-third of the total Va population. There, private ownership had been established, but with the remnant of a primitive communal system still existing.

The area on the edges of Ava Moutnain, covering Cangyuan, Gengma and Shuangjiang counties and part of Lancang and Menglian counties, and the Va area in the Xishuangbanna Dai Autonomous Prefecture, where two-thirds of the Va people live. There, the economy already bore feudal manorial characteristics.

In some areas in Yongde, Zhenkang and Fengqing, where a few Vas live with other ethnic peoples, the Va economy had developed into the stage of feudal landlord economy.

Post-liberation Development In December 1949, the Vas, together with other nationalities in Yunnan Province, were liberated. In 1951 the Central Government sent a delegation to the Ava mountainous areas, helping the Va people solve urgent problems in production and daily life, and to settle disputes among tribes. The Menglian Dai-Lahu-Va Autonomous County was set up in 1954 and the Cangyuan Va Autonomous County in 1955. They were followed by the founding of Ximeng Va Autonomous County in 1964 and the Cangyuan Va Autonomous County in 1965. In the course of practising regional autonomy, many Va cadres were trained, paving the way for implementing the Communist Party's united front policy, for further winning over and uniting with the patriots from the upper strata of the Vas, and for carrying out social reform in Va areas.

Different steps and methods were adopted by the People's Government in social reform, taking the unbalanced socio-economic development in various areas into consideration. The goal was socialism. In Zhenkang and Yongde the Vas, together with local Hans, carried out land reform and abolished the system of feudal exploitation and oppression. Then they carried out socialist reform in agriculture. In most of the areas in Ximeng, Cangyuan, Shuangjiang, Gengma and Menglian, exploiting and primitive backward elements were reformed in gradual steps through mutual aid and cooperation, with government support, so as to pass into socialism.

Two important economic measures were taken in the Va areas to improve production and people's life. One was to provide the poor Va peasants with food and seeds, draught cattle and farm tools, while helping them build irrigation projects to extend rice paddy fields. The other was to set up more state trading organizations to expand state trade. These measures brought changes to local production and daily life, enabling the people to do away with usury and exploitation by landlords.

Through transforming mountains, harnessing rivers and extending paddy fields, the Va people in the Ximeng area changed their primitive cultivation methods.

In pre-liberation days, eight out of 10 Va people were half-starved. For several months in a year they had to eat wild vegetables and wild starchy tubers. Their ordinary meal was thick gruel cooked with vegetables. However, by 1981 they owned 1,600 hectares of paddy fields, achieving good yields. In some fields the output per hectare came to 7.5 tons.

Industry was unheard of in the Ava mountainous areas in the past. Now there are hydro-electric power stations, tractor stations and locally-run workshops producing and repairing farm tools, smelting iron and processing food. The first generation of workers has come into being.

Industrial and agricultural development brought marked changes to the commerce, transport and communications, culture and education and health of the Va people. A case in point is Yanshi Village in Cangyuan County. There wasn't a presentable house except those owned by the village head. Now it has grown into a rising township, with a bank, a health centre, primary and middle schools, a farm tool plant and tailors' shops as well as many stores. The village has become an economic and cultural centre.

Many new schools have been set up in the Va areas. Nine out of 10 Va children are at school. Cultural centres, film projection teams and bookstores broaden the knowledge of the Va people and enrich their life. Every county in the Ava mountainous area has hospitals.

Over the past 30 years and more a new atmosphere of unity has prevailed in the Va areas. The old enmities, resulting from abduction of oxen and headhunting, have been replaced by mutual help in production and construction through mediation. Clan warfare which was common in pre-liberation days, seldom takes place.

The Lahus

The Lahu ethnic minority has a population of 304,200, mainly distributed in the Lancang Lahu Autonomous County in Simao Prefecture, Southern Lincang Prefecture and Menghai County in western Xishuangbanna in Yunnan Province. Others live in counties along the Lancang River.

The subtropical hilly areas along the Lancang River where the Lahu people live in compact communities are fertile, suitable for planting rice paddy, dry rice, maize, buckwheat as well as tea, tobacco, and sisal hemp. There are China fir and pine, camphor and nanmu trees in the dense forests, which are the habitat of such animals as red deer, muntjacs, wild oxen, bears, peacocks and parrots. Found here are also valuable medicinal herbs like pseudo-ginseng and devilpepper.

Mineral resources in the area include iron, copper, lead, aluminum, coal, silver, mica and tungsten.

The Lahu language belongs to the Chinese-Tibetan language family. Most of the Lahus also speak Chinese and the language of the Dais. In the past the custom of passing messages by wood-carving was prevalent. In some parts the alphabetic script invented by Western priests was in use. After liberation, the script was reformed and became their formal written language.

History   Legend says that the forbears of the Lahu people, who were hunters, began migrating southward to a lush grassland which they discovered while pursuing a red deer.

Some scholars hold that during the Western Han Dynasty more than 2,000 years ago, the "Kunmings," the nomadic tribe pasturing in the Erhai area in western Yunnan, might be the forbears of certain ethnic groups, including the Lahus. Then, the "Kunming" people still lived in a primitive society "without common rulers." They belonged to different clans engaged in hunting. The Lahu people once were known for their skill at hunting tigers. They roved over the lush slopes of the towering Ailao and Wuliang mountains.

In the 8th century, after the rise of the Nanzhao regime in Yunnan, the Lahu people were compelled to move south. By no later than the beginning of the 18th century they already had settled in their present-day places. Influenced by the feudal production methods of neighbouring Han and Dai peoples, they turned to agriculture. With economic development, they gradually passed into a feudal system, and their life style and customs were more or less influenced by the Hans and Dais.

Customs and Habits   Lahu men wear a collarless jacket buttoned on the right side, baggy long trousers, and a black turban. The women wear a long robe with slits along the legs. Around the collar and slits are sewn broad strips of colour cloth with beautiful patterns and studded with silver ornaments. Women's head dress extends a dozen feet long, hanging down the back and reaching the waist. Where the Lahus come into frequent contact with the Hans and Dais, they also are fond of the garments of those two nationalities.

Their houses are built on stilts, with the space below reserved for domestic animals. The style of building is similar to the Dais'.

Monogamy was practised. In some areas such as Bakanai Township in Lancang County and Menghai County in Xishuangbanna, young people were free to choose their marriage partners, and only a few marriages were arranged by parents. Women played the dominant part in marital relations. After the wedding, the husband stayed permanently in the wife's home, and kinship was traced through the mother's side. In other areas, men played the dominant part in marriage. Betrothal gifts were sent through a matchmaker before the wedding. On the evening of the wedding day the husband was required to stay in the bride's home with his production tools. After liberation, with the implementation of the marriage law, the old custom of sending betrothal gifts had been less strictly observed.

Traditionally, the dead were cremated. During the burial, mourners were led to the common cremation ground by women, who carried on their backs articles used by the deceased people during their life time. In some places, the dead person was buried, and the tomb piled with stones. The whole village stopped working in mourning on the burial day.

Religion The Lahu people used to worship many gods. Their supergod was "Exia," who was believed to have created the Universe and mankind, and had the power to decide the good or bad fortune of people. Exia was placed in a forbidden place in the depth of mountainous forests, unapproachable by non-Lahu peoples. They also worshipped the deities of earth, revenge and sotrm.

Bakanai Township in Lancang County has retained Lahu people's traditional facilities for making offerings — erect poles carved with geometric designs.

In the early Qing Dynasty, Mahayana (a sect of Buddhism) was introduced into the Lahu areas from Dali by Buddhist monks. These Han and Bai monks obviously were opposed to the Qing regime, and in the peasants' wars that followed Buddhism played an important part in mobilizing the people. In Shuangjiang and Lancang counties, religion had come to merge with politics. Military suppression by the Qing government and defeat of the peasant uprisings led to the disintegration of local Buddhist bodies. However, as a religion Mahayana still prevailed among the people.

The music and dances of the Lahu people have their unique styles and are permeated with life. There are many melodies and songs. Traditional musical instruments include the lusheng (a reed-pipe wind instrument) and three-stringed guitar. Their dances, numbering about 40, are characterized by foot tapping and swinging to the left. The Lahus have a rich stock of oral literature, most of which is related to physical labour. The most popular form of poetry is called "Tuopuke" or puzzle.

Socio-economic Forms The social economy in the Lahu areas had remained stagnant for a long time. Before liberation, it fell into two categories:

— Feudal landlord economy, which was prevalent among the Lahus in Lancang County as well as among those in Shuangjiang, Lincang, Jinggu, Zhenyuan, Yuanjiang and Mojiang counties, who accounted for one half of the total Lahu population in these areas. Compared with the other Lahu areas, economic development in these areas was faster. As a result of the influence by the Hans, a feudal landlord economy was formed between the 1880s and 1920s. The Lahus used the same farm tools as the Hans, but due to their relatively backward farming technique, yields were low.

Handicrafts included ironwork, weaving and bamboo handiwork, but few of the products were sold on the market. In agriculture, land ownership was rather concentrated. Besides Han landlords, there were a few Lahu landlords. Land rent came to 50 per cent of the crop yield. Han landlords and merchants exploited the Lahu peasants through usurious interest.

— Dai chieftain-dominated feudal manorial economy having remnants of primitive communes, which was prevalent in southwestern Lancang, Menglian, Gengma, Ximeng, Cangyuan and Xishuangbanna, where another half of the Lahu population lived. The Lahus led a poor life and their production was backward under the rule of Dai chieftains and the exploitation by Han landlords and merchants.

One of the ways in which the Dai chieftains ruled and exploited the Lahu peasants was through establishing the tribute-paying system. This made the peasants subordinate to them. Dai lords also reduced Lahu peasants to the status of serfs who were required to do such jobs for the chieftains as husking grain and clearing nightsoil and manure. Remnants of the primitive communal system included mutual aid in production, common ownership of land and matriarchal clan system.

New Life The liberation of the Lahu areas took place in early 1950. After wiping out the last bandits to restore social security, the People's Government distributed grain, seeds, cattle, farm tools, cotton cloth, salt and interest-free loans to help the Lahu people restore and develop production, and overcome difficulties in daily life.

Much effort was also made by the government to train Lahu cadres and to push on the policy of regional nationality autonomy. In April 1953, the Lancang Lahu Autonomous County was established. In June 1954 the Menglian Dai-Lahu-Va Autonomous County was set up. For the first time in history, the Lahu people had the right to manage their own affairs.

Land reform was later carried out under the leadership of the People's Government, to help the Lahu people end poverty. After some years, agricultural producers' cooperatives were organized throughout the Lahu areas.

A series of measures were adopted by the Lahu peasants to bring about fundamental changes in their agricultural production. These included the extension of paddy fields, applying scientific farming techniques, and the adoption of intensive cultivation.

Farm machines are now in extensive use, while small hydroelectric stations built over the years have brought electricity to most Lahu villages.

About a century ago, more than 1,000 households of Lahu, Dai and Han nationalities lived in Menglangba, the seat of present-day Lancang Lahu Autonomous County government. However, on the eve of liberation, this once flourishing city only had a population of about 200. It had become a desolate, disease-ridden land. The first batch of dwellings appeared soon after liberation. After the founding of the autonomous county, offices, department stores, food companies, hotels, a bank, bookshops, a post office, a hospital and a cinema were built along the broad main street.

In the past, practically all manufactured goods came from other areas. Now many enterprises run by the local government have gone up. Local industries include machine building, sugar refining, tea processing, mining, cement production, printing and power generating. The state-owned Lancang Lead Mine is a well-known enterprise in Yunnan Province.

Transport and communications have undergone changes, too. In addition to the trunk highway linking Simao with outlying counties, motor roads reach townships and villages.

A good number of primary and middle schools have been built since liberation. The overwhelming majority of the school-age children now attend school. In some schools minority students enjoy free tuition. The Lahu people now have their own college students. Four out of 10 primary and middle school teachers come from ethnic minorities.

Epidemic diseases were once rampant in the Lahu areas. Now hospitals and malaria prevention and treatment stations have been set up in all the autonomous counties of the Lahu people. Anti-epidemic teams have been dispatched by the People's Government to the areas, giving free medical care. Epidemic diseases have been controlled.

The Naxis

The Naxi nationality has a population of 245,200, most of whom live in concentrated communities in the Lijiang Naxi Autonomous County in Yunnan Province, the rest being scattered in Weixi, Zhongdian, Ninglang, Deqin, Yongsheng, Heqing, Jianchuan and Lanping counties in Yunnan Province, as well as Yanyuan, Yanbian and Muli counties in Sichuan Province. A small number live in Mangkang County of Tibet Autonomous Region.

The Naxi areas, traversed by the Jinsha, Lancang and Yalong rivers, and the Yunling, Xueshan and Yulong mountain ranges, have a complicated terrain. There are cold mountainous areas, uplands, basins, rivers and valleys, averaging 2,700 metres above sea level. The climate varies from cold and temperate to subtropical. Rainfall is plentiful.

Agriculture is the main occupation of the Naxi people. The chief crops are rice, maize, wheat, potatoes, beans, hemp and cotton. The bend of the Jinsha River is heavily forested, and Yulong Mountain is known at home and abroad as a "flora storehouse." The extensive dense forests contain Chinese fir, Korean pine, Yunnan pine and other valuable trees, as well as many varieties of herbs including fritillary bulbs, Chinese caterpillar fungus and musk.

There are rich reserves of such non-ferrous metals as gold,

silver, copper, aluminium and manganese. Water resources are abundant.

The Naxi language belongs to the Chinese-Tibetan language family. More than 1,000 years ago, the Naxi people had already created pictographic characters called the "Dongba" script and a syllabic writing known as the "Geba" script. With these scripts they recorded a lot of beautiful folklore, legends, poems and religious classics. However, they were difficult to master, and in 1957 the people's government helped the Naxi design an alphabetic script. Over the past few hundred years, as the Naxi people have come into closer contact with the people in other parts of China politically, economically and culturally, the oral and written Chinese has become an important means of communication in Naxi society.

History According to historical documents, the forefathers of the Naxi people were closely related to a tribe called "Maoniu Yi" in the Han Dynasty (206 B.C.-A.D. 220), "Mosha Yi" in the Jin Dynasty (265-420) and "Moxie Yi" in the Tang Dynasty (618-907).

Between the early 10th century and the middle of the 13th century, production in the Lijiang area underwent marked changes, as agriculture replaced livestock breeding as the main occupation of the people. Scores of agricultural, handicraft, mineral and livestock products were turned out, and the county presented a picture of prosperity. During that period, a number of slave-owning groups in Ninglang, Lijiang and Weixi counties gradually grew into a feudal manorial lord caste.

In 1278 the Yuan Dynasty (1206-1368) established Lijiang Prefecture representing the imperial court in Yunnan Province. This resulted in closer links between the Lijiang area and the centre of the empire.

In the early Ming Dynasty (1368-1644), the leader of the Naxi people, named Mude, was made the hereditary chieftain of Lijiang Prefecture, exercising control over the Naxi people and other ethnic groups in the vicinity. Throughout the Ming Dynasty, the hereditary chieftains from the Mu family kept taxes and tribute flowing to the Ming court in the form of silver and grain. The Ming, in turn, relied on the Mu family as the mainstay for the control of the people of various nationalities in northwestern Yunnan Province.

Later, with the development of the productive forces, buying, selling and renting of land began to take place in the Naxi areas, marking the beginning of a landlord economy.

From 1723, during the Qing Dynasty (1644-1911), hereditary local chieftains in the Lijiang area began to be replaced by court officials and the hereditary chieftain surnamed Mu thus became the local administrator.

Art and Literature   Naxi literature is rich in form and content. Besides works by Naxi scholars and writers, there is a repository of oral folk literature. "Genesis," "The Rich Steal Oxen," "Revenge" and "Song of Elopement" are characterized by simple and fresh expressions, and distinctive national flavour. The "Dongba Scripture," a religious work, dates back to the Tang Dynasty. Written in the pictographic script, it describes the various aspects of life of the Naxi people during their long transition from slavery to feudalism. It is extremely important for the study of Naxi literature, history and religion.

The Naxis are fond of singing and dancing, especially at weddings and funerals. The most popular songs are descriptive and short. They are sung at very high pitch and with strong rhythms, to the accompaniment of simple dances. The most common musical instruments are flutes, reed pipes and windstring instruments. The ancient musical piece, "Baishaxiyue," which dates back to the Yuan Dynasty, was rediscovered and preserved after liberation.

Naxi architecture, sculpture and painting have reached fairly high standards. Moreover, they are mixed with the traditional styles of the Hans and Tibetans. Some famous buildings preserved in Lijiang, such as the "Dabao Palace," "Glazed Hall," "Dading Pavilion" and "Five-Phoenix Chamber," were all built during the Ming Dynasty. All the murals in these buildings have the concise and harmonious strokes of Tibetan painting, and the style of Taoist and Buddhist paintings of the Tang Dynasty. Modern Naxi painting has made fresh progress since liberation.

Religion   Before liberation, most Naxi people were followers of the "Dongba" religion, which was a form of shamanism. Sorcerers, called "Dongba," were invited to chant scriptures at weddings, funerals, the New Year Day and other festivals. Some of the Naxis were followers of Lamaism. Buddhism, Taoism and Christianity only had limited access to the Lijiang area.

Customs and Habits Naxi women wear wide-sleeved loose gowns, with jackets and long trousers, tied with richly decorated belts at the waist. They often wear sheepskin slung over the shoulder, on which are seven stars exquisitely embroidered, with sun and moon symbols, one on each side. This reflects the Naxis' admiration for diligence — "people start working early in the morning and do not stop until late in the evening." Women in Ninglang County wear short jackets and long skirts reaching the ground, with many folds. They wrap large black cotton turbans around their heads and wear big silver earrings.

Men's garments are similar to those of the Han people.

The traditional festivals include the "Farm-Tool Fair" in January, "God of the Rain Festival" in March, and "Mule and Horse Fair" in July. There are also the Lunar New Year, the Pure Brightness Festival, the Dragon Boat Festival, the Mid-Autumn Festival and the Torch Festival — all being the same as those of the Hans.

Cremation has been a tradition since ancient times, but in some of the Naxi areas the custom of burying the dead was adopted in the late Qing Dynasty. It was common in the past to chant scriptures at the funeral ceremony to expiate the sins of the dead.

The monogamous family under the feudal landlord economy was the main type of Naxi family in Lijiang, Weixi and Yongsheng counties before liberation. However, the man enjoyed a predominant status in the family while the woman had little say and was denied the right to inherit property. Young people's marriages were all arranged by their parents.

Among some of the Naxi people in Yongning County in Yunnan Province and Yanyuan County in Sichuan Province, there still existed remnants of a matriarchal family structure until the eve of the democratic reform after liberation. The pedigree of the family was traced back through the maternal line, and children lived with the mother. The woman was the head of the family, and the property was passed to the children through the mother, or to the nephews through the mother's brothers. Women comprised the main labour force, respected at home and in outside society.

Social Economy The Naxi communities had reached the stage of feudal society long before the nationwide liberation in 1949, though the stages of development were not the same. In Lijiang, southern Weixi and Yongsheng counties where a feudal landlord economy was prevalent, certain factors of capitalism began to take shape. In Jinjiang and Sanba in Zhongdian County the remnants of manorial economy could still be found. In northern Weixi and part of Ninglang counties in Yunnan Province and Yanyuan County in Sichuan Province, the main form of economy was manorial.

The level of agricultural production was higher in the landlord economy areas. The landlords and rich peasants, who accounted for 10 per cent of the population, owned 60 to 70 per cent of the land. They exploited the peasants through land rent, usury and hiring them as farmhands. The rates of the rent ranged from 50 to 80 per cent of the crops harvested and the annual interest rates of the usury reached as much as 300 per cent. They also exploited the peasants through their privileges, with the backing of reactionary political rulers. They forced the peasants to work for them without pay, to present them with gifts, and to render various kinds of corvee labour.

In the manorial economy areas, the manorial lords owned almost all the land, water resources, grasslands and forests. In some places, each peasant had to do as many as 150 days of unpaid labour a year. The manorial lords in the Yongning area invented 35 pretexts to exploit the peasants. They included the so-called fish tax, water tax, firewood tax, death tax, and passer-by tax.

Under the manorial lord, the commoners were second-class citizens. Generally, the commoners did not own any land, and only after they had accepted merciless exploitation, such as heavy taxes and corvees, were they given a small piece of land. In this way they actually became serfs tied to the land of the lords. If they failed to pay their debts or committed crimes, they could be reduced to the status of household slaves. Completely under their masters' disposal, they could be sold, bought, exchanged or given as presents.

During the War of Resistance Against Japan, foreign trade in China's southeastern coastal area came to a standstill and transport between China and Burma was blockaded by Japan. This resulted in an unprecedented boosting of Sino-Indian trade, and Lijiang became a trading centre for India, Tibet and China's interior. Millionaire businessmen (some being Naxis) began to appear.

Lijiang County had a more developed handicraft industry than the other Naxi areas where landlord economy predominated. It covered iron, copper, carpentry, tanning, textiles, paper-making, tailoring, construction and sculpture. Copper articles and leather products were particularly famous.

Struggle for Liberation During the long period before liberation, the Naxi people, like people elsewhere in China, groaned under the oppression and exploitation of feudalism, imperialism and bureaucrat-capitalism. During the early 20th century, French imperialists grabbed the rights to exploit the Qifu mineral resources, and the British invaded Pianma in Yunnan Province. They met with strong opposition from the Lisu and Naxi peoples.

In April 1936, a Red Army unit under the Second Front Army led by Ren Bishi and He Long stopped over in Lijiang city on their march to the north to fight the Japanese aggressors. They were greeted warmly by the local people. They broke open prisons, distributed to the poor grain taken from landlords' barns, and acquainted the people with the Chinese Communist Party's stand on resisting Japanese aggression and its policy on national equality, thus greatly enhancing the understanding of the Party by the Naxi people.

In 1948, under the leadership of the Yunnan underground organizations of the Chinese Communist Party, the Naxi people set up in the countryside peasants' associations for fighting against Kuomintang rulers. They called on the peasants to refuse to pay rents and taxes, and refuse to be recruited into the Kuomintang army. Lijiang was eventually liberated on July 1, 1949.

In the early post-liberation days, while carrying out a series of measures to restore social order in the Naxi areas, the people's government helped the local people restore and develop production, and improve their living standards. Much was done to enhance the friendly relations among the different nationalities, paving the way for carrying out democratic reforms.

Land reform guided by prudence was carried out, and different measures were adopted according to specific conditions. The reform was completed in the Lijiang area in 1953, where landlord economy predominated. The land distributed to the poor peasants averaged two to three mu (or two- to three-fifteenths of a hectare) per capita, and grain produced averaged 840 kg per household.

Where a manorial economy predominated, feudal exploitation was abolished after peaceful negotiations with leaders of the upper strata.

The democratic reform greatly rallied the peasants' initiative in production. For example, the peasants in Yanjiao Village, Lijiang County, adopted the use of fertilizer right after reform. They also built eight big pools to extend their irrigated farmland. That year, their harvest averaged 240 kg per capita, more than doubling the figure of the previous year.

The reform was followed by socialist transformation, which was carried out in stages. By the end of 1957, socialist transformation in agriculture, handicrafts and capitalist commerce had been completed in the Naxi areas.

Liberation has also brought the Naxi people political equality and the rights to manage their own affairs. In 1954 the people in Lijiang County held their first congress, and Naxi delegates accounted for 59 per cent of the total. The Lijiang Naxi Autonomous County was set up in April 1961. The people's government has paid great attention to training local cadres, and today most of the leading cadres at various levels come from the Naxi nationality.

As a result of large-scale farmland capital construction, the Naxi areas had levelled 12,400 hectares of land for machine ploughing by 1981 and completed a number of small water-conservancy projects which extended the irrigated area by 7,000 hectares. These measures, plus scientific farming, have brought better harvests than ever before, and at the same time promoted forestry, animal husbandry, fishing and other sideline occupations.

There was no industry to speak of in the Lijiang area in pre-liberation days. In 1952, four small enterprises with a total annual output value of some 800,000 yuan were set up. The number of enterprises grew to 74 in 1981, and the output value came to over 20 million yuan. As a result, the number of Naxis working in industry keeps increasing.

There were no motor roads in the Naxi areas before liberation. Goods were carried by porters or on horseback along meandering paths. Now the county has a complete highway network.

Rapid development also was registered in education. In 1981, there were more than 600 primary schools and seven secondary schools in Lijiang County alone. In addition, there were 24 junior middle schools run by the township and village governments. The number of primary and middle school teachers totalled 2,570 — six times the pre-liberation figure. This provides a sharp contrast with the past, when not a single middle school was to be found in some of the counties and not a primary school in most of the villages in the Lijiang area.

The Naxi areas, where diseases were rampant, now have village clinics, health centres and epidemic-prevention stations. Local people enjoy free medical treatment, and most of the epidemic diseases have been brought under control.

The Jingpos

The Jingpos, numbering 93,000, live mostly in the Dehong Dai-Jingpo Autonomous Prefecture, Yunnan Province, together with the De'ang, Lisu, Achang and Han peoples. A few of them are found in the Nujiang Lisu Autonomous Prefecture.

The Jingpos mainly inhabit tree-covered mountainous areas some 1,500 metres above sea level, where the climate is warm. Countless snaking mountain paths connect Jingpo villages, which usually consist of two-storey bamboo houses hidden in dense forests and bamboo groves.

The area abounds in rare woods and medicinal herbs. Among cash crops are rubber, tung oil, tea, coffee, shellac and silk cotton. The area's main mineral resources are iron, copper, lead, coal, gold, silver and precious stones. Tigers, leopards, bears, pythons, pheasants and parrots live in the region's forests.

The Jingpos speak a language belonging to the Tibetan-Burmese family of the Chinese-Tibetan language system. Until 70 years ago, when an alphabetic system of writing based on Latin letters was introduced, the Jingpos kept records by notching wood or tying knots. Calculations were done by counting beans. The new system of writing was not widely used, however. After liberation, with the help of the government, the Jingpo people have started publishing newspapers, periodicals and books in their own language.

History According to local legends and historical records, Jingpo ancestors in ancient times inhabited the southern part of the Xikang-Tibetan Plateau. They gradually migrated south to the northwestern part of Yunnan, west of the Nujiang River. The local people, together with the newly-arrived Jingpos, were called "Xunchuanman," who lived mainly on hunting.

During the Yuan Dynasty (1271-1368), the imperial court set up a provincial administrative office in Yunnan, which had the Xunchuan area under its jurisdiction. As production developed, various Jingpo groups gradually merged into two big tribal alliances — Chashan and Lima. They were headed by hereditary nobles called "shanguan." Freemen and slaves formed another two classes. Deprived of any personal freedom, the slaves bore the surname of their masters and did forced labour.

During the early 15th century, the Ming Dynasty (1368-1644), which instituted a system of appointing local hereditary headmen in national minority areas, set up two area administrative offices and appointed Jingpo nobles as administrators. In the Qing Dynasty (1644-1911), the area inhabited by Jingpos was under the jurisdiction of prefectural and county offices set up by the Qing court.

Beginning from the 16th century, large numbers of Jingpo people moved to the Dehong area. Under the influence of the Hans and Dais, who had advanced production skills and practised a feudal economy, Jingpos began to use iron tools including the plough, and later learned to grow rice in paddy fields. This learning process was accompanied by raised productivity and a transition toward feudalism. Slaves revolted or ran away. All these factors brought the slave system to a quick end in the middle of last century.

Pre-Liberation Life Before China's liberation in 1949, there were primitive commune vestiges in Jingpo society. An area ruled by a "shanguan" was a rural commune. Each village in the commune was headed by a tribal chief who assisted the "shanguan" in administrative affairs. Even though private ownership had taken root, the waste land and mountain slopes within the boundaries of the rural commune belonged to all its members, who had the right to reclaim a piece of land and would forfeit it if left in waste again. Paddy fields, however, were either privately owned or tilled permanently by certain people. Often, noblemen or headmen, taking advantage of their privilege to allocate land, gradually gained more paddy fields for themselves, or even took paddy fields away from village members by force. This was followed by the selling, buying, mortgaging and leasing of paddy fields. At the time of the liberation of the Jingpo areas in 1950, landlords constituted one per cent of total Jingpo households, and rich peasants two per cent. The two groups had possession of 20 to 30 per cent of all paddy fields and 20 per cent of farm cattle. Of the common Jingpo peasants, only 15 per cent owned some paddy fields and farm cattle, while the majority were poor labourers with little land and few farm cattle and tools. Apart from being exploited in the way of land and cattle rent, usurers' interest rates and ultra-low pay, poor peasants each year had to pay a certain amount of "official rice" to their "shanguan" and do three to five days of corvee.

The basic unit of Jingpo society was the small family of husband and wife. Some "shanguans" and rich peasants practised polygamy. The family was headed by the father. A family with only daughters might have a son-in-law to live with it, but the son-in-law did not change his surname and his children would take his surname instead of that of his father-in-law. A childless family could adopt a son, who was required to support his foster parents and had the right to inherit their property. Elderly people without children were usually looked after by their relatives. The Jingpo family retained the system of inheritance by the youngest son. While the eldest son would set up a separate family after marriage, the youngest son would remain to support his parents and inherit most of their property. The youngest son had a definitely higher status than his brothers. Women had a low status in Jingpo society.

The Jingpos practised a hierarchical intermarriage system, that is, intermarriage between "shanguan" families and between common peasant households. While young people could freely socialize, their marriage, often involving many betrothal gifts, was arranged by their parents. Bride snatching was a common occurrence. When people died they were buried in the ground except for those who died an unnatural death. They were without exception cremated and their ashes buried.

Jingpo people lived in thatched cottages of bamboo and wood except a few "shanguans" and headmen, who had houses of brick and tile. The cottages, oblong in shape, had two storeys. The lower floor, about one metre above the ground, is for keeping animals, while the upper floor, usually partitioned into four to ten rooms with bamboo walls, is the living quarters for family members. In the middle of every room is a fireplace, around which people sleep. Every seven or eight years cottages have to be rebuilt. Rebuilding, having the help of all villagers, is completed in several days.

Rice is the staple food, although maize is more important in some places. Vegetables, beans, potatoes and yams are grown in cottage gardens. Jingpos also gather wild herbs and fruit as supplementary food.

Jingpo men usually wear black jackets with buttons down the front and short and loose trousers. Elderly people have a pigtail tied on top of their head and covered with a black turban. Young people prefer white turbans. Jingpo men going out invariably wear long knives on their waist or take rifles with them. All carry elaborately-embroidered bags containing items such as areca and tobacco. Jingpo women usually wear black jackets with buttons down the front middle or front left. Matching the jacket is a colourful knit skirt and a woolen shinguard. Women like wearing silver ornaments.

Jingpos are good singers and dancers. Group dancing, their major dancing form, reflects their life, work, war and sacrificial rites. It sometimes involves more than 1,000 people, their singing reverberating in nearby mountain valleys. Jingpo musicians use wooden drums, "elephant-leg" drums, gongs, cymbals and bamboo flutes.

Jingpos used to practise fetishism, believing that spirits live in the sun, moon, birds, animals, boulders and trees, bringing fortune or misfortune to human beings. As a result, superstition dominates their lives and taboos abound. Sacrificial rites accompanied sowing, harvesting, disease, weddings, funerals and combat.

Post-liberation Development   In 1950, liberation came to the Jingpo area. The Dehong Dai-Jingpo Autonomous Region was established in 1953 (changed to an autonomous prefecture in 1956). The Jingpo people elected their own representatives to the leading bodies of the autonomous region. In addition, the Jingpos have deputies to the Provincial People's Congress and National People's Congress.

To fundamentally change the backward conditions in Jingpo areas, the central and local governments helped the Jingpos get organized for cooperative production shortly after liberation. Measures were taken to do away with class exploitation and vestiges of primitiveness.

Since liberation, the Jingpo people have transformed virgin forests into tea plantations and orchards, and reclaimed barren mountain slopes into terraced fields. They have built tractor stations, reservoirs and power stations. Their grain production and income from sideline occupations have increased.

Industry, which was nonexistent in Jingpo areas before liberation, also has developed. The autonomous prefecture has built a number of small and medium-sized enterprises including a power plant, a motor factory, a farm tools factory and a factory producing daily-use chemicals.

There has been progress in other respects. Highways have been built on the formerly inaccessible Jingpo Mountain. High-tension power lines extend to many places, while a wire-broadcasting network covers almost every Jingpo household. Brick houses have begun to replace thatched cottages. Formerly poor peasants now have enough grain and different clothes for different seasons. Some more affluent peasants have bought radios, sewing machines and new hunting rifles. An increasing number of small hydroelectric stations have made electricity available to many Jingpo villages.

The ruling classes before liberation established no schools for the Jingpo people, resulting that very few people were literate. Now, however, there are middle schools in every county and primary schools in every community. Central and local ethnic minority institutes have trained group after group of Jingpo cadres. The

Dehong Prefecture boasts some 1,500 Jingpo cadres, accounting for 1.7 per cent of the total Jingpo population in the prefecture.

Violent epidemics, especially malaria, used to ravage the area. Since liberation, clinics have been set up in key Jingpo communities and many medical workers of Jingpo origin have been trained. Efforts have been made to improve environmental hygiene and drinking water. There has been a marked decrease in disease incidence. Formerly rampant epidemics such as cholera and the plague have been stamped out, and malaria, the most serious threat to local people's health, brought under control. The once desolate Jingpo Mountain is beginning to enjoy a prosperity it has never known before.

The Blangs

The Blang people, numbering 58,000, live mainly in Mt. Blang, Xiding and Bada areas of Menghai County in the Xishuangbanna Dai Autonomous Prefecture in southwestern Yunnan Province. There are also scattered Blang communities in the neighbouring Lincang and Simao prefectures. All the Blangs inhabit mountainous areas 1,500-2,000 metres above sea level. The Blangs in Xishuangbanna have always lived harmoniously with their neighbours of both the other minority nationalities and the majority Han.

The Blang people inhabit an area with a warm climate, plentiful rainfall, fertile soil and rich natural resources. The main cash crops are cotton, sugar-cane and the worldfamous Pu'er tea. In the dense virgin forests grow various valuable trees, and valued medicinal herbs such as pseudoginseng, rauwolfia verticillata (used for lowering high blood pressure) and lemongrass, from which a high-grade fragrance can be extracted. The area abounds in copper, iron, sulphur and rock crystal.

The Blangs speak a language belonging to the South Asian language family. The language does not have a written form, but Blangs often know the Dai, Va and Han languages.

According to historical records, an ancient tribe called the "Pu" were the earliest inhabitants of the Lancang and Nujiang river valleys. These people may have been the ancestors of today's Blangs.

Pre-liberation Life Before liberation, the Blang people were very superstitious. Ancestor worship was a part of their way of life. The Blangs in Xishuangbanna area believed in Hinayana Buddhism, as a result of the influence of the Dai tribe. The Blangs' Buddhist temples and social systems were similar to those of the Dais.

Blang men wear collarless jackets with buttons down the front and loose black trousers. They wear turbans of black or white cloth. Men have the tradition of tattooing their limbs, chests and bellies. Blang women, like their Dai sisters, wear tight collarless jackets and tight striped or black skirts. They tie their hair into a bun and cover it with layers of cloth.

Their staple diet consists of rice, maize and beans. They prefer their food sour and hot. Drinking home-brewed wine and smoking tobacco are their main pastimes. Blang women like chewing betel-nut and regard teeth dyed black with betel-nut juice as beautiful.

The Blangs live in two-storeyed balustraded bamboo houses. The ground floor is for keeping domestic animals and storing stone mortars used for hulling rice. The upper floor is the living quarters, and in the middle of the main room is a fireplace for cooking, heating and light. When a family builds a house, nearly all the grown-ups in the village offer help, completing the project in two or three days.

The Blang nationality has a rich store of folk tales and ballads transmitted orally. Their songs and dances show the strong influence of their Dai neighbours. Elephant-leg drums, cymbals and three-stringed plucked instruments provide musical accompaniment for dancing. People in the Blang Mountain area revel in their energetic "knife dance." Young people like a courting dance called the "circle dance." For the Blangs in the Mujiang area, New Year's Day and weddings are occasions for dancing and singing, often lasting the whole night.

The Blangs seek spouses outside their own clans and practise monogamy. With a few exceptions, mainly parental interference, young Blangs are fairly free to choose marriage partners.

The death of a person is followed by scripture chanting by

Buddhist monks or shamans to "dispel the devil," and the funeral is held within three days. Each village generally has a common cemetery divided according to clans or people having the same surnames. The dead are buried in the ground except for those dying a violent death, who are cremated.

Past Social Conditions Before liberation in 1950, social development was uneven in different Blang localities. The Blang communities in the Lincang and Simao prefectures were fairly developed socially and economically, as their members lived together with Hans and other more socially advanced peoples. Except for cemeteries and forests, which remained common property, land had become privately owned. A landlord economy had long been established, with landlords and rich peasants taking possession of the best land through exorbitant interest rates, mortgages, pawning and political privileges. Poor Blang peasants, aside from being at the mercy of landlords and rich peasants of Blang origin, were exploited by propertied classes of Han and other ethnic minorities. The Bao-Jia system (an administrative system organized on the basis of households, instituted by the Kuomintang government in 1932) tightened political control over all the Blang areas. The Kuomintang government, in collaboration with local landlords and tyrants, caused great suffering to the Blang people by excessive levying of taxes and forced conscription.

The Blang communities in Xishuangbanna's Mt. Blang, Xiding and Bada areas were less socially developed and more poverty-stricken. The Blangs had long been subjected to the rule of Dai feudal lords, who exacted from them an annual tribute of money and farm produce. The Dai landlords appointed a number of herreditary headmen called "Ba" from among the Blangs. Each "Ba" had several Blang villages under his rule and collected tributes for the Dai masters.

Blang society in Xishuangbanna retained varying degrees of public ownership of land by the clan or the village, aside from private ownership. A small number of villages had retained characteristics of the primitive commune, which was composed of 20-30 small families who had a common ancestor. Commune farmland, forests and pastures belonged to all the members. Families and individuals had the right to utilize this kind of land, but could not buy or sell it. As productivity developed, however, the patriarchs took advantage of their positions to gradually grab property for themselves, and began to exploit clan members.

Most Blang villages in Xishuangbanna had primitive commune features. Each village consisted of some 100 households belonging to several or a dozen clans of different blood relationships. While farm implements, houses and farm animals belonged to individual households, land, forests and water sources were the village's common property. The different clans took permanent possession of different parts of the public land and allocated their share to small families under them on a regular basis to enable farming on a household basis. The households were entitled to the harvest. Just as each small family depended on its clan membership for the use of land, each clan relied on its affiliation to the village for its right to use the village land. Once a clan moved elsewhere, its land reverted to the village. When a newcomer applied for land, a meeting of headmen would decide how much to allocate.

Members of a village commune were engaged in the same kind of political and religious activities. Public officials of the commune, namely the headmen, were elected.

Gradually, however, private ownership of land emerged. Many village commune members lost their land, becoming tenants of headmen or rich households. Their land henceforth assumed a completely private nature: it could be sold or bought, mortgaged or rented. Patriarchs or the elected headman of a village commune, taking advantage of their position, often took permanent possession of large amounts of good land.

Production was at an extremely low level before liberation in Xishuangbanna's Blang area. Agriculture was the economic mainstay of Blang society, with dry rice as the dominant crop, followed by tea and cotton. At the beginning of the spring ploughing season, patriarchs would organize clan members to clear forest land and allocate it among individual households for farming. Harvests were poor. The Blangs' low income contrasted sharply with their heavy economic burden, which included tribute, high interest to money lenders, different kinds of taxes and corvee.

Post-liberation Life In the spring of 1950, the Chinese People's Liberation Army entered the Blang area. By driving out bandits and local tyrants, and taking measures to protect the lives and property of the people of different nationalities, the army soon stabilized social order in this frontier region. This was followed by the people's government sending work teams to help the Blangs develop production and establish grassroots organs of power. Blangs sent their representatives to the prefectural and county people's congresses, where they exercised their rights as masters of their own affairs.

In light of the actual conditions in the Blang area, the people's government conducted a series of social reforms aimed at gradually eliminating feudal exploitation and vestiges of primitive backwardness hampering social development. Between 1952 and 1953, a land reform similar to that in the Han areas was carried out in Zhenkang, Lincang, Yanxian, Jingdong, Jinggu, Mujiang and other areas. In 1955-56, land reform of a more moderate nature was conducted in Gengma, Shuangjiang and some parts of Lancang, followed by the setting up of production cooperatives. In Xishuangbanna and Lancang's Nuofu area, where vestiges of primitive communism still existed, social reform progressed more slowly. It was not until 1958 that some cooperatives were set up there on a trial basis.

Since liberation, with the help of their Han and Dai neighbours, but mainly relying on themselves, the Blang people have made much progress in adopting more advanced farming methods. They have created paddy fields, built water-conservancy projects, begun using fertilizers and advanced farming tools, and adopted efficient management methods. As a result, the grain harvest has kept going up every year, as has the production of tea and cotton.

Commerce, education and health care have also developed rapidly. An ethnic minorities trading corporation has been set up in every prefecture; in some villages there are shops with a fairly complete stock of farm tools and daily-use items. State trading organizations purchase local produce in large quantities, resulting in increased income for the Blang people.

There were almost no schools in the Blang areas before liberation. In some places, young men were able to learn a little of the Dai language through chanting Dai Buddhist scriptures as trainee monks. Now all Blang children attend primary schools, which are evenly distributed in Blang villages.

The absence of any medical facilities in the Blang area before liberation used to compel sick people to seek help from shamans and other charlatans. In the early post-liberation days, the government sent medical teams to the area, providing free medical care. Later, clinics were set up, local medical teams formed, and medical workers of Blang origin trained. Epidemics such as dysentery, smallpox and malaria were basically brought under control. As a result, the general health conditions of the Blang people have greatly improved.

The Achangs

More than 90 per cent of the 20,400 Achangs live in Longchuan, Lianghe and Luxi counties in the Dehong Dai-Jingpo Autonomous Prefecture in southwestern Yunnan Province. The rest live in Longling County in the neighbouring Baoshan Prefecture.

These areas are on the southern tip of the Gaoligong Mountains. The climate is warm; the land fertile, crisscrossed by the Daying and Longchuan rivers and their numerous tributaries. The river valleys contain many plains, the Fusa and Lasa being the largest of them. Dense forests populated by deers, musk deers and bears cover the mountain slopes. Natural resources, such as coal, iron, copper, lead, mica and graphite, abound.

Achangs speak a language belonging to the Tibetan-Burmese language family of the Chinese-Tibetan system. Most Achangs also can speak Chinese and the language of Dais. Their written language is Chinese.

Achangs treasure their oral culture of ballads, stories and folk tales. Singing alternating duets is a favourite evening recreation of young men and women. Musical instruments used by Achangs include the bamboo qin (a stringed plucked instrument), the bamboo flute, the gourd-shaped sheng (a wind instrument), the sanxian (a three-stringed plucked instrument), the elephant-leg drum and the gong. Drum and monkey dances are among the most popular. Handicrafts include embroidery, lacquering, dyeing, weaving, engraving and silverware making and are known for their elaborate patterns and detail. Achang engraving is extraordinary and can best be seen on furniture, buildings and Buddhist shrines, on which workers have etched vivid forms of animals and plants.

Customs Achang men tend to wear blue, white or black jackets which button down the front, although on the Lasa plain many men wear jackets with buttons toward the left side. Achang women like to wear silver objects on festive occasions. Their clothes vary somewhat depending on where they live, but in general married women wear skirts and jackets with tight sleeves and wrap their heads with black or blue cloth that may go as high as three decimetres. Unmarried women wear trousers and tie their pigtails on top of their heads. Although the habit is disappearing, young men and women used to chew areca, blackening their teeth. For food, Achangs eat rice as their staple and prefer sour dishes. They live in courtyard houses of brick or stone with wood beam supports. Achang villages are connected by gravel paths or roads paved with stone slabs.

The basic unit of the Achang society is the patriarchal, monogamous family. Young men and women are free to choose their spouses. Courting rituals are quite specific. When dusk falls, young men go to bamboo groves near the homes of the young women they desire and play the sheng to win their favour. In some places, groups of young men and women gather around a bonfire, where couples flirt by singing alternate verses. This can go on until dawn. Before liberation, marriages were arranged by parents, which often led to forced marriage and misery for unlucky young lovers. The Achangs have a strict incest taboo: people with the same surname do not marry each other. But intermarriage with Hans and Dais has always been permitted.

Under the Han influence, Achangs generally practise ancestor worship. Most Achangs on the Fusa plain believe in Hinayana, a branch of Buddhism.

Achangs generally bury their dead. In Buddhist areas, funerals are scheduled on holy days and follow the chanting of scripture by monks. One monk leads the funeral procession. As he walks, he holds a long strand of white cloth tied to the coffin, as if he were guiding the dead into the "Heavenly Kingdom." The coffin is to be carried above the heads of the close relatives of the dead, figuratively providing the deceased with a "bridge" to cross the river to the netherworld. The dead are buried without their metal ornaments; even the gold coatings on false teeth must be removed to make sure nothing will contaminate their reincarnation. Those who die of infectious diseases or childbirth are cremated.

Past Socio-economic Conditions Before liberation Achangs in the Lianghe area lived within a familial organization called the "Jiahui" (family meeting). Similar to the patriarchal clan system, the Jiahui had written family rules and chose patriarchs to maintain the feudal order of exploitation. Regarded as inferiors to the men in the Jiahui, women had few rights. They had no right of inheritance. After liberation these practices were gradually eliminated.

The Achangs' ancestors once lived in the Jinsha, Lancang and Nujiang river valleys in northwestern Yunnan. Some of them moved west of the Nujiang River where they gradually evolved from hunters to farmers. According to legends, Achang forbears in those days lived in a matriarchal society with women having a dominant familial and social position and lovers living in group marriages.

During the Tang and Song dynasties (618-1279), the Achang area was controlled by Yunnan's Nanzhao and Dali principalities. During the Ming and Qing dynasties (1368-1911), the Achangs were ruled by Achang hereditary chiefs appointed by — and accountable to — the imperial court. After the bourgeois Revolution of 1911, warlords in Yunnan established an administrative bureau in the Achang area, installing the Bao-Jia system (an administrative system organized on the basis of households, each Jia being made up of 10 households, and each Bao of 10 Jia, by which the warlords enforced their rule at the primary level), oppressing and exploiting the Achang people in collaboration with local chiefs.

Before liberation, feudalism was the dominant economic form in the areas in which the Achangs lived. Farming was done according to the landlord system. Dai chiefs were the feudal lords; most landlords were Hans. Achang landlords were few in number.

Where they ruled, chiefs owned all the land. Aside from collecting taxes to enrich themselves, they used their political privileges to extort "gifts" from peasants on such occasions as holidays, weddings and funerals. The ruling classes, including Achang landlords, prospered through usury and the exploitation of labour.

Under the rule of chiefs, the Achang social structure was destroyed. Achangs were organized into the "gang" (township) and the "zuo" (district), through which the chiefs ruled them and levied tax upon them. "Official tax," "tax on opium," "tax on land" — these and other taxes and levies squeezed the people, draining them of whatever comforts they could accumulate. In addition, many Achang villages were burdened with a fixed amount of required, unpaid labour.

Post-liberation Life Liberation came for the Achangs in early 1950. Two years later, an Achang autonomous district was established in Longchuan County's Fusa area, where the Achangs were concentrated. This was followed by the establishment of three more Achang autonomous districts in the counties of Luxi and Lianghe in 1953 and 1954. When the Dehong Dai-Jingpo Autonomous Prefecture was created, the Achangs were amply represented in the prefectural people's congress.

Beginning in the autumn of 1955, a gradual land reform abolished feudal land ownership in the Achang area. Also abolished were feudal privileges, taxes and usury. Farmers were organized into cooperatives in 1958.

Achangs are famous for their rice cultivation. Before liberation, Achangs were kept so poor by the feudal system that they could not afford to eat rice. But since liberation, Achangs have been able to build irrigation systems that have transformed arid land into fertile paddy fields, ensuring steady rice harvests. They also have built small hydroelectric stations, and have bought farm machinery such as tractors, rice mills, diesel engines, threshers and winnowers.

Local industries, built up from nothing, are centred around Lianghe. They now include ironwork, oil pressing, dyeing, and farm tool, soap and rosin production. In Lasa, an ironworks produces water-powered fire blowers, replacing the manual ones that were in common use.

Development of education has been a priority. Before liberation, there was only one school, in Lasa, and that one mainly enrolled the children of chiefs. Today, however, several dozens of primary and middle schools have been set up and almost all Achang children are at schools.

In those areas, epidemics used to run rampant. After liberation, epidemic prevention stations and clinics have been established, and medical workers of Achang origin have been trained. Epidemics such as the plague, cholera and typhoid fever have been eliminated.

The Pumis

The 24,200 Pumis are concentrated in the Yunnan Province counties of Lanping, Lijiang, Weixi and Yongsheng, as well as in the Yi Autonomous County of Ninglang. Some live in Sichuan Province, in the Tibetan Autonomous County of Muli and Yanyuan County. They are on rugged mountains as high as 2,600 metres above sea level, cut by deep ravines.

According to Pumi legends and historical records, ancient Pumis were a nomadic tribe, roaming the Qinghai-Tibet Plateau. Their descendents later moved south to warmer, more verdant areas along valleys within the Hengduan Mountain Range. By the seventh century, the Pumis were living in Sichuan's Yuexi, Mianning, Hanyuan, Jiulong and Shimian areas, constituting one of the major ethnic minorities in the Xichang Prefecture. After the 13th century, the Pumis gradually settled down in Ninglang, Lijiang, Weixi and Lanping. They farmed and bred livestock. Later, agriculture gradually took a predominant place in their economy.

The Pumis speak a language belonging to the Tibetan-Burmese language family of the Chinese-Tibetan system. Although Pumis in the Muli and Ninglang areas once wrote with Tibetan characters, this was mainly for religious purposes. Gradually the Tibetan characters fell into oblivion, and most Pumis now use Chinese.

Pumi villages are scattered, usually at least 500 metres from one another, on gentle mountain slopes. Pumis generally build their houses from wood and with two floors, the lower for animals and the upper for people. Almost all family activities indoors take place around the fireplace, which is in the middle of the living room on the upper level.

In addition to maize, their staple food, Pumis also grow rice, wheat and highland barley. Their variety of vegetables and fruits is limited to Chinese cabbage, carrots, eggplant and melons. A favourite food of the Pumis' is "pipa meat" — salted pork wrapped in pork skin in the shape of a pipa, a plucked string Chinese instrument with a fretted fingerboard. They also like tobacco, tea and liquor. Liquor, in fact, is used both as a sacrificial offering and as a gift for the living.

Pumi women in Ninglang and Yongsheng often wrap their heads in large handkerchiefs, winding their plaited hair, mixed with yak tail hairs and silk threads. They consider plait beautiful, the more so the bigger it is. Normally, they wear jackets with buttons down one side, long, plaited skirts, multi-coloured wide belts and goatskins draping over their backs. In the Lanping and Weixi areas, women tend to wear green, blue or white long-sleeved jackets under sleeveless jackets, trousers and embroidered belts. Often, they wear silver earrings and bracelets. Pumi men wear similar clothes: linen jackets, loose trousers and sleeveless goatskin jackets. The more affluent wear woolen overcoats. Most carry swords.

Before liberation in 1950, Pumi society was in many ways still organized according to the pre-feudal clan system. In Yongsheng County, for example, clan members lived together, with different clans having different names. Families belonging to the same clan regularly ate together to commemorate their common ancestry. Marriage was primarily between clans. Internal disputes were arbitrated by the patriarch or other respected elders. Clan members shared a commitment to help one another through difficult times. In Yongsheng, ashes of the dead of each clan were placed in the same forest cave.

Pumi communities in Yongsheng and Ninglang counties were

primarily made up of big families, while in Lanping and Weixi counties, small families prevailed. Only sons were entitled to inherit property, and the ancestral house usually was left to the youngest son. Monogamy was customary, although some landlords were polygamous. Parents chose their children's spouses, and marriage between cousins was preferred. Most women married at 15, while most men at 18. After liberation such objectionable practices as forced marriage, engagement of children not yet born and burdensome marriage-related costs were gradually done away with.

Pumis who live with Naxis and Yis in the Ninglang area cremate their dead, while those inhabiting the Lanping area bury them. Pumis in the Weixi area lying between the two do both.

Pumis celebrate the beginning of Spring Festival (the Chinese Lunar New Year) and the 15th of the first month of the lunar calendar. On the latter festival all Pumis, young and old, clad in their holiday best, go camping on mountain slopes and celebrate around bonfires. The holidays are devoted to sacrifices to the "God of the Kitchen" and to feasting, horse racing, shooting contests and wrestling.

Pumis are good singers and dancers. Singing contests in which partners alternate verses are a feature of wedding ceremonies and holidays. They dance to the flute, incorporating in their movements gestures tied to their work as farmers, hunters and weavers.

Pre-liberation Life Their main work was farming crops. More than 90 per cent of the Pumis, in fact, farmed land scattered on hill slopes. The Pumis' major crops were maize, wheat, broad bean, barley, oats, Tibetan barley and buckwheat. However, their output, relying largely on natural conditions, was generally very low. Their farm tools came mainly from Han areas. Their farming techniques were similar to those of their neighbouring Hans, Naxis and Lisus, although the few Pumis who lived in isolated communities still farmed primitively.

Pumis also raised livestock, primarily cattle and sheep. Non-farm activities included manufacture of wool sweaters, linen, bamboo articles, liquor, charcoal and medicinal herbs. Hunting, beekeeping, pig and poultry raising were also common. Some Pumis make fine crafts: lacquered wooden bowls made in Ninglang County are known for their fine workmanship. Before liberation, Pumis had no blacksmiths. Local tools were made of wood. All trade was bartered.

In the decades prior to liberation, landlords dominated the economy in Pumi areas in Lanping and Lijiang counties. Except for a limited number of "public hills," the landlords owned the land, and they exploited peasants by extorting rent in kind, that accounted for at least 50 per cent of the harvest. Pumi landlords and Naxi chiefs owned domestic slaves whom they could sell or give away.

Post-liberation Development Since liberation, Pumis have become their own masters. They have been amply represented in local people's congresses and government agencies as well as in the National People's Congress. Democratic reforms were completed between 1952 and 1956. The reforms were accompanied by a large-scale construction program, which included irrigation projects, factories, schools and hospitals. Their arid land was transformed into terraced fields. Even in the cold, high-altitude Maoniushan area of Ninglang County, the Pumis reaped good harvests from 1,120 hectares of new paddy fields. New industries have been developed: ironwork and salt and aluminium mining. Highways have been built linking Pumi communities with neighbouring areas.

The educational opportunities and health care facilities for Pumis are rapidly expanding. Most children now attend primary schools and many of them go on to middle schools. Medical workers at clinics and health-care stations have replaced witches as primary providers of care.

The Nus

The Nu nationality, numbering some 23,200, live mainly in Yunnan Province's Bijiang, Fugong, Gongshan and Lanping counties, which comprise the Nujiang Lisu Autonomous Prefecture. Others are found in Weixi County in the Diqing Tibetan Autonomous Prefecture.

The Nu people speak a language belonging to the Tibetan-Burmese group of the Chinese-Tibetan language family. It has no written form, and, like many of their minority-nationality neighbours, the Nus used to keep records by carving notches on sticks; educated Nus nowadays use the Han language (Chinese) for administrative purposes.

The Nu homeland is a country of high mountains and deep ravines crossed by the Lancang, Dulong and Nujiang rivers. The famous Grand Nujiang Canyon is surrounded by mountains, which reach 3,000 metres above sea level. Dense virgin forests of pines and firs cover the mountain slopes and are the habitat of tigers, leopards, bears, deer, giant hawks and pheasants.

The area is rich in mineral deposits and valuable medicinal herbs. In addition, with a warm climate and plentiful rain, it promises great hydroelectric potential.

Origins and History In the eighth century, the area inhabited by the Nus came under the jurisdiction of the Nanzhao and Dali principalities, which were tributary to the Tang (618-907) court. During the Yuan and Ming dynasties it came under the rule of a Naxi headman in Lijiang. From the 17th century, rulers comprised various Tibetan and Bai headmen and Tibetan lamaseries. These rulers usurped the Nus' land and carried many of them off as slaves.

From the mid-1850s, the British colonialists who had conquered Burma pushed up the Nujiang River valley. They were followed by American, French and German adventurers. This caused friction with the Nu and other minority peoples in the area, such as the Lisu, Tibetan and Drung nationalities. In 1907, these peoples banded together to stage a mass uprising against the encroachments of French missionaries.

Culture and Customs Before liberation, social development was uneven among the various Nu communities. The Nu people in Lanping and Weixi counties had long entered the feudal stage, and their methods of production and standard of living were similar to those of the Hans, Bais and Naxis. There were vestiges of primitive communalism in the Nu communities in Bijiang, Fugong and Gongshan, where private ownership and class polarization had only just begun.

Bamboo and wooden farm tools were the main implements of production, and major crops were maize, buckwheat, barley, Tibetan barley, potatoes, yams and beans. Output was low, as fertilizer was not used and crop techniques were primitive. The annual grain harvest was some 100 kg short of the per capita need and the diet was supplemented by hunting and fishing using bows and poisoned arrows.

Industry was represented by handicraft products made on a cottage-industry basis — linen, bamboo and wooden articles, iron tools, and liquor. Surplus handicrafts were bartered for necessities in the small markets.

Before liberation, land ownership took three forms: primitive communal type, private and group-ownership. The older Nu vil-

lages in Bijiang and Fugong retained vestiges of the ancient patriarchal clan system; there were ten clan communes located in ten
separate villages, which each had communal land. According to
a 1953 survey, a landlord economy had emerged in Bijiang County,
with an increasing number of land sales, mortgages and leases. In
some places, rich peasants exploited their poorer neighbours by a
system called "washua," under which peasants laboured in semi-serf
conditions. Slavery was practised in a fraudulant form of son
adoption.

Monogamy was the general practice, although a few wealthy
landlords and commune headmen sometimes had more than one
wife. After marriage, men would move out of the family dwelling
and set up a new household with some of the family property. The
new family, however, still retained a cooperative relationship with
the parental family and the whole clan. The youngest son lived
with his parents and inherited their property. Women had low
social status, doing the household chores and working in the fields
but having no economic rights at all.

The traditional burial forms dictated that males be buried face
upward with straight limbs, while females lay sideways with bent
limbs. In the case of a dead couple, the female was made to lie
on her side facing the man and with bent limbs — symbolizing the
submission of the female to the male. When an adult died, all the
members of the clan or village commune observed three days of
mourning.

The Nus live in wooden or bamboo houses, each usually consisting of two rooms. The outer one is for guests and also serves as
the kitchen. In the middle is the fireplace, with an iron or stone
tripod for hanging cooking pots from. The inner room is used as
a bedroom and grain storage, and is off-limits to outsiders. The
houses are built by the common efforts of all the villagers and are
usually erected in one day.

Before liberation, both men and women wore linen clothes.
Girls after puberty wore long skirts and jackets with buttons on the
right side. Nu women in Gongshan wrapped themselves in two
pieces of linen cloth and stuck elaborately-worked bamboo tubes

through their pierced ears. Married women in Bijiang and Fugong wore coral, agate, shell and silver coin ornaments in their hair and on their chests. For earrings they used shoulder-length copper rings. Besides, all Nu women like to adorn themselves with thin rattan bracelets, belts and anklets. Nu men wear linen gowns and shorts, and carry axes and bows and arrows.

The staple food of the Nus is maize and buckwheat. They rarely grow vegetables. In the past, just before the summer harvest they had to gather wild plants to keep alive. Both men and women drink large quantities of strong liquor.

The Nus were animists, and objects of worship included the sun, moon, stars, mountains, rivers, trees and rocks. The shamans were often clan or commune chiefs and practised divination to ensure good harvests. Apart from that, their duties also included primitive medicine and the handing down of the tribe's folklore. Any small mishap was the occasion for holding an elaborate appeasement rite, involving huge waste and hardship to the Nu people. In addition, Lamaism and Christianity had made some headway among the Nus before liberation.

The Nus practise an extempore type of singing accompanied on the lute, flute, mouth organ or reed pipe. Their dances are bold and energetic — mainly imitations of animal movements.

Liberation and a New Life   Liberation came to the Nu areas in 1950. Local governments gave out free food grains, seeds, farm implements and articles of daily use to the Nu people to help them tide over their difficulties and boost production. In 1954 the Nujiang Lisu Autonomous Prefecture was established, which had under its jurisdiction the counties of Bijiang, Fugong, Gongshan, Lushui and Lanping (this last incorporated in 1957). On October 1, 1956 the Gongshan Drung and Nu Autonomous County was set up.

The pace of social reform varied in the different Nu areas. For instance, in the more-developed Lanping County, where feudalism had gained a strong hold, land reform was carried out, followed by the establishment of cooperatives in 1956. In Bijiang, Fugong and Gongshan counties, where vestiges of primitive communalism still survived, the government adopted a policy of first developing production and then gradually eliminating exploitation and primitive practices.

Beginning in 1953, local governments started sending cadres to Nu villages to promote advanced production techniques, and start up educational and public health projects. Special funds were earmarked for irrigation projects, land reclamation, paddy-field development and sideline production. By 1958, all the Nu areas had been organized into cooperatives.

Light industries and mining, too, have gained a foothold among the Nus, and grain production has increased several times owing to the transformation of poor land into paddy fields. The formerly isolated Nu communities are now linked to each other by a network of highways, and some 20 chain bridges now span the Nujiang, Lancang and Dulong rivers.

At the time of liberation, only about 20 people of Nu origin had received primary education. Now there are primary schools in all townships and most villages, and a middle school in every county. The majority of Nu children are in school.

Four hospitals and a network of clinics and community health-care centres have done much to control dysentery, typhoid, cholera and other epidemics.

The De'angs

The number of De'ang people in China totals 12,300. Small as their population is, the people of this nationality are quite widely distributed over Yunnan Province. Most of them dwell in Santai Township in Luxi County of the Dehong Dai-Jingpo Autonomous Prefecture and in Junnong Township in Zhenkang County of the Lincang Prefecture. The others live scattered in Yingjiang, Ruili, Longchuan, Baoshan, Lianghe and Gengma counties. Some De'angs live together with the Jingpo, Han, Lisu and Va nationalities in the mountainous areas. And a small number of them have their homes in villages on flatland peopled by the Dais

The De'ang language belongs to the South Asian family of languages. The De'angs have no written script of their own, and many of them have learned to speak the Dai, Han or Jingpo languages, and some can read and write in the Dai language. An increasing number of them have picked up the Han language over the post-liberation years.

In the mountainous areas of Gaoligong and Nushan ranges in western Yunnan Province, the De'ang people have been living there for generations. The climate here is subtropical, and there is fertile soil, abundant rainfall, rich mineral resources and dense forests.

The dragon bamboo here grows very long and has a stem with a diameter of 10 cm to 13 cm. The Zhenkang area has been famed for this kind of bamboo for the past 2,000 years. It is used to build houses and make household utensils and farm implements. Bamboo shoots are a famed delicacy.

The De'angs, who took to farming since very ancient times, grow both wet and upland rice, corn, buckwheat and tuber crops as well as walnut and jute. And they have learned to cultivate tea, cotton, coffee, and rubber after the founding of the People's Republic in 1949.

The De'angs have been great tea drinkers since very early times, and now every family has tea bushes growing among vegetables, banana, mango, jack fruit, papaya, pear and pomegranate trees in a garden around the house.

History De'ang was a name given to this ethnic group in the Qing Dynasty (1644-1911). Before that time the De'angs along with the Blang and Va nationalities speaking a south Asian language inside Yunnan Province were called "Pu people," according to historical records. In those bygone times the "Pu people" were distributed mainly in the southwestern part of Yunnan Province, which was called Yongchang Prefecture in the Han Dynasty (206 B.C.-A.D. 220). Their forefathers settled on the banks of the Nujiang River (upper reaches of the Salween that flows across Burma) long before the arrival of the Achang and Jingpo ethnic minorities.

Development of De'ang society has been uneven. Since the De'angs have lived in widely scattered localities together with the Han, Dai, Jingpo, Va and other nationalities, who are at different stages of development, they have been influenced by these nationalities politically, economically and culturally. Dai influence is particularly strong since the De'angs had for a long period lived in servitude under Dai headmen in feudal times. However, some traces of the ancient clan and village commune of the De'ang ethnic minority are still to be found in the Zhenkang area.

The production unit of the De'ang nationality is the family, and there is marked division of labour according to sex and age. The farm tools used are bought from Han and Dai regions. General-

ly speaking, the De'angs practise intensive farming on flatland and
on farms near the Han and Dai regions or in paddy fields.   Dry
land is not cultivated meticulously.

In De'ang villages in the Dehong area, the cultivated land used
to be communally owned.   The wasteland around each village was
also communally owned, but people could freely open up the land
for crop-growing.   If the land was left uncultivated, it automatically
reverted to communal ownership again.   In later times, the selling
or mortgaging of paddy fields and gardens led to the emergence of
private ownership.   As a result, most of the paddy fields came into
the possession of Han landlords, rich peasants and Dai headmen.

Without either draught animals or funds, and burdened down
with taxes and debts, the De'angs could not open up hillside land
and gradually became the tenants or farmhands of the landlords, rich
peasants and headmen.   Many cut firewood, burned charcoal and
weaved in the off-hours to make ends meet.

In the Zhenkang Prefecture, which had plenty of dry land and
little paddy land, private ownership of land and usury had been
uncommon.   Yet feudalist ownership and tenancy show such traces
of communal ownership of land as strict demarcation lines between
the land of different villages and clearly-marked signs between communally owned land, woods and small privately owned plots.   Communal land in each village was managed by headmen.   And anyone,
from other villages who wanted to rent the communal or private
plots, had to get the permission of village headmen.

Some De'ang people still retain some traces of the communal
system in the way they live.   A clan commune was formed by many
small families with blood relations.   Usually thirty to fourty people
shared one outsized communal house, but each individual family
had its own fireplace and kept its own account.   Primitive distribution on an equal basis was practised in farming.   But exploitation
had appeared with some families owning more cows and working
less.

The De'ang people everywhere used to live under the sway of
the feudal lords of the Dai nationality.   De'ang headmen in the
Dehong region were either appointed by Dai chieftains or were

hereditary. To control and exploit the De'ang people, Dai chieftains granted official titles to De'ang headmen and let them run the villages, impose levies, and collect tributes. Some De'ang people who lived in or near areas under the Jingpo's jurisdiction had to pay "head taxes." This constituted another burden for the De'angs who were bled white by heavy taxes and rents collected by Dai chiefs or the Kuomintang government.

Landlords and rich peasants of the De'ang nationality made up only two per cent of the population. Many of them were appointed headmen of Dai chiefs. Being tenants or farmhands of either Han landlords and rich peasants or Dai headmen, most De'angs lived in dire poverty.

Post-liberation Development A new day dawned for the De'ang people when Yunnan Province was liberated in 1951. The first thing the De'angs did was to restore social order and develop farm production after helping the government round up remnant KMT troops who had turned bandits. In 1955 land was distributed to the De'ang people who made up half of the population on the flatland and in the semi-hilly areas of Zhenkang, Gengma, Baoshan and Dehong in an agrarian reform in which both the De'ang and Dai people participated. Not long afterwards, the De'angs set up agricultural cooperatives. At the same time, the rest of the De'ang people living in the mountainous areas of Dehong, like the Jingpos dwelling there, formed mutual aid groups to till the land, carried out democratic reforms and gradually embarked on the socialist road.

The De'ang people, who lived in compact communities in Santaishan in Luxi County and Junnong in Zhenkang County, established two ethnic township governments. In July 1953, the Dehong Dai-Jingpo Autonomous Prefecture was established, and the De'angs had 12 representatives in the government. Many functionaries of the De'ang nationality are now serving in government offices at various levels. Some De'angs in Yunnan Province have been elected deputies to local people's congresses and the National People's Congress.

The economy in the De'ang areas has been developing apace.

Take Santaishan in Luxi County for example. People here started farmland construction on a big scale with their Han and Jingpo neighbours in the wake of agricultural cooperation. Today, the land here is studded with reservoirs and crisscrossed by canals, and hillslopes have been transformed into terraced plots. Tea and fruit are grown, and large numbers of goats, cows and hogs are raised. The cropped area has increased enormously, and grain production is four times the 1951 level.

As the people of this minority nationality could scarely make enough to keep body and soul together, no De'angs went to school in pre-liberation days. Those who could read some Dai words in those days were a few Buddhist monks. Pestilence and diseases due to poor living conditions were rampant, and there were no doctors. People had but to ask "gods" to cure them when falling sick.

Today De'ang children can attend primary schools established in villages where the De'angs live. Priority is given to enrolling De'ang children in other local schools. Large numbers of illiterate adults have learned to read and write, and the De'ang people now have even their own college students, teachers and doctors.

Small-pox which had a very high incidence in localities peopled by the De'ang nationality has been eradicated with the assistance of medical teams despatched by the government. Malaria, diarrhoea and other tropical diseases have been put under control.

Life Style Like most people in the sub-tropical regions, the De'angs live in houses made of bamboo. While some dwell in large communal houses, those in the Dehong area have a two-storey house to every family. The upper floor serves as living quarters, kitchen and storeroom, and beneath it is a stable for animals and poultry. There are also outhouses in which are stored firewood and foot-pedalled mortars used in husking rice.

People dress in traditional costumes studded with silver ornaments. Men wear turbans. Boys look handsome with their silver necklaces. Most women wear dark dresses lined with extra large silver buttons at the front, and skirts with red and black flower patterns. Rattan waistbands and silver earrings add grace and charm. Nowadays, De'ang boys have the same hair style as the Hans and do not like to burden their bodies with heavy ornaments. Men have the custom of tattooing their bodies with designs of tiger, deer, bird and flower.

Monogamy is practised. People of the same clan do not marry with one another. Intermarriage is rare with people of other nationalities.

Young people have the freedom to choose their own partners, and courtship lasts for a long time. When a girl hears a love song under her window, she either ignores it or responds. If she likes the boy singer, she tosses a small blanket down to him. Then she opens the door and lets him in. The boy covers his face with the blanket, enters her room, and meets the girl by the side of the fire. The parents are happy and do not interfere.

The lovers often meet and chat until midnight or dawn. After a few dates, the boy gives her a necklace or waistband as a token of his love. The more waistbands a girl gets, the more honoured she is. To show his devotion, the boy wears earrings. The number she gives him is a mark of her love.

If the courtship goes well, the boy would offer gifts to the girl's family and send people to propose marriage. Even if the girl's parents disagree, the girl can decide for herself and go to live in the boy's house.

A De'ang wedding party is gay and interesting. Each guest is sent two packages, one containing tea and the other cigarettes. This is an invitation. They bring gifts and firecrackers to the bride and groom.

The new couple first enter the kitchen and put some money in a wooden rice tub. This means they have been nurtured by the cereal, and now show their gratitude. Water-drum dancing is an important part of the wedding ceremony. The drums are made of hollowed trunks into which water is poured to wet the skin and centre to determine its tone. Water-drum dancing has a legend behind it. In ancient times a young De'ang man's beautiful fiancee was snatched away by a crab monster. He fought the crab, vanquished it, ate it, and made a drum of its shell. At today's wedding ceremonies, water-drum dancing symbolizes true love.

The De'angs bury their dead in public cemeteries but those who die of long illness or difficult labour are cremated.

The De'angs are Hinayana Buddhists. Most villages have a temple. The monks live on the offerings of their followers. Their daily needs are provided by the villagers in turn. Formerly the De'angs did not raise pigs or chickens. A rooster was kept in each village to herald the break of day. Today this old custom has died, and chickens are raised. People do not work during religious holidays or sacrificial days. Being Buddhists, the De'angs in some localities do not kill living creatures. This has its minus side — wild boars that come to devour their crops are left unmolested. This at times results in quite serious crop losses.

The Drungs

The Drungs, numbering about 4,700, live mainly in the Dulong River valley of the Gongshan Drung and Nu Autonomous County in northwestern Yunnan Province. Their language belongs to the Tibetan-Burmese group of the Chinese-Tibetan language family. Similar to the language of the Nu people, their neighbours, it does not have a written form and, traditionally, records were made and messages transmitted by engraving notches in wood and tying knots.

History   During the Tang Dynasty (618-907), the places where the Drungs lived were under the jurisdiction of the Nanzhao and Dali principalities. From the Yuan Dynasty (1271-1368) to the end of the Qing Dynasty (1644-1911), the Drungs were ruled by court-appointed Naxi headmen. In modern times, the nationality distinguished itself by repulsing a British military expedition in 1913.

Natural Environment   The Dulong River valley extends 150 km from north to south. It is flanked on the east by Mt. Gaoligong, 5,000 metres above sea level, and on the west by Mt. Dandanglika, 4,000 metres above sea level.

The area has abundant rainfall due to the influence of monsoon winds from the Indian Ocean; the annual precipitation is 2,500 mm. Virgin forests cover the mountain slopes, and medicinal herbs, wild animals and mineral deposits abound. Crops grown in the area used to be limited to maize, buckwheat and beans, but after liberation rice and potatoes were introduced.

Customs and Traditions Before liberation, Drung society maintained many vestiges of the primitive commune system. There were 15 patriarchal clans called "nile." Each nile consisted of several family communes, and each commune occupied a separate territory marked off by boundaries such as streams and mountain ridges. The clan was further divided into "ke'eng," or villages, where people dwelt in common long houses.

Agricultural production remained at a very low level until liberation, due mainly to the primitive nature of the Drungs' farm tools. Every year saw several lean months when their diet had to be supplemented by food gathering, hunting and fishing.

The ke'eng members pursued collective farming on common land and held their hunting, fishing and gathering grounds in common. However, in modern times this system was slowly giving way to ownership of the means of production by blood-related families. Following financial difficulties due to illness or debt as a result of the imposition of taxes, land sales gradually led to the emergence of oppressive landlords. And rich households used to make seasonal workers and destitute children work for them.

The Drungs produced some primitive handicrafts, including bamboo and rattan articles and engaged in the weaving of linen. But the absence of both traders and towns made barter the only form of exchange.

The ke'eng was the grassroots organization of Drung society. Its members regarded themselves as being descended from the same ancestor. A Drung's personal name was preceded by that of the family and his father's name. In the case of a woman, her mother's name was included.

Each ke'eng was headed by a "kashan" whose duties were both administrative and ceremonial. He also directed warfare and mediated disputes. The ke'engs were politically separate entities, which formed temporary alliances in times of great danger threatening from outside communities.

Marriage within the clan was forbidden and monogamy was

the rule in recent times, but vestiges of primitive group marriage remained, such as several sisters marrying one man. Polygamy was also not unknown.

The dead were buried in the ground in hollow logs, except in cases of death from serious disease, when the corpses were cremated or disposed of in the rivers. Funerals were attended by all the relatives, who brought sacrificial offerings of food.

The Drung people, male and female, wear their hair down to their eyebrows in front and down to their shoulders behind. Both sexes used to wrap themselves in a covering of striped linen fastened with straw ropes or bamboo needles. The poorer ones would often have no other clothing but a skirt of leaves.

Girls tattooed their faces at the onset of puberty, with the patterns varying according to the clan.

The traditional ke'eng long house — made of logs in the northern areas and of bamboo further south — is made up of a large, oblong room which serves as the ke'eng's common quarters, with two rows of smaller rooms at the back. Each small room has a fireplace in the middle and is the home of an individual family.

At one time, each ke'eng had a common granary, but this was replaced by granaries owned by small groups of families.

The Drungs are animists and make sacrificial offerings to appease evil spirits. Shamans, and sometimes the kashan, performed such rites. The Drung New Year falls in December of the lunar calender. The exact dates are not fixed, nor is the duration of the celebration, which lasts as long as the food does. Cattle are slaughtered as an offering to Heaven, and the Drungs dance around the carcasses.

New Life A new life began for the Drung nationality with liberation in 1949. The year 1956 saw the establishment of the Gongshan Drung and Nu Autonomous County, with a Drung as the county magistrate. The first task for the people's government was to provide the Drungs with clothing and farm tools, and promote farm production and education.

In light of the conditions in Drung society, the government decided that land reform would be inappropriate, and concentrated on the development of production.

Beginning in 1954, about 6,000 hectares of arable land was brought under cultivation in the Dulong River valley. Irrigation projects transformed part of the land into paddy fields, which had been non-existent up until then. A few years later, the area began to sell surplus grain to the state. Along with the increased farm production went a boost for livestock raising (cattle, goats and pigs), the cultivation of medicinal herbs and the processing of animal hides.

Primary schools, unknown in the Drung area in the past, now number 20. Clinics and health stations have put the shamans out of business.

Special attention has been paid to making the mountainous Drung area accessible to the outside world. Some 150 km of roads have been constructed, and ferries and bridges now span the roaring torrents of the hill streams. Modern commodities are now available to the Drungs. There is also a post office, bookstore and film-projection team in the valley. Several small hydroelectric power stations, built in the last couple of decades, have brought electricity to the Drung villages.

By 1980 some 100 Drung cadres worked in government, industrial, educational and health organizations. Some are prefectural and county leaders.

The Jinos

Numbering 12,000 in all, the Jinos live in the Jinoluoke Township of Jinghong County in the Xishuangbanna Dai Autonomous Prefecture, Yunnan Province.

The language of this ethnic minority belongs to the Tibetan-Burmese group of the Chinese-Tibetan language family. Its structure and vocabulary have much in common with Yi and Burmese. Without a written language of their own, the Jino people used to keep records by notching on wood or bamboo.

Jinoluoke is a mountainous area stretching for 70 kilometres from east to west and 50 kilometres from north to south. The climate there is rainy and subtropical with an average annual temperature of 18 to 20°C. The rainy season lasts from May to September with July and August having the heaviest rainfall. The rest of the year is dry.

Jino land is crisscrossed by numerous rivers and streams, the longest being the Pani and the Small Black rivers. The major crops are upland and wet rice and corn. The famous Pu'er tea grows on Mount Jino. Jinoluoke also has a long history of cotton-growing and is abundant in such tropical fruits as bananas and papayas. Elephants and wild oxen roam the dense primeval forests which are also the habitat of monkeys, hornbills and other birds. Jinoluoke is also rich in mineral resources.

History	It is said that the Jinos migrated to Jinoluoke from Pu'er and Mojiang or places even farther north.	It seems likely that they still lived in a matriarchal society when they first settled around the Jino Mountain.	Legend has it that the first settler on the mountain ridge was a widow by the name of Jiezhuo.	She gave birth to seven boys and seven girls who later married each other. As the population grew, the big family was divided into two groups to live in as many villages, or rather two clans that could intermarry. One was called Citong, the patriarchal village, and the other was Manfeng, the matriarchal village.	With the passage of time, the Jino population multiplied and more Jino villages came into existence.

Until some 40 years ago, Jino people from far and near still went to offer sacrifices to their ancestors in the matriarchal and patriarchal villages every year.

The Jino matriarchal society gave way to a patriarchal one some 300 years ago.	But the Jinos were still in the transitional stage from primitivity to a class society at the time the People's Republic was founded in 1949.

Most Jinos are farmers.	In 1949 they still cultivated land by a slash and burn method, not knowing how to irrigate their crops. Land was communally owned by clans or villages and farmed collectively except in some villages where land was privately owned.

The Jonos are great hunters.	When men go out hunting, they shoulder crossbows with poisoned arrows or shot-guns.	They are also experts in the use of traps and nooses to catch wild animals. They hunt in groups and divide the game equally among the participants.	But the pelts of animals go to the men who shot them. While the men hunt, the women gather wild fruit in the forests. Edible herbs are also collected for soup.

The early ancestors of the Jinos, united by ties of consanguinity into a big family, dwelled in the Jizhuo Mountains in very ancient times.	But the social structure of the Jinos had changed by 1949. The basic unit of society was no longer the clan by blood-ties following the emergence of the communal village in which people of different clans lived together. The boundaries of the villages were marked with wooden or stone tablets on which swords and spears were carved. The land within the boundary was commnual property, and each village was inhabited by at least two clans whose members could intermarry. Two elders were elected to take care of village administration as well as sacrificial rites and production. Each village was a small, self-contained world.

Primitive egalitarianism still manifests itself to these days in Jino customs. The meat of wild beasts brought back by hunters is divided equally among all adults and children in a village. Even a small deer is cut into very tiny pieces and shared out among all the villagers, including new-borns. Because of low crop-yields resulting from primitive farming methods and extortion by the Kuomintang and Dai overlords, there was always a shortage of grain for three or four months every year. But despite that, the Jinos stored what little grain they had in unguarded straw sheds outside their houses, and never worried that it would be stolen.

Zhuoba (the village father) and Zhuose (the village mother) were the leaders in a communal village. Being the oldest people in the village, they were respected by all. They became village leaders by virtue of their seniority, not because they were brave in war or eloquent in speech. No matter how mediocre they might be, even if they were blind or deaf, they had to serve as village elders so long as they were the oldest people in the community. After their death, the next eldest in the same clan would be chosen as successors.

Their functions were tinged with time-honoured traditions or religion. For instance, the yearly sowing could only begin after the elders had animals slaughtered and offered to the spirits at a ceremony during which the elders put a few seeds in the soil, before the other villagers could start sowing on a big scale. The elders also fixed the dates for holidays. The beating of a big drum and gong in elders' homes ushered in the new year, and all the villagers, young and old, would rush to the elders' homes to sing and dance.

Life Style The Jinos live in bamboo houses built on stilts on flat hill-tops. The men usually wear collarless white jackets and white or blue trousers made of flax or cotton. Before liberation most men divided their hair into three tufts. Women, as a rule, prefer multi-coloured and embroidered collarless short gowns and short black skirts rimmed in red and opened at the front. Many wear long skirts and puttees. They also wear their hair in a coil just above the foreheads, and sling across their shoulders sharp-pointed flax hats. Both men and women go barefooted, and have thick bamboo or wooden sticks plugged into the holes in their earlobes. Those with big holes in their earlobes are considered most beautiful. The Jinos carry things in baskets on their backs with straps tied on their foreheads.

Monogamy is practised in Jino society. But before marriage the prospective brides and grooms are permitted to have sex. If a woman brings her illegitimate child to live in the home of her husband, both the mother and child are not looked down upon. In some villages, special houses are built for unmarried young men and women to spend the night. But once married, a woman must remain faithful to the husband throughout life. Divorce is rare.

A dead body is put in a coffin carved out of a single log and buried in a communal cemetery. The personal belongings of the dead — work tools and clothing, and a copper pot of silver for some of the rich — are buried as sacrificial objects. Above the grave, a small thatched hut with bamboo tables inside is set up to provide a place for the relatives of the dead to offer meals to the departed soul for a period of one to three years.

Being animists, the Jinos believe that all things on earth have souls. Ancestral worship constitutes an important part of their religious activities. When there was a drought or something untoward happend, a shaman was sent for to mumble prayers and kill oxen, pigs or dogs to appease the trouble-making spirits. Shamans also used to cure diseases with herbal medicines.

The Jinos learn to sing when still very young. They are good at improvising poems and set them to agreeable melodies extemporaneously. At holiday gatherings, the young dance to songs sung by elders. There are many Jino festivals. The biggest one takes place on New Year's Day in March and is celebrated at different dates in different villages. There are worships for "Large Dragon" and "Small Dragon," both of which meant to get rid of disasters and pray for good harvests. A festival is held annually in the wake of a harvest, at which all Jinos gather to help themselves to newly harvested rice.

Better Times Begin Changes began to take place in Jino life in 1954 when teams sent by the people's government arrived for the first time in the out-of-the-way mountainous areas. They brought relief supplies and helped the local people to step up production. After winning over the powerful village elders, they helped the Jinos undertake democratic reforms to put an end to outdated institutions that had kept them backward for centuries.

And in 1955, the Jinos set up cooperative teams to work the land more effectively. Formerly upland rice was cultivated in small jungle clearings where the trees were felled and burnt before each sowing. Today the crop is grown on well-prepared paddy fields, and the yield has jumped up enormously. The paddy is irrigated by water lifted by electric pumps. The service of prayer-mumbling priests is no longer needed, nor was the slaughtering of animals, to appease evil spirits in times of drought.

Small reservoirs and hydro-electric power installations have been built, and electric lamps have replaced the flickering oil-lamps that once lit Jino homes. The wooden mortars formerly used for pounding rice have gone, too, with the advent of milling equipment powered by electricity.

In 1981 there were 14 primary schools and middle schools with an enrolment of 1,600 in the mountainous areas where most people used to be illiterate. The Jinos now boast their own college students and university-trained doctors.

Another thing the Jinos welcome most is the emergence of a network of trading stores that offer farm implements, clothing, food, salt and a long list of goods at moderate prices. Gone are the travelling cut-throat merchants who used to squeeze every cent out of the pockets of the Jino people.

The Miaos

With a population of more than five million, the Miao people form one of the largest ethnic minorities in southwest China. They are mainly distributed across Guizhou, Yunnan, Hunan and Sichuan provinces and Guangxi Zhuang Autonomous Region, and a small number live on Hainan Island in Guangdong Province and in southwest Hubei Province. Most of them live in tightly-knit communities, with a few living in areas inhabited by several other ethnic groups.

On the Yunnan-Guizhou Plateau and in some remote mountainous areas, Miao villages are comprised of a few families, and are scattered on mountain slopes and plains with easy access to transport links.

Much of the Miao area is hilly or mountainous, and is drained by several big rivers. The weather is mild with a generous rainfall, and the area is rich in natural resources. Major crops include paddy rice, maize, potatoes, Chinese sorghum, beans, rape, peanuts, tobacco, ramie, sugar cane, 'cotton, oil-tea camellia and tung tree. Hainan Island is abundant in tropical fruits.

History As early as the Qin and Han dynasties 2,000 years ago, the ancestors of the Miao people lived in the western part of present-day Hunan and the eastern part of present-day Guizhou. They were referred to as the Miaos in Chinese documents of the

Tang and Song period (A.D. 618-1279).

In the third century A.D., the ancestors of the Miaos went west to present-day northwest Guizhou and south Sichuan along the Wujiang River. In the fifth century, some Miao groups moved to east Sichuan and west Guizhou. In the ninth century, some were taken to Yunnan as captives. In the 16th century, some Miaos settled on Hainan Island. As a result of these large-scale migrations over many centuries the Miaos became widely dispersed.

Such a wide distribution and the influence of different environments has resulted in marked differences in dialect, names and clothes. Some Miao people from different areas have great difficulty in communicating with each other. Their art and festivals also differ between areas.

Language The Miao language belongs to the Miao-Yao branch of the Chinese-Tibetan language family. It has three main dialects in China — one based in west Hunan, one in east Guizhou and the other in Sichuan, Yunnan and part of Guizhou. In some places, people who call themselves Miao use the languages of other ethnic groups. In Chengbu and Suining in Hunan, Longsheng and Ziyuan in Guangxi and Jinping in Guizhou, about 100,000 Miao people speak a Chinese dialect. In Sangjiang in Guangxi, some 30,000 Miaos speak the Dong language, and on Hainan Island, 100,000 speak the language of the Yaos. Due to their centuries of contacts with the Hans, many Miaos can also speak Chinese.

Custom Their clothing has distinctive features which vary from place to place. In northwest Guizhou and northeast Yunnan, Miao men usually wear linen jackets with colourful designs, and drape woollen blankets with geometric patterns over their shoulders. In other areas, men wear short jackets buttoned down the front or to the left, long trousers with wide belts and long black scarves. In winter, men usually wear extra cloth leggings known as puttees. Women's clothing varies even from village to village. In west Hunan and northeast Guizhou, women wear jackets buttoned on the right and trousers, with decorations embroidered on collars, sleeves and trouser legs. In other areas, women wear high-collared short jackets and full- or half-length pleated skirts. They also wear various kinds of silver jewellery on festive occasions.

In southeast Guizhou, west Hunan, Rongshui in Guangxi and on Hainan Island, the Miaos eat rice, maize, sweet potatoes and millet as staple foods. In northwest Guizhou, Sichuan and northeast Yunnan, they mainly eat maize, potatoes, buckwheat and oats. In southeast Guizhou, Miao cooks make a sour mixture of glutinous rice and vegetables by packing them tightly into jars for up to two months. Before 1949, for lack of salt, many Miao people had to flavour their food with pepper or a sour taste. Many even had to live on wild vegetables.

Because timber resources are plentiful in most Miao areas, houses are usually built of wood, and roofed with fir bark or tiles or are thatched. In central and western Guizhou, houses are roofed with stone slabs.

Houses vary greatly in style. In mountainous areas, they are usually built on slopes and raised on stilts. Animals are kept under the stilted floors. In the Zhaotong area in Yunnan and on Hainan Island, most Miaos live in thatched huts or "branch houses," made of woven branches and twigs or bamboo strips plastered with mud.

The typical Miao family is small and monogamous. Aged parents are usually supported by their youngest son.

In some areas, a son's name is followed by his father's, but generally a Miao person uses only his or her own name. Influenced by the Han feudal patriarchal clan system, the Miaos made efforts to maintain their family pedigrees, built ancestral halls and adopted words in their names to indicate their position in the family hierarchy.

Marriages are usually arranged by parents, but unmarried young men and women have the freedom to court. Mass courting occasions sometimes take place during holidays, when young women from a host village gather to sing antiphonal love songs with young men from neighbouring villages. If a couple are attracted to each other, they exchange love tokens. But they must still win the approval of their parents before they can marry.

In Chuxiong, Yunnan Province, the practice of setting up public courting houses for unmarried men and women prevailed until a few decades ago. After a day's work, they would visit these houses to sing, dance and court with their partners. The Miaos there also practised the custom of "kidnapping brides." If the kidnapped girl consented to an offer of marriage, a grand wedding feast was held. If she did not, she was free to go.

Different Miao communities celebrate different festivals. Even the same festivals may fall on different dates. In southeast Guizhou and Rongshui County in Guangxi, the Miao New Year festival is celebrated on "Rabbit Day" or "Ox Day" on the lunar calendar. The festivities include beating drums, dancing to the music of a lusheng (a wind instrument), horse racing and bull-fighting. In counties near Guiyang, people dressed in their holiday best gather at the city's largest fountain on April 8 of the lunar year to play lusheng and flute and sing of the legendary hero, Yanu.

In many areas, the Miaos have Dragon Boat festivals and Flower Mountain festivals (May 5), Tasting New Rice festivals (between June and July), Pure Brightness festivals and the Beginning of Autumn festivals. In Yunnan, "Stepping over Flower Mountains" is a popular festivity for the Miaos. Childless couples use the occasion to repeat vows to the god of fertility. They provide wine for young people, who sing and dance under a pine tree, on which hangs a bottle of wine. Young men and women may fall in love on this occasion, and this, it is hoped, will help bring children to the childless couples.

The Miaos used to believe in many gods, and some of their superstitious rituals were very expensive. In west Hunan and northeast Guizhou, for instance, prayers for children or for the cure of an illness were accompanied by the slaughter of two grown oxen as sacrifices. Feasts would then be held for all the relatives for three to five days.

Culture The Miao have a highly diversified culture developed from a common root. They are fond of singing and dancing, and have a highly-developed folk literature. Their songs, which do not rhyme and vary greatly in length from a few lines to more than 15,000, are easy to understand and are very popular among the Miaos.

The lusheng is their favourite musical instrument. In addition, flutes, copper drum, mouth organs, the xiao (a vertical bamboo flute) and the suona horn are also very popular. Popular dances include the lusheng dance, drum dance and bench dance.

The Miaos create a variety of colourful arts and crafts, including cross-stitch work, embroidery, weaving, batik, and paper-cuts. Their batik technique dates back 1,000 years. A pattern is first drawn on white cloth with a knife dipped in hot wax. Then the cloth is boiled in dye. The wax melts to leave a white pattern on a blue background. In recent years, improved technology has made it possible to print more colourful designs, and many Miao handicrafts are now exported.

Socio-economic Structure Miao areas differ in their scale of economic and educational development. Early Miao society went through a long primitive stage in which there were neither classes nor exploitation. Totem worship survived among Miao ancestors until the Jin Dynasty 1,600 years ago. By the Eastern Han Dynasty (A.D. 25-220), the ethnic minorities in the Wuxi area had begun farming, and had learned to weave with bark and dye with grass seeds, and trade on a barter basis had emerged. But productivity was still very low and tribal leaders and the common people remained equal in status.

Primitive Miao society changed rapidly between the third and tenth centuries A.D. Communal clans linked by family relationships evolved into communal villages formed of different regions. Vestiges of the communal village remained in the Miao's political and economic organizations until liberation in 1949. Organizations known as Men Kuan in the Southern Song Dynasty (1127-1279), and as Zai Kuan during the Qing Dynasty (1644-1911), were formed between several neighbouring villages. Kuan leaders were elected by its members, who met regularly. Rules and regulations were formulated by all members to protect private property and maintain order. Anyone who violated the rules would be fined, expelled from the community or even executed. All villages in the same Kuan were dutybound to support one another, or else were punished according to the relevant rule.

By the end of the Tang Dynasty (618-907), the Miaos had divided into different social classes. Communal leaders had authority over land, and frequent contacts with the Hans and the impact of their feudal economy gave impetus to the development of the Miao feudal-lord economy. The feudal lords began to call themselves "officials," and called serfs under their rule "field people."

During the Song Dynasty (960-1279), some upper-class Miaos were appointed prefectural governors by the imperial court, thus providing a political guarantee for the growth of the feudal economy. Under the rule of feudal lords, the ordinary people paid their rent in the form of unpaid service. The lords had supreme authority over them, and could punish them and bring them to trial at will. If feuds broke out between lords, the "field people" had to fight the battles.

By this time, agriculture and handicrafts had been further developed. Grain was traded for salt between prefectures, and Xi cloth was sent as a tribute to the imperial court. High-quality iron swords, armour and crossbows came into use. By the end of the Song Dynasty, the Miaos in west Hunan had mastered the technique of iron mining and smelting. Textiles, notably batik, also flourished. Regular trade sprung up between the Miaos and Hans.

The Miao feudal-lord economy reached its peak and began to decline during the Ming Dynasty (1368-1644). A landlord economy had taken shape and was in its early stage of development. In 1502, the Ming Court began to abolish the rule of Miao feudal lords, and appointed officials who were subject to recall. During the early years of the Qing Dynasty, these measures were applied to many Miao areas, contributing a great deal to the disintegration of the feudal-lord system and the growth of a landlord economy. In west Guizhou and northwest Yunnan, however, some lords still retained their power, and the feudal-lord economy continued to exist there until the end of the Qing Dynasty.

After the 1880s, imperialists began to increase their political influence on and economic infiltration into Miao areas. They imported capital and plundered raw materials, and this resulted in a semi-colonial economy. At the same time, they stimulated the growth of the Miao commodity economy, which gave birth to a capitalist economy. In west Hunan, for instance, big landlords who possessed more than 135 hectares of land also ran business enterprises such as oil pressing, dyeing, tung oil trading and wine-making. Some of them accumulated several thousand silver dollars. Some maintained armed forces, and were appointed officials by the Kuomintang government, thus becoming landlords, bureaucrats and bandits all in one. Under the ruthless oppression of such landlords, many poor peasants were forced to leave their homes and wander about looking for food and shelter. Many died.

Struggle Against Oppression Throughout their history, the Miaos have taken up arms on many occasions to fight against the oppression of reactionary rulers. In 1795, Shi Liudeng, Shi Sanbao, Wu Bansheng and Wu Bayue led an insurrection in west Hunan and northeast Guizhou against the Qing rulers. A huge rebel force swept across a vast area, and dealt corrupt Han and Manchu officials and local tyrants a crushing blow. The Qing Court had to assemble armies from seven provinces to suppress the insurrection, which later joined forces with the White Lotus Society, another rebel army. Supported by Han, Tujia and other ethnic groups, the insurrection lasted 12 years. The Xian Feng and Tong Zhi reigns (1851-1874) witnessed the biggest Miao insurrection, which was led by Zhang Xiumei. Its forces seized almost the entire northwestern part of Guizhou, and continued their struggle from 1855 to 1873.

Since its early years, the Chinese Communist Party has shown concern for the liberation of ethnic minorities. In December 1926, a draft resolution concerning the liberation of the Miao and Yao peoples was adopted at the first peasant representative assembly in Hunan. The resolution called on the Miaos and Yaos to join or form peasant associations, and asked all peasant associations to support the struggles of these minorities. When the Red Army passed through the Miao area during the Long March in December 1934, its General Political Department ordered the whole army to observe revolutionary discipline and respect the customs and habits of minority peoples. The army also promised that land would be confiscated from the landlords and given to the peasants, and that self-determination and equality with the Hans would be implemented to oppose oppression by Han landlords. Many Miao people volunteered to help and join the Red Army. Some organized themselves into self-defence units to engage in armed struggle in their areas.

During the revolutionary war period, many Miaos joined the Communist-led armed forces to fight against conscription, taxation and grain levies.

After liberation, the Miaos helped the People's Liberation Army to suppress the bandits who had been rampant in west Hunan. These bandits, some of them armed by the Kuomintang before their retreat, took part in killing, looting and sabotage. The Miaos helped guard strategic checkpoints and comb the mountains for bandits. By 1951, all these bandits had been eliminated.

Progress After Liberation From the autumn of 1950 to the spring of 1951, a campaign urging landlords to cut rents and return peasants' deposits on leased land was carried out in Miao areas. Feudal exploitation had mainly taken the form of rent in kind. Tenants had to pay 50 to 70 per cent of their crops in an "unfixed rent" contract, or pay a fixed proportion regardless of the harvest.

Rent reduction was a preparatory move for more thorough land reform, a process which was usually milder in the Miao areas than in Han areas. Attention was paid to arousing the political consciousness of the masses and directing the spearhead of the struggle at a very small minority of landlords. During the land reform in the former West Hunan Miao Autonomous Region alone, 230,000 families were given more than 67,000 hectares of land and 85,000 houses. More than 1,850 tons of grain, 13,000 cattle and 230,000 farm tools were also distributed. This redistribution helped the Miao people solve their immediate living problems and gave incentive to production.

Since 1951, a number of Miao autonomous divisions have been established in Guizhou, Yunnan, Guangxi, Guangdong, and Hunan. Most of these autonomous divisions have taken the form of multi-ethnic autonomy, as the Miaos have for a long time lived harmoniously with the Tujia, Bouyei, Dong, Zhuang, Li and Han peoples.

In some Miao areas, before autonomous authorities were established, priority was given to such things as the election of delegates to the People's congress and the training and appointment of minority administrative staff. Now a large number of Miao people have been promoted to leading posts. In Northwest Guizhou Autonomous Prefecture alone, Miaos account for 68 per cent of the district and township officials.

In 1953, the cooperative transformation of agriculture began in Miao areas, and was completed by the spring of 1957.

Before 1949, textiles, iron-forging, carpentry, masonry, pottery, alkali-making and oil-pressing were the only industries in the area. After the birth of New China, many factories and hydroelectric power stations were built. Now electricity is widely used for lighting, irrigation and food processing.

In mountainous areas, the Miaos have built reservoirs, dug canals and created new farmland. They have also developed a diversified economy according to local conditions. As a result, grain production as well as oil, fibre and starch crops and medicinal herbs have all flourished. This has helped to open up new sources of raw materials and supplies for industry and commerce, and improved the Miao people's living standards.

Sheep-raising has a long history in Weining Autonomous County, Guizhou, where 265,000 hectares of grassland and trees provide an ideal grazing area. Herds have grown rapidly as a result of the introduction of improved breeds and better veterinary services.

The construction of railways between Guiyang and Kunming, and between Hunan and Guizhou has boosted the development of the Miao areas along the routes. Before 1949, more than half the counties in Qiandongnan Autonomous Prefecture had no bus services. But by 1981, more than 4,400 kilometres of highways had been built there.

Cultural, educational and public health provisions have also expanded rapidly. At present, there are 23,000 teachers in Qiandongnan alone, of whom over half are of the Miao or Dong minorities. They have set up schools in mountainous areas and brought education to the formerly illiterate mountain villages. Before 1949, the incidence of malaria was as high as 95 per cent in Xinchi village in Ziyun County, Guizhou Province. But since liberation, the disease has been eradicated through massive health campaigns. This is giving rise to the rapid emergence of clean, hygienic and literate Miao villages.

The Bouyeis

Most of China's 2,100,000 Bouyei people live in several Bouyei-Miao autonomous counties in Xingyi and Anshun prefectures and Qiannan Bouyei-Miao Autonomous Prefecture in Guizhou Province. Others are distributed in counties in the Qiandongnan Miao-Dong Autonomous Prefecture or near Guiyang, the capital of Guizhou.

The Bouyei region is on the Yunnan-Guizhou Plateau, which slopes from an altitude of 1,000 metres in the north to 400 metres in the south. The Miaoling Mountains stretch across the plateau, forming part of its striking landscape.

The famous Huangguoshu Falls cascade down more than 60 metres near the Yunnan-Guizhou highway in Zhenning Bouyei-Miao Autonomous County. The thunder of water can be heard several kilometres away, and mists from the falls contribute to a magnificent view.

The Bouyei are blessed with fertile land and a mild climate. The average annual temperature is 16 degrees Centigrade, and an essentially tropical environment, receiving between 100 and 140 centimetres of rain a year, is ideal for farming. Local crops include paddy rice, wheat, maize, dry rice, millet, sorghum, buckwheat, potatoes and beans. Farmers also grow cotton, ramie, tobacco, sugar cane, tung oil, tea and oil-tea camellia as profitable cash crops.

As the Red River valley is low-lying and tropical, paddy rice yields two harvests annually. Silk, hemp, bamboo shoots and bananas complement the local economy, and coffee and cocoa have also been planted there recently.

The valley is also rich in trees, yielding a variety of timber, which is good for construction, such as pines and China firs. The remote, heavily-forested mountain and river areas provide a habitat for tigers, leopards, bears, musk deers, foxes, golden pheasants and others. Medicinal herbs are abundant in the woods, and the area is also rich in mineral resources, such as coal, iron, zinc, antimony, copper, petroleum, asbestos and mercury.

The Bouyei language is of the Zhuang-Dai branch of the Zhuang-Dong group belonging to the Chinese-Tibetan family of languages. In the past, the Bouyeis had no written language of their own, and used Han characters instead. After 1949, the People's Government helped formulate a Bouyei writing system based on Latin letters.

This ethnic group possess a rich folk literature, which includes fairy tales, fables, folk songs, proverbs and poems. During weddings, scores of young men and women are invited to join in antiphonal singing of a rich ethnic quality. In the Biandan Mountain area of Zhenning County, old women are invited to sing songs of blessing by firesides. They can sing day and night for up to a week without repeating the words of their ballads. Popular musical instruments of the Bouyeis include the suona horn, yueqin, dongxiao, short xiao, and sister xiao (all vertical bamboo flutes) and a copper drum. Their favourite dances include the weaving dance and the lion dance.

The Bouyeis are skilled in arts and crafts. Their colourful and beautifully-patterned batik dates far back to ancient times. In 1953, a batik factory was built in the city of Anshun with the help of the local authorities, and traditional technology was improved. Now, batik has become one of their best-selling handicrafts, popular both on domestic and foreign markets. In addition, their colourful embroidery, exquisite summer sleeping mats and bamboo hats are not only durable and attractive, but also highly artistic.

They live mostly on plains or in river valleys in villages composed of families from several different clans, in two-storeyed houses, bungalows or a combination of the two. Often people live on an upper floor, and keep livestock on the lower.

Young Bouyei males generally wear short buttoned jackets and long trousers, with scarves on their heads. Women wear jackets buttoned on the right (although some young women prefer lace-trimmed jackets buttoning down the middle), and long trousers or pleated skirts. They also wear scarves and a variety of silver jewellery.

They are monogamous, but young people of opposite sexes mix freely. When they go to fairs or other festivities, unmarried young men and women get together to sing songs. If a woman is attracted to a man, she will throw him a ball made of silk strips which she has embroidered herself. If the man is agreeable, they then make a date at which they will sing love songs to each other. After several dates, they may announce their engagement. Under the feudal system of the past, however, most marriages were arranged by parents.

In the past, the Bouyeis believed in spirits and worshipped ancestors, although many living near missionary outposts were converted to Christianity. In general, they observe the same festivals as the Hans. On June 6 and April 8, however, they celebrate their own festivals in commemoration of the leaders of ancient uprisings and their ancestors. On "Ox King Festival," April 8, special cakes and glutinous rice dyed in five different colours are made and offered to ancestors. After the ceremony, half of these offerings are given to their cattle, which are also granted a day of rest as a reward for their hard work.

History Studies of the language, names and geographical distribution of the Bouyeis indicate that they have a common ancestry with the Zhuangs. The ancient Yue people, who were widely distributed, were composed of such ethnic groups as the Xiou and Louyue in Guangdong and Guizhou provinces and Guangxi Zhuang Autonomous Region. The similarity between the modern Zhuang and Bouyei languages and the ancient Louyue tongue is a strong indication of the origin of the Bouyeis. In addition, many habits and customs of the Yues still prevail among the Bouyeis.

For several centuries before the Tang Dynasty (A.D. 618-907), both the Zhuang and Bouyei peoples were referred to as "the alien barbarians," but long separation eventually led to development of different cultures and lifestyles. After A.D. 900, they became recognised as separate minority groups.

After the second century B.C., increasing contacts between the Bouyeis and the Hans boosted the former's productivity, and feudal economic relationships were established.

By the Tang Dynasty, the central imperial court had established in the Bouyei region an administrative system, under which local feudal lords were appointed prefectural governors, and land became their hereditary property. The system lasted for more than 1,000 years, until the Qing court forced minority officials to surrender their powers. Under the rule of minority headmen, the Bouyei society had retained its feudal lord presence until 1911. Feudal lords and local officials owned all the land, but not literally the peasants or serfs within their territories. Lords still subjected peasants to cruel exploitation, but were no longer allowed to kill them at will. Each peasant household was given a piece of land to support itself, but was forbidden to purchase it. Peasants and serfs were thus bound to the land and made to work for the feudal lords for generations.

During the Qing Dynasty (1644-1911), the imperial court abolished the rule of minority headmen, and appointed officials with limited tenures. As a result, the feudal lord economy collapsed and a landlord economy took its place. As most land was owned by the rich few and exploitation of the peasants by landlords became even crueler, class conflicts intensified and led to many peasant uprisings, the biggest of which was the Nanlong Uprising in 1797.

Under the rule of imperialism, feudalism and bureaucratic capitalism before 1949, the Bouyeis were discriminated against politically, and remained economically backward.

In 1932, the Chinese Communist Party sent party workers to the area to mobilise the peasants for the struggle against feudalism. When the Red Army passed through the area on its Long March (1934-36), many Bouyeis volunteered to help by working as guides or delivering food supplies and messages.

In 1948, the Bouyei people in Anlong County organised a 700-strong armed group to fight against conscription, taxation and grain levies. The same years, the column of Yunnan-Guangxi-Guizhou Border Areas of the People's Liberation Army (PLA) was formed, and the Luopan guerrilla area was established. In 1949, the Bouyeis in Anlong County rose up in an armed rebellion against the Kuomintang, and drove its forces out of Guizhou. About the same time, the PLA moved into Guizhou to tackle the remnants of the Kuomintang forces, and brought complete liberation to the whole Bouyei region in 1951.

By 1954, land reform had been completed there, and three years later, the area had achieved a socialist transformation of agriculture, the handicraft industry and capitalist industrial and commercial enterprises.

Post-liberation Development   In the early years of the People's Republic, few Bouyeis took part in management. By 1981, however, there were 8,220 Bouyei administrators, accounting for 65 per cent of the total minority managerial staff in the area.

Before 1949, Bouyei agriculture was backward, especially in remote mountain areas, where slash-and-burn farming methods still dominated. Since liberation, tremendous changes have taken place. By 1982, grain output totalled 720,000 tons, nearly twice as much as the 1949 figure, and 12,880 water conservancy projects had been built. These stored 200 million cubic metres of water, and brought 56,600 hectares of land under irrigation — a six-fold increase over the 1949 area.

Before 1949, there was virtually no industry in the Bouyei region. Since then, however, many industries have been developed, including iron and steel, coal, machine-building, chemicals, electronic products, building materials and plastics.

In 1949, the total length of roads came to only 296 kilometres in what is now Qiannan Prefecture. By 1981, 6,100 kilometres of new roads had been built. And three main railway lines (Guizhou-Guangxi, Yunnan-Guizhou and Hunan-Guizhou) run through Bouyei areas in Qiannan, Anshun and Guiyang. In addition, air services now link Guiyang with Beijing, Shanghai and other big Chinese cities.

Education and medical care have also improved greatly since liberation. By 1981, the numbers of secondary and primary schools had risen to 150 and 3,789 respectively, compared with hardly any in 1949. Teacher training schools and colleges teaching modern farming methods have also been established.

In the past, medical facilities in the area were very poor. Epidemic diseases, such as smallpox, cholera and dysentery were rampant, with malaria alone affecting 58 per cent of the local population. After 1949, the People's Government supplied financial aid, equipment and large numbers of medical workers to help the Bouyeis improve health care. Now, besides major hospitals at prefectural level, every county has its own hospital, epidemic prevention station and maternal health centre, and every district has a clinic.

The Dongs

Nestling among the tree-clad hills dotting an extensive stretch of territory on the Hunan-Guizhou-Guangxi borders are innumerable villages in which dwell the Dong people.

The population of this ethnic group in China is 1.425 million. Situated no more than 300 km north of the Tropic of Cancer, the area peopled by the Dongs has a mild climate and an annual rainfall of 1,200 mm. The Dong people grow enormous numbers of timber trees which are logged and sent to markets. Tong-oil and lacquer and oil-tea camellia trees are also grown for their edible oil and varnish.

The most favourite tree of the people of this nationality is fir, which is grown very extensively. Whenever a child is born, the parents begin to plant some fir saplings for their baby. When the child reaches the age of 18 and marries, the fir trees, that have matured too, are felled and used to build houses for the bride and groom. For this reason, such fir trees are called "18-year-trees."

With the introduction of scientific cultivation methods, a fir sapling can now mature in only eight or 10 years, but the term "18-year-trees" is still current among the Dong people.

Farming is another major occupation of the Dongs, who grow rice, wheat, millet, maize and sweet potatoes. Their most important cash crops are cotton, tobacco, rape and soybean.

With no written script of their own before 1949, many Dongs learned to read and write in Chinese. Philologists sent by the Central People's Government helped work out a Dong written language on the basis of Latin alphabet in 1958.

Customs and Habits   The Dongs live in villages of 20-30 households located near streams. There are also large villages of 700 households. Their houses, built of fir wood, are usually two or three storeys high. Those located on steep slopes or river banks stand on stilts; people live on the upper floors, and the ground floor is reserved for domestic animals and firewood. In the old days, landlords and rich peasants dwelled in big houses with engraved beams and painted columns. Paths inside a village are paved with gravels, and there are fishponds in most villages. One lavish feature of Dong villages are the drum towers. Meetings and celebrations are held in front of these towers, and the Dong people gather there to dance and make merry on New Year's Day. The drum tower of Gaozhen Village in Guizhou Province is especially elaborate. Standing 13 storeys high, it is decorated with carved dragons, phoenixes, flowers and birds.

Equally spectacular is folk architecture that goes into the construction of bridges. Wood, stone arches, stone slabs and bamboo are all used in erecting bridges. The roofed bridges which the Dongs have dubbed "wind and rain" bridges are best-known for their unique architectural style. The Chengyang "Wind and Rain" Bridge in Sanjiang is 165 metres long, 10 metres across and 10 to 20 metres above the water. Roofed with tiles engraved with flowers, it has on its sides five large pagoda-like, multi-tier pavilions beautifully decorated with carvings.   It is a covered walk-way with railings and benches for people to sit on and enjoy the scenes around.

A typical Dong diet consists mainly of rice. In the mountainous areas, glutinous rice is eaten with peppers and pickled vegetables. Home-woven cloth is used to make traditional Dong clothing; finer cloth and silks are used for decoration or for making festival costumes.   Machine-woven cloth printed black and purple or blue is becoming more popular.

Men usually wear short jackets with front buttons. In the mountainous localities in the south, they wear collarless skirts and turbans.

The females are dressed in skirts or trousers with beautifully embroidered hems. Women wrap their legs and heads in scarves, and wear their hair in a coil.

Many popular legends and poems, covering a wide spectrum of themes, have been handed down by the Dongs from generation to generation. Their lyrics tend to be very enthusiastic, while narrative poems are subtle and indirect, allusive and profound. Songs and dances are important aspects of Dong community life. Adults teach traditional songs to children, and young men sing them.

Prior to 1949, the feudal patriarchal family was the basic social unit. Women were on the lowest rung of the social ladder, and they were even forbidden to touch sacrificial objects. Girls lived separately on the upper floors allowing no men to visit them. After marriage, women were given a little share of "female land" for private farming. Monogamy was and is practised. Childless couples were allowed to adopt sons, and only men were entitled to inherit family property.

A newlywed woman continued to live with her own parents. She went to her husband's home only on holidays and on special occasions. She would go to live with her husband permanently after giving birth to her first child.

Dong funeral rituals are similar to those of the Hans, but in Congjiang the deceased is put in a coffin which is put outdoors unburied. Before liberation, funeral ceremonies were very elaborate and wasteful. They have been much simplified since 1949. The Dongs believe in ancestor worship and revere many gods and spirits. They have special reverence for a "saint mother" for whom altars and temples have been erected in the villages.

The Dongs have many festivals — Spring Festival, Worshipping Ox Festival, New Harvest Festival, Pure Brightness Festival and Dragon Boat Festival.

History At the time of the Qin and Han dynasties (221 B.C.-A.D. 220) there lived many tribes in what is present-day Guangdong and Guangxi. The Dong people, descendants of one of these tribes, lived in a slave society at that time. Slavery gradually gave way to a feudal society in the Tang Dynasty (618-907).

...aditional Dai wed-
...ng ceremony.

...oung people of
...e Va nationality.

A Lisu girl making a handbag.

A skilled pottery maker of the Lahu nationality.

Two young Naxi embroideresses.

A young Jingpo measuring precipitation.

Thread tying — a Blang ritual for blessing the newborn.

Achang women busy weaving and spinning.

A Pumis fetching water.

Benglongs picking papayas.

Young Drung women.

Melon shells are used by the Nus as water containers.

Pupils of the Jino nationality.

Intrigued by a Miao bride's dowry.

Young women of the Bouyei nationality.

Among young happy Dongs.

A Shui happy with the harvest.

A worker of the Zhuang nationality.

Gelo women during a work break.

A Yao teacher.

A Mulam girl.

A Maonan mother with her son.

A Tujia singer.

Jing farmers.

Li workers busy harvesting rubber.

She women making the best choice in a village store.

Gaoshans carrying water on head.

Agriculture developed rapidly during the Qing Dynasty (1644-1911) in the Dong areas in southeast Guizhou and southwest Hunan provinces. Rice production went up with improved irrigation facilities. And self-employed artisans made their appearance in Dong towns. Markets came into existence in some bigger towns or county seats, and many big feudal land owners also began to do business. After the Opium War of 1840-42, the Dong people were further impoverished due to exploitation by imperialists, Qing officials, landlords and usurers.

The Dongs, who had all along fought against their oppressors, started to struggle more actively for their own emancipation after the founding of the Chinese Communist Party in 1921. They served as guides and supplied grain to the Chinese Red Army when it marched through the area during its Long March in the mid-1930s. In 1949, guerilla units organized by the Dong, Miao, Han, Zhuang and Yao nationalities fought shoulder to shoulder with regular People's Liberation Army forces to liberate the county seat of Longsheng.

Post-liberation Period   A momentous event in Dong history took place on August 19, 1951 when the Longsheng Autonomous County of the Dong, Zhuang, Miao and Yao peoples was founded. This was followed by the setting up of the Sanjiang Dong Autonomous County in Guangxi, the Tongdao Dong Autonomous County in Hunan, the Miao-Dong Autonomous Prefecture in southeastern Guizhou, and the Xinhuang Dong Autonomous County in Hunan.

The establishment of autonomous counties enhanced relations between various nationalities and eliminated misunderstanding, mistrust and discord sowed by the ruling class between the Dongs and other ethnic minorities. In Congjiang County, Guizhou, the Dongs in one village once warred against the Miaos in another for the possesion of a brook. The people of the two villages remained hostile to each other for over a century until the dispute was resolved through negotiations after the setting up of the Miao-Dong Autonomous Prefecture.   They have been living in harmony since.

Another eventful change in Dong life is the carrying out of the agrarian reform, which put an end to feudal oppression under which members of this nationality had been groaning for centuries.

The Dongs who were ruled and never ruled have their own people holding posts in the governments of the autonomous counties. Dong cadres in Guangxi number 2,950, and those in Hunan 3,040. Many Dong women, who had no political status formerly, now hold responsible government posts at the county or prefectural levels.

Achievements have also been made in many other fields in the post-liberation period. With the opening of schools, all children between 7 and 10 in Longping village, for example, are attending classes. Malaria and other diseases, which used to take a heavy toll of lives, have by and large been eliminated, thanks to improved health care and the disappearance of witch doctors. There was no industry in the Dong areas formerly. Today, small factories are turning out farm implements, chemical fertilizer, cement, paper and other products. Electricity generated by small power installations drives irrigation pumps and light homes in many Dong villages.

The Shuis

There are in China 286,500 Shuis, the majority of whom dwell on the upper reaches of the Longjiang and Duliu rivers that meander across plains and rolling land interspersed with vast expanses of forests in southern Guizhou Province. They live in compact communities in the Sandu Shui Autonomous County and in Libo, Dushan and other counties. Some Shuis have their homes in the northwestern part of the Guangxi Zhuang Autonomous Region.

The areas in which the Shuis live are a land of plenty, abounding in fish and rice. Wheat, rape, ramie are also grown besides a great variety of citrus and other fruits. The forests are a source of timber and medicinal herbs. The Duliu and other rivers teem with fish.

The Shui language belongs to the Zhuang-Dong branch of the Chinese-Tibetan language family. The Shuis used to have an archaic writing script. Some of their words were pictographs, while others resembled Chinese characters written upside down. Except for scores of these ancient words that are still used for religious purposes, the Shuis use Chinese in their daily lives.

The Shuis boast a treasure house of colourful oral literature and art. Their literature includes poetry, legends, fairy tales and fables. Among the various forms, poetry, which consists of long narrative poems and extemporaneous ballads, are generally considered the most prominent.

Stories and fables in prose style praise the diligence, bravery, wisdom and love of the Shui ethnic group and satirize the stupidity of feudal rulers. With rich content and vivid plots Shui tales are usually highly romantic.

Their songs, which are usually sung without the accompaniment of musical instruments, fall into two categories. The "grand songs" are sung while they work, whereas the "wine songs" are meant for wedding feasts or funerals.

The Shui people are good dancers. "Lusheng Dance" and "Copper Drum Dance" are the most popular dances enjoyed by all on festive occasions. Traditional musical instruments include gongs, drums, lusheng, huqin and suona horns. The Shui people make beautiful handicrafts — embroideries, batiks, paper cuts and wood carvings.

Life Style   The Shuis usually dress in black and blue. Men have long gowns and black turbans, and women wear collarless blue blouses, black trousers and aprons, all of which are embroidered. On festive occasions, the females put on skirts and a variety of silver earrings, necklaces and bracelets. They usually wear their hair in buns.

Shui diets consist of rice and fish, supplemented with corn, barley, wheat and sweet potatoes. A kind of liquor made of rice goes to entertain guests or is offered to dead ancestors at sacrificial ceremonies.

A Shui house is either a one-storeyed affair or a two-storeyed building. Dwellers of two-storeyed houses usually live upstairs and reserve the ground floor for livestock, dogs and chickens.

Monogamy is practised. Young people had the freedom to choose their spouses three centuries ago. Such freedom came to an end with the growth of the feudal economy, and children of rich landed families could only marry those of wealthy ones, and marriages were arranged by parents.

On wedding day, the groom's family sent some unmarried men to escort the bride home. The bride walked all the way to her husband's home under an umbrella and returned to her parent's home on the same day or the day after. The bride, as a rule, did not live very often with her husband until six months after marriage. Such feudal ways as parental arrangement of children's marriages and extortion of big payments by parents of brides from the grooms' families have ceased to exist following the establishment of the People's Republic in 1949.

Shui funerals used to be extremely elaborate. Livestock were killed as sacrificial offerings to the dead. Singing, dancing and performance of local operas went on and on until an auspicious day was found to bury the dead. Such wasteful funerals have been simplified in the post-liberation years.

The Shuis are believers of polytheism. In former days a shaman would be employed to say prayers and animals slaughtered to be offered to evil spirits when someone fell ill or died or when something bad happened. Catholicism that came to the area in the late Qing Dynasty (1644-1911) won very few converts.

The Shuis have a calendar of their own which takes the ninth lunar month as the beginning of a new year, and their biggest festival is the "duan" holiday which is celebrated with great pomp after the autumn harvest at the beginning of the 11th lunar month every year. Garbed in their colourful costumes, the Shuis gather in their village to watch horse-races and plays, and to feast for days on end.

History The Shuis are probably the descendants of the Luo-yues, one of the early tribes that lived along China's southeastern coast before the Han Dynasty (206 B.C.-A.D. 24). They adopted their present name at the end of the Ming Dynasty (1368-1644).

In the Song Dynasty (960-1279) villages were formed and rice-growing began. By the end of the Song, the Shuis had entered the early stage of feudalism. The nobles bearing the surname of Meng initiated in the upper reaches of the Longjiang River a feudal system which bore the distinctive vestiges of the communal village. The Yuan rulers (1271-1368) established local governments at the pre-fectural level in an attempt to appease the ethnic groups. The Ming period witnessed a marked economic growth in Shui communities. The introduction of improved farm tools made it possible for farmers to open up paddy fields on flatland and terraced fields on moun-.

tain slopes. The primitive "slash and burn" farming gave way to more advanced agriculture characterized by the use of irrigation and draught animals. As a result, grain output increased remarkably.

The Ming imperial court followed the preceding dynasty's practice of appointing hereditary Shui headmen. Under this system, the Shuis had to pay taxes to and do corvee for these court-appointed headmen as well as for the imperial court.

During the two centuries between 1640 and 1840 the Shui economy continued to develop. Farm production registered a marked increase, with per hectare yield of rice on flatland reaching 2,250 kilogrammes. Some quit farming and became handicraftsmen.

After the Revolution of 1911, national capitalism gained some ground in the area. In what is now the Sandu Shui Autonomous County, iron mines and plants processing iron, mercury and antimony were set up, but later they were either taken over by Kuomintang monopolist capital or went bankrupt. The comprador capitalists plundered the rich natural resources, while big landowners annexed large areas of farmland. Ruthless exploitation through usury, hired labour and high land rent robbed farmers of 60 to 70 per cent of their crops, thus ruining a great many farmers.

Changes After 1949   The founding of New China brought a revival and further growth in production. During the land reform in the early 50's, full respect for Shui customs was emphasized and public land was reserved for festive horse-racing and dancing. In 1957 the Sandu Shui Autonomous County was established.

Formerly only 13 per cent of the arable land was irrigated. Now thousands of water conservancy facilities have been built to bring most arable land under irrigation.

Abundant mineral resources have been found and mined. Today local industries include chemical fertilizer, coal-mining, farm machinery, sulphur, casting, sugur refining, wine-making and ceramics. Handicraft industries such as ironwork, masonry, silver jewelry, carpentry, textiles, papermaking, bamboo articles have also developed.

In the past, transportation was very difficult in this mountainous area, with only one 17-km highway traversing the county. Now all the seven districts in the county are connected by highways or waterways, and many towns and factories have bus services. The Hunan-Guizhou and Guizhou-Guangxi railways have further facilitated the interflow of commodities between the Shui community and other areas and strengthened ties between the Shui and other nationalities.

Before 1949 there were few schools in the area. By 1981, apart from 10 secondary schools and 145 primary schools with a total enrolment of 27,700, there was one nationality school and one nationality teachers' school. Cadres of the Shui nationality now number 900, or 32.7 percent of the county's total administrative staff.

In the past malaria was rampant in the area with an 80 per cent incidence rate, but the only medical facility was a small hospital with three medical workers. After 1949 a large number of clinics and hospitals were set up. Thanks to the persistent efforts in the past years, malaria has been brought under control.

The Gelos

The 54,000 Gelos live in dispersed clusters of communities in about 20 counties in western Guizhou Province, four counties of the Wenshan Zhuang-Miao Autonomous Prefecture in southeastern Yunnan Province and the Longlin Multi-National Autonomous County in Guangxi Zhuang Autonomous Region.

Only about a quarter of the Gelos still speak the Gelo language belonging to the Chinese-Tibetan language family. Yet, because of close contact with other ethnic groups, their language has not remained pure — even within counties. There are Gelo-speaking people unable to converse with each other. For this reason, the language of the Hans, or Chinese, has become their common language, though many Gelos have learned three or four languages from other people in their communities, including the Miaos, Yis and Bouyeis Living among other ethnic groups, the Gelos have become largely assimilated to the majority Han customs.

How the Gelos Live The Gelos' living quarters, like those of their Han neighbours, usually consist of a central kitchen and two bed-rooms built on a hillside or at the foot of a mountain. Before liberation, poor Gelos lived in mud, bamboo or stone houses, some with thatched roofs. Landlords and wealthier peasants lived in houses with wooden columns and thick stone slabs, with tile or stone roofs.

Now, nearly everyone lives in houses of wood.

Gelos continued to wear their ethnic costumes until 30 or 40 years ago. Women wore very short jackets with sleeves embroidered with patterns of fish scale. They wore tight skirts divided into three sections, the middle one of red wool and the upper and lower ones of black-and-white striped linen. Gelo women also wore short, black sleeveless gowns which hung longer in the back. Their shoes had pointed, upturned toes. Men wore front-buttoned jackets, and both sexes wore long scarves.

In the mountain areas, the Gelos eat mostly maize, while in the flatlands, they eat wheat, rice, millet and sorghum. All the Gelos — like many other Chinese — love to eat hot and sour dishes as well as glutinous rice cakes.

Before liberation, Gelo marriage customs were feudal, with matches made by parents at childhood, regardless of the desires of the children involved. As Gelos were so few and so scattered, marriages were usually made among cousins. To celebrate the marriage, the bride would walk with her relatives, carrying an umbrella, to the groom's home, where they would live apart from their parents.

While funeral customs in most Gelo communities are the same as in Han areas, singing and dancing still marks funerals in a few places, such as Zunyi and Renhuai counties in Guizhou. There, mourners dance in groups of three, one playing a lusheng (reed pipe), one beating a bamboo pole, the third brandishing a sword, and all singing as they dance. In other areas, mourners sing in front of the coffin; family members of the deceased serve wine in gratitude to them. In some places, a shaman who chooses the time and place of burial recites scriptures at the grave. Animal sacrifice usually accompanies the burial. Trees, rather than stones, mark the grave.

Gelo folk literature consists of poetry, stories and proverbs. Poems are of three, five or seven-character lines. Most Gelo folk tales eulogize the intelligence, honesty, diligence and bravery of the Gelo people, and satirize the upper classes. Typical are "The Brave Girl" and "Deaf Elder Brother and Blind Younger Brother Stealing Sheep." Gelo dances are simple and graceful, accompanied by the erhu, horizontal xiao, suona, gong, drum and other string and wind instruments.

"Flower Dragon" and "Bamboo-Strip Egg" are two favourite Gelo games. "Flower Dragon," in fact, is a ball of woven bamboo, a little larger than a ping-pong ball. Inside are bits of broken porcelain, coins and sandstones. The game, especially popular in Zunyi and Renhuai, is played by groups of pairs on hillsides. "Bamboo-Strip Egg" is also a ball, larger and stuffed with rice straw. Two teams of three or five throw and kick the ball, avoiding contact except with the hands or feet.

Most Gelo festivals echo Han traditions, but some practices differ. At Spring Festival — the Lunar New Year — Gelos offer a huge rice cake to their ancestors and after it is made, it remains untouched for three days. In Guizhou's Anshun, Puding and Zhenning, Gelo communities also celebrate the sixth day of the sixth lunar month by sacrificing chickens and preparing wine to bless the rice crop already in the fields.

The sixth day of the seventh lunar month marks the second most important event of the year, a festival of ancestor worship in Wozi and Gaoyang villages of Puding County. Oxen, pigs and sheep are slaughtered for ritual sacrifices to ancestors.

On the first day of the tenth lunar month, Gelos give their oxen a day of rest. This is the day of the Ox King Buddha, and in some communities on this day oxen are honoured and fed special rice cakes.

Prior to liberation, Gelos had a number of distinctive taboos. During Spring Festival, for example, they did not allow themselves to sweep floors, carry water, cook food, clean houses, plough, ride horses or pour water from their houses. In some areas on other holidays, Gelos would not transplant rice or build houses if they heard thunder.

History Over the last 2,000 years or more, Gelos have lived in many places in China. Bridges, graves, wells, and even villages in Guizhou Province still bear Gelo names, even where no Gelo still lives. The group's name dates back to the Ming Dynasty (1368-1644). Before then, they were called the "Liaos." Descended from the Yelang, the strongest tribe in the Han Dynasty's Zangke Prefecture, the Liaos moved out of Zangke to Sichuan, where they became subject to the feudal regime, between the third and fifth centuries.

By the fifth century, the Liaos had developed metal spears, shields and fishing tools and copper cooking vessels. They could weave fine linen. At this time, the Liao people elected their kings, who later became hereditary rulers. As with other south-central minorities, the Gelos were ruled in the Yuan and Ming periods (1271-1644) by appointed chiefs, who lost their authority to the central court when the Qing Dynasty came to power.

Until 1949, most Gelos were farmers. They grew rice, maize, wheat, sweet potatoes, and millet. Before the founding of New China, Gelo farmers had no irrigation or ways of storing water. As a result, their maize output was only about 675 kg per hectare. Droughts inevitably brought about devastating consequences. Side businesses, especially cork production, bamboo weaving and making straw sandals were essential to the Gelos for survival.

Before liberation, land mainly belonged to landlords of other ethnic groups. In Pingzheng village of Zunyi County, for example, landlords and rich peasants owned 50 per cent of the land, even though they constituted only nine per cent of the population. Rent was usually paid in kind and every year over half of the harvest went for rent. Gelo farmers also had to pay additional tributes as high as 200 per cent of a year's rent. In western Guizhou, farmers not only paid in maize, opium, soybeans and peppers, but they also had to work — unpaid — for 50-80 days a year.

Liberation Gelo areas were liberated in 1949. Relief food and emergency funds from the Central People's Government were sent there and invested to enhance production and improve living standards. Reservoirs and other irrigation systems were built, and water turbines were installed.

Most Gelos were illiterate before 1949. Now there are schools in all Gelo communities for school-age children. Some Gelo youths have gone on to college.

CENTRAL SOUTH AND SOUTHEAST CHINA

The Zhuangs

The Zhuang nationality is China's largest minority group. Its population of 13.38 million approaches that of Australia. Most of the Zhuangs live in southwest China's Guangxi Zhuang Autonomous Region, which is nearly the size of New Zealand. The rest have settled in Yunnan, Guangdong, Guizhou and Hunan provinces.

While most Zhuang communities concentrate in a compact area in Guangxi, the others are scattered over places shared by other nationalities such as Han, Yao, Miao, Dong, Mulao, Maonan and Shui.

Lying in Guangxi's mountainous regions, the Zhuang area is high in the northwest, undulating in the middle and low in the southeast. Limestone is widely distributed in the area, which is known round the world for its karst topography. Many rocky peaks rise straight up from the ground, and the peaks hide numerous fascinating grottoes and subterranean rivers. Guilin, a tourist attraction in Guangxi, is an excellent example of such landscape. As the saying goes: "The landscape at Guilin is the best on earth; and the landscape at Yangshuo is the best in Guilin." Wuming, Jingxi and Lingyun counties are also known for their scenic splendours.

Crisscrossing rivers endow the Zhuang area with plentiful sources of water for irrigation, navigation and hydropower. The coastline in south Guangxi not only has important ports but also yields many valuable marine products including the best pearls in China.

The Zhuang area enjoys a mild climate with an average annual temperature of 20 degrees centigrade, being warm in winter and sweltering in summer in the south. Plants are always green, blossoming in all seasons. Abundant rainfall nurtures tropical and subtropical crops such as rice, yam, corn, sugar cane, banana, longan, litchi, pineapple, shaddock and mango. The mountains in southwest and northwest Guangxi abound in Liuzhou fir, silver fir and camphor trees, rare elsewhere. Mineral resources include iron, coal, wolfram, gold, copper, tin, manganese, aluminium, stibium, zinc and petroleum. The area is also rich in tung oil, tea, tea oil, mushroom, Chinese cinnamon, pseudo-ginseng, Chinese gecko (used in traditional Chinese medicine to help regain vitality), fennal and fennal essence. The last four items are the Zhuang area's special products.

History "Zhuang" was one of the names the ancestors of the nationality gave themselves. The term was first recorded some 1,000 years ago, in the Song Dynasty. The Zhuangs used to call themselves by at least a dozen other names, too.

The Zhuang areas first came under the administration of China's central authority 2,000 years ago. In 221 B.C., Qin Shi Huang, China's first feudal emperor to unify the country, conquered the area and established three prefectures there. The emperor had the Lingqu Canal built to facilitate irrigation. He also started a project to move people from other places to the area, strengthening its political, economic and cultural ties with the central-south part of the country.

In the centuries that followed, a number of powerful clans emerged in this area, who owned vast tracts of land and numerous slaves and servants. Still later, during the Tang and Song dynasties, social and economic development was such that irrigated rice paddies, farm cattle, iron, copper and spinning and weaving spread far and wide.

However, the Zhuang area still lagged behind central China economically. Quite a number of places retained the primitive mode of production, including slash-and-burn cultivation and hunting. The dominant social system was feudal serfdom and people were classified into three strata: hereditary land-owners, tenant farmers and house slaves. The system was eliminated during the Qing Dynasty (1644-1911), the last feudal monarchy in China.

Administratively, most of the Zhuang area was governed by the headmen system all through the over 1,000 years from the Tang to Qing dynasties. Backed by the central authorities, the local headmen oppressed and exploited the Zhuangs, forcing them into hundreds of uprisings.

In 1851, the Taiping Revolution, the biggest of peasant uprisings in Chinese history, broke out in this area. Thousands of Zhuangs joined the Taiping Army, forming its spine in its march to the north. Many of them became important leaders of the army and the Heavenly Kingdom of Taiping.

Inhabiting China's southern frontier areas, the Zhuangs have played an important role in defending the country's territory. In the 1070s, they repulsed the Annamese aggressors; in the middle 16th century, they beat back the invading Japanese pirates.

Towards the end of the 19th century, French troops that had occupied south Vietnam pushed northward and invaded China. People of Zhuang and Han nationalities in Guangxi formed the Black Banner Army and trounced the French invaders near Hanoi in 1873. They again routed the French at Hanoi in 1882.

When the French invaders made new incursions into China in 1885, the local Zhuang and Han people helped the Chinese army win a crucial victory at Zhennanguan, a pass on the Sino-Vietnamese border.

The Zhuangs also made great contributions to the Revolution of 1911, China's first democratic revolution led by Dr. Sun Yat-sen. Many Zhuangs became key members of the Tong Meng Hui, an organization Dr. Sun formed to advance his revolutionary cause.

After the Chinese Communist Party was founded in 1921, revolutionary bases were set up under its leadership in the Zhuang area. The first Communist Party organization was established there in 1925. In the following years, the Zhuangs' revolutionary endeavours grew from strength to strength and finally triumphed in 1949, helping found New China and ushering in a new life for the local people.

Culture The Zhuang language belongs to the Chinese-Tibetan language family. Ancient Zhuang characters appeared in the South Song Dynasty (1127-1279), but never got popularized. So, the Zhuangs wrote in the Han script until 1955, when the Central People's Government helped them create a writing system based on the Latin alphabet. The Romanized script has been used in books, magazines and newspapers.

The Zhuang nationality's ancient culture and art are not only rich and colourful but also outstanding with their indigenous characteristics. For example, 2,000-year-old frescoes have been found at more than 50 spots on the precipices hanging over the Zuojiang River running through southwest Guangxi. The best known of them is the Huashan fresco in Ningming County which is over 100 metres long and 40 metres wide, featuring 1,300 figures. Drawn in rugged and vigorous lines, it reflects the life of the Zhuangs' ancestors.

Bronze drum, a special relic of minority groups in central-south and southwest China, dates back well over two millennia. Guangxi alone has unearthed more than 500 of such drums, which are in different designs and sizes. The largest exceeds one metre in diameter and the heaviest weighs over half a ton while the lightest several dozen kilogrammes. The tops and sides of the drums are decorated with designs done in relief.

However, explanations are diverse in so far as the use of these drums is concerned. Some people believe that they were meant for military music, others argue that they were for folk music, and still others think they were for religious rites or to symbolize power and wealth.

Zhuang brocade is a splendid handicraft which originated in the Tang Dynasty (618-907). Woven in beautiful designs with natural cotton warp and dyed velour weft, the brocade is excellent for making quilt covers, table-clothes, braces, aprons and handbags. Winning national fame during the Ming and Qing dynasties (1368-1911), Zhuang brocade has been steadily improved and at least 40 new designs have been developed in the past few decades.

Legends, fairy tales, stories and ballads frame the folk literature of the Zhuangs who have also been reputed for their singing. Sweet songs can be heard wherever you go in the Zhuang area. Extemporaneous melodies and lyrics and clever use of metaphors, riddles and cross-examinations add charm to their songs. It is said that, in the Tang Dynasty, a Zhuang woman singer called Third Sister Liu became known not just for her beautiful singing but especially for the courageous exposure in her songs of the crudeness of local tyrants. Today her name is a household word throughout China thanks to a successful film about her made in the 1950s.

In the old days, every Zhuang community held its regular songfests at given venues. On those occasions, young people from nearby villages would come together in their holiday best to meet each other and choose their lovers through songs.

Common Zhuang musical instruments include *suona* (Chinese cornet), bronze drum, cymbal, gong, *sheng* (Chinese wind pipe), *xiao* (vertical bamboo flute), *di* (Chinese flute) and *huqin* (a stringed instrument) made of horse bones.

Zhuang dances are characterized by distinct themes, forceful and nimble steps, jocular and humorous gestures and true-to-life emotions. The Rice-Husking Dance, Silk-Ball Dance, Shrimp-Catching Dance, Tea-Picking Dance, Shoulder-Pole Dance and Bronze-Drum Dance not only vividly depict the Zhuangs' life and work, but also display their straightforward, unbending nature.

Yet what combines the Zhuangs' folk literature, music, dance and other forms of art is the Zhuang Opera, which first originated from religious rites in the Tang Dynasty.

Customs and Habits Most Zhuangs now live in one-storey houses the same as the Hans. But some have kept their traditional two-storey structures with the upper storey serving as the living quarters and the lower as stables and storerooms. The old housing style, they think, suits the mountainous terrain and the humid climate.

Contemporary Zhuang clothing is in general close to the wear of the Han people. But traditional dresses remain in many places or are worn for special occasions. In northwest Guangxi, for instance, elderly women like collarless, embroidered and trimmed jackets buttoned to the left together with baggy trousers, embroidered belts and shoes and pleated skirts. They fancy silver ornaments. Women of southwest Guangxi prefer collarless, left-buttoned jackets, square kerchieves and loose trousers — all in black.

Tattoo used to be an ancient Zhuang custom. A great writer of Tang Dynasty, Liu Zongyuan, mentioned it in his writings. Chewing betel nuts is a habit still popular among some Zhuang women. In places such as southwest Guangxi, betel nuts are a treat to guests.

Rice and corn make up the Zhuangs' staple food, and glutinous rice is particularly favoured by those in south Guangxi.

The Zhuangs are monogamous. But they have a strange custom — the wife stays away from the husband's home after marriage. At the wedding, the bride is taken to the bridegroom's home by a dozen girls of the same generation. She returns to live with her parents the next day and visits her husband only occasionally during holidays or the busy farming seasons. The woman will move permanently to the man's home two or three years later. This convention, which often impairs the harmony between husband and wife, has been going out of existence.

While sharing many festivals with the Hans, the Zhuangs have three red-letter days of their own: the Devil Festival, the Cattle Soul Festival and the Feasting Festival. The Devil Festival, which falls on July 14 on the lunar calendar (usually in August on the Gregorian calendar), is an important occasion next only to the Spring Festival. On that day, every family would prepare chicken, duck and five-coloured glutinous rice to be offered as sacrifices to ancestors and ghosts.

The Cattle Soul Festival usually follows the spring ploughing, when every family would carry a basketful of steamed five-coloured glutinous rice and a bundle of fresh grass to the cattle pen. After a brief sacrificial rite, they would feed the cattle with the grass and half of the rice. They believe that the cattle have lost their souls because of the whipping during the spring ploughing and that the ritual would call back the lost souls.

The Feasting Festival is celebrated only by people who live near the Sino-Vietnamese border. Legend has it that a group of Zhuang soldiers, having repulsed the French invaders in the late 19th century, returned in late January and missed the Spring Festival. To pay tribute to them and celebrate the victory, their neighbours prepared a sumptuous feast for them.

The Zhuangs are polytheists, worshipping among other things giant rocks, old trees, high mountains, land, dragons, snakes, birds and ancestors. Taoism has also had a deep influence on the Zhuangs since the Tang Dynasty. In the old days, there were semi-professional Taoist priests in the countryside, and religious rites cost a lot of money. Foreign missionaries came to the area in the 19th and early 20th centuries, but their influence was limited to cities and towns.

Development After Liberation Land reforms began in the Zhuang area immediately after the founding of the People's Republic. Land was confiscated from evil landlords and distributed among the poor peasants. Later producers' cooperatives were formed while the socialist transformation of handicrafts and private industry and commerce was carried out.

Starting from 1952, the policy of regional national autonomy was implemented in the area. At first, a Zhuang autonomous region was set up in the western part of Guangxi, which was enlarged to cover the whole of Guangxi and renamed the Guangxi Zhuang Autonomous Region in 1958. Shortly afterwards, the Wenshan Zhuang-Miao Autonomous Prefecture was established in Yunnan Province and the Lianshan Zhuang-Yao Autonomous County in Guangdong Province. According to statistics tabulated in 1984, there were more than 207,208 Zhuang government employees at various levels in Guangxi, making up one-third of the total number in the region. The case in Wenshan Prefecture and Lianshan County was about the same.

The Zhuang area is basically agricultural, but before liberation the local people never had enough to eat despite their hard work and the favourable natural conditions. By 1983, they had raised grain output by 158 per cent thanks to improved field management and the 500,000 water conservancy projects built since liberation.

Forestry in the Zhuang area has grown even more rapidly, with timber output 150 times what it was before 1949.

The rapid growth of agriculture and forestry has contributed to the development of modern industry, which started from scratch after liberation. In the early 1980s, Guangxi annually produced 4,400 tractors and 3,600 farm lorries.

Guangxi's total agricultural and industrial output today is 40 times the figure for 1950.

In transportation, highways now reach every township in the region, railway mileage has almost quadrupled and shipping services have been opened on the main rivers.

Education and medical services have also taken on a new look. There were three colleges in Guangxi in the early 1950s but higher education was still beyond the reach of the minority groups because of their lack of elementary and secondary education. Today the autonomous region has 19 universities and colleges, and the Guangxi Nationalities Institute alone has turned out over 14,000 minority graduates, half of whom were Zhuangs. Elementary and middle schools have increased in large numbers so as to enroll all school-age children. The number of minority primary school pupils in the region is 15 times the pre-liberation figure. The number of middle school and college students has increased 44 and 170 times respectively.

In the past, the Zhuangs had such a shortage of medical services that for generations they suffered from infectious or contagious diseases like cholera, smallpox, snail fever and malaria. The incidence of malaria, for example, exceeded 90 per cent. Now these diseases have almost been eliminated since hospitals cover all cities, counties and townships, and every village has its clinic. The region as a whole has 84,778 medical workers, over 20 per cent of them being Zhuangs. The number of medical workers in the Zhuang areas of

Yunnan and Guangdong provinces has also grown considerably since liberation.

The Yaos

The Yaos, with a population of 1.4 million, live in mountain communities scattered over 130 counties in five south China provinces and one autonomous region. About 70 per cent of them live in the Guangxi Zhuang Autonomous Region, the rest in Hunan, Yunnan, Guangdong, Guizhou and Jiangxi provinces.

Historically, the Yaos have had at least 30 names based on their ways of production, life styles, dresses and adornments. The name "Yao" was officially adopted after the founding of the People's Republic in 1949.

Half of the Yaos speak the Yao language belonging to the Chinese-Tibetan language family, others use Miao or Dong languages. As a result of close contacts with the Hans and Zhuangs, many Yaos also have learned to speak Chinese or Zhuang language.

Before liberation, the Yaos did not have a written language. Ancient Yaos kept records of important affairs by carving notches on wood or bamboo slips. Later they used Chinese characters. Hand-written copies of words of songs are on display in the Jinxiu Yao Autonomous County in Guangxi. They are believed to be relics of the Ming Dynasty (1368-1644). Ancient stone tablets engraved with Chinese characters can be found in a lot of Yao communities.

Most Yaos live in beautiful, humid mountain valleys densely covered with pines, firs, Chinese firs, Chinese cinnamons, tung oil trees, bamboos and tea bushes. The thickly forested Jianghua Yao

Autonomous County in Hunan is renowned as the "home of Chinese firs." The places inhabited by the Yaos also abound in indigo, edible funguses, bamboo shoots, sweetgrass, mushrooms, honey, dye yam, jute and medical herbs. The forests are teeming with wild animals such as boars, bears, monkeys, muntjacs and masked civets. Rich as they are in natural resources, the Yao mountain areas are ideal for developing a diversified economy.

History   Called the "savage Wuling tribes" some 2,000 years ago, the Yao ancestors lived around Changsha, capital of today's Hunan Province. Two or three centuries later, they were renamed the "Moyao." One of China's foremost ancient poets, Du Fu (712-770), once wrote:

> *"The Moyaos shoot wild geese,*
> *With bows made from mulberry trees."*

As time went on, historical accounts about the Yaos increased, showing growing ties between the Yao and the Han people. In the Song Dynasty (960-1279), agriculture and handicrafts developed considerably in the Yao areas, such that forged iron knives, indigo-dyed cloth and crossbow weaving machines became reputed Yao products. At that time, the Yaos in Hunan were raising cattle and using iron farm tools on fields rented from Han landlords.

During the Ming and Qing dynasties (1368-1911), farm cattle and iron tools spread among the Yaos in Guangxi and Guangdong, who developed paddy fields and planted different kinds of crops on hillsides. They dug ditches and built troughs to draw water from springs for daily use and irrigation. Sideline occupations such as hunting, collecting medical herbs, making charcoal and weaving were pursued side by side with agriculture.

Before the founding of the People's Republic, the Yao economy could be divided into three types:

The first and most common type, with agriculture as the base and forestry and other sideline occupations affiliated, was concentrated in places blessed with fine natural conditions and the greatest influence of the Hans. Here farming methods and social relations very much resembled those of the Han and Zhuang nationalities.

The second type was centred on forestry, with agriculture as a sideline. A few landlords monopolized all the forests and hillside fields, while the foresters and farmers had to pay taxes and rents no matter whether they went ploughing, hunting or fishing, built their houses, buried their dead, collected wild fruits and herbs, drank from mountain streams or even walked on the mountains. When the poor opened up wasteland, for instance, they had to plant saplings between their crops. As soon as the saplings grew into trees, they were paid to the landlords as rent. These exactions caused many Yaos to be continually wandering from place to place.

The third type, engaged in by a tiny percentage of the Yao population, was the primitive "slash-and-burn" cultivation. Although most land was owned by Han and Zhuang landlords, the Yao farmers had some of their own. In such cases, the land belonged to ancient communes, each formed by less than 20 families descended from the same ancestor. The families in a commune worked together and shared the products equally.

The Yaos practised an interesting form of primitive cooperation called "singing-while-digging." This can still be seen in Guangxi today. At times of spring ploughing, 20 to 30 households work together for one household after another until all their fields are ploughed and sown. While the group is working, a young man stands out in the fields, beating a drum and leading the singing. Everyone sings after him.

Today hunting remains an important part of Yao life. On the one hand, it provides them with a greater variety of food; on the other, it prevents their crops and forests from being damaged by too many wild animals. After hunting, the bag is divided equally among the hunters. Sometimes portions are given to the children carried on the elders' backs, but the hunter who caught the animal is awarded a double portion. Sometimes, part of the bag is put aside for the aged people back in the villages.

For nearly 1,000 years before this century, most Yaos were ruled by hereditary headmen. The headmen obeyed the central government, which was always dominated by the Han or other large nationalities. After the Kuomintang took power early in this century, it pursued a system similar to the previous one, which meant rule through puppet Yao headmen and "divide and rule." These policies incited endless conflicts among the Yaos and caused them a great deal of hardship. It was not until the birth of New China that the Yaos realized equality with other nationalities as well as among themselves.

Customs and Habits   The Yaos have such unique life styles that the various communities are quite different from each other. According to the *Book of the Later Han Dynasty* (25-220), the ancient Yaos "liked five-coloured clothes." Later historical records said that the Yaos were "barefoot and colourfully dressed."

In modern times, the Yao costumes maintain their diversity. Men wear jackets buttond in the middle or to the left, and usually belted. Some men like trousers long enough to touch their insteps; some prefer shorts akin to knee breechs. Men's dress is mainly in blue or black. However, in places such as Nandan County in Guangxi, most men wear white knee-length knickerbockers. Men in Liannan County, Guangdong Province, mostly curl their long hair into a bun, which they wrap with a piece of red cloth and top with several pheasant feathers.

Women's dress varies more. Some Yao women fancy short collarless jackets, cloth belts and skirts either long or short; some choose knee-length jackets buttoned in the middle, belts with both ends drooping and either long or short slacks; some have their collars, sleeves and trouser legs embroidered with beautiful patterns. In addition to the silver medals decorating their jackets, many Yao women wear silver bracelets, earrings, necklets and hairpins.

Rice, corn, sweet potatoes and taros make up their staple food. Common vegetables include peppers, pumpkins and soybeans. Alcoholic drinks and tobacco are quite popular. In northern Guangxi, a daily necessity is "oily tea." The tea leaves are fried in oil, then boiled into a thick, salty soup and mixed with puffed rice or soybeans. The oily tea serves as lunch on some occasions. Another favourite dish is "pickled birds." The cleaned birds are blended with salt and rice flour, then sealed into air-tight pots. Beef, mutton and other meat are also pickled this way and considered a banquet delicacy. Many Yaos think it taboo to eat dog meat. If they do eat it, they do the cooking outside the house.

A typical Yao house is a rectangular wood-and-bamboo structure with usually three rooms — the sitting-room in the middle, the bedrooms on both sides. A cooking stove is set in a corner of each bedroom. Some hillside houses are two-storeyed, the upper storey being the sitting-room and bedrooms, the lower storey stables.

For those families who have a bathroom built next to the house, a bath in the evening is an everyday must, even in severe winters.

The Yaos have intriguing marriage customs. With antiphonal singing as a major means of courting, youngsters choose lovers by themselves and get married with the consent of the parents on both sides. However, the bridegroom's family used to have to pay a sizeable amount of silver dollars and pork as betrothal gifts to the bride's family. Some men who could not afford the gifts had to live and work in the bride's families and were often looked down upon.

In old Yao families, the mother's brothers had a decisive say in crucial family matters and enjoyed lots of other privileges. In several counties in Guangxi, for example, the daughters of the father's sisters were obliged to marry the sons of the mother's brothers. If other marriage partners were proposed the betrothal gifts had to be paid to the mother's brothers. This, perhaps, was a remnant of matrilineal society.

Festivals take place one after another in the Yao communities, at a rate of about once a month. Although festive customs alter from place to place, there are common celebrations such as the Spring Festival, the Land God Festival, the Pure Brightness Festival, "Danu" Festival and "Shuawang" Festival. The "Danu" Festival, celebrated in the Yao Autonomous County of Duan in Guangxi, is said to commemorate ancient battles. The "Shuawang" Festival, held every three or five years in the tenth month by the lunar calendar, provides the young people with a golden opportunity for courtship.

The Yaos worshipped a plethora of gods, and their ancestors. Their belief in "Panhu," the dog spirit, revealed a vestige of totemism. Yao communities used to hold lavish rites every few years to chant scriptures and offer sacrifices to their ancestors and gods. In some communities, a solemn ceremony was performed when a boy entered manhood. Legend has it that at the ceremony he had to jump from a three-metre-high platform, climb a pole tied with sharp knives, walk on hot bricks and dip a bare hand into boiling oil. Only after going through these tests could he get married and take part in formal social activities.

With growing scientific and cultural knowledge, the Yaos have, on their own initiative, discarded irrational customs and habits during recent decades, while preserving healthy ones.

The Yaos cherish a magnificent oral literary tradition. As mentioned above, singing forms an indispensible part of their life. When a group of people are opening up wasteland, one or two selected persons stand aside, beating drums and singing to enliven the work. Young males and females often sing antiphonally all through the night. Extremely rich in content, some of the folk songs are beautiful love songs, others recount the history of the Yao nationality, add to the joyous atmosphere at weddings, synchronize working movements, tell legends about the creation of heaven and the earth, ask meaningful questions with each other or tell humorous stories. In many of them, the words have been passed down from generation to generation.

Besides drums, gongs and the *suona* horn (a woodwind instrument), the long waist drum, another traditional musical instrument, is unique to the Yaos. It was said to have been popular early in the Song Dynasty (1127-1279). The revived waist drum dance has been frequently performed both in China and abroad since the 1950s.

The Yaos are expert weavers, dyers and embroiderers. In the Han Dynasty (206 B.C.-A.D.220), they wove with fabrics made from tree bark and dyed it with grass seeds. In the Song Dynasty, they developed delicate designs dyed on white cloth with indigo and beeswax. The product became famous all over the country later.

Post-liberation Life The Yaos have an age-old revolutionary tradition. As early as the Han Dynasty, they fought feudal imperial oppression. During the Tang and Song dynasties, they waged more rebellions against their Han rulers. Still later, in the 15 years from 1316 to 1331, they launched more than 40 uprisings. The largest revolt lasted for a century from 1371. The frightened Ming (1368-1644) emperors had to send three huge armies to conquer the rebels.

The famous Taiping Rebellion, led by Hong Xiuquan in the 1850s against the Qing (1644-1911) feudal bureaucrats, got effective support from the Yaos. Many Yao people joined the Taiping army and were known for their bravery.

The Yaos played an active role in China's new democratic revolution which finally led to the founding of the People's Republic. In the 1920s, after the birth of the Chinese Communist Party, Mao Zedong presided over a meeting which passed the *Resolution to Liberate the Miao and Yao People.* The Yao Autonomous County of Bama in Guangxi today used to be the base area of the 7th Red Army commanded by Deng Xiaoping.

On the eve of the founding of New China, thousands of Yaos joined the guerrillas, expelled local Kuomintang rulers and set up their own governments under the leadership of the Communist Party.

Democratic reforms were carried out after 1949 according to the different characteristics of the three types of Yao economy. The reforms abolished the feudal exploitation system and enhanced the progress of agriculture, forestry, animal husbandry and other forms of production.

Meanwhile, autonomous localities were gradually formed for the Yaos.

In August 1951, when a central government delegation visited Guangxi, it helped the local government set up Longsheng Autonomous County, the first one for the Yaos. From 1952 to 1963, eight Yao autonomous counties appeared, and over 200 autonomous townships covered smaller Yao communities. The policy of regional autonomy enabled the Yaos to be their own masters, ending the history of discrimination and starting an era of national equality and unity.

Local autonomous governments have made successful efforts to improve the people's lives. The Yao Autonomous County of Duan in Guangxi is a fine example. There the Yaos live in karst valleys. The soil is stony, erosive and dry. An old saying went that "the mountains start burning after three fine days; the valleys get flooded after a heavy rain." Now the saying is nothing more than history, as the government has helped remove the jeopardy of droughts and floods by building tunnels, dams and reservoirs.

Before 1949, the Yao area only had a few handicraft workshops. But now, there are many medium- and small-sized power plants and factories making farm machines, processing timber, and making chemicals and cement.

In the early 1950s, few Yao people had any education, but today, schools can be found in all villages. Almost every child of school age gets elementary and secondary education. Some elite students go on to colleges.

In the old days, the Yaos never knew such a thing as a hospital. As a result, pestilence haunted the region. Now, government-trained Yao doctors and nurses work in hospitals or clinics in every Yao county, township and village. Epidemics such as smallpox and cholera have been eliminated. With the people's health well protected, the Yao population has doubled since the founding of the People's Republic.

The Mulams

The Mulam nationality has a population of 90,400, of which 90 per cent live in Luocheng County in the Guangxi Zhuang Autonomous Region. Others are scattered in neighbouring counties.

The Mulam language is a member of the Zhuang-Dong language group of the Chinese-Tibetan language family, but because of extensive contacts with the majority Han and local Zhuangs many Mulams speak one or both of these languages in addition to their own.

Their homeland is one of rolling hills interspersed with lush green valleys. The Wuyang and Longjiang rivers cross their territory, which has an ideal climate for growing paddy rice, maize, beans, potatoes, melons and cotton. The area is famous for its tea and medicinal herbs, as well as mineral resources such as coal, iron and sulphur.

History Historical records trace the Mulam nationality back to the period of the Yuan Dynasty (1271-1368), when their society seems to have been entering the feudal stage. The Mulam villages paid tribute in grain to the imperial court twice a year.

In the Qing Dynasty (1644-1911) the Mulam areas were divided into "Li," under which were "Dongs" — units of ten households.

The Dong chief was responsible for collecting taxes and law and order. The Dongs were mostly inhabited by families sharing the same surname. Later, when they increased in size, the Dongs were divided into "Fangs."

Economy Even prior to liberation, the farming economy of the Mulams was comparatively advanced. Farming techniques, crop varieties and tools were basically the same as those of their Han and Zhuang neighbours. Oxen and water buffalos were the main draught animals, although horses were sometimes used also. Some 60 per cent of arable land was taken up by paddy fields, and the Mulams had long known the use of manure fertilizer.

The Mulams' well-developed irrigation system, unfortunately, was under the control of the rich landlords, who syphoned most of the water off for themselves. The encroachment of insects and wild animals was a serious problem for the Mulam farmers.

In the past, each household was a basic production unit. The division of labour between men and women was not strict, but ploughing, carrying manure and threshing were usually men's jobs, while women did the rice transplanting, sowing and housework.

Also well developed were sideline products, which included collecting medicinal herbs, raising livestock, blacksmithing, making pottery and weaving cloth.

Prior to liberation, land in the Mulam areas was heavily concentrated in the hands of the rich landlords, especially the most fertile parts. The landlords demanded that their tenants pay rent in kind and provide unpaid labour service. They also exploited the poorer peasants by means of usury.

Customs and Culture Mulam houses consist of three rooms, usually one-storied, with mud walls and tile roofs. Inside, on the left of the door, the ground is dug away to form a cooking pit. The livestock are kept away from the living quarters.

Rice, maize and potatoes are the staple diet of the Mulams, who also enjoy eating hot peppers and glutinous rice. It is taboo to eat cats or snakes. Mulams who bear the surnames Luo and Wu are forbidden to eat dog meat or the internal organs of animals.

The Mulams used to be famous for their spinning, weaving and dyeing, and their favourite colour is deep blue. Traditionally, men wore jackets with large buttons down the front, long, baggy trousers and straw sandals. Young girls wear their hair in braids, which is coiled up onto their heads after marriage. Women's jewelry includes silver earrings, bracelets and finger rings.

Early marriage arranged by the parents was common before liberation. Brides did not live with their husbands until the first child was born. Intermarriage with the Hans and Zhuangs was permissible, but weddings were costly affairs which drained the wealth of a family.

The Mulams used to be animists, and celebrated a festival every month, the most important of which was the Yifan Festival. At this celebration, pigs and sheep were slaughtered, dramas and lion and dragon dances were performed, and the shamans chanted incantations. The lunar New Year's Day was the Mulam's New Year, and the eighth day of the fourth lunar month was "Ox Birthday," when the oxen were given a rest and fed glutinous rice, and wine and meat were offered to the Ox God. On the fifth day of the fifth lunar month the Dragon Boat Festival was celebrated. Unlike the Han and Zhuang Dragon Boat festivals, the Mulams used to carry a paper boat into the fields and a shaman would chant spells to drive away insects and ensure a good harvest. The 15th day of the eighth lunar month was Youth Festival, when young people gathered to sing folk songs and make lovers' trysts.

Folk songs and "Caidiao" (a form of local drama) are very popular among the people. The songs are antiphonal and sung in the Han language.

Liberation and Progress　The Mulam area was liberated in the winter of 1949. After local bandits and tyrants had been eliminated, land reform was set in motion in 1952. By 1956, the task of organizing the Mulam farmers into cooperatives had been completed. Attention was paid particularly to irrigation systems. In 1981, in Dongmen and Siba townships in Luocheng County, 13 water-conservancy projects were completed, increasing the irrigated area from 266 hectares to 3,300 hectares and ensuring a steady growth in grain output. Farm mechanization went hand in hand with other development projects.

Industries, mainly connected with the farming sector, have also sprung up . By 1981, Luocheng County had four factories, turning out cement, chemical fertilizers and pesticides, repairing farm machinery, processing timber and making iron castings. Collective enterprises are also taking shape.

Before the People's Republic was founded, transportation in the region was solely horse- and man-power. Now, highways connect all the major towns and a 65-km railway links the Mulams and their products with the outside world.

Much progress has also been made in recent years in education and health. There were only a few primary schools and two middle schools for the Mulams before 1949, but nowadays, more than 95 per cent of Mulam children are in school.

Medical facilities have been set up to cover the area, and endemic diseases brought under control.

These achievements are due in no small part to the efforts of the Mulam people and their cadres who represent them at all levels of local and national government.

The Maonans

The Maonan nationality has a population of 38,100, living in the northern part of the Guangxi Zhuang Autonomous Region.

The Maonan communities are located in sub-tropical areas characterized by a mild climate and beautiful scenery, with stony hills jutting up here and there, among which small patches of flatland are scattered. There are many small streams which are used to irrigate paddy rice fields. Drought-resistant crops are grown in the Dashi Mountain area where water is scarce. In addition to paddy rice, agricultural crops include maize, wheat, Chinese sorghum, sweet potatoes, soybean, cotton and tobacco. Special local products include camphor, palm fibre and musk. The area abounds in mineral resources such as iron, manganese, stibium and mercury. The Maonans are experts in raising beef cattle, which are marketed in Shanghai, Guangzhou and Hongkong.

People surnamed Tan take up 80 per cent of the population. Legend has it that their ancestors earlier lived in Hunan Province, then emigrated to Guangxi and multiplied by marrying the local women who spoke the Maonan tongue. There are other Maonans surnamed Lu, Meng, Wei and Yan, whose ancestral homes are said to have been in Shandong and Fujian provinces.

The Maonan language belongs to the Dong-Shui branch of the

Zhuang-Dong language group of the Chinese-Tibetan language family. Almost all the Maonans know both the Han and the Zhuang languages because of long contact with those people.

History Long subjected to the oppression of the reactionary ruling class, the Maonan areas developed very slowly. At the end of the Ming Dynasty (1368-1644), the Maonans still used wooden hoes and ploughs. Various iron tools were in use by the time of Qing Dynasty (1644-1911), when land was gradually concentrated and the division of classes became distinct. There began to appear farm labourers who did not own an inch of land, poor peasants who had a small amount of land, self-sufficient middle peasants, and landlords and rich peasants who owned large amounts. The landlords and rich peasants cruelly exploited farm labourers and poor peasants by means of land rent and usury. There were also slave girls either bought by the landlords or forced by unpaid debts to serve landlords all their lives.

The Maonans waged struggles in order to resist the oppression of the feudal ruling class. During the Liberation War (1946-1949), the Maonan people, led by the Chinese Communist Party, together with the local Hans and Zhuangs, organized armed forces, effectively helping the People's Liberation Army liberate their homeland.

Economy The Maonan people are chiefly engaged in agriculture, but also have sidelines which yield more than half their total income, such as weaving bambooware, raising beef cattle, making wooden articles and casting iron. Before liberation, their major farm tools were ox-pulled ploughshares, iron hoes, foot-pedalled ploughs, scrapers and scythes. Backward tools and farming techniques kept the agricultural production at a very low level for a long time.

The land ownership in the Maonan areas was highly concentrated before 1949. In Yuhuan Township, Huanjiang County, the landlords and rich peasants — some 3.8 per cent of the township population — occupied 36.1 per cent of the total arable land; whereas the farm labourers and poor peasants who took up 53.4 per cent of the population only owned 18.7 per cent of the land. Land rent was mostly paid in kind at an exploitative rate.

Customs and Culture The Maonans with the same surnames

and from the same clans usually live together in small villages with only a few households. The biggest village consists of not more than 100 households. Their houses and clothes are basically identical to those of their Han and Zhuang neighbours. Houses have two storeys, with mud walls and tile roofs. The second floor is used as living quarters and the ground floor for livestock.

The major staples of the Maonans are rice and maize, and then millet, sweet potatoes and pumpkins. They all enjoy tobacco, alcohol, tea and hot peppers. They pick out big sweet potatoes with no injuries, dry them in the sun and leave them in the open at night to be drenched by dew. Twenty or 30 days later, The potatoes are put into cellars or above the cooking stoves. After another 20 days or so, they are steamed and enjoyed as a delicacy.

The Maonan families are generally small and monogamous. In the past, marriages were all decided and arranged by the parents. There were customs like "not settling in the home of the husband," and a younger brother would marry the deceased elder brother's wife or vice versa. The remarriage of widows was greatly restricted. When a person died, a Taoist priest would be invited to recite scriptures and join in the funeral procession, the son of the dead person would "buy water" at a river or in a well to wash the body. Before the burial, chicken blood was sprayed into the grave to bless the spirit of the deceased and protect his or her offspring.

The Maonans celebrate the Spring Festival, Zhongyuan Festival and Pure Brightness Day, similar to those of their Han and Zhuang neighbours. However, the Fenglong Festival is unique to the Maonans and is celebrated by offering sacrifices to God and their ancestors to pray for a good harvest. Married daughters and relatives living in other places return to their home villages for the celebration. A special treat is five-coloured rice. In the past, there were many taboos, such as suspending productive labour on festivals, which hindered the development of production. After liberation, weddings and funerals were simplified, and some superstitious activities were reformed.

Singing is a popular recreational activity of the Maonans. In addition, they also enjoy "Maonan opera," based on folklore and legends and portraying love affairs, anti-feudal struggles, joys and sorrows, partings and reunions, and the lofty ideals of the people.

Maonan carving and weaving have unique styles. The former comprises wood and stone varieties, delicate and vivid in imagery. The latter is famous for flowery bamboo hats and bamboo mattresses.

The Maonans are polite and hospitable, calling each other brothers and sisters when they meet. When guests visit, they entertain them with oranges and sweet potatoes. Guests, important or not, are always solicitously invited to dine with their hosts.

Liberation and New Life The Maonan areas were liberated in October 1949. From then on, they started a new life. In the spring of 1950, a people's government was established in Xianan District, the biggest Maonan area. The agrarian reform, which started in the autumn of 1952, obliterated feudal land ownership, raised the Maonans' enthusiasm for productive labour and improved their life. By February 1952, more than 99 per cent of the farm households had joined the agricultural cooperatives. The change of productive relations spurred the Maonans to build water-conservancy projects and farm scientifically, raising output rapidly.

The political status of the Maonans also changed rapidly. Maonan deputies are elected to attend the National People's Congress and the people's congresses at all levels of the region. Many Maonan cadres have come of age, and some of them have taken on leading positions at the county level.

Since liberation, the Maonan people have scored gratifying achievements in the development of industrial and agricultural production, education and medical care. Huanjiang used to be a poor mountainous area where "there were more stones than soil, and water was as dear as oil; three straight days of rainfall would cause a flood, and streams ran dry if the rain stopped for half a day." But this problem has been solved by the construction of the Nanchuan Reservoir and a related irrigation network. Helped by Han workers, three small hydraulic power stations have been completed, providing electricity for irrigation and lighting.

There are bus services connecting 11 of the 14 Maonan villages in Huanjiang County. In the past, there were only two schools in the whole of Xianan, and only children from rich families could afford to attend them. Now there are several middle and primary schools. There are also some 100 Maonan college graduates working in the area.

Medical care for the Maonans used to be very poor and smallpox, cholera, malaria, measles and typhoid were endemic. Since liberation, the Maonans have had their own doctors and medical-care network. The incidence of diseases has been greatly reduced, and such contagious diseases as smallpox and cholera eradicated.

The Jings

The 12,000 people of this tiny nationality live in compact communities primarily in the three islands of Wanwei, Wutou and Shanxin in the Fangcheng Multi-National Autonomous County, the Guangxi Zhuang Autonomous Region, near the Sino-Vietnamese border. About one quarter of them live among the Han and Zhuang nationalities in nearby counties and towns.

The Jings live in a subtropical area with plenty of rainfall and rich mineral resources. The Beibu Gulf to its south is an ideal fishing ground. Of the more than 700 species of fish found there, over 200 are of great economic value and high yields. Pearls, sea horses and sea otters which grow in abundance are prized for their medicinal value. Sea water from the Beibu Gulf is good for salt making. The main crops there are rice, sweet potato, peanut, taro and millet, and sub-tropical fruits like papaya, banana and longan are also plentiful. Mineral deposits include iron, monazite, titanium, magnetite and silica. The large tracts of mangroves growing in marshy land along the coast are a rich source of tannin, an essential raw material for the tanning industry.

The Jing people had their own script which was called *Zinan*. Created on the basis of the script of the Han nationality towards the end of the 13th century, it was found in old song books and religious scriptures. Most Jings read and write in the Han script because they have lived with Hans for a long time. They speak the Cantonese dialect.

The ancestors of the Jings emigrated from Viet Nam to China in the early 16th century and first settled on the three uninhabited islands since the neighbourhood had been populated by people of Han and Zhuang nationalities. Shoulder to shoulder with the Hans and Zhuangs there, they developed the border areas together and sealed close relations in their joint endeavours over the centuries.

Pre-liberation Days   Before liberation, the Jings made a living by fishing, with farming as a secondary occupation. On Shanxin island, 70 per cent of the villagers' income came from fishing, 27 per cent from farming and the remaining three per cent from other productive operations. Output of the fishing industry was low due to the fishermen's poor equipment, backward methods and inability to operate in deep waters. Farm production averaged only 750 kg per hectare and the harvest could provide the peasants with only three or four months' provision.   The Jings had to make ends meet by bartering fish for food grain and other daily necessities and by handicrafts like carpentry and bamboo weaving.

Class polarisation among the Jings was glaring. Most farmland, fishing gear and grounds and salt pans were in the hands of landlords of Jing or Han nationalities. Land rent came as high as 50 per cent of the harvest plus free labour services. Under the rule of a headman, all villagers were required to pay taxes and perform military service, with violations severely punished.

This brutal system left the villagers half-starving in their thatched huts and gunny-sack clothes. Four hundred of the 450 families on the three islands were in dire poverty by the time of liberation in 1949. Some 80 families had had to sell their children, and 75 others fled the area due to famine. One hundred and twenty men had been pressganged into the reactionary army and 69 others had been jailed.

Post-liberation Life   The first campaign after liberation was to rid the Jing areas of bandits and despots. Then rent reduction was initiated and by the spring of 1952 redistribution of land had been completed. This was followed by democratic reform among the fishermen.

The Dongxing Multi-National Autonomous County for the Jing, Zhuang and Yao nationalities was set up in 1958. It was renamed the Fangcheng Multi-National Autonomous County.

Great changes have taken place on the three islands peopled by the Jings. The most significant projects undertaken on the poor alluvial islands were the construction of 11 dykes to reclaim land from the sea and connect the islands with the mainland. A total of 400 hectares of land was created, equivalent to four times the original cultivated land on the islands. The Jing people who used to be grain deficient, now have a surplus to sell to the state.

New motorized junks and fishing gear have been added for deep sea operations. Pearl cultivation has been a thriving industry since 1958, when pearl oyster farms were built in a deep water harbour ideal for the growth of such shells. Trees planted over an area of 433 hectares since the same year now form a shelter belt against winds and shifting sands. Over the years tropical fruits such as banana, papaya, coconut and longan, introduced from elsewhere, have been doing well on the islands.

The Jings, who were all illiterate before liberation, are now going to school, and many young people have moved onto college education. Each village now has a clinic, and paramedics have been assigned to each fishing vessel.

Jing people like antiphonal songs which are melodious and lyrical. Their traditional instruments include the two-stringed fiddle, flute, drum, gong and the single-stringed fiddle, a unique musical instrument of the nationality. Folk stories and legends abound. Their favourite dances feature lanterns, fancy coloured sticks, embroidery and dragons.

Jing costume is simple and practical. Traditionally, women wear tight-fitting, collarless short blouses buttoned in front plus a diamond-shaped top apron and broad black or brown trousers. When going out, they would put on a light coloured gown with narrow sleeves. They also like earrings. Men wear long jackets reaching down to the knees and girdles. Now most people dress themselves like their Han neighbours though a few elderly women retain their tradition and a few young women coil their hair and dye their teeth black.

Many Jings are believers of Buddhism or Taoism, with a few followers of Catholicism. They also celebrate the Lunar New Year—Spring Festival — and the Pure Brightness Festival, the Dragon Boat Festival and the Mid-Autumn Festival like the Hans.

Fish sauce is a favourite condiment the Jing people use in cooking, and a cake prepared with glutinous rice mixed with sesame is a great delicacy for them.

There used to be some taboos, such as stepping over a fishing net placed on the beach, sitting on a new raft before it was launched, and stepping on the stove. But many old habits that hampered the growth of production have died out bit by bit.

The Tujias

In the Wuling Range of western Hunan and Hubei provinces, at elevations from 400 to 1,500 metres, dwell 2.83 million people called the Tujias. They live mainly in the Xiangxi Tujia-Miao Autonomous Prefecture, Exi Tujia-Miao Autonomous Prefecture and some counties in southeastern Hunan and western Hubei. In these areas, the climate is mild but rainy, and the land is well-forested. The Youshui, Fengshui and Qingjiang rivers intersect there, and on the terraced mountainsides and in the green valleys grow rice, maize, wheat and potatoes. Cash crops include beets, ramie, cotton, tung oil, oil tea and tea, with oil tea and tung oil playing key commercial roles. Timber includes pine, China fir, cypress and the nanmu tree. The area is rich in rare medicinal herbs, minerals, aquatic products and giant salamanders.

About 20,000-30,000 people living in remote areas such as Longshan speak Tujia, a language which is similar to that spoken by the Yis and belongs to the Chinese-Tibetan language system. But the large majority have come to speak the Han and Miao languages, now that the Tujias have been largely assimilated. Their clothing and customs are very much like those of the Hans. Old Tujia ways survive only in remote areas.

Life Style Traditionally, Tujia women wear jackets trimmed with lace and with short, broad sleeves. They wear long skirts, and wrap their coiled hair in cloth. They adorn themselves with necklaces, earrings, bracelets and ankle bracelets. Tujia men wear short jackets with many buttons in front. The traditional handwoven "xi" and "tong" cloth with intricate designs are the main material for clothing. In pre-liberation times, the gentry wore furs in winter, while the poor peasants wore thin garments and were cold.

In the old society Tujia chiefs and officials had wooden homes with tiled roofs and carved columns, while ordinary people lived in thatched bamboo-woven houses.

At one time, young Tujias could select their marriage partners fairly freely, and courting involved a great deal of singing and dancing. Only approval of a wizard was necessary for a match. But as the feudal economy developed, marriage became more a matter of economics. Parents would calculate the value of their children as potential partners, and choice became limited by wealth. The new marriage law promulgated in the early days of the People's Republic made mercenary marriages illegal.

In feudal times, cremation of the dead was a basic custom of the Tujias. During a funeral, a Taoist priest would walk in front of a procession while a wizard chanted scripture. Burial was later adopted following association with the Hans.

The Tujias had some rather distinctive taboos. Young girls or pregnant women were not permitted to sit on thresholds, while men could not enter a house wearing straw raincoats or carrying hoes or empty buckets. Nor were people allowed to approach the communal fire or say ostensibly unlucky things on auspicious days. Young women were not allowed to sit next to male visitors, although young girls could. At worship ceremonies, cats were kept away as their meowing was considered unlucky.

Although they are dying out as the Tujias become more assimilated, religious beliefs have included Taoism, ancestor worship and a shamanistic belief in gods, ghosts and demons. Formerly, prayers were said before hunting, and when a person died, wizards were invited to expel evil spirits and ghosts from the house.

The Tujias are well-known for a hand dance with over 70 ritual gestures to indicate war, hunting, farming and feasting. The dance is popular at Spring Festival, the Lunar New Year, when several thousand people participate. Tujia epics, which are imaginative, tell of the origins of mankind and of the migrations and aspirations of the Tujias in dramatic and poetic ways. Tujia folksongs are usually about love and work, battles and grief. Virtually all Tujias can compose and sing songs.

Embroidery and weaving stand high among Tujia crafts and their patterned quilts are especially beautiful. The Tujia gunny cloth is valued for its durability.

History There are several conflicting versions of the origin of the Tujias. Some say they are the descendants of the ancient Ba people; others claim they come from the Wuman, who moved to western Hunan from Guizhou Province; yet another tale claims they came from Jiangxi Province in the east at the end of the Tang Dynasty (618-907). In any case, the Tujias were a distinct ethnic group in western Hunan by the early Five Dynasties period, around the year 910. After early contact with Hans, they developed metal smelting and commercial crafts.

Han peasants migrated to western Hunan in the early 12th century, bringing with them modern tools and farming expertise. In western Hubei, feudal lords sold some of their lands to Han peasants and businesspeople, some of whom became landlords. The feudal lords also commanded the economy. So the Tujias were exploited by their own chieftains, feudal lords and Han landlords.

During the Ming Dynasty (1368-1644), Tujia soldiers, together with Han, Zhuang, Miao, Yao, Mulam and Hui fighters, were sent to the country's coastal provinces to fight against Japanese pirates pillaging the areas.

In the 20th century, peasant movements gathered momentum under the Chinese Communist Party's leadership. In 1928, Communist Party organizer He Long led an armed rebellion in western Hunan and Hubei, and Tujias fought as guerrillas in Sanzhi, Hefeng, Xianfeng, Enshi and Jianshi. Toward the end of 1934, He Long's forces joined the Central Red Army in the 12,500-kilometre Long March. Many young Tujias joined the Red Army when it passed through Tujia areas in 1935, and after 1938 they went north to the Anti-Japanese front in Yanan.

During the liberation war (1946-49), Tujia guerrillas, alongside the Chinese People's Liberation Army, defeated reactionary local armed forces and Kuomintang troops and helped overthrow the Kuomintang rule.

Post-Liberation Development   Since ancient times, the Tujias have been a distinct ethnic group, but they were not recognized officially as such until after liberation in 1950. They were granted "minority nationality" status in 1956; in the following year, the Xiangxi Tujia-Miao Autonomous Prefecture was established, where Tujia laws and institutions were protected. The Laifeng and Hefeng Autonomous counties were chartered in Hubei in May 1980.

Most Tujias were illiterate before liberation. Now there are 4,000 primary schools, and 91 per cent of Tujia children of school age are enrolled. At the same time, there are 93,000 secondary school students in 276 schools. Since 1959, the number of medical facilities available to Tujias has increased by 90 per cent, that of hospital beds by 120 per cent, and that of medical personnel by 900 per cent.

Industry in Tujia areas, which was nonexistent before liberation, has developed since 1950. Tujia enterprises are involved in metallurgy, machinery, coal, electric generation, textiles, plastics, papermaking, chemicals, building materials, boat building and wines.

Before 1949, transportation through the high mountains and forests where the Tujias live was very difficult. Goods had to be carried by hand or on people's backs. Now remote areas are linked by roads and bridges. The Hunan-Guizhou railway has made the Tujia area accessible to the rest of China.

The Lis

Hainan, China's second largest island after Taiwan, is the home of the Li nationality with a population of about 817,600. Most of them live in and around Tongze, capital of the Hainan Li-Miao Autonomous Prefecture, and Baoting, Ledong, Dongfang and other counties under its jurisdiction; others live among people of the Han and Hui nationalities in other parts of the island.

Lying at the foot of the Wuzhi Mountains, the Li area is a tropical paradise with fertile land and abundant rainfall. Coconut palms and rubber trees line the beaches and people in some places reap three crops of rice a year and grow maize and sweet potatoes all the year round. The area is the country's major producer of tropical crops such as coconut, arica, sisal hemp, lemon grass, cocoa, coffee, rubber, oil palm, cashew, pineapple, casava, mango and banana.

The island is abundant in minerals like copper, tin, crystal quarts, phosphorus, iron and tungsten. There are numerous salt pans and many fine harbours along the coast, and good fishing grounds off the shore. Pearls, coral and hawksbill, turtles of commercial value are found in the coastal waters. Black gibbons, civets and peacocks live in the primeval forests which abound with valuable timber trees.

The Lis had no written script. Their spoken language belongs to the Chinese-Tibetan language family. But many of them now speak the

Chinese language. A new romanized script was created for the Li nationality in 1957 with government help.

History   According to historical records, the term "Li" first appeared in the Tang Dynasty (618-907). The Lis are believed to be descendants of the ancient Yue nationality, with especially close relations with the Luoyues — a branch of the Yues — who migrated from Guangdong and Guangxi on the mainland to Hainan Island long before the Qin Dynasty (221-206 B.C.). Archaeological finds on the island show that Li ancestors settled there some 3,000 years ago during the late Shang Dynasty or early Zhou Dynasty when they led a primitive matriarchal communal life. Ethnically, the Lis are closely related to the Zhuang, Bouyei, Shui, Dong and Dai nationalities, and their languages bear resemblance in pronunciation, grammar and vocabulary. People of the Han nationality began to settle on the island also before the Qin Dynasty as farmers, fishermen and merchants. Together, people of the two nationalities contributed to the development of Hainan. Later, the Han Dynasty sent troops under Lu Bode and Ma Yuan to set up prefectures and strengthen government control there and enhance relations between the mainland and the island.

In the 6th century, Madame Xian, a political leader of the Yues in southwest Guangdong, Hainan and the Leizhou Peninsula, pledged allegiance to the Sui Dynasty. Her effort in promoting national unity and unification of the country not only enhanced the relationship between Hainan Island and the central part of China but also helped the development of the primitive Li society by introducing feudal elements into it.

The Tang Dynasty (618-907) further strengthened central control over the Li areas by setting up five prefectures which consisted of 22 counties. In the Song Dynasty (960-1279), rice cultivation was introduced and irrigation developed, and local farmers were able to grow four crops of ramie annually. Brocade woven by Li women became popular in central China.

In the early Yuan Dynasty, Huang Daopo, the legendary weaver in Chinese history, achieved her excellence by learning weaving techniques from the Lis. Running away as a child bride from her home in Shanghai, she came to Hainan and lived with the Lis there. Returning to Shanghai, she passed on the Li techniques to others and invented a cotton fluffer, a pedal spinning wheel and looms, which were the most advanced in the world at the time.

The feudal mode of production became dominant in Hainan during the Ming and Qing dynasties as elsewhere in China. Most of the land was in the hands of a small number of landlords, and peasants were exploited by usury and land rent. Large tracts of land were seized by the government for official use. Only in the Wuzhi Mountains did people still work the land collectively, but even this remnant of the communal system was used by feudal landlords as a means of exploitation.

Heavy oppression of the Li people kindled flames of uprising. In the Song and Yuan dynasties, the Lis in Hainan staged 18 large-scale uprisings; during the Ming and Qing dynasties 14 major rebellions took place. After the Opium War in 1840, Hainan was invaded by foreign imperialists who brought untold sufferings to the local Li and Han people, who rose repeatedly against feudal lords and foreign invaders.

The first Communist Party cell was organized in Hainan in 1924. In 1926, the Communist Party Committee for the Qiongya Area came into being. This was followed by the establishment of the trade union, peasant and women's organizations in Lingshui County. The Party organized revolutionary armed forces on the island and liberated the county seat of Lingshui in February of 1928. The first worker-peasant democratic county government in Hainan was founded there, and revolutionary base areas were set up in the rural areas. Soon afterwards, the Qiongya Worker-Peasant Revolutionary Army was formed.

The Japanese invaded Hainan Island in February 1939. People of various nationalities in Hainan rose in resistance led by the Communist Party. In the spring of 1944, an anti-Japanese guerrilla force — the Qiongya Column — was formed. It grew into an army of 7,000 towards the end of the war, liberating three-fifths of the island. In 1946, the Qiongya Column led by the Special Party Committee of Qiongya and with the support of the Li and other nationalities, repulsed the repeated attacks of Chiang Kai-shek's reactionary troops.   A large number of Li cadres were tempered in the protracted struggle. Hainan was liberated by People's Liberation Army forces coming down from the mainland in the spring of 1950.

Customs   Li women wear buttonless blouses and tight-fitting long skirts.   Women in some places wear pullovers. They do their hair in a coil at the back and pin it with bone hairpins and wear embroidered kerchiefs.   They like silver jewellery, and some still tattoo their faces. Men wear collarless jackets, and those in Dongfang County wear much the same kind of jackets as women.

The Li people like roast meat and pickled sour meat mixed with rice meal and wild herbs.   Arica is a favourite with women, who chew it with shell ashes wrapped in green leaves; the juice dyes their lips red.   The Lis are also heavy smokers and drinkers.

Several families related by blood live together, pooling their labour and sharing the harvest. They dwell in boat-shaped thatched bamboo houses with woven bamboo or rattan floors half a metre above the ground.   These houses have mud plastered walls.

The Li people are monogamous, and close relatives are not allowed to marry each other.   Before liberation, marriages were arranged by parents when their children were still young and brideprices were as high as several hundred silver dollars or several head of cattle.   Those who could not afford the bride-price were indentured to the bride's family for several years. Shortly after the wedding, the bride went back to live with her own parents until she knew she had become pregnant. These old customs have gradually gone out of practice since liberation.

Death was announced by the firing of guns, and the body was put into a coffin hewed out of a single log and was buried in the village cemetery.   Before 1949, animism and ancestor worship were common among the Lis who also believed in witchcraft. All this has been abolished since the island was liberated in 1950.

The Lis are known for their skill in weaving kapok. They are also famed for their knowledge of herbal medicine. Their remedies for snakebites and rabies have proved very effective.

They keep a primitive calendar and calculate according to a 12-

day cycle, with each day named after an animal, similar to the 12 earthly branches used by the Han nationality.

Socio-economic Conditions   The Li economy was backward and development was lopsided before liberation. Over 94 per cent of the Li area was in semi-colonial, semi-feudal society and the landlord economy was fairly developed. In general, the level of development in agriculture and handicraft there was lower than that of the Han areas, so were commerce and animal husbandry. People were impoverished under feudal exploitation and the Kuomintang government's heavy taxation.

In the heart of the Wuzhi Mountains, 13,000 Lis still lived a primitive communal life of collective farming by the time of liberation. A communal farm consisted of several families related by blood. They worked collectively and shared the harvests. This area was more backward than the rest of the island economically. The communal farms — the "Hemus" — fell into two major categories: smaller farms based on maternal or paternal blood relations and larger farms which admitted "outsiders" who had no blood ties with the original member families.

Each commune had a headman who was in charge of production and distribution and officiated at religious ceremonies with his wife's assistance. He was also a social leader who mediated disputes and was empowered to admit "outsiders" as communal members. Headmen and members were equals in the old days but, under the influence of feudalism, some headmen began to seize public grain reserves as their own and exploit "outsiders." Some later became government officials and degenerated into local tyrants.

While farm cattle remained public property, farm tools, hunting and fishing gear and work tools were privately owned by families. With the inception of private ownership of cattle and land, the practice of selling and pawning land became popular, as did the leasing of cattle and land. Rent was paid in kind. The exploitation of hired labour began to appear, and the primitive communal system gave way to serfdom and slavery. The establishment of prefectures and counties accelerated class differentiation among the Li people.

A social unit called "kom" existed for a long time in the Li areas.

Koms were different in size, and had strict territorial boundaries between each other. A big kom consisted of several small ones which in turn were usually formed by two villages. Most disputes between the koms arose over infringement of each other's territory for hunting, fishing or wood-cutting purposes. Like many of the communal farms, the koms were based on blood relations, and each had one or several headmen chosen for their administrative ability or seniority. Headmen chaired meetings, settled disputes and formulated regulations. With the growth of the feudal economy, the headmen of the koms gradually came to represent those in power.

Hainan's liberation in May was followed by the campaign to wipe out remaining bandits and fight local despots. The Hainan Li-Miao Autonomous Prefecture was founded in July 1952 and the People's Government provided the local people with seeds, farm tools, cattle and grain to help them develop production. Land reform brought tremendous changes to the Li areas. New water conservancy projects and improved farming methods have contributed tremendously to the growth of the rural economy over the years.

There are now throughout the prefecture 380 mining and industrial enterprises covering plastics, matches, food, sugar refining products, pottery, cement, radio, iron and steel, textile, drugs and machinery.

Poor peasants were mostly illiterate in the past. They made knots on ropes or counted beans to keep records and notes. Now the more than 18,000 primary schools provide education for almost all school-age children. Middle schools number more than 200. An increasing number of young Lis are attending colleges.

Hospitals, epidemic prevention stations and clinics have been set up in the prefecture and all the counties. Smallpox and cholera, once rampant here, have been brought under control while the incidence of malaria which once took the lives of a whole village, has been reduced drastically.

The Shes

The 370,000 Shes are scattered in Zhejiang, Jiangxi, Anhui and Guangdong provinces. They live in villages of several dozen households or live along with Hans. Most reside in hilly country 500 to 1,500 metres high. Rivers have carved out their valleys. The climate is mild and humid, the frost season brief, and the land fertile. Agricultural products abound: rice, sweet potatoes, wheat, rape, beans, tobacco and potatoes are just a few.

Timber and bamboo are important commercial commodities for the Shes; other native produce include tea, oil tea, dried and cured bamboo shoots, peanuts, ramie, mushroom, camphor and medicinal herbs. Mineral resources include coal, iron, gold, copper, alum, graphite, sulphur, talcum, mica and many other non-ferrous metals.

The She language is very close to the Kejia dialect of the Hans, and most Shes speak Chinese instead of their ethnic tongue; a few Guangdong Shes speak a language similar to the Miao.

How the Shes Live Shes like to sing. They sing in the fields as well as on special festival occasions. and every year Shes participate in several singing festivals. Shes like to sing duets, but they sing alone as well.

Women wear clothes with flowers, birds and geometric embroidery. Often they wear bright-coloured sashes or bamboo hats,

411

decorated with pearls and trimmed with white or red silk lace. Lace is also used to trim clothing.

In some areas, women wear shorts year-round. When they do so, they wrap their legs and wear colourful waist sashes and jackets with lace. They coil their hair on top of the heads and tie it with red wool thread. On her wedding day, a She bride will wear a phoenix coronet held in place by silver hairpins.

The She families are organized by "ancestral temples" together with people of the same surname or clan. Each such temple has a chief responsible for settling internal disputes, administering public affairs and presiding over sacrificial ceremonies. Within each temple are the "fangs," under which blood-related groups live together.

The basic living and production unit remains the patriarchal family, led by the eldest man. Still, She women enjoy a higher status than their Han sisters. In fact, She men often live with their wives' families and adopt their surnames.

Today, She marital customs are much like those of the Hans. But under pre-liberation feudal conditions, parent-arranged marriages were common, as were outright sales of daughters. Brides' dowries usually included farm tools, bamboo hats and rain capes. The wedding ceremony was simple. The groom would go to the home of the bride's family for a feast. Finding the table empty, he would sing out what he wanted, calling for chopsticks, wine and traditional wedding food. At the end of the banquet, he would sing again, this time ordering the dishes to be removed. The cook, in turn, would return his songs with melodies of his own. The newlyweds would say prayers to their ancestors and bid farewell to the bride's relatives. With the groom in front, they would walk to his family's home, each holding an umbrella and singing in echo. The groom's parents would welcome them at the front door, completing the wedding ceremony.

As the feudal landlord system evolved, parents and matchmakers became more important in making "correct" marriages; bride prices became exorbitant, and the poorest peasants were unable to afford marriage. Because of so many pre-arranged, loveless marriages, folk-singing gatherings became a means for people to spend time with their lovers — in defiance of the feudal marriage system.

Centuries ago, Shes cremated their dead, but by the 1940s earth burial was common.

Like Hans, Shes celebrate the Spring Festival, Lantern Festival, Pure Brightness Festival (in memory of the dead), Dragon Boat-Racing Festival, Moon Festival and the Double-Ninth Festival. In addition, the third day of the third lunar month is a holiday on which no work is done. Ancestor worship is the centre of another festival on the eighth day of the fourth lunar month. Sacrifices are offered to the "Duobei King" in October, and people have a day off on the 19th of the second lunar month to mark the Buddha's attainment of Nirvana.

Traditionally, every clan was symbolized by a dragon-headed stick, a sign of the Shes' totemic beliefs. Moreover, Shes used to trace their ancestry to a legendary "Panhu," who helped an emperor put down a rebellion and won the love of his princess. Legend has it that Panhu and the princess had three sons and a daughter, who became the ancestors of the Shes. Shes used to worship a painting of their legendary ancestors and make sacrificial offerings to them every three years.

Until education became widespread after the founding of New China, Shes believed in ghosts and spirits. Superstition used to hamper people's minds and production. Among the old and the uneducated, it still does.

History Scholars disagree about the true origins of the Shes. Are they descendants of the ancient Yues? Do they share common ancestry with the Yaos? Most believe that the Shes' ancestors originally lived in the Phoenix Mountains in Chaozhou, Guangdong Province. They left their native place to escape the oppression of their feudal rulers. That's why they called themselves "guests from the mountains."

In their new homes, the Shes were ruled by the central government for the first time in the 7th century, when the Tang court organized prefectures in Zhangzhou and Tingzhou in Fujian Province. Feudal patterns among the Shes were well established by the Song Dynasty (960-1279). At that time, the Shes were planters of rice, tea, sugarcane and ramie.

By the 14th century, many Shes had migrated into the mountain areas in eastern Fujian, southern Zhejiang and northeastern Jiangxi. Although they worked hard alongside Hans, many were impoverished by feudal lords who seized large tracts of land. Others had to work as hired labourers, or fled to find a living. The situation improved under the Ming Dynasty (1368-1644). Some prosperous Shes were picked to govern the rest in the interests of the Ming court.

Throughout history, the Shes struggled against exploitation and oppression imposed by their rulers. During the First Revolutionary Civil War (1924-27), She peasants in eastern Guangdong organized to fight landlords, and similar uprisings sprang up in Fujian and Zhejiang provinces. Revolutionary activities exploded in eastern Fujian during the Agrarian Revolution (1927-37), and most of the She areas were under the worker-peasant democratic power. The Shes made great contributions to the Anti-Japanese struggle (1937-45) and in the struggle against the Kuomintang. Most She areas were revolutionary bases during the war for China's liberation.

Post-liberation Life   After the founding of New China in 1949, irrigation systems and improved farming methods boosted agricultural production, and machines were brought in to grind feed, mill rice and process tea. Now the Shes are among the country's major tea producers, and much of their tea is for export.

Before 1949, there were no highways in She areas. Now a road network connects all counties. The Yingtan-Xiamen railway passes through the She mountains.

On the eve of liberation, only two of the more than 20,000 Shes in Lishui County, Zhejiang Province, were primary school graduates, and only seven out of a thousand of She children in Fujian Province were able to attend primary schools. Today virtually all She school-age children are enrolled. The Shes now have three ethnic minority schools for senior education and many college graduates of their own.

The Gaoshans

The Gaoshan people, about 300,000 in total, account for less than 2 per cent of the 17 million inhabitants* of Taiwan Province. The majority of them live in mountain areas and the flat valleys running along the east coast of Taiwan Island, and on the Isle of Lanyu. About 1,500 live in such major cities as Shanghai, Beijing and Wuhan and in Fujian Province on the mainland.

The Gaoshans do not have their own script, and their spoken language belongs to the Indonesian group of the Malay/Polynesian language family.

Taiwan Island, home to the Gaoshans, is subtropical in climate with abundant precipitation and fertile land yielding two rice crops a year (three in the far south). Being one of China's major sugar producers, Taiwan also grows some 80 kinds of fruit, including bananas, pineapples, papayas, coconuts, oranges, tangerines, longans and arecas. Taiwan's oolong and black teas are among its most popular items for export.

The Taiwan Mountain Range runs from north to south through the eastern part of the island, which is 55 per cent forested. Over

---

* This is based on statistics published by Taiwan authorities in June 1982.

70 per cent of the world's camphor comes from Taiwan. Short and rapid rivers flowing from the mountains provide abundant hydro-power, and the island is blessed with rich reserves of gold, silver, copper, coal, oil, natural gas and sulphur. Salt is a major product of the southeast coast, and the offshore waters are ideal fishing grounds.

The Gaoshans are mainly farmers growing rice, millet, taro and sweet potatoes. Those who live in mixed communities with people of the Han nationality on the plains work the land in much the same way as their Han neighbours. For those in the mountains, hunting is more important, while fishing is essential to those living along the coast and on small islands.

Gaoshan traditions make women responsible for ploughing, transplanting, harvesting, spinning, weaving, and raising livestock and poultry. Men's duties include land reclamation, construction of irrigation ditches, hunting, lumbering and building houses.

Flatland inhabitants entered feudal society at about the same time as their Han neighbours. Private land ownership, land rental, hired labour and the division between landlords and peasants had long emerged among these Gaoshans. But, in Bunong and Taiya, land was owned by primitive village communes. Farm tools, cattle, houses and small plots of paddy field were privately owned. A primitive cooperative structure operated in farming and the bag of collective hunting was distributed equally among the hunters with an extra share each to the shooter and the owner of the hound that helped.

Gaoshan communities were known as "communes" which con-sisted of some 70 households on the average. The Malan Commune in Amei, one of the biggest, had well over 500 households. The size of the households ranged from five or six people to 30 or more. The communes' territories were clearly defined and each commune had public land which was available for use by its members.

The commune headman, usually the oldest man in the village elected by the commune membership, was responsible for settling internal disputes, officiating at sacrificial rites and presiding over commune discussions of internal and external affairs.

Customs and Habits The Gaoshans are monogamous and patriarchal in family system, though the Amei tribe still retains some of the vestiges of the matriarchal practice. Commune heads are elected from among elderly women and families are headed by women, with the eldest daughter inheriting the family property and male children married off into the brides' families. In the Paiwan tribe, either the eldest son or daughter can be heir to the family property. All the Amei young men and some of the Paiwan youths have to live in a communal hall for a certain period of time before they are initiated into manhood at a special ceremony.

Gaoshan clothes are generally made of hemp and cotton. Men's wear includes capes, vests, short jackets and pants, leggings and turbans decorated with laces, shells and stones. In some areas, vests are delicately woven with rattan and coconut bark. Women wear short blouses with or without sleeves, aprons and trousers or skirts with ornaments like bracelets and ankle bracelets. They are skilled in weaving cloths and dyeing them in bright colours and they like to decorate sleeve cuffs, collars and hems of blouses with beautiful embroidery. They also use shells and animal bones as ornaments. In some places, the time-honoured tradition of tattooing faces and bodies and denting the teeth has been preserved. Some elderly Gaoshan women, though having lived on the mainland among the Han people for many years, still take pride in their distinctive embroidery.

For transportation in rugged terrain, the Gaoshans have built bamboo and rattan suspension or arch bridges and cableways over steep ravines. They are also highly skilled in handicrafts. Their rattan and bamboo weaving, including baskets, hats and armours, pottery utensils, wooden mortars and pestles and dugout canoes are unique in design and decoration. In the mountains, the Cao and Bunong tribes are experts in tanning hides, while the Taiya tribe makes excellent fishing nets.

Songs and dances are very much a part of Gaoshan life. On holidays, they would gather for singing and dancing. They have many ballads, fairy tales, legends, odes to ancestors, hunting songs, dirges and work songs. Instruments include the mouth organ, nose flute, and bamboo flute. One musical form unique to the Gaoshans is a work song accompanying the pounding of rice.

Gaoshan art includes a great deal of carving and painting of human figures, animals, flowers and geometric designs on wooden lintels, panels, columns and thresholds, musical instruments and household utensils. Hunting and other aspects of life are also depicted, and figures with human heads and snake bodies are a common theme.

The Gaoshans are animists who believe in immortality and ancestor worship. They hold sacrificial rites for all kinds of occasions including hunting and fishing. The dead are buried without coffins in the village graveyard. There are vestiges of the worship of totems — snakes and animals — and certain taboos still remain.

History The name Gaoshan was created for the minority people in Taiwan following victory over Japan in 1945. There have been several versions of the origin of the nationality. The main theories are: they are indigenous, they came from the west, or the south, or several different sources. The theory that they came from the west is based on their custom of cropping their hair and tattooing their bodies, worshipping snakes as ancestors and their language, all of which indicate that they might have been descendants of the ancient Baiyue people on the mainland. Another theory says that their language and culture bear resemblance to the Malays from the Philippines and Borneo, and so the Gaoshans must have come from the south. The third and more reliable theory is that the Gaoshan nationality originated from one branch of the ancient Yue nationality living along the coast of the mainland during the stone age. They were later joined by immigrants from the Philippines, Borneo and Micronesia.

Cementing close economic and cultural ties through living and working together over a long period of time, these peoples had by the time of the Ming and Qing dynasties (1368-1911) welded themselves into a new nationality known as Fan or Eastern Fan, which is today called the Gaoshan nationality.

Archaeological evidence suggests that the Gaoshan nationality has all along maintained close connections with the mainland. Until the end of the Pleistocene Epoch 30,000 years ago, Taiwan had been physically part of the mainland. Fossils of human skulls belonging to this period and old stone age artifacts found in Taiwan show that humans probably moved there from the mainland during the Pleistocene Epoch. Neolithic adzes, axes and pottery shards unearthed on the island suggest that new stone age culture on the mainland was introduced into Taiwan 3,000 to 4,000 years ago.

In A.D. 230, two generals of the Kingdom of Wu, Wei Wen and Zhuge Zhi, led a 10,000-strong army across the Strait to Taiwan, and brought back several thousand natives from the island. At that time, the ancestors of the Gaoshans belonged to several primitive, matriarchal tribes. Public affairs were run collectively by all members. Their tools included axes, adzes and rings made of stone and arrowheads and spearheads made of deer antlers. Animal husbandry was still in an embryonic stage.

By the early 7th century, the Gaoshans had started farming and livestock breeding on top of hunting and gathering. They planted cereal crops with stone farm tools. Each tribe was governed by a headman who summoned the membership for meetings by beating a big drum. There was neither criminal code nor taxation. Criminal cases were tried by the entire tribe membership. The offender was tied with ropes, flailed for minor offences or put to death for serious crimes.

These early Gaoshans had no written language, nor calendar; they kept records by tying knots. People worshipped the Gods of Mountain and Sea, and liked carving, painting, singing and dancing.

In the Song and Yuan dynasties (960-1368), central government control was extended to the Penghu Islands and Taiwan, which were placed under the jurisdiction of Jinjiang and Tongan counties in Fujian Province. During the Ming Dynasty (1368-1644), farming, hunting and animal husbandry further developed in Taiwan. In the early 17th century, an increasing number of Hans from the mainland moved to Taiwan, lending a great impetus to economic development along the island's west coast.

The Gaoshan and Han people in Taiwan worked closely together in developing the island and fighting against foreign invaders and local feudal rulers. Japanese pirates invaded Keelung, the major seaport in Northern Taiwan, in 1563. In 1593 the Japanese rulers tried to coerce the Gaoshan people into paying tribute to them but this demand was firmly rejected. The invasions of Japanese pirates from 1602 to 1628 were repeatedly beaten back.

Towards the end of the Ming Dynasty (1368-1644), the Dutch and the Spanish time and again made forays into Taiwan, but were repulsed by the islanders. Finally, in 1642, the Dutch defeated the Spanish, seized the island and imposed tyrannical rule on the local people. This touched off immediate resistance. The anti-Dutch armed uprising led by Guo Huaiyi in the mid-17th century was the largest in scale. In April 1661, China's national hero Zheng Chenggong led an army of 25,000 men to Taiwan and liberated it from under the Dutch with the assistance of the local Gaoshan and Han people, ending the Dutch invaders' 38-year-old colonial rule over Taiwan.

After recovering Taiwan from the Dutch, Zheng Chenggong instituted a series of measures to advance economic growth and cultural development there. He forbade his troops engaged in reclamation to encroach on the Gaoshan people's land, helped the local people improve their farm tools and learn more advanced farming methods from the Han people, encouraged children to attend school, and expanded trading. With the growth of production, the feudal system of land ownership came into being, and the gap between the rich and the poor was getting wider and wider. The feudal landlord economy developed in the Qing Dynasty (1644-1911), when the Gaoshans began using ox-driven carts, ploughs and rakes developed by the Hans.

Zheng died five months after recovering the island, and his son succeeded him. The Zhengs governed Taiwan for 23 years. In 1683, the Qing court brought the island under central government control and this rule lasted for 212 years till Taiwan fell under Japanese rule following the signing of the Sino-Japanese Treaty of Shimonoseki in 1895.

After the Opium War of 1840, British, American, Japanese and French colonialists invaded and plundered Taiwan one after another. The foreign invasion and plundering were met with fierce resistance. To fight the British invaders, the local people formed a volunteer army of 47,000 troops who beat back all the five British invasions.

Taiwan fell into the hands of the Japanese in 1895 after China's defeat in the Sino-Japanese War. Fighting shoulder to shoulder for five months, Gaoshan and Han people inflicted 32,315 casualties on the Japanese invaders.

During the 20 years from 1895 to 1915, the people of Taiwan staged some 100 armed uprisings against Japanese occupation. One of them was the Wushe Uprising mounted by the Gaoshan people in Taizhong County in 1930 under the leadership of the Chinese Communist Party. Enraged by the murder of a Gaoshan worker by Japanese police, over 300 Gaoshan villagers wiped out the 130 Japanese soldiers stationed there and held Wushe for three days. In the following months, the insurgents killed and wounded more than 4,000 Japanese occupationists. In retaliation, the Japanese moved in most of their garrison forces in Taiwan along with planes and big guns and crushed the uprising. They slaughtered over 1,200 Gaoshans including all the insurgents.

After victory over Japan in 1945, Taiwan was returned to China and placed under Kuomintang rule.

Gaoshans on the Mainland Fifteen hundred Gaoshans now live on the mainland. Though small in number, these Gaoshans have three deputies to the National People's Congress, China's supreme organ of power. They enjoy equal rights in the big family of all nationalities on the mainland.

The Gaoshan people share the aspiration of all other nationalities in China for peaceful reunification of the motherland, so that people on both sides of the Taiwan Strait will be reunited.

APPENDIXES

NOTES

1. The Taiping Rebellion was a peasant revolutionary war waged against the Qing Dynasty in the middle of the 19th century. Hong Xiuquan, Yang Xiuqing and others staged an uprising in Guangxi in January 1851 and proclaimed the founding of the Taiping Heavenly Kingdom. In 1853 they captured Nanjing, a city on lower Yangtze River. The Taiping Forces then continued the drive north and pushed to the vicinity of Tianjin. After establishing its capital in Nanjing, the leaders of the kingdom made many political and military errors. Unable to withstand a joint attack organized by the Qing government and foreign imperialists, the rebellion suffered defeat and collapsed in 1864.

2. The Revolution of 1911 was a Chinese bourgeois democratic revolution that overthrew the imperial regime of the Qing Dynasty. On October 10 of that year, a section of the New Army of the Qing, at the urging of revolutionary societies, rose up in Wuchang. This was followed by uprisings in other provinces throughout China, and very soon the rule of the Qing Dynasty crumbled. On January 1, 1912, the Provisional Government of the Republic of China was set up in Nanjing with Sun Yat-sen as president.

3. On May 4, 1919, students in Beijing held a mass rally and demonstrated against the victorious powers of the First World War allowing Japan to assume all the special "rights" in Shandong previously arrogated by Germany. The Northern Warlord government suppressed the students and arrested more than 30 of them. In Beijing, classroom strikes were organized in a protest that evoked the immediate response of students all over

China. Beginning June 3, more students were arrested, precipitating a stronger protest by people throughout the country. Workers in Shanghai and other places struck, and merchants closed their shops. Launched by the intellectuals, the May 4th Movement soon became a country-wide patriotic movement embracing the proletariat and the petty bourgeoisie. Concurrently with this, the New Culture Movement unfolded in opposition to feudalism.

4. An army organized in August 1937 under the leadership of the Chinese Communists, it was then designated as "8th Route" Army under the National Revolutionary Army in accordance with an agreement between the Communist Party and the Kuomintang after the founding of the National United Front for Fighting Japanese Aggression.

5. The New Fourth Army was formed of guerrilla units fighting under the leadership of the Chinese Communist Party in Jiangxi, Guangdong, Hunan, Hubei, Henan, Anhui, Zhejiang and Fujian during the War of Resistance Against Japan. In October 1939, the various guerrilla units began to be assembled and to use this designation.

6. The United Anti-Japanese Army was composed of various anti-Japanese guerrilla units fighting in the Northeast, the Northeast People's Revolutionary Army and the Communist Party-led Anti-Japanese Volunteers.

7. The Opium War: During the first few decades of the 19th century, Britain shipped increasing quantities of opium to China. This not only ruined the health of the Chinese people but also drained lots of silver out of China. It aroused fierce opposition in the country. In 1840, under the pretext of safeguarding its trade with China, Britain launched armed aggression against her. Chinese troops under the command of Lin Zexu put up resistance, and the people in Guangzhou (Canton) organized "Quell-the-British Corps", which dealt serious blows to the British invading forces. In 1842, however, the corrupt Qing

government signed with Britain the humiliating Treaty of Nanjing, under which Britain exacted a huge indemnity from China and annexed Hong Kong, while Shanghai, Fuzhou, Xiamen (Amoy), Ningbo and Guangzhou were opened as treaty ports, and tariffs on British goods shipped to China were fixed jointly by China and Britain.

8. The Second Opium War: From 1856 to 1860 Britain and France jointly waged a war of aggression against China, with the backing of the United States and Tsarist Russia. Qing government, which was then devoting all its energies to suppressing the Taiping Revolution adopted a policy of passive resistance towards the foreign aggressors. The Anglo-French forces, which occupied such major cities as Guangzhou, Tianjin and Beijing, looted and razed to the ground the Yuan Ming Yuan Palace in Beijing and forced the Qing government to conclude the treaties of Tianjin and Beijing. The main provisions of these treaties included the opening of Tianjin, Niuzhuang, Dengzhou, Taiwan, Danshui, Zhaozhou, Qiongzhou, Nanjing, Zhenjiang, Jiujiang and Hankou as treaty ports, and the granting to foreigners of prerogatives to travel and carry out missionary activities in China's interior and to sail in Chinese inland rivers. This opened the way for the imperialist forces to penetrate into both the maritime provinces and the interior of China.

While the Anglo-French forces were attacking Tianjin, Tsarist Russia compelled Qing court by force of arms to sign the "Sino-Russian Treaty of Aigun" on May 28, 1858, under which it annexed more than 600,000 square kilometres of Chinese territory north of the Heilong River and south of the Outer Hinggan Mountains.

And when Beijing was captured by the Anglo-French forces two years later, Tsarist Russia forced the "Sino-Russian Treaty of Beijing" on the Qing government. By this treaty it grabbed some 400,000 square kilometres of Chinese territory east of the Wusuli River.

Under the 1864 "Tahcheng Protocol on the Delimitation of

Sino-Russian Boundary" forced on the Qing government by Tsarist Russia, the latter annexed 440,000 square kilometres more of Chinese territory in western China.

9. The Boxer Movement: The Boxer Movement was an anti-imperialist armed struggle waged by peasants and handicraftsmen in north China in 1900. The movement first started in Shandong and Henan provinces and then spread to the whole of north China. But it was put down with incredible savagery following the occupation of Beijing and Tianjin by the joint forces of eight imperialist powers.

10. The "September 18th Incident": On September 18, 1931, the Japanese Army stationed in northeast China mounted a surprise attack on Shenyang. Under Chiang Kai-shek's order of "absolute non-resistance," the Chinese troops in Shenyang and elsewhere in the Northeast withdrew to south of the Great Wall, and consequently the Japanese forces occupied the provinces of Liaoning, Jilin and Heilongjiang. The Japanese attack on Shenyang is thus known as the "September 18th Incident."

11. Northeast-China Anti-Japanese Volunteer Army: Responding to the call of the Communist Party of China to take up arms against the Japanese invaders who occupied northeast China in 1931, people and some troops of the Northeastern Army formed resistance forces such as the Volunteers' Army, Salvation Army and Self-Defence Army. These armies had grown into a 300,000-member force in 1932, and they are known as "Northeast-China Anti-Japanese Volunteer Army."

12. December 9th Movement (1935): Several thousand students in Beijing (Peking), under the leadership of the Communist Party of China, held a patriotic demonstration on December 9, 1935, putting forward such slogans as "Stop the civil war, get united to resist foreign aggression" and "Down with Japanese imperialism." The students were suppressed by the Kuomintang government. The next day, students in Beijing went on strike. And on 16th, some 10,000 students and Beijing residents held another

demonstration and very quickly won people's support throughout the country. This pushed the anti-Japanese movement in China to a new height.

13. The Chinese National Liberation Vanguard Corps: It was a revolutionary youth organization formed under the leadership of the Chinese Communist Party in September 1936 by progressive youths who participated in the December 9th Movement of 1935. After the outbreak of the Anti-Japanese War in 1937, many of its members fought and helped build up base areas behind the enemy lines. The organizations of the National Liberation Vanguard Corps in the Kuomintang areas were forcibly dissolved by the Chiang Kai-shek government in 1938; those in the Liberated Areas were later merged to form the Association of Youth for National Salvation.

14. The Northern Warlords (1912-1928): After the Qing Dynasty was overthrown by the Revolution of 1911, Yuan Shih-kai, a big warlord in north China, usurped the presidency of the Republic of China. A warlord clique controlling the central and local administrations thus came into being. The Northern Warlords split into several factions after the death of Yuan Shih-kai. These factions, each backed by an imperialist power, continuously warred against one another. The Northern Warlords ruled for 17 years until they were overthrown in 1928.

15. "Letting a hundred flowers blossom and develop the new through the old" is a policy put forward by the Communist Party of China to reform and develop China's traditional operas during the early post-liberation period, and it is applicable to other divisions of literature and art as well.

Originating from the slogan "Develop the new through critical assimilation of the old" proposed in the Shaanxi-Gansu-Ningxia Border Region during the Anti-Japanese War, the "Hundred Flowers" policy advocates that operas of different genres, schools, forms and styles should be developed simultaneously through free competition and that a critical attitude should be taken toward literary and art heritages, namely, rejecting their feudal dross and absorbing their democratic essence.

The implementation of this policy promoted the development of China's traditional operas, literature and art of various nationalities. A good number of local opera genres were revived, and many folk literary and art forms were collected and popularized. The policy gave an impetus to the creation and performance of works of various styles and themes and enabled literature and art in China to display a stronger national and popular character. The "Hundred Flowers" policy also fostered a rapid growth of literature and art of China's minority nationalities.

16. This refers to a February 1923 general strike on the Peking (Beijing)-Hankou Railway. Railway workers, under the leadership of the Communist Party, demanded freedom to organize a regional trade union. On February 7, Northern Warlords Wu Peifu and Xiao Yaonan, who were backed by British imperialism, butchered the strikers. This became known as the February 7th Massacre.

17. On June 19, 1925, 250,000 workers in Hong Kong staged a general strike in support of the "May 30th Movement." They were joined two days later by workers in a foreign concession in Guangzhou (Canton). The strike lasted until October 1926.

18. A form of folk song popular among the Han, Hui, Dongxiang, Tu, Salar and Bonan peoples in northwest China's Gansu and Qinghai provinces and Ningxia Hui Autonomous Region. Love songs of this type used to be sung in the wild beyond the earshot of elders. Since liberation odes and songs have also taken this form.

CENSUS OF CHINA'S NATIONALITIES ON JULY 1, 1982

Nationality	Population (in thousand)	Percentage against national total
Total number of population in 29 provinces, municipalities and autonomous regions	1,003,940	100
Han	936,703.8	93.30
Mongolian	3,411.7	0.34
Hui	7,219.4	0.72
Tibetan	3,870.1	0.39
Uygur	5,957.1	0.59
Miao	5,030.9	0.50
Yi	5,543.4	0.54
Zhuang	13,378.2	1.33
Bouyei	2,120.5	0.21
Korean	1,763.9	0.18
Manchu	4,299.2	0.43
Dong	1,425.1	0.14
Yao	1,402.7	0.14
Bai	1,131.1	0.11
Tujia	2,832.7	0.28
Hani	1,058.8	0.11
Kazak	907.6	0.09
Dai	839.8	0.08
Li	817.6	0.08
Lisu	481.0	0.05
Va	298.6	0.03
She	368.8	0.04
Gaoshan	1.5	...
Lahu	304.2	0.03

Nationality	Population (in thousand)	Percentage against national total
Shui	286.5	0.03
Dongxiang	279.4	0.03
Naxi	245.2	0.02
Jingpo	93.0	0.01
Kirgiz	114.0	0.01
Tu	159.4	0.02
Daur	94.0	0.01
Mulam	90.4	0.01
Qiang	102.8	0.01
Blang	58.5	0.01
Salar	69.1	0.01
Maonan	38.1	...
Gelo	53.8	0.01
Xibe	83.6	0.01
Achang	20.4	...
Pumi	24.2	...
Tajik	26.5	...
Nu	23.2	...
Uzbek	12.5	...
Russian	2.9	...
Ewenki	19.3	...
De'ang	12.3	...
Bonan	9.0	...
Yugur	10.6	...
Jing	12.0	...
Tatar	4.1	...
Drung	4.7	...
Oroqen	4.1	...

Nationality	Population (in thousand)	Percentage against national total
Hezhe	1.5	...
Moinba	6.2	...
Lhoba	2.1	...
Jino	12.0	...
Unidentified nationalities	879.2	0.09
Chinese citizens with foreign origin	4.8	...

NATIONAL AUTONOMIES IN CHINA

Five autonomous regions, 31 autonomous prefectures and 96 autonomous counties and banners

	Name of Autonomy	Location of People's Government	Date of Establishment	Major Minority Nationalities
	Inner Mongolia Autonomous Region	Hohhot	May 1, 1947	Mongolian, Hui, Korean, Manchu, Daur, Oroqen, Xibe and Russian
Inner Mongolia Autonomous Region	Oroqen Autonomous Banner	Alihe	Oct. 1, 1951	Oroqen, Daur, Ewenki, Korean, Manchu and Mongolian
	Ewenki Autonomous Banner	Bayantuohai	Aug. 1, 1958	Ewenki, Mongolian and Daur
	Morin Dawa Daur Autonomous Banner	Nirji	Aug. 15, 1958	Daur, Ewenki, Oroqen, Manchu and Mongolian
	Dorbod Mongolian Autonomous County, Heilongjiang Province	Taikang	Dec. 5, 1956	Mongolian, Hui, Manchu, Korean and Daur
Jilin Province	Yanbian Korean Autonomous Prefecture	Yanji	Sep. 3, 1952	Korean, Manchu, Hui and Mongolian
	Changbai Korean Autonomous County	Changbai	Sep. 15, 1958	Korean and Manchu
	Qian Gorlos Mongolian Autonomous County	Qianguo	Sep. 1, 1956	Mongolian, Manchu, Hui, Korean and Xibe

	Major Minority Nationalities	Location of People's Government	Date of Establishment	Major Minority Nationalities
Liaoning Province	Harqin Left Wing Mongolian Autonomous County	Dachengzi	Apr. 1, 1958	Mongolian and Hui
	Fuxin Mongolian Autonomous County	Fuxin	Apr. 7, 1958	Mongolian, Manchu, Hui and Korean
	Xiuyan Manchu Autonomous County	Xiuyan	Jun. 11, 1985	Manchu
	Fengcheng Manchu Autonomous County	Fengcheng	Jun. 13, 1985	Manchu
	Xinbin Manchu Autonomous County	Xinbin	Jun. 7, 1985	Manchu and Korean
Hebei Province	Dachang Hui Autonomous County	Dachang	Dec. 7, 1955	Hui
	Mengcun Hui Autonomous County	Mengcun	Nov. 30, 1955	Hui
Ningxia	Ningxia Hui Autonomous Region	Yinchuan	Oct. 25, 1958	Hui, Dongxiang, Bonan, Salar, Tu and Manchu
Gansu Pro.	Linxia Hui Autonomous Prefecture	Linxia	Nov. 19, 1956	Hui, Dongxiang, Bonan, Salar, Tu and Tibetan

Name of Autonomy	Location of People's Government	Date of Establishment	Major Minority Nationalities
Gannan Tibetan Autonomous Prefecture	Hezuo	Oct. 1, 1953	Tibetan, Hui, Mongolian, Salar, Dongxiang, Tu, Manchu and Bonan
Tianzhu Tibetan Autonomous County	Huazangsi	May 6, 1950	Tibetan, Tu, Hui and Mongolian
Sunan Yugur Autonomous County	Hongwansi	Feb. 20, 1954	Yugur, Tibetan, Hui, Mongolian and Tu
Subei Mongolian Autonomous County	Dangchengwan	Jul. 29, 1950	Mongolian, Hui and Tibetan
Aksay Kazak Autonomous County	Bolozhuanjing	Apr. 27, 1954	Kazak and Hui
Dongxiang Autonomous County	Suonanba	Sep. 25, 1950	Dongxiang and Hui
Zhangjiachuan Hui Autonomous County	Zhangchuan	Jul. 6, 1953	Hui
Jishishan Bonan-Dongxiang-Salar Autonomous County	Chuimatan	Sep. 30, 1981	Bonan, Dongxiang and Salar
Haibei Tibetan Autonomous Prefecture	Haomen	Dec. 31, 1953	Tibetan, Mongolian and Hui

Gansu Province

Qinghai Pro.

	Name of Autonomy	Location of People's Government	Date of Establishment	Major Minority Nationalities
Qinghai Province	Huangnan Tibetan Autonomous Prefecture	Tongren	Dec. 22, 1953	Tibetan, Hui, Salar, Mongolian and Tu
	Hainan Tibetan Autonomous Prefecture	Gonghe	Dec. 6, 1953	Tibetan, Hui, Mongolian, Tu and Salar
	Golog Tibetan Autonomous Prefecture	Maqen	Jan. 1, 1954	Tibetan
	Yushu Tibetan Autonomous Prefecture	Yushu	Dec. 25, 1951	Tibetan and Hui
	Haixi Mongolian-Tibetan-Kazak Autonomous Prefecture	Delingha	Jan. 25, 1954	Mongolian, Tibetan, Kazak, Hui, Tu and Salar
	Huzhu Tu Autonomous County	Weiyuan	Feb. 17, 1954	Tu, Tibetan, Mongolian and Hui
	Hualong Hui Autonomous County	Bayan	Mar. 1, 1954	Hui, Tibetan and Salar
	Xunhua Salar Autonomous County	Jishi	Mar. 1, 1954	Salar, Tibetan and Hui
	Henan Mongolian Autonomous County	Youganning	Oct. 16, 1954	Mongolian, Tibetan and Hui

	Name of Autonomy	Location of People's Government	Date of Establishment	Major Minority Nationalities
Qinghai Province	Menyuan Hui Autonomous County	Haomen	Dec. 19, 1953	Hui, Tibetan, Tu, Mongolian and Salar
	Datong Hui-Tujia Autonomous County	Qiaotou	To be set up.	Hui, Tu and Tibetan
	Minhe Hui-Tujia Autonomous County	Shangchuankou	To be set up.	Hui and Tu
Xinjiang Uygur Autonomous Region	Xinjiang Uygur Autonomous Region	Urumqi	Oct. 1, 1955	Uygur, Kazak, Hui, Kirgiz, Uzbek, Mongolian, Daur, Xibe, Tajik, Tatar, Russian and Manchu
	Changji Hui Autonomous Prefecture	Changji	Jul. 15, 1954	Hui, Kazak, Uygur, Mongolian, Uzbek, Russian, Tatar, Kirgiz and Tajik
	Bayingolin Mongolian Autonomous Prefecture	Korla	Jun. 23, 1954	Mongolian, Uygur, Kazak, Russian, Kirgiz and Hui
	Kizilsu Kirgiz Autonomous Prefecture	Artux	Jul. 14, 1954	Kirgiz, Uygur, Uzbek, Tajik and Hui
	Bortala Mongolian Autonomous Prefecture	Bole	Jul. 13, 1954	Mongolian, Kazak, Uygur, Hui, Russian, Xibe, Kirgiz, Tatar and Uzbek
	Ili Kazak Autonomous Prefecture	Yining	Nov. 27, 1954	Kazak, Uygur, Mongolian, Hui, Russian, Xibe, Kirgiz, Tatar, Manchu, Daur and Tajik

	Name of Autonomy	Location of People's Government	Date of Establishment	Major Minority Nationalities
Xinjiang Uygu Autonomous Region	Barkol Kazak Autonomous County	Barkol	Sep. 30, 1954	Kazak, Mongolian, Uygur, Hui, Uzbek, Manchu and Kirgiz
	Taxkorgan Tajik Autonomous County	Taxkorgan	Sep. 17, 1954	Tajik, Kirgiz and Uygur
	Mori Kazak Autonomous County	Mori	Jul. 17, 1954	Kazak, Uygur, Hui, Manchu, Uzbek, Tatar, Russian and Kirgiz
	Yanqi Hui Autonomous County	Yanqi	Mar. 15, 1954	Hui, Uygur, Mongolian, Kazak, Russian, Xibe, Tatar, Kirgiz, Manchu, Uzbek and Tibetan
	Qapqal Xibe Autonomous County	Qapqal	Mar. 25, 1954	Xibe, Kazak, Uygur, Hui, Kirgiz and Mongolian
	Hoboksar Mongolian Autonomous County	Hoboksar	Sep. 10, 1954	Mongolian, Kazak, Uygur, Tatar, Hui and Uzbek
Tibet Autonomous Region	Tibet Autonomous Region	Lhasa	Sep. 9, 1965	Tibetan, Hui, Moinba and Lhoba
Sichuan Province	Aba Tibetan Autonomous Prefecture	Barkam	Jan. 1, 1953	Tibetan, Hui and Qiang
	Liangshan Yi Autonomous Prefecture	Xichang	Oct. 1, 1952	Yi, Miao, Hui and Tibetan

Name of Autonomy	Location of People's Government	Date of Establishment	Major Minority Nationalities
Garze Tibetan Autonomous Prefecture	Kangding	Nov. 24, 1950	Tibetan, Yi and Hui
Muli Tibetan Autonomous County	Bowa	Feb. 19, 1953	Tibetan, Yi and Miao
Maowen Qiang Autonomous County	Fengyi	Jul. 7, 1958	Qiang, Hui and Tibetan
Xianjiang Tujia-Miao Autonomous County	Lianhe	To be set up.	Tujia and Miao
Pengshui Miao-Tujia Autonomous County	Hanjia	To be set up.	Miao and Tujia
Shizhu Tujia Autonomous County	Chengguan	To be set up.	Tujia
Youyang Tujia-Miao Autonomous County	Zhongduo	Nov. 11, 1983	Tujia and Miao
Xiushan Tujia-Miao Autonomous County	Zhonghe	Nov. 7, 1983	Tujia and Miao
Mabian Yi Autonomous County	Chengguan	To be set up.	Yi

Sichuan Province

	Name of Autonomy	Location of People's Government	Date of Establishment	Major Minority Nationalities
Si-chuan	Ebian Yi Autonomous County	Chengguan	To be set up.	Yi
Yunnan Province	Xishuangbanna Dai Autonomous Prefecture	Jinghong	Jan. 24, 1953	Dai, Hani, Blang, Yi, Yao, Va, Hui, Lahu and Jino
Yunnan Province	Wenshan Zhuang-Miao Autonomous Prefecture	Wenshan	Apr. 1, 1958	Zhuang, Miao, Yao, Hui and Yi
Yunnan Province	Honghe Hani-Yi Autonomous Prefecture	Gejiu	Nov. 18, 1957	Hani, Yi, Miao, Zhuang, Yao, Dai and Hui
Yunnan Province	Dehong Dai-Jingpo Autonomous Prefecture	Luxi	Jul. 24, 1953	Dai, Jingpo, Achang, Lisu and De'ang
Yunnan Province	Nujiang Lisu Autonomous Prefecture	Lushui	Aug. 23, 1954	Lisu, Nu, Bai, Drung, Yi and Tibetan
Yunnan Province	Chuxiong Yi Autonomous Prefecture	Chuxiong	Apr. 15, 1958	Yi, Miao Dai, Zhuang, Hui, Lisu and Bai
Yunnan Province	Deqen Tibetan Autonomous Prefecture	Zhongdian	Sep. 13, 1957	Tibetan, Lisu, Naxi, Yi, Bai, Nu and Pumi
Yunnan Province	Dali Bai Autonomous Prefecture	Xiaguan	Nov. 22, 1956	Bai, Yi, Hui, Lisu, Miao and Dai

Name of Autonomy	Location of People's Government	Date of Establishment	Major Minority Nationalities
Eshan Yi Autonomous County	Chengguan	May 12, 1951	Yi, Hani, Hui and Miao
Lunan Yi Autonomous County	Dongfanghong	Dec. 31, 1956	Yi, Hui and Miao
Cangyuan Va Autonomous County	Mengyong	Feb. 28, 1964	Va, Lahu, Dai and Hui
Gengma Dai-Va Autonomous County	Hongwei	Oct. 16, 1955	Dai, Va, Lahu, Blang, Yi and De'ang
Lijiang Naxi Autonomous County	Dayan	Apr. 10, 1961	Naxi, Lisu, Yi, Bai, Tibetan and Pumi
Ninglang Yi Autonomous County	Daxing	Sep. 20, 1956	Yi, Naxi, Pumi and Tibetan
Jiangcheng Hani-Yi Autonomous County	Mengliejie	May 18, 1954	Hani, Yi, Dai, Yao and Lahu
Lancang Lahu Autonomous County	Menglang	Apr. 7, 1953	Lahu, Va, Hani, Yi, Dai, Blang, Hui and De'ang
Menglian Dai-Lahu-Va Autonomous County	Menglian	Jun. 16, 1954	Dai, Lahu, Va, Hani and Yi

Yunnan Province

Name of Autonomy	Location of People's Government	Date of Establishment	Major Minority Nationalities
Ximeng Va Autonomous County	Ximeng	Mar. 5, 1965	Va, Lahu and Dai
Hekou Yao Autonomous County	Chengguan	Jul. 11, 1963	Yao, Miao, Yi, Zhuang and Dai
Pingbian Miao Autonomous County	Yuping	Jul. 1, 1963	Miao, Yi, Yao and Zhuang
Gongshan Drung-Nu Autonomous County	Cikai	Oct. 1, 1956	Drung, Nu, Lisu, Tibetan, Naxi and Bai
Weishan Yi-Hui Autonomous County	Weicheng	Nov. 9, 1956	Yi, Bai, Hui, Miao and Lisu
Xundian Hui-Yi Autonomous County	Rende	Dec. 20, 1979	Hui, Yi and Miao
Mojiang Hani Autonomous County	Jiulian	Nov. 28, 1979	Hani, Dai, Yi and Hui
Nanjian Yi Autonomous County	Chengzhen	Nov. 27, 1965	Yi, Hui, Dai, Bai, Lisu and Miao
Xinping Yi-Dai Autonomous County	Chengguan	Nov. 25, 1980	Yi, Dai and Hani

Yunnan Province

Name of Autonomy	Location of People's Government	Date of Establishment	Major Minority Nationalities
Yuanjiang Hani-Yi-Dai Autonomous County	Chengguan	Nov. 22, 1980	Hani, Yi and Dai
Shuangjiang Lahu-Va-Blang-Dai Autonomous County	Chengguan	Dec. 30, 1985	Lahu, Va and Blang
Weixi Lisu Autonomous County	Baohe	Oct. 13, 1985	Lisu
Jingdong Yi Autonomous County	Jinping	Dec. 20, 1985	Yi
Puer Hani-Yi Autonomous County	Ninger	Dec. 15, 1985	Hani and Yi
Yangbi Yi Autonomous County	Shangjie	Nov. 1, 1985	Yi
Jinping Miao-Yi-Dai Autonomous County	Chengguan	Dec. 7, 1985	Miao, Yao and Dai
Jinggu Dai-Yi Autonomous County	Weiyuan	Dec. 25, 1985	Dai and Yi
Luquan Yi-Miao Autonomous County	Pingshan	Nov. 25, 1985	Yi and Miao

Yunnan Province

Guizhou Province

Name of Autonomy	Location of People's Government	Date of Establishment	Major Minority Nationalities
Qiandongnan Miao-Dong Autonomous Prefecture	Kaili	Jul. 23, 1956	Miao, Dong, Shui, Zhuang Bouyei, Yao and Mulam
Qiannan Bouyei-Miao Autonomous Prefecture	Duyun	Aug. 8, 1956	Bouyei, Miao, Shui, Dong and Yao
Qianxinan Bouyei-Miao Autonomous Prefecture	Xingyi	May 1, 1982	Bouyei and Miao
Songtao Miao Autonomous County	Chengguan	Dec. 31, 1956	Miao
Zhenning Bouyei-Miao Autonomous County	Chengguan	Sep. 11, 1963	Bouyei and Miao
Ziyun Miao-Bouyei Autonomous County	Songshan	Feb. 11, 1966	Miao and Bouyei
Weining Yi-Hui-Miao Autonomous County	Chengguan	Nov. 11, 1954	Yi, Hui, Miao and Bouyei
Sandu Shui Autonomous County	Chengguan	Jan. 2, 1957	Shui, Miao, Bouyei and Yao
Guanling Bouyei-Miao Autonomous County	Guansuo	Feb. 16, 1982	Bouyei and Miao

	Name of Autonomy	Location of People's Government	Date of Establishment	Major Minority Nationalities
Gui-zhou Pro.	Yuping Dong Autonomous County	Chengguan	To be set up.	Dong
Guangxi Zhuang Autonomous Region	Guangxi Zhuang Autonomous Region	Nanning	Mar. 15, 1958	Zhuang, Yao, Miao, Dong, Mulam, Maonan, Hui, Yi, Shui, Jing and Gelo
	Du'an Yao Autonomous County	Anyang	Dec. 15, 1955	Yao, Zhuang, Miao, Mulam, Maonan and Hui
	Rongshui Miao Autonomous County	Rongshui	Nov. 26, 1952	Miao, Zhuang, Dong, Yao, Shui and Mulam
	Sanjiang Dong Autonomous County	Guyi	Dec. 3, 1952	Dong, Miao, Yao and Zhuang
	Longsheng Multi-National Autonomous County	Longsheng	Aug. 19, 1951	Dong, Zhuang, Miao and Yao
	Fangcheng Multi-National Autonomous County	Fangcheng	May 1, 1958	Zhuang, Yao and Jing
	Longlin Multi-National Autonomous County	Xinzhou	Jan. 1, 1953	Zhuang, Miao, Yao, Yi and Gelo
	Jinxiu Yao Autonomous County	Jinxiu	May 28, 1952	Yao and Zhuang

	Name of Autonomy	Location of People's Government	Date of Establishment	Major Minority Nationalities
Guangxi Zhuang Autonomous Region	Bama Yao Autonomous County	Bama	Feb. 6, 1956	Yao and Zhuang
	Luocheng Mulam Autonomous County	Dongmen	Jan. 10, 1984	Mulam
	Fuchuan Yao Autonomous County	Fuyang	Jan. 1, 1984	Yao
Guangdong Province	Hainan Li-Miao Autonomous Prefecture	Baoting	Jul. 1, 1952	Li, Miao and Hui
	Liannan Yao Autonomous County	Sanjiang	Jan. 25, 1953	Yao
	Lianshan Zhuang-Yao Autonomous County	Jitian	Sep. 26, 1962	Zhuang and Yao
	Ruyuan Yao Autonomous County	Rucheng	Oct. 1, 1963	Yao
Hunan Province	Xiangxi Tujia-Miao Autonomous Prefecture	Jishou	Sep. 20, 1957	Tujia, Miao, Yao and Hui
	Jianghua Yao Autonomous County	Tuojiang	Nov. 25, 1955	Yao and Zhuang

	Name of Autonomy	Location of People's Government	Date of Establishment	Major Minority Nationalities
Hunan Province	Chengbu Miao Autonomous County	Rulin	Nov. 30, 1956	Miao, Yao, Dong, Zhuang and Hui
	Tongdao Dong Autonomous County	Shuangjiang	May 7, 1954	Dong, Miao and Yao
	Xinhuang Dong Autonomous County	Chengguan	Dec. 5, 1956	Dong, Miao, Yao and Hui
Hubei Prov.	Exi Tujia-Miao Autonomous Prefecture	Enshi	Dec. 1, 1983	Tujia
Zhejiang Province	Jingning She Autonomous County	Hexi	Dec. 24, 1984	She

LANGUAGE FAMILIES OF MINORITY NATIONALITIES*

Chinese-Tibetan Language Family	I. Zhuang-Dong Language Group: 1. Zhuang-Dai Language Branch: Zhuang, Bouyei and Dai 2. Dong-Shui Language Branch: Dong, Mulam, Shui and Maonan 3. Li Language Branch: Li II. Tibetan-Burmese Language Group: 1. Tibetan Language Branch: Tibetan and Moinba 2. Yi Language Branch: Yi, Lisu, Naxi, Hani, Lahu, Jino and Bai 3. Jingpo Language Branch: Jingpo and Drung 4. Qiang Language Branch: Qiang and Pumi 5. Unidentified Language Branch: Lhoba, Nu and Achang III. Miao-Yao Language Group: 1. Miao Language Branch: Miao and She 2. Yao Language Branch: Yao** 3. Unidentified Language Branch and Group: Tujia and Gelo IV. Chinese Language Group: Hui and Manchu***
Altaian Language Family	I. Tujue Language Group: Uygur, Salar, Uzbek, Kazak, Tatar, Yugur (Yaohuer) **** and Kirgiz II. Mongolian Language Group: Mongolian, Tu Dongexiang, Daur, Bonan and Yugur (Enger)**** III. Manchu-Tungusic Language Group: 1. Manchu Language Branch: Manchu,*** Xibe and Hezhe 2. Tungusic Language Branch: Oroqen and Ewenki 3. Unidentified Language Branch: Korean
South Asian Language Family	Va, De'ang and Blang
Nandao Language Family	Gaoshan

Indian-European Language Family	I.	Slavonian Language Group: Eastern Slavonian Branch: Russian
	II.	Iranian Language Group: Tajik
Unidentified Language Branch, Group and Family		Jing

* The table lists all of China's 55 minority nationalities and is arranged according to the similarity of their languages and the size of their populations.

** The Yaos have three languages. The Lajia language belongs to the Zhuang-Dong Language Group and the Bunu to the Miao Language Group.

*** All the Huis and most of the Manchus speak Chinese while a small group of Manchus stick to their native language.

**** The Yugurs speak two languages that fall into two different language groups.

中国少数民族

马寅　主编

*

外文出版社出版

（中国北京百万庄路24号）

外文印刷厂印刷

中国国际图书贸易总公司

（中国国际书店）发行

北京399信箱

1989年（大32开）　第一版

（英）

ISBN　7-119-00001-2/Z・1（外）

02180

17-E-2112 S